An Introduction to
World Religions

R.B. Chamberlain, PhD, ThD

"although [their practices] may seem abhorrent to some, religious belief need not be acceptable, logical, consistent, or comprehensible to others in order to merit First Amendment protection."
— *US Supreme Court Associate Justice Anthony Kennedy*

Notice

An Introduction to World Religions

Copyright © 2013
Robert B. Chamberlain, PhD, ThD

All rights reserved. No portion of this book may be reproduced or transmitted in any form or by any means, digital, electronic or mechanical, including transcription, recording, photocopying, digitization, or by any information storage and retrieval system, without permission in writing from the author.

The world map on the cover is used under the copyright notice of the creator (vectortemplates.com). The globe on the frontispiece is in the public domain, and was downloaded from www.clker.com (a trademark of Rolera, LLC, an Illinois Limited Liability Corporation) in full compliance with their terms of usage.

Independently Published 2013
Charleston, South Carolina, USA
ISBN-13: 978-1484891605
ISBN-10: 1484891600

An Introduction to World Religions

Table of Contents

Foreword	i
Section I – Religious Concepts	1
1 The What & Why of Religion	3
2 Religious Experience	13
3 Religious Ontology	25
4 Proposed Proofs: The Existence of God	41
5 Ancient & Classic Religions	57
Section II – Judaism	71
6 Jewish Foundations	73
7 Historical Development	89
8 Scripture, Concepts, Practices & Holidays	101
9 Modern Divergence	113
Section III – Christianity	123
10 Christian Foundations	125
11 Historical Development	135
12 Scripture, Concepts, Practices & Holidays	155
13 Modern Divergence	171
Section IV – Islam	191
14 Islamic Foundations	193
15 Historical Development	201

Table of Contents
[continued]

16	Scripture, Concepts, Practices & Holidays	207
17	Modern Divergence	217
Section V – Hinduism		231
18	Hindu Foundations	233
19	Historical Development	239
20	Concepts, Scripture & Holidays	251
21	Divergence	261
Section VI – Buddhism		273
22	Buddhist Foundations	275
23	Historical Development	279
24	Scripture, Concepts & Holidays	291
25	Modern Divergence	299
Section VII – Other Paths		307
26	East Asian Faith	309
27	African Faith	327
28	Neo-Pagan Faith	337
Appendix: Photo Credits		347

Foreword

This text began as a collection of lecture notes that were printed, bound, and made available to students to supplement their text in an *Introduction to World Religions* class at what was then called Brevard Community College (now Eastern Florida State College). These notes were instructor-specific, and were used initially on the Cocoa, Florida campus; they were revised several times, and were finally used at the Palm Bay campus.

The high cost of text books in this field resulted in the conversion of these notes into a more cohesive format so that they could serve as the primary text for this course. A traditional college semester runs about 16 weeks; so, with classes lost as a result of holidays and examinations, there are generally 28 class sessions. This presentation of the material is therefore divided into 28 chapters — intended to correspond to 28 class meetings.

The organizational structure is to divide the material into seven distinct sections: an initial section introducing basic concepts in the field of religion, five sections focused on the "major" world religions (Judaism, Christianity, Islam, Hinduism, and Buddhism), and a final section introducing other faith systems from East Asia, Africa, and the Neo-Pagan movements.

Each of the five Major Religions sections is divided into four chapters: Foundations (covering the founder, people, and early history of the movement); Historical Development (covering the growth and development of the faith, including a review of the major sects or divisions within the tradition); Scripture, Concepts and Holidays (covering the written texts on which the faith relies, the primary ethical and theological concepts which they promulgate, and the principle holidays which they observe); and, Divergence (a look at two or three faith traditions that are related to, spawned by, or separated from, the main body of the faith – to see the variety and breadth within each of the major traditions).

Section I
Religious Concepts

Why take a class in "World Religions"?

Although there are estimated to be in excess of 5,000 religions in the world, you will likely never come face to face with more than a handful of them — probably no more than 10 or 20. So, why learn about the variety of religions in the world today?

The simple answer is that — as communication improves, transportation becomes more efficient, and personal travel evolves — people are meeting and working with people from backgrounds that they never would have met if they had lived a hundred years earlier. A second reason has become more apparent since 9/11: religion is often a convenient means to identify scapegoats for the problems of the world; and, insufficient or incorrect knowledge is frequently a primary reason why this scapegoating is successful in demonizing these "others". Although you may only ever meet people who practice a small number of these belief systems, you have no idea which of the world's many faiths you may encounter. Being able to understand and appreciate what others have to offer can go a long way toward life being productive, efficient and peaceful; and, that makes scapegoating much less likely.

The goal here is not to make you an expert in any of these religions, but to provide some basic information regarding the history, beliefs, practices, and issues confronting them. It serves also to introduce you to what it is that a religion holds sacred; what it is that is important to them. Specifically, it is designed to increase exposure to some of the larger religions, and to provide an introduction to some of the divergent faiths that are often overlooked. Hopefully, broadening our understanding of a "strange religion" will enable us to appreciate how those who practice it function in the world, and why they do what they do. This may not have seemed important 200 years ago, 100 years ago, or even when your parents were in school; but, it certainly is now.

More than likely, simply presenting religion after religion would only tend to confuse the average student. What can help to reduce the likelihood of this is an overview of a few concepts that underlie all of these various religions. So, Section I (the first 5 chapters) is dedicated to addressing a number of issues that impact all religions. Hopefully, these introductory points will help to clarify such questions as:

- How can a religion be atheist?
- How can one be agnostic?
- Why is Confucianism considered a religion?
- Why do some religions often seem to 'look like' another religion in so many ways?
- *et cetera*

That said, our exploration into *Religious Concepts* will address several major points:

- What do we mean by the term *religion*?
- Why do humans appear to be inherently religious?
- What is meant by the term *cult*?
- What is a *religious experience*, and can they be verified?
- How can religions be grouped and organized?
- What are *parody religions*, and are they real religions?
- Is there a God (or gods), and is there any proof?
- How similar are ancient (or classical) religions to those that people practice today?

Chapter 1
The *What* and *Why* of Religion

Religion is excellent stuff for keeping common people quiet.
Religion is what keeps the poor from murdering the rich.
— Napoleon Bonaparte

A frequent dictionary definition of religion is 'the belief in, and worship of, a god or gods'. This definition is certainly applicable to theistic religions such as Christianity, but may not accurately reflect other religious systems (such as Jainism, which is effectively agnostic); but, religion can also be defined as "a particular system of faith and worship". A third view is that it can be any "system of beliefs held to with ardor and faith". Although these are all very similar, there are differences.

The Romans used the Latin word *religiō* to mean 'an obligation, or bond'. This, in turn, was derived from the earlier word *religāre*, a verb that meant to 'tie back', or 'bind tightly'. The more specialized meaning of a 'bond between human beings and the gods' evolved sometime around the 5th century, and generally referred to a monastic life. It wasn't until around the 16th century that it came to represent this type of bond for all people (essentially, the 'modern meaning').

So, for the purpose of this text, we will combine the definitions into the more comprehensive *"worship of a god or gods; any system of beliefs regarding the metaphysical; or, any form of perceived spiritual obligation"*.

Why Religion?

Why humans follow a religion is a little more complex, and depends primarily on the answers to a few simple questions:

o   Is there, in truth, a God, gods, or Ultimate Reality?
   ▶ yes – some form of religion is probably advisable;
   ▶ no – religious practices are either a waste of time or serve a strictly sociological purpose.

Why is religion advisable if the answer was "yes"? The answer to that could be called **the three F's**. These are:

- Fear (God will "get you" if you don't);
- Function (you expect to "get something out of it"); or,
- Faith (God, as the Ultimate Being, simply *deserves* your respect and honor).

If the answer was "no", then only the second option (function) makes much sense as a justification for religion (*e.g.* Jainism and some forms of Buddhism). Several philosophers, however, have proposed their suggestions as to why humans follow a religion even when a deity is denied.

In the Beginning ...

Once upon a time, in a land far, far away ... or, to be more accurate, during the first half of the 19th century in Germany, there was a philosopher by the name of *Ludwig Andreas Feuerbach* [1804–1872]. Feuerbach was the first philosopher to apply what is often called *philosophical anthropology* to religion. This first appeared in a highly influential work titled The Essence of Christianity [1841], and in this he presented what religious philosophers today refer to as "projection".

Projection is just what the name implies: the concept that subjective internal human experiences are *projected* out onto the objective world. He used this to explain how certain religious beliefs and practices came to be. Although later philosophers would have other human experiences that they thought were the source of this projection, for Feuerbach it was basic human qualities. He saw the basic qualities and needs of humans as the initial source for their projections: wisdom, love, strength, *et cetera*. As a result, he said humans perceive God as omniscient (all knowing), omniagape (all loving), omnipotent (all strength), and so on. Feuerbach saw God as the external projection of humanity's internal qualities, needs and experiences; and, in the first part of his text, he wrote that "if man is to find contentment in God, he must find himself in God."

If that were not clear enough, Feuerbach went on to explain the absurdity of the idea that God could have any existence whatsoever separate from man. In other words, Feuerbach (who actually first entered university as a theology student) was saying that God is the projection, the invention, the creation of man; man was not, is not, and could not be the creation of God. He also branded revelation as poisonous and destructive to rational thought and reason, and declared all sacraments and rituals as little more than pandering to immorality and superstition.

Feuerbach was never particularly successful as a philosopher while he was alive, so why should we care about him now? We care because this concept of projection is one that has reappeared again and again with other philosophers. The only difference is what they believe is being projected; *i.e.* the source of religion.

Was Feuerbach an atheist? Yes and no. Although he believed that God exists; he also thought man had created Him "in his own image". Therefore, he was more properly a *scientific materialist* — *i.e.* someone who believes all reality springs from a physical, material basis as a consequence of discernible, scientific principles.

How did this influence future religious philosophers? Several of them adopted Feuerbach's basic premise, and then 'ran with it'.

Individual Intellectualism

"Religion ... stands in fundamental antagonism ... to science."
– Sir James George Frazer

  EB Tylor (left) and Sir James Frazer (right) were among the first to look at religion from the viewpoint of Feuerbach's scientific materialist method. Neither of them believed in God, so they had eliminated *a priori* the possibility that religion might exist because God exists, and thus only looked for material explanations. The conclusion they reached was that each religion emanated from a single, solitary, human mind. Tylor called this primordial thinker the *savage philosopher*. This was an individual who tried to determine the answers to the great questions of life, and then passed his conclusions on to the next generation of thinkers to be refined. In this approach, religion (the body of his ideas and conclusions) became part of the social environment once a sufficient number of people heard of the ideas

and came to agree with them (sort of a *social critical mass*). As such, they saw religious groups as collectives of individuals who share a large number of related beliefs. Religion, to Tylor and Frazer, was a set of these beliefs that — although sincerely believed at one point — must now be seen as foolish, ignorant, illogical and absurd. Tylor and Frazer were highly respected philosophers in the 1800s and early 1900s; but, they certainly were not "religion friendly".

Functional Projection

"Religion [is] the universal obsessional neurosis of humanity."
– Dr. Sigmund Freud

"Religion is an illusion, and it derives its strength from the fact that it falls in with our instinctual desires." – Dr. Sigmund Freud

Dr. Sigmund Freud (left), the developer of psychoanalysis, had some very definite opinions about religion. Freud saw everything in terms of psychology — including religion. Since Feuerbach had so cavalierly dismissed the spiritual, and Freud's contemporaries (Tylor and Frazer) insisted that religion was inherently absurd, the question became: "why, if it is utterly absurd and foolish, has humanity clung to these superstitions so tenaciously?"

This was the area where Freud felt he could contribute to the discussion. A pioneer of the inner workings of the human mind, Freud was certain that if anyone could answer this question, he was the one. Freud thought that the real attraction of religion, the ultimate source of its appeal, was the human subconscious — maintaining that faith arose from the emotional and psychological conflicts that originated in early childhood. Therefore, he concluded that religion was best seen as an *obsessional neurosis*. If Freud was correct, and if it is as he maintained, pointing out that it was superstitious and illogical would be no more likely to dissuade a believer than pointing out the disadvantages of short fingernails would alter the behavior of an obsessive fingernail biter.

Social Encapsulation

> *"Society is the soul of religion."*
> – David Émile Durkheim

Émile Durkheim (right) is often referred to as the *father of sociology*; and, Durkheim, a noted French scientist, saw religion as a predominantly social function. He wrote that, although we all make personal choices and decisions, we make these choices within the social framework we inherit at birth. He saw a kind of *social treasury*  present in all societies — including such items as language, habits, rights, inventions, *et cetera*. What is of interest here is that chief among these cultural treasures, as Durkheim saw them, was religion. Rather than a peripheral factor, he believed religion actually serves a crucial role in the cultural life of society — providing the ideas, rituals and sentiments that guide us throughout our lives.

Durkheim's idea of the inter-relatedness of culture and religion may seem rather obvious to us today; but, at the time he proposed it in the early 1900s, this was a radical idea. Tylor and Frazer had seen religion as the consequence of a single individual's thoughts and ideas (that *savage philosopher*); Freud saw it as evidence of an obsessional neurosis; but, Durkheim introduced the idea that it was an integral part of the social fabric — essentially, an encapsulation of society's structure. To Durkheim, it wasn't foolish, ignorant, or absurd; neither was it a form of mental illness. It was a normal, healthy social function — a 'social treasure'.

Social Opiate

> *"Religion is the sigh of the oppressed creature, the feeling of a heartless world, and the soul of soulless circumstances. It is the opium of the people."*
> — Dr. Karl Heinrich Marx

Karl Marx is often remembered as the economic philosopher whose primary work, <u>Das Kapital</u>, served as a basis for modern communism. Marx, however, also had a great deal to say about religion — particularly in his later writings. Marx was not very interest-

ed in what people believed, how they put it into practice, or why they believed what they did. What did interest him was the role that beliefs played in what he saw as an inevitable class struggle. Marx agreed whole heartedly with Tylor and Frazer that religious beliefs were absurd; he also agreed with Freud and Durkheim that what was more important was determining why people held them anyway — what *function* they served. He thought he knew.

Marx saw religion as meeting an inherent need for security. He was convinced that, once the economically oppressed people of the world resolved their class struggle, religious beliefs would wither away as an unnecessary remnant of the capitalist burden they had escaped. Marx thought religion got people to tolerate economic subjugation now in return for some future reward in heaven. That was the primary reason Lenin and others who established communist governments officially made their states atheist. Expecting that the class struggle had been resolved by their revolution, they considered religion no longer relevant.

Spiritual Reality

"I myself do nothing. The Holy Spirit accomplishes all through me."
– William Blake

Dr. Mircea Eliade (left) took a different approach from Tylor, Frazer, Freud, Marx or Durkheim. Most of them began with the assumption that religious belief was absurd; and, the exception to this (Durkheim) regarded the "validity" of religious belief to be irrelevant. Eliade argued that you could not legitimately take either position. He argued that, just as only an Egyptian can truly appreciate Egyptian architecture, or only a skilled musician can appreciate Mozart, we can only truly appreciate religious beliefs through the eyes of a believer. He acknowledged that individual psychology, economic factors, social constructs, and other forces all have their effects on religion; but, he maintained that they neither cause it nor dictate its fundamental beliefs.

Eliade clearly believed in God. Although he was very discreet as to what form those beliefs took, he never backed away from his fundamental belief in God (his PhD was from India, and his thesis was on yoga). Some scholars claim that this gave his work a pro-religious bias, and skeptics therefore maintain his views must be summarily dismissed. This, however, is unacceptable when these same critics rarely had a problem with admittedly anti-religious biases on the part of others (who were often openly atheist).

Cultural System

"Religion is a candle inside a multicolored lantern. Everyone looks through a particular color, but the candle is always there."
– Mohammed Neguib

Clifford Geertz (right) was an American anthropologist who took Durkheim's ideas one step further: seeing religion as not only having a cultural meaning for society, but actually serving as the vehicle which conveys it. He objected strenuously to the views of Marx and others in the sense that he believed trying to reduce all human religion to economic struggles, social demands, or psychological neuroses had no real value at all. He declared that these grand approaches neglect the *system of meanings* conveyed in religion, and that this is equivalent to trying to explain the workings of a computer without mentioning software, or trying to explain a book without ever mentioning the presence of words.

To Dr. Geertz, *religion was what conveyed cultural meaning* for a given society. This differed from Durkheim's approach in that Geertz did not need to propose the non-existence of God to legitimize his view. Although generally accepting the existence of God as axiomatic, he was more concerned with how religion was structured to convey cultural values within a society once that recognition was acknowledged.

Genetic Religiosity

"Although self-transcendence might seem a bit 'flaky' to some readers, it successfully passes the tests for a solid psychological trait. It basically is a yardstick for what is often referred to in the West as faith, or in the East as the search for enlightenment."
– Dr. Dean Hamer

Perhaps the most controversial proposal regarding why humanity appears to be innately religious is that of Dr. Dean Hamer.

Dr. Hamer (below left) was the Director of the Gene Structure and Regulation Unit of the *National Cancer Institute* (a part of the *National Institutes of Health*). In his book  The God Gene: How Faith is Hardwired into our Genes (right), Dr Hamer proposed that religiosity is actually a result of the efficiency of the presynaptic cells in the reuptake of the neurotransmitter serotonin (something which is genetically determined).

Presynaptic Serotonin Receptors Bear with it as we get a little technical for a minute. In 2003, the *American Journal of Psychiatry* published an article by a Swedish team of researchers (Lars Farde; Bengt Andrée; Henrik Soderstrom; Jacqueline Borg) about a study that was done at the Karolinska Institute. What they had discovered was that religiosity appears to be inversely correlated to the degree of serotonin reuptake in the brain. In other words, the greater the reuptake (absorption) of serotonin, the less likely someone was to display religiosity or spirituality.

Serotonin (also known as 5-hydroxytryptamine) is a neurotransmitter that helps to regulate brain function in a number of areas — most notably, mood and sleep. Serotonin is fabricated from the amino acid *tryptophan* (found in large quantities in foods such as turkey and chocolate). This partially explains the sleepiness often associated with large Thanksgiving dinners involving turkey, and the relationship of chocolate to mood.

Put simply, the more serotonin circulating in the blood, the more mellow, sleepy, and contented you tend to be. This is why SSRIs (an abbreviation *for Selective Serotonin Reuptake Inhibitors*) have the effects that they do: they stimulate the creation of additional serotonin, and diminish the body's ability to reabsorb it. In other words, they flood the brain with serotonin. This causes a feeling of well-being. Users report that these drugs often produce euphoria, a sense of connection with other people, and a marked increase of love, happiness and other positive emotions.

Normally, these receptors (presynaptic cells) 'take up' serotinin in a process known as *reuptake*. If something blocks this process, the result is the same as if there were more serotonin being created: *i.e.* a general sense of well-being. Some of the better known drugs that block this reuptake of serotonin in this manner are *Prozac*®, *Paxil*® and *Zoloft*® (all commercial SSRIs). It would stand to reason that biologically having fewer receptors would also create this feeling of "connection", also known as *self transcendence*.

One conclusion that can be drawn (after eliminating all of the technical jargon) is that the serotonin system in the brain may provide a biological impetus for religiosity. Since the concentration of serotonin receptors is genetically determined, this is one possible way in which religiosity may be genetically based.

Religion is a social construct made up of culture, historical events, and meaningful ritual. It is a combination of biology, spirituality, and culture. Dr. Hamer's The God Gene does not speak specifically to religion; he is actually more interested in what was just described as *self transcendence*. This is the process by which someone is able to go beyond their own narrow interests and experiences and 'touch the hem of reality'. It's the ability to see oneself as an integral part of the greater whole.

Dr Hamer makes no attempt to base spirituality, faith, or religion on a single gene, however. Although scientists know that there are some features that appear to be based on a single gene (*e.g.* eye color), there are also many human characteristics that are based on multiple genes (*e.g.* language ability). By far the most important aspect of Dr Hamer's research is his attempt to determine the practical function of human spirituality. This is important because, if spirituality is found to be tied to our genetic code in some way, evolutionary theory would predict that a high level of spirituality must have a beneficial impact on human life. Dr Hamer concludes in his book that 'religiosity makes people happier'. There appears to be a physical response to self-transcendence that has been described as "elation"; and, when someone is feeling elated (*i.e.* "spiritually exalted"), they want to live. The desire to live impels a person to do all the things necessary to survive. and thus serves as a classic example of what Darwin described as "natural selection", and Herbert Spencer rendered as the "survival of the fittest".

If Dr Hamer is correct, it could explain why recovering alcoholics and drug addicts often turn to religiosity. It seems, as was just reviewed in the section on serotonin, that religion, psychotropic drugs, alcohol, Prozac©, Zoloft©, Paxil©, and so forth all yield essentially the same result: self transcendence and euphoria. In his book, Dr Hamer maintains that spirituality and religiosity are neither an accident, a neurosis, an economic response, nor the result of youthful training. He believes they are, instead, largely a consequence of genetic makeup. He suggests that religiosity even perhaps provides an advantage to humans by giving them a sense of purpose and the drive necessary to overcome obstacles.

Summary

All seven of these approaches attempt to explain why religion exists. Why is it so important to humanity? Why does it inevitably appear in cultures across the world and across the centuries?

o Scientific materialists expected religion would simply fade away once humanity became more "scientifically enlightened"; but, some of the most respected scientists have exhibited a strong, personal, religious nature (*e.g.* Albert Einstein, Werner von Braun, Sir Isaac Newton, and Galileo).

o Social reformers expected religion to fade from view once the social conflicts were resolved or eliminated. For example, Marx thought of religion as a tool of the oppressor over the oppressed in a perpetual class struggle; and, a communist state should have therefore eliminated the human need for religion. But, when Cuba revised its constitution in 1992 after 33 years without religion, thousands of churches appeared almost without notice. The original communist state, the Soviet Union, was officially atheist for 69 years, and yet the Russian Orthodox faith proved to be still very much alive and well when the Soviet government fell.

Perhaps, just maybe, the reason religion is so strong is that humans recognize that there truly is a spiritual basis for existence. Maybe science can't answer all of our questions to our satisfaction; maybe sociology can't explain it all away; and, maybe it is neither an economic struggle nor a mental aberration. Maybe.

Chapter 2
Religious Experience

The eye through which I see God is the same eye through which God sees me; my eye and God's eye are one eye, one seeing, one knowing, one love. — Meister Eckhart

Early in the 20th century, Dr William James was invited to be the Gifford Lecturer on Natural Religion at the University of Edinburgh. His role was to conduct 10 lectures in each of 2 semesters. After his appointment ended, James compiled and edited his notes on the twenty lectures, and Harvard University Press published them in what has become a classic in the field of religion: The Varieties of Religious Experience.

William James had a remarkable pedigree. He was:
o the son of the well-known British writer Henry James, Sr.;
o the brother of Alice, noted for her posthumous diaries;
o the brother of American novelist Henry James, Jr;
o a graduate of Harvard Medical School;
o part of naturalist Louis Agassiz' Amazonian expedition;
o a student of both von Helmholtz and Freud;
o an anatomy and physiology professor at Harvard;
o fluent in five languages;
o psychology & philosophy professor (35 years) at Harvard;
o guest lecturer at Edinburgh, Oxford and Stanford; and,
o often in discussion with luminaries such as Emerson, Carlyle, Thoreau, Greeley, Hawthorne, Tennyson, and J.S. Mill (all friends of his father).

James had become a renowned philosopher and psychologist on his own. The value of his book was that it looked at religion — without preconceived biases — from a psychologist's perspective.

James' exploration of religious experience was expansive, but what is most relevant here are his lectures on *mysticism*. It was in these lectures (Gifford Lectures XVI and XVII) that James asked: "What does the expression 'mystical states of consciousness' mean? How do we part off mystical states from other states?"

Dr. James, unlike many of his contemporaries (as well as many scientists today), did not use the word *mystical* with any sense of ridicule or derision. James was sincerely interested in understanding the mystical state of mind — particularly as it related to religious experience, understanding, and revelation. Here, consider *mystical state* and *religious experience* to be virtually synonymous.

What identifies a 'mystical state'?

James identified 4 characteristics correlated with the mystical state. He considered the first two to be sufficient to definitively mark a state of mind as *mystical*, whereas he believed the second two were less consistently required, but generally applied.

Ineffability

It "defies expression, and no adequate report of its contents can be given in words." James readily admitted that this was a negative trait (since it describes a state by what it is not, rather than what it is), but he felt it was clearly the most significant. He added that "mystical states are more like states of feeling than states of intellect." He made it clear, however, that this did not detract from the legitimacy of the mystical state. It requires ears to appreciate and fully comprehend a symphony; and, it takes someone who has been in love to fully understand what it feels like to be in love. Similarly, James believed that it requires one who has had a religious experience (*i.e.* has experienced a mystical state of mind) to truly understand it [compare this to Mircea Eliade on page 8].

Noetic Quality

Despite a distinct resemblance to states of feeling, they convey a strong sense of being a state of knowledge. "They are states of insight into depths of truth unplumbed by the discursive intellect. They are illuminations, revelations, full of significance and importance, all inarticulate though they remain"

Transiency

James maintained that mystical states generally can not be long sustained, and tend to be rather fleeting — he suggests a half hour to 2 hours at their longest. However, they may be sequential, with later ones building upon and expanding earlier experiences.

Passivity

When one of these *mystical states* occurs, the individual has no control over their experience. It seems to 'evolve' without any level of control or direction on the part of the participant, and the experiencer becomes a passive participant in the experience.

Modes of Religious Experience

James essentially identified two forms, or modes, in which a mystical state of consciousness, or *religious experience*, can occur: revelatory and acceptant. The Noetic Quality described above may be 'something new'; it might be, for lack of a better description, a revelation. But, it might also simply be an awareness of something that had previously been known, but had not been fully realized; and, it is likely that the overwhelming majority of human religious experiences fall into this second category. As such, they constitute an acceptance of insight into something already basically understood. Revelatory experiences, however, are sudden realizations, glimpses of truth, or flashes of great understanding.

Revelatory religious experiences are of limited value to anyone other than the one who experiences them unless they are recorded somehow. This is particularly true since the memory of revelatory specifics seems to fade quickly. It is like the dream that, when you awake, is so vivid that you are convinced it would make a great novel; but, after breakfast, you can only recall pieces of it, and it has lost its intensity. Some experiences are recorded in the first moments after the experience; others are recorded *during* it.

Verbal

Some religious experiences have been recounted verbally by the subject in the very first moments following their experience. 40 year old Muhammad experienced visits by the angel Jibra'il (Gabriel) throughout more than 20 years. Muhammad was illiterate; he could neither read nor write. Following each experience, he would *recite* what he had been told to friends and family members. Eighteen years passed after Muhammad's death before a group of reciters had these recitations (which Muhammad had his followers memorize) written down in the volume known to us today as the *Qur'an* (Arabic: "recitations").

Written

Some religious experiences were never voiced, but were initially written out. John [or someone using that *nom de plume*] stated that he "was in the spirit" [Rev 1:10] when instructed to write what he saw and "send it to the churches". Being *in the spirit* was a religious experience, a mystical state of consciousness. What he *wrote* is now known as the *Apocalypse*, or *Book of Revelation* — the final book of the Christian New Testament.

Joseph Smith was just 18 when he reported a visit by the angel Moroni. This angel guided Smith to golden plates inscribed in a foreign language, and provided a translation key. Smith was told to write out the translation of the text engraved on the plates, and to share it with the world. We now call that transcription *The Book of Mormon*.

Auto-writing

Mary Baker Eddy wrote an explanatory handbook, or biblical commentary, for what became Christian Science. Mrs. Eddy later insisted that she had to go back and read *Science and Health with Key to the Scriptures* because she had no idea what she had written, stating that it was "as if [her] hand had been guided".

Channelling

In her religious experience, Dr Helen Schucman served as the channel for the voice of a disembodied spirit that identified itself as *Yeshua* (Aramaic for *Jesus*). Her *channelled experiences* were tape recorded and transcribed over a period of 7 years until they were collected, bound, and published as *A Course in Miracles*. William James had refused to consider mystical states of consciousness (*i.e.* religious experiences) as something to be ridiculed, or that occurred only to the uneducated and superstitious, and Schucman was a good example of what James had meant. Schucman: held a PhD in psychology; was raised Jewish, but was not religiously active, and had publicly declared herself an atheist; was a professor of medical psychology at Columbia University; and, at the time of the channeling, worked on it with Dr. William Thetford [Director of Clinical Psychology at Columbia-Presbyterian Hospital].

Historical Spontaneous Religious Experiences

Looking at this chronologically, there are numerous historical religious experiences that could be used as examples (strictly for convenience, these are all pre–1800). In fact, most religions have resulted from someone's religious experience. To understand the breadth, diversity, and similarities of these experiences, consider these as being at least potentially representative of the event.

Muhammad [570–632]

Muhammad was an Arab born into the Quraysh tribe, the group that controlled the local commercial and political scene. At the age of 40, Muhammad was standing vigil in a cave in the mountains near his home when he had a religious experience — a personal visit by the angel Jibra'il (Gabriel). These nightly visitations continued for the remainder of his life, and what the angel spoke was later recorded as the Muslim scripture, the *Qur'an*. These serialized experiences resulted in what is currently the second largest religion in the world.

Joan of Arc [1412–1431]

Known as the *Maid of Orléans*, she forced the English to break their military siege of that city. Joan "heard voices"; and, later, even saw the angels and saints who frequently talked to her. At the age of 19, the English convicted her of witchcraft and heresy; she was executed by being burned at the stake. However, her religious experiences appear to have been spontaneous, and she was later canonized (recognized as a Saint) by the Roman Catholic church.

George Fox [1624–1691]

Fox was a member of an English group known as the Seekers. Fox experienced a realization that every human possessed a divine spark, or inner light. As a result, he completely separated from the official Church of England (Anglican) as well as the sectarian alternatives that flourished in England during the mid-1600s. Fox taught the sanctity of human life, and the inherent superiority of God-given inspiration to scriptural edict. Ridiculed, jailed, and condemned, his following (known as *The Religious Society of Friends* or *The Friends of Truth*) grew. Derisively called *Quakers* by their critics, Fox led the group until his death.

Emanuel Swedenborg [1688–1772]

Born Emanuel Svedberg, Swedenborg was born into a Swedish Lutheran family. A scientist (geologist) respected by both royalty and his peers, Swedenborg began having "spiritual experiences" (as he described them) at the age of 48. Lasting for about 11 years, these dreams, mystical journeys, and communication with the spirit world provided him with revelatory insight into the nature of reality and the fate of the soul after death.

The Theosophical Society was created in England for the sole purpose of studying his revelations. After his death, this group evolved into the *Church of the New Jerusalem* (commonly called the *Swedenborgian Church*).

John Wesley [1703–1791]

Wesley was an ordained Anglican priest. While a fellow at Lincoln College (Oxford), he joined a Bible study group known as the *Holy Club* (known to critics as *Bible Bigots*). He experienced what can be described as a religious experience on 24 May 1738. Wesley was listening to Martin Luther's preface to the *Epistle to the Romans* being read at a Moravian meeting when he "felt [his] heart strangely warmed". This convinced him of the personal relationship with Christ one attains when saved by faith alone.

Wesley began writing and preaching on his experience, and this evolved into organized groups and associations. Technically a society of the Anglican church until 3 years after his death (1794), he had drawn up rules for governing these associations as early as 1743, and had started ordaining "Methodist" ministers in 1784.

Induced Religious Experiences

Religious experience is not a unique event impacting only select individuals. Many faiths consider it to be a key facet of their belief system. As such, they have devised means to aid an adherent in having this experience. This may be done physically, chemically, psychologically, *et cetera*. Consider the following (there are many others).

Sweat Lodge

The *sweat lodge* is a tradition that is common in many early religious practices, although it is perhaps best known from the Native American practice. It may be a temporary structure or a permanent one, and can be made of birch bark, animal skins, earthen mounds, cedar boards, *et cetera*.  A Navajo sweat lodge (right) most often resembles a simple tent; others, such as the Hopi, may just be an excavated, covered pit which may reach more than 130°F and 100% humidity. In both cases, rocks, fire, and occasionally water (in a Hopi sweat lodge) are used to bring the internal temperature and humidity well above that of the outside.

Shamans, elders, chiefs, leaders, and (at times) all male adults in the community may enter the sweat lodge for a ceremony. It is considered a preparation or purification rite by most users, and generally results in a religious experience for those involved. This usually involves several days of prayer and chanting in the extreme heat — often without food or water.

Organic Drugs

Peyote is an organic hallucinogen derived from a common Mexican cactus. It has been used in sacramental rituals by Toltecs and other MesoAmerican natives for a minimum of 3,000 years — producing visions, healings, and religious experiences.

The psilocybin mushroom was more often the plant of choice by North American natives. Again, this was used primarily in sacramental rituals. Marijuana is often used in the Rasta faith for similar rituals.

Smoke

Smoke is often symbolic — rising from the human smoker to the spiritual heavens. Although the Hopi combine it with the sweat lodge experience, it also often occurs alone. Tobacco — in sufficient concentration — is hallucinogenic. Religious practitioners around the world use tobacco (and other hallucinogens) in nearly every way imaginable: smoked, blown, drunk, snorted, chewed, eaten, sucked, licked, and even injected rectally.

The Taino *caciques* (the ancient native tribal chiefs of Puerto Rico) smoked as a means to communicate with the spirits of their ancestors, whom they recognized as having become tutelary spirits (*i.e.* guardian angels). This human–spirit contact was a religious experience for them as they communed with *cemíes* (wood or stone idols; many carved from the ancestor's bones) with smoke.

Many of the natives of the American plains (such as the Lakota Sioux) would use smoking as a ritual preparation or purification, and as a *seal* upon the completion of an important event (leading to the settlers' concept of a *peace pipe*). When at war, or moving, natives would bring a pipe with them already packed with tobacco for future sacramental use — sealed with buffalo fat until needed.

Trance

Working oneself into a trance, a hypnotic-like state, has been a common method of gaining a religious experience. The group of Sufi masters often disrespectfully called *whirling dervishes* (left, in Turkey) spin and dance until they literally fall from exhaustion — often entering a trance leading to religious experience.

An excellent Western example of this form of religious experience was embodied in the thousands of visions and *ecstatic transports* of Ellen Gould White [1827–1915], the prophetess and founder of the Seventh Day Adventist movement. Mrs. White was baptized as a Methodist, but soon followed the charismatic millennial leader, William Miller. Her visions led her followers to a life of vegetarianism, abstinence from alcohol and tobacco, avoidance of drugs in treating illness, and an unparalleled missionary zeal.

Asceticism & Deprivation

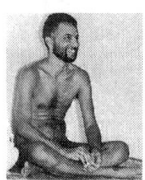

Ascetics are found world-wide. The practice of asceticism consists of the renunciation of all physical pleasures, as well as self-denial of all but the most fundamental level of material subsistence (*e.g.* Jain monk, left). It is generally regarded as an aid to spiritual development, and often as a precursor to religious experience. In the Oglala Sioux nation, the individual (under the guidance of a shaman) would go to a totally isolated spot (such as a specific hill, or clearing), and would remain there to practice *hanbleceya* (literally, "crying out for a vision"). He would remain there — without any food or water — until he had his vision (usually ~4 days). Often known as a *Vision Quest*, this was essentially a deprivation induced religious experience. He would then return to the village and ask the shaman (sacred person) for assistance in interpreting the vision he had.

Dance

The Hopi nation (and related natives) in the US southwest, fashion *Katchinas* to embody certain spirits for them. During ceremonial functions, members of the Hopi wear costumes to play the part of a particular katchina during a ritualistic dance (*e.g.* the Hopi rain dance). Frequently, these dances result in visions or other experiences for those who take part.

Meditation

Meditation is viewed as a means of putting the conscious mind "on hold" so that the soul is not distracted by earthly interference, and is commonly used in a number of religious expressions (such as Raja Yoga, Jnana Yoga, and several Christian groups); but, it is probably best known as the means used by His Holiness Maharishi Mahesh Yogi (right) in his *Transcendental Meditation* movement. Touted in the west for its ability to lower blood pressure, reduce heart rate, and even produce spontaneous healings, it is used in the east primarily for its value in attaining *moksha* (spiritual release).

Sex

Perhaps one of the most unexpected means of inducing a religious experience is sex! Rajneesh Chandra Mohan (right) was born in India into a Jain family. After obtaining a Masters Degree in Philosophy, he was employed as a Philosophy Professor at an Indian university for

9 years. During this time, he gradually became the spiritual advisor to a small group, and changed his name to Baghwan Shri Rajneesh [1931–1990]. This translates roughly into English as 'Master Rajneesh, the Blessed One'.

Rajneesh left the university in the early 1960s, moved to Mumbai, and established the Rajneesh Foundation. In 1974, the group moved to Pune (a regional city not far from Mumbai) to establish an ashram (a large, communal teaching center). Although his unique brand of spirituality has been described as a syncretic mix of Taoist, Hindu, and Christian beliefs, his central teaching was *dynamic meditation*. This 'no-effort meditation' was accomplished by participating in some physical activity that totally occupied the physical senses to the point of exhaustion — to 'get the physical senses out of the way' so that the unhampered mind would be free to experience communion with God. Periods of meditation follow this strenuous physical period, with the physical body "falling away" and leaving the spirit free to commune with God.

Some of the ways of inducing exhaustion with which he experimented at the ashram included hours of continuous laughter, crying, primal screaming, and hours of — you guessed it — continuous sex. This required volunteers to help adherents prepare for meditation; and, still today, the Pune ashram boldly places a sign on the streetside entrance that reads "Free sex — with AIDS-free government issued certificate of health."

Contemporary Religious Experiences

Dr. Timothy Leary [1920–1996]

Dr. Leary (left) taught psychology at the University of California in Berkeley. When his wife committed suicide in 1955, Leary was totally distraught. In time, he left California and returned to his home state of Massachusetts — accepting a position as Professor of Psychology at Harvard University in 1959. While on a research field study in México in 1960, Leary was first introduced to psilocybin mushrooms, a naturally occurring hallucinogenic. When he returned to Harvard that year, he initiated what became known as the *Harvard Psilocybin Project* to investigate the effect that hallucinogenic drugs have on the mind — an official, University sanctioned project.

Leary first took LSD in 1962, describing it as "the most shattering experience of my life". Let go by Harvard in 1963, Leary founded several groups that tried to find the 'psychedelic utopia' described by Aldous Huxley in *Island*. Using LSD in place of the mushrooms (a cheaper, synthetic form of the drug), Leary maintained that hallucinogens had altered his views on life (a religious experience?), but with side effects. Leary was quoted as once saying that "There are three side effects of acid: enhanced long term memory, decreased short term memory, and I forget the third."

Dr. Richard Alpert [1931–]

Dr. Alpert (right) was a peer and fellow professor with Leary at Harvard in the early 1960s. He joined with Leary in the *Harvard Psilocybin Project*, was let go by Harvard with Leary, and joined with him in the attempt to find that psychedelic utopia. Deeply impacted by his drug induced experiences, and disappointed in their failure to find utopia psychedelically, Alpert left for India in 1967. There, he met his guru, Neem Karoli Baba, and changed his name to Ram Dass. Upon returning to the US, Dass founded several service charities, lectured, taught, and authored a number of books — all clearly Hindu in nature.

Dr. Ralph Metzner

The third member of the *Harvard Psilocybin Project* was Dr. Ralph Metzner (right). Metzner co-authored *The Psychedelic Experience* with Leary and Alpert in 1964. This book, the result of their experiments, was essentially a modern rewrite of the *Tibetan Book of the Dead*. In reflecting back, Metzner said that "To die and be reborn is a metaphor for the most radical and total transformation that consciousness and identity can undergo." Since his life changing experiences, Metzner has founded several ecological groups, and conducts seminars and lectures on *The Unfolding Self*, *Shamanism*, and *Consciousness Studies*.

Edgar Cayce [1877–1945]

Edgar Cayce (left) demonstrated an uncanny ability to put himself into a kind of self-induced sleep by lying down on a couch, closing his eyes, and folding his hands over his stomach. This state of relaxation-meditation-trance reportedly enabled him to place his mind in contact with all time and space. In this state, he responded to questions as diverse as, "What are the secrets of the universe?" to "How can I remove a wart?" His answers to these questions were called "readings", and were often used to explore the great religious questions of life. Cayce was a devout Christian and a dedicated Sunday School teacher (Disciples of Christ); but, his readings were widely divergent from traditional Christianity.

Verification

By their very nature, religious experiences can not generally be verified. You'll recall that James compared them to the wonder of a symphony and the feeling of being in love; the former is not understandable to someone without ears, and the second is foreign to someone who has never been in love. Similarly, a mystical state of consciousness can truly only be appreciated by someone who has had their own religious experience.

Verify comes from the Latin *vērus* (which meant "true"). But, as James said, these experiences are "more like states of feeling than states of intellect", and determining if a *feeling* is true is much different from assessing an intellectual fact. So, asking if they can be verified is inappropriate.

Those that believe there is no God, and that religious experiences are therefore inherently absurd and ludicrous, often claim a person who says that they had such an experience was drunk, insane, stoned, stupid, or perhaps experiencing a psychotic break.

Those that accept the implications of another's religious experience generally point to the otherwise unexplained changes in their life, the increase in spiritual devotion that often follows, and the perceived impact that their experience had indirectly on the lives of others. In other words, they consider the only way that an experience can ever be verified is by the results that it engenders.

Chapter 3
Religious Ontology

Organization charts and fancy titles count for next to nothing.
— *Colin Powell*

Ants have the most complicated social organization on earth next to humans.
— *E. O. Wilson*

Before specific religious traditions can be reviewed, which belief systems and groups should be considered needs to be determined. To do this, a basic *religious ontology* needs to be agreed upon. This is a systematic grouping of religions similar to how the physical world is classified by kingdom, family, species, genus, *et cetera*. This will provide an overview of some of the ways in which religions are "related". To start, what is included in the general "religion" group in the first place? There are several items that are religious, but do not necessarily constitute "religion".

Spirituality

Spirituality is a person's innate desire to "make a connection" with Ultimate Reality. It typically has no organized physical form.  There doesn't need to be an organized group or structure (*i.e.* religion) for spirituality to flourish. Jiddu Krishnamurti (left) was very popular as a speaker on college campuses throughout nearly all of the 20th century. He began his public career as the religious icon of a group of Theosophists. After having a dramatic, personal, religious experience, Krishnamurti disbanded this group – a group which had been financing both the movement and his personal needs. In doing so, in a speech he gave to the core group on August 3rd, 1929, he said the following:

> I maintain that truth is a pathless land, and you can not approach it by any path whatsoever, by any religion, by any sect. That is my point of view, and I adhere to that absolutely and unconditionally. Truth, being limitless, unconditioned, unapproachable by any path whatsoever, can not be organized; nor should any organization be formed to lead or to coerce people along any particular path. If you first understand that, then

you will see how impossible it is to organize a belief. A belief is purely an individual matter, and you cannot and must not organize it. If you do, it becomes dead, crystallized; it becomes a creed, a sect, a religion, to be imposed on others.

Krishnamurti's position is an excellent example of the class of beliefs here being called *spirituality*. Note that this is describing an approach, and not an actual set of beliefs.

Dr. Peter Singer (right) is a world renowned ethicist, and is currently (since 1999) Professor of Bioethics at Princeton University. He is well known for:
- o writing the book *Animal Liberation*, which others (*e.g.* PETA) adopted as virtually scriptural for the animal rights movement;
- o authoring the macropædia article on Ethics for the *Encyclopædia Britannica*;
- o authoring numerous books (*e.g. In Defense of Animals, Embryo Experimentation, Practical Ethics,* and *The Great Ape Project*) and professional articles in the field of ethics;
- o founding the Great Ape Project – a movement to get great apes (Gorillas, Chimps, *et cetera*) legally declared "persons" by the UN and countries around the world so they would be accorded basic rights (*e.g.* right to life, prohibition of torture, no medical experimentation, individual liberty); and,
- o being one of the best known atheists in the world.

Singer's belief system would also fall under spirituality – even though some may find the use of the term *spiritual* to be oxymoronic when applied to an atheist. Nevertheless, his obvious desire to 'make a connection' with Ultimate Reality (which his many writings clearly illustrate) certainly puts him into this category as much as it does Krishnamurti.

Religiosity

Religiosity is an adherence to a set of religious beliefs or practices that may or may not be organized. Typically, there are two forms that religiosity can take: a lack of association with any organized religious body; or, association with multiple bodies. This is perhaps best understood by looking at an example of each form.

Ch 3 – Religious Ontology

Dr. Huston Smith (below) is probably the most recognized religious scholar in the US (perhaps the world). Dr. Smith served as a professor at MIT, Syracuse, Washington University, and the Universities of Colorado, Denver, and California at Berkeley. He has  written extensively, and was the focus of a 1996 PBS television mini-series with Bill Moyer. Personally, Smith practices Advaita Hinduism, Buddhism, Sufi Islam, Taoism, and Methodist Christianity — *simultaneously!* It would be difficult, if not impossible, to pin a specific religious label on Dr Smith; and yet, he is clearly religious. This seeming paradox can be summed up in a quote from an interview published in the November-December 1997 issue of *Mother Jones* magazine:

> Institutions are not pretty. Show me a pretty government. Healing is wonderful, but the American Medical Association? Learning is wonderful, but universities? The same is true for religion... religion is institutionalized spirituality.

At the opposite extreme are those who have no association with any religious organization. An example of this would be any of the million Americans who are classified as Wiccan solitaries. These are followers of the Pagan faith of Wicca (witchcraft) who practice and worhip as individuals – not having established a tie to any formal Wiccan group. These are not often known to the public; however, one who is would be Edwin Courtenay, a popular English witch who often facilitates Wiccan retreats and festivals in the UK. Courtenay is clearly religious, but maintains no formal association with any organized religious group.

Religion

An organized religious belief system is, by definition, a religion. Be careful with this term, however; this does not imply, by labeling something a *religion*, the value of the belief system. It is merely a recognition of the fact that there is some level of organizational structure related to the belief system in question. Examples abound, and are well known to virtually every American student — *e.g.* Christianity, Hinduism, Judaism, Taoism, Zoroastrianism, Islam, Buddhism, *et cetera*..

Cult

To most religious people today, "cult" is a four letter word (in more ways than one). The Roman Catholic faithful often consider the more liberal Protestant bodies to be cults; some of the more conservative Protestants consider Roman Catholicism a cult; the German government calls Scientology a cult; the media called Heaven's Gate a cult; the US government (or, at least the ATF) considered the Branch Davidians a cult; Congress saw People's Temple as a cult; ... The "anti-cult" groups on the internet seem to think that nearly everything is a cult; while, at the same time, the most unbiased religious resources refuse to use the term at all. The problem is obvious: it isn't simple! So, what do those people who use the word mean when they say "cult"; and, are these all really cults? And, why are there others who seem to avoid the term altogether? To answer this, we need to be able to define the term.

What People Mean

The *Cult Awareness and Information Centre* specializes in "warning" people about what they consider to be cults. On their website, they give the following analogy:

A goldfish living in a bowl that is painted black on the outside will never know it lives in a bowl unless someone takes it out and shows it the rest of the world. Mindsets can be like that — locked into a 'thinking box', unable to see outside because the web of beliefs is so all-encompassing ...

In the USA alone there are an estimated 5,000 cults actively recruiting people of all ages, from all walks of life, at the rate of thousands of new recruits every year.

It is important at the outset when viewing this web site to know that the woman who founded it provided numerous religious organizations as examples — religions which are generally recognized as perfectly legitimate religious expressions by most theological experts. Examples of these include:

- Jehovah's Witness
- Latter-Day Saints (Mormon)
- Christian Science
- Seventh Day Adventist
- Scientology
- Readers of Deepak Chopra
- Baha'i
- ...

The CAIC arrived at this list by using the following definition: "Any group which deviates from Biblical, orthodox, historical Christianity – *i.e.* any who deny: the Deity of Christ; His physical resurrection; His personal and physical return to earth, and salvation by FAITH alone." Clearly, this puts many groups in line to be classified as cults — including Islam, Buddhism, Hinduism, Taoism, Judaism, and many of the Protestant denominations.

Other examples of the misuse of the word appear in hundreds of books. For example, the book *Fast Facts on False Teachings* by Ron Carlson and Ed Decker provides a definition for cult as a group that "espouses false teachings". They then list groups they believe espouse false teachings; they identify specific cults:

- Atheism
- Buddhism
- Confucianism
- Hindusism
- Judaism
- Jehovah's Witnesses
- Taoism
- Quakers
- Christian Scientists
- Baha'i
- Mormons
- 7th Day Adventists
- Islam
- Neo-Pagan
- Unitarian Universalism
- New Age
- Roman Catholicism

In total, they identify more than 5 billion people as belonging to cults; that is roughly ¾ of the entire human population on earth! When anyone, for any reason, stretches a definition this far, it ceases to have any meaningful value.

Derivation

Those who spend time and money warning people about cults often show that the word comes from the Latin *cultus*. This is claimed to involve "worship, ritual, emotion, liturgy and attitude." In fact, however, this meaning comes more likely through the Old French *culte*. It turns out that the Latin verb *cultivare* (of which *cultus* is the past participle) has diverged widely and taken on many modern forms: *e.g.* culture, colony, and cultivate. Thesauri commonly list sect, religion, and denomination as synonyms. The most critical term with which it is usually equated is *schism*. Since a cult is a group that was "cultivated from" some parent group, it should be expected to disagree with the parent group's beliefs, practices and liturgy (otherwise, it wouldn't have split from it).

How can *cult* be reasonably defined?

A reasonable definition for "cult" is the *Anthropological Definition*. Typically, anthropologists look to see how many of five criteria are met. These criteria are that a cult has:
  (1) a charismatic, powerful leader(s);
  (2) a group mentality that denies individuality and personal, independent thought;
  (3) a denial of intimacy through exclusion or alienation of friends and relatives;
  (4) financial pressure and abuse for the welfare of the group (often at the personal expense of the adherent); and,
  (5) separation and isolation from the surrounding community.

To the extent that a group meets these criteria, it may properly be called a "cult"; but, to the degree it does not, you are likely being unnecessarily derisive and relying on a connotation rather than what it actually means.

Summary

> "God has made different religions to suit different aspirations, times and countries...one can reach God if one follows any of the paths with wholehearted devotion." – Swami Ramakrishna

There are thousands of religions in the world today. With regard to the US (according to one of the few reliable and respected internet web sites in this area[1]), "The total number of faith groups in the U.S. cannot be calculated. The value depends upon exactly how one defines *faith group* or *religion*. Perhaps we can say that every person's religion is, to some degree, unique. Thus there are over 200 million religions in the U.S." In terms of organizations, there are at least 2,000 in the US, and more than 5,000 world wide.

Before simply taking somebody's word for it, use the above criteria whenever you hear a group called a cult. You may be surprised to discover that, in most cases, the use of the term *cult* is more often indicative of the speaker's bias and wishful thinking than it is of reality.

---

[1] Ontario Consultants on Religious Tolerance (www.religioustolerance.org)

A Proposed Ontology

Having defined spirituality, religiosity, religion and cult, it is now possible to define a proposed *ontology* (or *taxonomy*) of religions. In such a form (next page), expressions of spirituality or religiosity which are not organized into structured bodies are not included. Only organized *religions* are included.

The remainder of the chapters will focus entirely on the *Natural* religions. So, before we move on, let's take a look at some examples of both spurious and parody religions.

Spurious Religions

Organized religions formed for purposes other than spiritual beliefs are spurious religions. Although often considered a derogatory classification, there may be no disputing the reason why a particular religious organization was formed. When that reason is not primarily to spread or encourage the beliefs of a particular faith system, that organization may properly be called a *spurious religion* — without any derogatory connotation.

The **Church of Satan** was founded in California in 1966 by Anton Szandor LaVey. Although this religion technically still exists (LaVey died in 1997), it has never had any appreciable membership. Those who do claim to belong to the faith appear, more often than not, to be young people using membership to upset friends and relatives, or actors seeking exposure in the entertainment press. It began during the early years of the counter-culture movement of the sixties; and, the founder, LaVey (real name: Howard Levey), used the church primarily as a source of income. After having worked as a circus roustabout, burlesque theater organist, and several other jobs, the Church of Satan provided him with a lifelong income. Many of LaVey's autobiographical claims can not be verified. The primary church scripture, *The Satanic Bible*, was assembled by LaVey (not 'written' due to extensive plagiarism from the writings of Ragnar Redbeard, Ayn Rand, and John Dee). In fact, the book itself was not originally intended as a satanic scripture; Avon Books© approached LaVey and asked him to write it to coincide with the release of their movie, Rosemary's Baby. This is an example of a *petitionary spurious religion*.

A 5-Level Religious Ontology

- Metaphysical Beliefs
  - ♦ Agnosticism (*existence of god unknown*)
    - Open Agnosticism (*existence of god is unknown*)
    - Closed Agnosticism (*existence of god is unknowable*)
  - ♦ Atheism (*god does not exist*)
  - ♦ Theism (*a god or gods exists*)
    - Polytheism (*multiple gods*)
      - ➢ Animism (*all entities have a spirit or soul*)
      - ➢ Soft Polytheism (*deities are aspects of a single god*)
      - ➢ Hard Polytheism (*deities are distinct and separate*)
        - o Monolatry (*acknowledge many; worship just one*)
        - o Henotheism (*situational worship of just one*)
        - o Kathenotheism (*temporal worship of just one*)
    - Monotheism (*one God*)
      - ➢ Natural (*exist to worship God*)
        - o Pantheism (*all is God*)
        - o Panentheism (*all is in God, but God is much more*)
        - o Inclusive (*all gods are seen as ethnic variants of one God*)
        - o Exclusive (*only one God, and 'our God' is that God*)
        - o Physical (*focus is on nature and how to control & use it*)
        - o Social (*focus of faith is on how to co-exist with others*)
        - o Psychological (*focus is on personal relationship with God*)
      - ➢ Spurious (*exist for reasons other than worship*)
        - o Constructive (*purpose is to ensure access to privileges*)
        - o Protective (*purpose is to protect against discrimination*)
        - o Petitionary (*purpose is to secure tangible benefits*)
      - ➢ Parody (*exist to mock natural religion*)
        - o Earnest (*created for a religious or practical reason*)
        - o Frivolous (*created for amusement or non-practical reason*)

- ❖ Eutheism (*God is good*)
- ❖ Maltheism (*God is evil*)
- ❖ Dystheism (*God may be good or evil at different times*)

The ***Universal Life Church*** was founded in California in 1959 by the Reverend Kirby J. Hensley. Reverend Hensley was an ordained Baptist minister, but the ULC was formed to accept "all peoples" — it has no formal dogma or creed, and no set beliefs (except for everyone to get along). Although it initially operated out of Henley's garage, he ran for President of the United States on the Universal Party ticket in both 1964 and 1968. Although Hensley later admitted to Morley Safer on the CBS show *60 Minutes* "Why sure, I'm a con man.", he did not mean that the *Universal Life Church* was fraudulent. His statement, however, does establish it as a spurious religion – a faith started for reasons other than to propagate a belief system. There were 2 primary reasons why Henley began the church: as a means to enable him to get his house declared a church to avoid paying property taxes; and, to serve as the sponsoring body for others to be ordained – enabling them to pursue personal religious careers by making it legal for them to perform marriages, funerals, prison chaplain services, *et cetera* (as a *constructive spurious religion*). Although they do raise money by selling some highly questionable items (*e.g.* sainthood), ordination is – and always has been – free.

Finally, an example of a *protective spurious religion* is the ***Covenant of the Goddess***. This Pagan association was founded in 1975 "to secure for Witches and covens the legal protection enjoyed by members of other religions." It is expected that members will already have a set of pagan beliefs (not specified by the CoG) prior to requesting membership. Once admitted, however, they provide assistance and support to member groups and individuals to ensure that they are not discriminated against. They provide legal aid, legal counseling, recognized ordination, and a host of other services often denied non-mainstream religions.

In each of these examples, the spurious religion in not a false religion, but a faith organization whose goal and intent is something other than propagation of faith. It may be *protective* (such as ensuring the legal protection requisite to practice in peace), *constructive* (to enable members to perform tasks legally reserved for recognized religious structures), or *petitionary* (*e.g.* financial gain).

Parody Religions

A religion organized to ridicule, point out flaws, or parody either a specific religion or religion in general is known as a parody religion. These may be founded or supported by devout people who simply want a faith to recognize its flaws (and do something about them), by people who are thoroughly anti-religion (and want to harm them), by people trying to produce public entertainment, or one of any number of other groups of people.

The **Church of the SubGenius** is one of the earliest of the current crop of parody religions – founded in 1953 by the Sub-Genius Foundation of Dallas, Texas. Some of the better known people who have been formally ordained as ministers of the church include Paul Reubens (actor *Pee Wee Herman*), Penn Jillette (the speaking half of the magi-comedy team of *Penn & Teller*), Frank Zappa (leader of the *Mothers of Invention* rock group), and David Byrne (founding member of the *Talking Heads* band). One of the more important ministers of the church, however, was Philip Gale (the whiz who developed the technical basis for *Earthlink*). The central figure of the faith is J.R. "Bob" Dobbs (left) who was, in fact, a piece of 1950's pre-computer, publishing clip art.

The purpose of the church is to parody two specific religious systems: Evangelical faiths (of whatever persuasion); and, the Church of Scientology (Gale was raised as a Scientologist until he committed suicide while at MIT – in fact, his technical brainchild, Earthlink, was founded by Scientologist Sky Dalton).

The church is unashamedly commercial – selling clerical ordination for $30, and making blatant, often crass appeals for funds. If you are interested in ordination, there is no financial risk with that $30 fee: they guarantee salvation or triple your money back (*i.e.* you collect $90 at the pearly gates if you're denied admission).

The *Mark of Dobbs* (or the *Dobbs Icon*) is their logo (left), and the satirical resemblance to a patriarchal Christian cross is typical of the disregard often displayed for virtually all religions – encouraging humor that seems to have no bounds, and often results in what may be seen as very bad taste.

It's not certain exactly when the **Church of the Invisible Pink Unicorn** was founded, although it first appeared in print on 7 July 1990. The central figure of the church is an Invisible Pink Unicorn (or IPU), and utterance of her name is always followed by "Peace Be Upon Her" (or "Peace Be Upon Her Holy Hooves"). Their web site opens with a vague image of the IPU and the following:

> *Invisible Pink Unicorns are beings of great spiritual power. We know this because they are capable of being invisible and pink at the same time. Like all religions, the Faith of the Invisible Pink Unicorns is based upon both logic and faith. We have faith that they are pink; we logically know that they are invisible because we can't see them.*

The church is an atheist creation intended to parody all organized religions by showing what atheists consider to be the inherent logical flaws of faith: because She is invisible, nobody can prove that She doesn't exist nor that She is pink (even if that appears oxymoronic). This is a parody on the near universal belief in a non-material God. A few of the beliefs they espouse include:

- Her preferring pineapple & ham pizza, detesting pepperoni;
- Her "rapture" of socks (explaining their otherwise inexplicable tendency to disappear (*e.g.* 2 go into the dryer, but only 1 comes out);
- Her evil opponent, the Purple Oyster – once one of her minions, but cast out of Her Pastures for the Great Evil of claiming pepperoni & mushroom pizza is preferable to pineapple and ham; and,
- pricking non-believers with Her horn (humans often blame mosquitos for this, as they are generally present because they are attracted to the Goddess).

The **Western Branch of American Reform Presbylutheranism** is not only a parody religion (frivolous), it is fictional. It is the 1st Church of Springfield (on *The Simpsons* TV show); and, it is the church led by the Reverend Lovejoy, and attended by most of the residents of Springfield. It is a Protestant denomination that split with Catholicism over the right to come to church with wet hair.

Basic beliefs include:
- that Pagans, Jews, Hindus, and Homosexuals are hedonistic, and all going to hell;

- o engaging missionaries who serve by ridiculing away the beliefs of native peoples;
- o seeing monogamous gays and stem cells as domestic enemies of the faith; and,
- o denying evolution and believing in Creationism.

The fourth and final example of a parody religion here is one that was created originally as a political protest. It was so clever and well received, however, that it has quickly gained a sizeable following – particularly among college students.

Pastafarianism, also known as ***The Church of the Flying Spaghetti Monster,*** was founded by Bobby Henderson in 2005. It was introduced in a letter he sent (and later made public) to the Kansas State Board of Education. At the time, they were debating whether to grant equal time to the teaching of evolution and Intelligent Design in the Kansas public schools. In November 2005, the Board voted to include Intelligent Design as part of their core science curriculum; but, objections (largely a result of Henderson's parody) reversed that decision just 15 months later (February 2007).

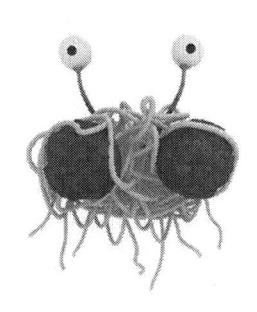

The Flying Spaghetti Monster (left), resembles spaghetti with two meatballs, and is God to this church – also known as His Noodliness, and Spagedeity. Following success in Kansas, Pastafarians next focused attention on the Polk County, Florida School Board which, in December 2007, began consideration of an approach similar to the one in Kansas (under pressure, they dropped the plan).

Henderson followed up on his original letter by writing *The Gospel of the Flying Spaghetti Monster,* which has sold more than 100,000 copies. Collectively, the letter and gospel reveal some interesting facts regarding Pastafarianism – *e.g.* that:
- o there is an invisible, undetectable Flying Spaghetti Monster, which created the universe "after drinking heavily";
- o evidence for evolution was planted by the Flying Spaghetti Monster in an effort to test Pastafarian faith;

Ch 3 – Religious Ontology   37

- o the Flying Spaghetti Monster "is there changing the results with 'His Noodly Appendage'" when scientific measurements, such as radiocarbon dating, are made;
- o heaven contains a beer volcano, and a stripper factory;
- o Hell is similar, but the beer is stale, and the strippers all have VD;
- o the 'Bible' of Pastafarianism is known as the *Loose Canon*;
- o in place of the *Ten Commandments*, there are the *Eight I'd Really Rather You Didn'ts*; and,
- o the official conclusion to prayer is *R'amen* – a portmanteau of the Semitic *Amen* and *Ramen*, the instant noodle.

Michelangelo's *Creation of Adam* was adapted (right) by Niklas Jansson (a follower) for use by Pastafarianism, and has become the virtual brand of the church..

The less stringent alternative to the Mosaic ten commandments begin with "I'd really rather you didn't…" (abbreviated below as IRRYD) rather than "Thou shalt not…". These are:

- o IRRYD act like a sanctimonious holier-than-thou ass when describing my noodly goodness. If some don't believe in me, that's okay. Really, I'm not that vain.
- o IRRYD use my existence as a means to oppress, subjugate, punish, eviscerate, and/or, you know, be mean to others.
- o IRRYD judge people for the way they look, or how they dress, or the way they talk, or, well, just play nice,
- o IRRYD indulge in conduct that offends yourself, or your willing, consenting partner of legal age AND mental maturity.
- o IRRYD challenge the bigoted, misogynistic, hateful ideas of others on an empty stomach. Eat, then go after the bitches.
- o IRRYD build multi-million-dollar churches-temples-mosques-shrines to my noodly goodness when the money could be better spent (take your pick): a) Ending poverty b) Curing diseases   c) Living in peace, loving with passion, and lowering the cost of cable
- o IRRYD go around telling people I talk to you. You're not that interesting. Get over yourself. And I told you to love your fellow man; can't you take a hint?
- o IRRYD do unto others as you would have them do unto you if you are into, um, stuff that uses a lot of leather-lubricant-Las Vegas.

Bottom line on Parody Religions

Parody religions may be classified as Frivolous and have no followers (*e.g. The Western Branch of American Reform Presbylutheranism*), or be classified as Earnest with a loyal and devoted following with a specific purpose in mind (*e.g. Pastafarianism* or the *Church of the SubGenius*). What makes them parody religions is their goal to entertain, ridicule, or point out the flaws of established religion.

Text Structure

This text is divided into seven concentrations: Religious Concepts, Judaism, Christianity, Islam, Hinduism, Buddhism, and Other Paths. A logical question would be: 'Why these seven concentrations?' Why were these religious paths chosen?

As humans, there are several organizational schemes that are commonly employed to organize large amounts of data; but, none of these appear to have been used:
- o **Alphabetical** — Cao Dai would come before Christianity, and Juche would come before Judaism.
- o **Chronological** — Australian Aboriginal faiths are older than most of the faiths chosen, but are not included
- o **Numerical** — there are more followers of Juche or Falun Dafa than there are of Judaism; and,
- o **Geographical** — all of the faiths chosen originated in Asia or Africa, and no faiths were chosen from North or South America, Australia, *et cetera*.

The selection used is based on size and, in large part, on the 3 different focal orientations shown in the ontology chart: physical, social and psychological. The faiths chosen provide an overview of faiths that come from each of these three different perspectives.

Physical Religion   Typically, western cultures (which are largely populated by the so-called Western religions) exercise a desire and intent to control the natural forces around them. They have tended to seek to "have dominion over the fish of the sea, and over the fowl of the air, and over every living thing that moveth upon the earth." [Genesis 1:28] Their attempts to do this have led to scientific discoveries, inventions, weather prediction, reclamation of marsh and wetlands (*e.g.* the Netherlands), dredging of harbors, damming of rivers, flooding of valleys for reservoirs, *et cetera*. These faiths typically perceive that the physical world is there for humanity to use, exploit and control.

Social Religion   East Asian cultures (overwhelmingly populated by East Asian religions) are recognized for their strong, hierarchical family structures, their respect for elders and others in authority, their apparently inherent demand for social structure, *et cetera*. Although some of this may be seen as a politically incorrect stereotype, much of it is nonetheless true. And, their religious beliefs deal with the issues of culture, the issues of people living and working with one another without friction. For example, Confucianism stresses relationships and respect, while Taoism strives for a balance between opposing extremes (the *yin* and *yang*).

Psychological Religion   The South Asian religions (and the cultures they dominate) see humanity's goal as one of trying to perfect the self — to attain release from endless cycles of rebirth, and to reach ultimate union with the godhead. Although the methodologies of Hindus, Buddhists and Jains vary, their ultimate goal is extremely consistent: they view salvation as a personal quest, and this affects their politics, their religion and their culture.

A Closing Thought on the Number and Variety of Religious Systems

> "The same individual might couch the same point in different ways, depending on the audience to which he is speaking. A father talking about the same general subject might speak in different language to his wife or to his five-year-old child or to a professional audience. Such diversity is appropriate, indeed essential, for communication. If the primordial truth had delivered itself in the same idiom to all humankind, it would have been understood by none.. ...One could say that God, to connect with the different temperaments of the different civilizations, perforce must meet them on their own ground. ... We could say that the deepest truths ... are filtered through the distinctive sensibilities of the various civilizations, which we know are different, or there would only be one civilization."   — *Primoridal Tradition*, Huston Smith (1976)

Chapter 4
Proposed Proofs: The Existence of God

Question with boldness even the existence of god; because, if there be one, he must more approve of the homage of reason than that of blindfolded fear.   — *Thomas Jefferson*

I do not feel obliged to believe that same God who endowed us with sense, reason, and intellect had intended for us to forgo their use.   — *Galileo*

Attempts have been made so far to explore what religion is, why humans practice religion, what it means to have a religious experience, and how to sort religions ontologically. These usually rely on one basic assumption: there is someone or something to which this respect is owed. But, is that a reasonable assumption? Scholars, philosophers, scientists, theologians — all have a vested interest in the anwer to that question. The scientific materialist insists that the answer is "no, that is not a reasonable assumption". The problem that they face is that they are left trying to prove a negative, and this is something that is extremely difficult to do.

In the classic 1950 movie *Harvey* (remade in 1972), Elwood P. Dowd (*i.e.* Jimmy Stewart) is befriended by a *pwca* (poo'-kah). In Welsh folklore, the pwca is a mischievous fairy that often stands 6 to 8 feet tall, speaks with a human voice, and takes the form of a giant, hairy animal (*e.g.* a rabbit) — invisible and inaudible to all but those he chooses to befriend. In the film, Elwood's sister, the police, and the doctors at an asylum are all out to prove to Elwood that Harvey is a product of his inebriated imagination. But, they found out how difficult it can be to prove that something nobody can see, hear, smell, taste or touch doesn't exist. This is the problem scientific materialists have in proving that God doesn't exist — *i.e.* they can't.

But, is it any easier to prove that God does exist? It wasn't for Elwood with Harvey (the pwca); but, that hasn't stopped some great minds (and some not so great) from attempting to offer arguments to make God's existence probable, if not indisputable.

There are 15 to 20 reasonably good atempts in this field. This chapter will review 5 of the best known and most convincing.

These cover a span of more than 900 years, and vary widely in their approach. Those covered here are:
- *Intelligent Design* — by William Paley (1800);
- *The Wager* — by Blaise Pascal (1670);
- *Reductio ad Absurdum* — by Saint Anselm (1063);
- *Kalām* — by William Lane Craig (1984); and,
- *Moral Law* — by Clive Staples Lewis (1952).

Intelligent Design

Sometimes referred to as the *watch-maker argument*, this was first presented in 1800 by William Paley [left] in *Natural Theology*. This is a little long, so what follows is an edited and abridged version of his original presentation in his own words.

In crossing a heath, suppose I pitched my foot against a stone and were asked how the stone came to be there. I might possibly answer that for anything I knew to the contrary it had lain there forever; nor would it, perhaps, be very easy to show the absurdity of this answer. But suppose I had found a watch upon the ground, and it should be inquired how the watch happened to be in that place. I should hardly think of the answer which I had before given, that for anything I knew the watch might have always been there. Yet why should not this answer serve for the watch as well as for the stone? Why is it not as admissable in the second case as in the first? For this reason, and for no other, namely, that when we come to inspect the watch, we perceive – what we could not discover in the stone – that its several parts are framed and put together for a purpose, *e.g.* that they are so formed and adjusted as to produce motion, and that motion so regulated as to point out the hour of the day; that if the different parts had been differently shaped from what they are, of a different size from what they are, or placed after any other manner or in any other order than that in which they are placed, either no motion at all would have been carried on in the machine, or none which would have answered the use that is now served by it. ... This mechanism being observed — it requires indeed an examination of the instrument, and perhaps some previous knowledge of the subject, to perceive and understand it; but being once, as we have said, observed and understood — the inference we think is inevitable, that the watch must have had a maker — that there must have existed, at some time and at some place or other, an artificer or artificers who formed it for the purpose which we find it actually to answer, who comprehended its construction and designed its use.

Nor would it, I apprehend, weaken the conclusion, that we had never seen a watch made — that we had never known an artist capable of

Ch 4 – Proposed Proofs: The Existence of God 43

making one — that we were altogether incapable of executing such a piece of workmanship ourselves, or of understanding in what manner it was performed; all this being no more than what is true of some exquisite remains of ancient art, of some lost arts, and, to the generality of mankind, of the more curious productions of modern manufacture. ...

Neither, secondly, would it invalidate our conclusion, that the watch sometimes went wrong or that it seldom went exactly right. ... It is not necessary that a machine be perfect in order to show with what design it was made: still less necessary, where the only question is whether it were made with any design at all.

Nor, thirdly, would it bring any uncertainty into the argument, if there were a few parts of the watch, concerning which we could not discover or had not yet discovered in what manner they conduced to the general effect; or even some parts, concerning which we could not ascertain whether they conduced to that effect in any manner whatever. ... The indication of contrivance remained, with respect to them, nearly as it was before.

Nor, fourthly, would any man in his senses think the existence of the watch with its various machinery accounted for, by being told that it was one out of possible combinations of material forms; that whatever he had found in the place where he found the watch, must have contained some internal configuration or other; and that this configuration might be the structure now exhibited, namely, of the works of a watch, as well as a different structure.

Nor, fifthly, would it yield his inquiry more satisfaction, to be answered that there existed in things a principle of order, which had disposed the parts of the watch into their present form and situation. ...

And not less surprised to be informed that the watch in his hand was nothing more than the result of the laws of *metallic* nature. It is a perversion of language to assign any law as the efficient, operative cause of any thing. A law presupposes an agent, for it is only the mode according to which an agent proceeds: it implies a power, for it is the order according to which that power acts. Without this agent, without this power, which are both distinct from itself, the *law* does nothing, is nothing. ...

Neither, lastly, would our observer be driven out of his conclusion or from his confidence in its truth by being told that he knew nothing at all about the matter. He knows enough for his argument; he knows the utility of the end; he knows the subserviency and adaptation of the means to the end. ...

Suppose, in the next place, that the person who found the watch should after some time discover that, in addition to all the properties which he had hitherto observed in it, it possessed the unexpected property of producing in the course of its movement another watch like itself — the thing is conceivable; that it contained within it a mechanism, a system of parts — a mold, for instance, or a complex adjustment of lathes, baffles, and other tools — evidently and separately calculated for this purpose; let us inquire what effect ought such a discovery to have upon his former conclusion.

The first effect would be to increase his admiration of the contrivance, and his conviction of the consummate skill of the contriver. ...

He would reflect, that though the watch before him were, *in some sense*, the maker of the watch, which, was fabricated in the course of its movements, yet it was in a very different sense from that in which a carpenter, for instance, is the maker of a chair — the author of its contrivance, the cause of the relation of its parts to their use. With respect to these, the first watch was no cause at all to the second; in no such sense as this was it the author of the constitution and order, either of the arts which the new watch contained, or of the parts by the aid and instrumentality of which it was produced. ... Therefore,

Though it be now no longer probable that the individual watch which our observer had found was made immediately by the hand of an artificer, yet does not this alteration in anyway affect the inference that an artificer had been originally employed and concerned in the production. The argument from design remains as it was. Marks of design and contrivance are no more accounted for now than they were before. ...

Nor is anything gained by running the difficulty farther back, that is, by supposing the watch before us to have been produced from another watch, that from a former, and so on indefinitely. Our going back ever so far brings us no nearer to the least degree of satisfaction upon the subject. Contrivance is still unaccounted for. We still want a contriver. A designing mind is neither supplied by this supposition nor dispensed with... Contrivance must have had a contriver, design a designer, whether the machine immediately proceeded from another machine or not. That circumstance alters not the case. ... And the question which irresistibly presses upon our thoughts is, whence this contrivance and design? The thing required is the intending mind, the adapting hand, the intelligence by which that hand was directed. ...

Our observer would further also reflect that the maker of the watch before him was in truth and reality the maker of every watch produced from it: there being no difference, except that the latter manifests a more exquisite skill, between the making of another watch with his own hands, by the mediation of files, lathes, chisels, *etc.*, and the disposing, fixing, and inserting of these instruments, or of others equivalent to them, in the body of the watch already made, in such a manner as to form a new watch in the course of the movements which he had given to the old one. It is only working by one set of tools instead of another.

The conclusion which the *first* examination of the watch, of its works, construction, and movement, suggested, was that it must have had, for cause and author of that construction, an artificer who understood its mechanism and designed its use. This conclusion is invincible. A *second* examination presents us with a new discovery. The watch is found, in the course of its movement, to produce another watch similar to itself; and not only so, but we perceive in it a system of organization separately calculated for that purpose. What effect would this discovery have or ought it to have upon our former inference? What, as has already been said, but to increase beyond measure our admiration of the skill which had been employed in the formation of such a machine? Or shall it, instead of this, all at once turn us round to an opposite conclusion, namely, that no art or skill whatever has been concerned in the business, although all other evidences of art and skill remain as they were, and this last and supreme piece of art be now added to the rest? Can this be maintained without absurdity? Yet this is atheism.

Every observation which was made concerning the watch may be repeated with strict propriety concerning the eye, concerning animals, concerning plants, concerning, indeed, all the organized parts of the works of nature.

When we are inquiring simply after the *existence* of an intelligent Creator, imperfection, inaccuracy, liability to disorder, occasional irregularities may subsist in a considerable degree without inducing any doubt into the question; just as a watch may frequently go wrong, seldom perhaps exactly right, may be faulty in some parts, defective in some, without the smallest ground of suspicion from thence arising that it was not a watch, not made, or not made for the purpose ascribed to it. ... these are different questions from the question of the artist's existence; or, which is the same, whether the thing before us be a work of art or not; and the questions ought always to be kept separate in the mind. So likewise it is in the works of nature. Irregularities and imperfections are of little or no weight in the consideration when that consideration relates simply to the existence of a Creator. When the argument respects His attributes, they are of weight; but are then to be taken in conjunction ...[There is] evidence which we possess of skill, power, and benevolence displayed in other instances; ... though we be ignorant of it, other than defect of knowledge or of benevolence in the author.

This may not rise to the level of a conclusive proof; but, it certainly makes an interesting argument. And, this is not solely an opinion for a course in *World Religions*; some highly intelligent people in the physical sciences agree. Dr. Wernher von Braun, the

German rocket scientist who went on to lead the US space program for many years, once said:

> One cannot be exposed to the law and order of the universe without concluding that there must be design and purpose behind it all ... [Some would] challenge science to prove the existence of God. But must we really light a candle to see the sun ?

The Wager (Blaise Pascal)

In pursuit of "Is there a God ?" the next step is to take a look at an argument that is probably best suited for those who prefer to spend their free time in a gambling casino.

Wager first appeared in a collection known as *Pensées*. Blaise Pascal [left], a noted mathematician (after whom the Pascal programming language is named), was in poor health. Although *Pensées* (French: "thoughts") was incomplete at the time of his death, Pascal had published an interim version in 1670, and a much more professional version was published posthumously in 1844.

Pascal proposed a "wager" in his writings. He maintained that this was a wager which all humans make; it is not optional. Basically, he said you must bet on whether or not God exists. You can bet that He does, or you can bet that He does not; but, since you must decide how to live your life, you can not simply refuse to bet.

Now, in reality, either God does exist, or God does not exist; and, you either believe God exists or not. . Both must be one or the other; Pascal framed these two choices essentially as a 2 by 2 matrix (Pascal had invented matrix algebra).

	I accept that God exists	I reject God's existence
God does exist	Eternal bliss, but incurs the cost of living a good life	Damnation, but saves the cost of living a good life
God does not exist	With no reward or penalty, the cost of living a good life is wasted	No costs; no reward; no penalty.

Basically, what Pascal was saying can be shown this way:

(1)   There are two basic alternatives:
    (a) God exists; or,
    (b) God does not exist.

(2) Human reason and logic can not decide between (a) and (b).

(3) But, you must choose between (a) and (b) to determine how to live your life.

(4) The stakes in this choice are:
(a) the costs of living a "good" life (in behavior, effort, *et cetera*); and,
(b) the potential payback of having lived that life.

(5) If you accept that God exists, and He does (top left block of the matrix), you
(a) earn eternal bliss with God; but,
(b) probably have a slightly harder life here on earth by adhering to a "good" life.

(6) If you accept that God exists, and it turns out that He does not (bottom left), you
(a) forego the wanton life you could have lived and incur the cost of a "good life"; and,
(b) gain or lose nothing.

(7) If you deny that God exists, and in fact He does not exist (bottom right), you
(a) forego the costs incurred by living a "good" life (*i.e.* do whatever you want); and,
(b) gain or lose nothing.

(8) If you deny that God exists, and later learn that He does (top right), you
(a) save the marginal costs of living a "good" life; but,
(b) lose any chance at eternal bliss (and perhaps earn eternal damnation).

(9) Therefore, only an idiot would wager that God does not exist! To save only the marginal costs of living a "good" life, you risk eternal damnation, and forego the possibility of eternity in heaven.

There are a couple of assumptions that are built into this argument; and, they are not trivial. First, it is implied that acceptance of God's reality and living an appropriate lifestyle go together;

second, it is assumed that believing and living this way are sufficient for eternal bliss.

Critics have raised the question that if you only believe in God out of self-interest, why would God reward you with eternal bliss? They also often deny that a belief in God will automatically encourage adherence to a totally different lifestyle; they are quick to point out Catholic priests molesting children, televangelists having extramarital affairs, and so on. They also dispute whether you can have a belief simply because you see the logic of it being in your best interests to have that belief. Finally, how do you really know what it is that God wants of you? The "good life" you assume God wants may, in fact, be totally misdirected.

Reductio ad Absurdum (Saint Anselm)

Reductio ad absurdum is a Latin phrase which means "to reduce to the absurd". This is a highly respected form of logical argument in which one shows that an argument, if carried through to the end, is inherently self-contradictory. Saint Anselm [left], the Archbishop of Canterbury from 1093 to 1109, proposed to show the existence of God through this logical process. An updated version of what Anselm offered goes as follows:

To be proved: *God exists.*

Proof by: *reductio ad absurdum*

Proof:
1) Joe asserts that God does not exist.
2) He understands that what is called *God* is "a being than which nothing greater can be conceived."
3) Joe understands that "a being than which nothing greater can be conceived" at least exists in his mind, since he understands the words, the thought, the concept.
4) To say that "a being than which nothing greater can be conceived" does not exist in reality is to say that such a being is only an idea, since it does not exist in both the mind and reality.

Ch 4 – Proposed Proofs: The Existence of God   49

5) But such a being, if it exists in the mind alone, is in fact "a being than which something greater <u>can</u> be conceived" — because it is inherently greater for something to exist in both the mind and reality than to exist in the mind alone.

6) So, Joe believes that "a being than which nothing greater can be conceived" is, in fact, "a being than which something greater can be conceived". This is inherently self-contradictory, oxymoronic, and logically impossible.

7) Therefore, since "a being than which nothing greater can be conceived" cannot exist in the mind alone (because it leads to this contradiction), such a being must exist in both mind <u>and</u> reality.

8) Therefore, God <u>does</u> exist in reality, and not just as an idea or concept.

Typically, the arguments against Saint Anselm's logic usually go something like this: "I don't know what he did wrong; but, he must have done something, because I don't like the answer he got, or how he got it." Too bad.

Kalām (William Lane Craig)

Although the name assigned to this proof may not sound it, the creator of this argument is a fundamentalist Protestant theologian by the name of Dr. William Lane Craig [right]. Dr. Craig is currently the Research Professor of Philosophy at the Talbot School of Theology in La Mirada, California. He first published this argument in *The Kalām Cosmological Argument* in 1979.

Craig's argument is stated as a *syllogism* (*i.e.* three step proof) as follows:

(1) Anything that *begins* to exist must have a cause, or 'reason for beginning';

(2) at some point, the universe *began* to exist; therefore,

(3) the universe must have had a *cause* for having come into being.

The first point in this syllogism is virtually never disputed; it seems indisputably logical that an effect must have a cause. The second point, however, may not be so readily accepted. Did the universe ever begin? If we take the word of scientists, there definitely was a beginning. Today, the most generally accepted scientific theory of that origin is the so-called *Big Bang* hypothesis. In fact, after the launch of the Hubble telescope into high earth orbit, scientists even began to calculate the point in time when that most likely happened.

It is a mathematical rule that infinity can never be reached by addition. That rule is called *the impossibility of traversing the infinite*. Dr. Craig illustrates it this way:

> Imagine a man running up a flight of stairs and every time his foot strikes the top step, another step appears above it. It is clear that the man could run forever, but he would never cross all the steps because you could always add one more step

It thus follows from this rule that a series of events in time similarly can not be actually infinite. 2018 would never arrive if it were preceded by an infinite number of years because one cannot cross an infinity of years to reach 2018 any more than the man running up the stairs can cross an infinity of steps. Thus the number of years before 2018 must be finite — really, really, really, really big, but finite nonetheless. If it is finite, then there must have been a first year (*i.e.* there was a beginning).

It had to begin because any beginningless series of events in time is actually an infinite series; for, if the series of past events had no beginning and went on forever, it would be mathematically infinite. But, for history, this can not be. Why not? President Kennedy was elected in 1960. Barack Obama won in 2012 — 52 years later. If the series of universal events is truly infinite, then JFK's election was preceded by an infinite number of events; but, so was the election of Obama. So, the set of events prior to the 1st election is the same as the set of events prior to the 2nd (and every event in between). How can that be? Fifty two years separated those two events; *i.e.* 52 years full of events were added to the set of events prior to Kennedy's election. *Nothing can be added to an actual infinite*, however (this is another of those mathematical rules). This means the series of events prior to the 1st election can not actually be infinite. Dr. Craig thus draws the perfectly valid mathematical conclusion that:

the series of all past events must be finite and have a beginning. But the universe *is* the series of all events, so the universe must have had a beginning.

Another way of looking at this is that history is a collection of times and events that is formed by adding one member after another. A collection formed by adding one member after another cannot be actually infinite (you guessed it: another of the mathematicians' rules); therefore, history can not be actually infinite (*i.e.* again, it had a beginning).

Mathematicians and scientists (who often tend to be scientific materialists) do not appreciate philosophers using "their" tools to establish a proof for God; but, this proof is not intended to be a conclusive proof, but just to establish a likely proof through provision of a *sufficiency of evidence*. Consider this evidence:

- o In the early 20th century, Edwin Hubble (right; the man for whom the telescope was named) observed that light from distant galaxies is red–shifted — which tells scientists they are moving away from us (*i.e.* that the universe is expanding from an initial state which took place some finite time ago). This is the *Doppler Effect* (with sound, a car horn changing to a lower tone as it speeds away). This is seen as confirmation of the "Big Bang" theory of 'the beginning'.

- o This so–called *Big Bang* theory also predicted what astronomers know as "three-degree blackbody radiation". Although initially just a theory, this has now — to the surprise of many — been discovered empirically.

- o Robert C. Newman, a noted astrophysicist, suggested that if a process existed which caused the universe to lose energy at <u>any</u> rate, then the minimum age of the universe would guarantee that it would have already run out of energy. This would make it extremely unlikely that the universe as we know it is part of an infinite series of universal expansions and contractions.

- o Even if Newman could be shown to be wrong, there is no viable explanation for why a contracting universe would suddenly begin to expand, or *vice–versa*. Recent evidence (including that from the Hubble telescope) confirms that the galaxies are moving away from each other too quickly for gravity to ever reverse this process and pull them back.

So, their conclusion? The universe is expanding, and will continue to do so.

o American scientists, in April 1992, discovered what they described as "ripples of matter at the edge of the universe". These 'ripples' are evidence that the universe was given its structure very early in its history, and further confirms that the universe had a definite beginning.

o Dr Stephen William Hawking [right], one of the most brilliant men ever, is credited with having been the primary developer of the *singularity theorem* — a theorem that, at its core, affirms that space and time must, of necessity, have had a beginning.

That brings us to the third step in the *kalām* argument: there must have been a cause. But, is that certain? GWF Leibniz wrote that "no fact can be real of existing and no statement true unless it has a sufficient reason why it should be thus and not otherwise." In other words, *every effect has a cause*. Or, stated in still another way, if something had a beginning (the effect), then it must have had a cause. This is not simply a philosopher's game: engineers rely on this to design machines; meteorologists assume it to forecast the weather; doctors depend on it to treat disease; and, pilots would be devastated if they could not depend on it.

This *principle of sufficient reason,* as it is known, has never been falsified; and, it is supported by a ton of empirical evidence. Why should anyone object to the use of this principle with regard to the beginning of the universe? Why would they prefer to disregard such a fundamental principle of rational thought? Primarily because it is clear that if they (many of whom are atheists) accept that the universe had a beginning, they must also accept that there was a cause for this beginning.

But, was that cause *personal* or *impersonal*? Consider the alternatives. If it were impersonal, the cause would have to be a *natural* one. Natural causes (*i.e.* impersonal, physical causes), however, exist <u>within</u> the universe. If something existed prior to the universe (a rather obvious and necessary condition for it to serve as the cause of the universe), then it could not be a natural cause because the laws of nature would not have existed prior to the universe. Also, if a natural cause were sufficient (where the very existence of the cause is enough to guarantee the beginning of the universe), the universe would have always existed. The example Craig gives is that when a match is struck, it ignites; and thus striking a match is a sufficient cause of a lit match. Note that as soon as a sufficient cause exists, the effect follows immediately; there is no gap between the cause and the effect. This means that if the sufficient cause of the universe had always existed, then the universe would also have always existed.

The alternative to this is that the cause is a *personal agent* — an agent that "willed" the creation of the universe. To again use the match example: once the match is struck, the effect immediately follows; but, if a personal agent does not strike the match, the effect will not follow. Similarly, if the cause of the universe is a personal agent, the universe does not have to be eternal like its sufficient cause. Instead, the universe could have been willed into existence — as a person wills a match to light (by striking it). Once the cause is set into motion, the effect follows; but, if and only if that cause is set into motion. Only a personal agent can choose whether or not to set the cause in motion. Dr Craig maintains that we can conclude, therefore, that the cause of the universe must be an agency — *i.e.* it must be personal.

In summary, anything that begins must have a cause for beginning (Liebniz' *principle of sufficient reason*); an abundance of evidence shows that the universe clearly had a beginning; therefore, the universe was *caused* to begin; and, this cause must, of necessity, be *personal* (*i.e.* not inanimate). In short, God (specifically, a Personal God) exists!

Moral Law (C.S. Lewis)

The final "proof" of God's existence to be covered here was developed by Clive Staples Lewis [left]. More commonly known as CS Lewis, he was a Fellow in English Literature at Oxford University until 1954, when he was unanimously elected to chair Mediæval and Renaissance Literature at Cambridge University. He authored over thirty books in children's literature and popular theology. His two best known theological works were *Mere Christianity* and *The Screwtape Letters* (although he is probably better known as the author of the multi-book *Chronicles of Narnia* series). Lewis participated in a series of BBC radio programs in England that were transcribed into three books published in the early 1940s. *Mere Christianity*, an amalgamation of these books, was first published in 1952. His *Moral Law* derivation for the existence of God comprised the first four chapters of Book One (the first of four distinct segments of the composite text).

Lewis essentially proposed two types of law: *pseudo–law* (actually just an accounting of empirical facts); and, *actual–law* (which, by contrast, is a statement of what "ought to be", but does not compel that it be obeyed). The difference between these two types of law is best seen through illustration. Examples of *pseudo–laws* would be:
- the Law of Gravity;
- Mathematical Rules; and,
- Newton's Laws of Mechanics.

These are each simply statements of empirical fact. A rock released 3 feet above the ground can not choose to defy the Law of Gravity; two plus two can not elect if it wants to be four; and, a billiard ball rolling across a billiard table can not suddenly just decide to stop in mid roll. By contrast, the following are examples of *actual–laws*:
- Traffic Laws;
- the Ten Commandments; and,
- public event Ticket Rules.

These *laws* instruct us in what ought to be, and usually even prescribe penalties for violating them; but, you are essentially free to choose whether or not to obey or follow them — *i.e.* whether to *obey*, or *pay the penalty*. You can choose whether or not to drive too fast or through stop signs without stopping; Exodus says "Thou shalt not steal", but prisons are full of people who decided that they would; and, the tickets to many public events provide a list of attendance rules that people often simply ignore (such as bringing candy from home into the movie theater rather than pay $6 for Junior Mints®).

Human beings adhere to what has been variously called a *Law of Human Nature*, *Rule of Decent Behavior*, or *Moral Law*. It isn't written down for people to follow; it is simply understood. When someone says "How would you like it if someone did that to you?" or "Come on, you promised" or "Leave him alone, he isn't hurting anyone, is he?" you are hearing the speaker indirectly acknowledge that there is some underlying set of rules for appropriate behavior. Our innate biological instincts and inculcated sociological instincts may provide us with a sense of obligation or desire; but, they direct what we shall do, not what we ought to do.

If you come upon a burning tanker truck loaded with fuel on your way home from a class, you have a biological instinct to flee from what appears to be an impending explosion; however, you have a sociological instinct to rush to the aid of the trapped driver to save him from certain death. Your instincts in this case are in conflict; and, when instincts are in conflict, we normally follow the stronger — self-preservation. But, Lewis said that there is a *Moral Law* guiding what we "ought to do" in this circumstance; and, people around the world make that choice every week by rushing in to save the driver.

Feeling a *desire* to do something is not the same thing as feeling that you *ought* to do something. We have a desire to provide for a child's every want; but, we know that would only lead them to a selfish and greedy lifestyle as an adult. We have the *desire* to supply their wants; but, we know that we *ought* to let them earn at least some portion of what they want.

If *Moral Law* were just another name for one of our instincts, then there should be some (at least one) action that would be considered good all the time; but, there is not. Every instinct is at times enhanced by Moral Law, and at other times suppressed by it. Killing is bad — unless someone is about to murder someone we love; patriotism is good — unless it causes us to do something unnecessarily destructive to another country or people; motherly love is good — unless it leads to harm for the child of another. Support or suppression of these instincts arises from Moral Law.

There may appear to be differences in what is right and wrong (what constitutes our Moral Law) by ethnicity or nationality. Lewis maintained that these differences can be shown, without exception, to be differences in our understanding of facts, rather than a fundamental difference in Moral Law. As a result of history or current events, the perception and interpretation of facts may differ by societal group. That does not mean that Moral Law is different as much as it implies that Moral Law is being *applied* differently based on individual perceptions of fact.

As humans, we can study and analyze anything in the universe; but, there is only one thing where we have an edge, an advantage, beyond mere observation. In analyzing rocks, trees, stars, *et cetera*, we learn through external observation. But, in the case of humanity, we also have "inside information". In addition to our external observations, Lewis maintained that we also know there is a Moral Law which we did not make, which we can not quite forget even when we try, and which we know we ought to obey.

Does the world simply exist as it does by chance? Or, is there a power of some sort behind it that chose to have the universe exist? If such a power does exist, we should not expect it to be one of these observable facts, but the reality that causes them. A controlling power outside the universe would not be observable within that universe any more than an architect is observable within a building, or an artist is observable in a painting. Their skill, talent and intent might be observable in their work; but, they would not.

> The only way in which we could expect it to show itself would be inside ourselves as an influence or a command trying to get us to behave in a certain way. — Lewis

And, we do. In other words, the only place and time when we could logically expect to get an answer, the answer is *yes*.

> I should expect to find that there was ... a Power behind the facts, a Director, a Guide. — Lewis

Chapter 5
Ancient and Classic Religions

Experts in ancient Greek culture say that people back then didn't see their thoughts as belonging to them. When ancient Greeks had a thought, it occurred to them as a god or goddess giving an order: Apollo was telling them to be brave; Athena was telling them to fall in love. Now, people hear a commercial for sour cream potato chips and rush out to buy, but now they call this free will. At least the ancient Greeks were being honest. — American novelist Chuck Palahniuk

Your sad devotion to that ancient religion has not helped you
— Darth Vader (Star Wars IV: A New Hope)

The term "primitive religion", which is so common in comparative religion texts, has been avoided for a very simple reason: it's an insult. The dictionary tells us that *primitive* means "ancient, archaic, little evolved." By contrast, *ancient* means "belonging to times long past." This isn't a problem; and, in part, that's why the word 'ancient' was used in the title of this chapter. The problem comes with the terms 'archaic' and 'little evolved'. Using this same dictionary, 'archaic, little evolved' could easily be rendered as 'obsolete, under-developed'; and, that is demeaning.

The epigraphs at the top of the page take two totally different views of ancient religions: Chuck Palahniuk (American author and journalist) maintains that there was an ethical consistency to ancient faiths; Darth Vader belittles them (little surprise). Darth Vader, since he is a fictional character in a science fiction novel and movie might not seem to be relevant; but, that quote reflects how many people view ancient religions.

Now, how do we determine if a religion is ancient or classic? Quite honestly, it is highly arbitrary. Because the United States is primarily descended from European peoples, there is a natural tendency in the west to consider the religions of the Romans and Greeks as *classic*, while considering the faiths of the Incans and Aztecs as *ancient*. If we were predominantly descended from Native Americans, it is likely that Incan and Aztec would be classic and Roman and Greek ancient. So, trying to be as sensitive as possible, they are divided here in the following manner:

Ancient
- o Andean (Incan)
- o Mesoamerican (Aztec)
- o Mesopotamian (Sumerian)

Classical
- o Hellenic (Greek)
- o Jovian (Roman)
- o Kemetic (Egyptian)

Extinct Religious Beliefs

Ancient religions actually began long before any recorded history. Archæologists have discovered artifacts, relics and remains of early human settlements which clearly indicate that these people had some form of religious practice, obviously believed in a life after death, and must have accepted a god (or gods) greater than themselves. They have even discovered funerary practices that provided the deceased with everything they would need in the next life. This period extends roughly from about 10,000 BCE back in time to the earliest modern humans (pre 100,000 BCE). There is far more reliable data on societies much more recent than that, so this review will be restricted to begin much more recently — looking at 3 ancient religions and 3 classic religions. For that reason, there won't be excessive detail on any of them; it will be presented in broad strokes, for comparison purposes only.

Andean

The Andean peoples (that is, those groups that inhabited the Andes mountains of South America) were a highly developed people by the time that the Spanish arrived about 500 years ago. The Inca, the chief nation of this group at the time the Spanish arrived, had highly developed trade, road systems, language, cities, culture and religion. Although South American religion was varied (just as it was in Europe), most of the Andean peoples shared a number of common religious beliefs (just as Europeans did).

> The central ... religious concept throughout Peruvian [*i.e.* Andean] history was that of the creator ... best known [as] ... **Viracocha** [Foam on the Sea], describing how his power to create ... floated like the earth [on the] waters surrounding it.

This description [Parrinder, Geoffrey. *World Religions: from Ancient History to the Present.* New York: Facts on File inc., 1985] describes Viracocha in transcendent terms: like foam on the ocean, or fat on a pot of water (*i.e.* over, covering all). In addition to Viracocha, the Incans offered worship and honor to the Sun (his elder son), the Moon (his younger son), Venus/Thunder (his daughter), Amaru (sort of a cross between a dragon and an Earth Mother goddess), and a few other lesser deities.

Despite appearances to the contrary, Andean religion was virtually monotheistic. Viracocha was the one, indivisible, creative power; and, all of the other "deities" were simply seen as aspects, emanations, or representations of Him. Viracocha was the 'invisible sun', the 'invisible moon', *et cetera*. In other words, he was all of these things *in their spiritual essence*. Incan worship of the sun, the moon and Venus thereby constituted worship of visible 'stand ins' for Viracocha — think of it as a sort of *proxy worship*.

Mesoamerican

The religions of Meso-America (modern México & Central America) were even more diverse than those of the Andes; however, they too had their innate similarities. There was often a linguistic relationship among the various nations (*e.g.* Tepaneca, Acolhua, Tlaxcalteca, Xochimilca, and Aztec — all speaking dialects of Nahuatl); there was frequent trade, intermarriage and cultural exchange; and, it is likely that they are genetically related as well — possibly descended from peoples from the so-called four corners area of the American southwest. However, due to the fact that they were the most powerful when the Spanish arried, it is the Aztec about whom we know the most.

Unlike the Andean nations, the mesoamerican nations were unabashedly polytheistic. Gods included *Xiuhtecuhtli* (the fire god), *Quetzcoatl* (right; god of wind and science), *Tlaloc* (rain god), *Tezcatlepoca* (god of the night sky), *Xipe Totêc* (phallic fertility god), and *Tlazolteotl* (the goddess of childbirth). The Aztec concept of this pantheon of gods and goddesses was extremely complex, and changed over the years. It seems apparent, however, that Tezcatlepoca was at the top of the hierarchy. Unlike the Inca, the other deities were not aspects of Tezcatlepoca, but independent *teotl* (literally, "stoney ones"; but, figuratively, something that was 'permanent, immortal'). This can be seen in an ancient Aztecan text (tramslated by Parrinder– see source at top of preceding page).

> This one was considered a real *teotl*, he lived everywhere, in hell, on earth, and in heaven. On earth he brought dust and dung to life, and caused many sufferings among men, he set people against each other, therefore he is said to be hostile on both sides. He created all things; he brought evil things upon men, thus placing them into his shade, and asserting himself as their master, he mocked men. Sometimes he gave them riches, dominance and power to rule, nobility and honor.

Mesopotamian

Mesopotamia (Greek: "between the rivers") refers to the land between and either side of the Euphrates and Tigris rivers. Today, most of Mesopotamia is in Iraq (with some portions of it in Iran). It was from this area that Abraham, patriarch to Judaism, Christianity, Baha'i and Islam, emigrated around 2100 BCE. Peoples of this area include the Sumerians, Babylonians, Assyrians, *etc.*

The southern end of this area was once all marsh land. This region gradually filled in with silt from the two rivers, the rivers merged, and the coastline receded south with the new fill. If you look at a modern map of the point where the rivers enter the Persian Gulf, you need to realize that 4,000 years ago, the two rivers did not meet before reaching the gulf, and the shore line was about 150 miles further north (where the rivers are still separate). The area between them near their mouths was a wet, frequently flooded, marshy plain. This natural environment led the early Sumerians to believe that the whole universe had sprung from the sea. They pictured the land as 'floating on the sea' (after all, if they dug a hole, they struck water).

The Sumerian creation described the separation of the dry land from the waters beneath the land and the waters above (ocean & ground water from rivers & rain), the creation of the sun, moon, planets and stars; and then, 'as in heaven, so on earth', came forth plant, animal and human life. The deities, however, were definitely plural.

There was Anu, god of the heavens and (originally) supreme god; Enlil, god of the air and wind, who became the supreme god when the Sumerian city-state which housed his temple (Nippur) conquered the Sumerian city-state which housed the temple of Anu (Uruk); and, Enki, god of the underworld. As god of the underworld, Enki was also god of the primeval waters. Since this was seen as the source for all creation, Enki was also seen as the god of infinite wisdom. It was Enki to whom the Sumerians gave thanks for their many creations and inventions (the wheel, cart, fire, boat, writing, cities, *etc*).

There were many others – many, many others. Sin was the moon god; Marduk, the son of Enki, the local protector of what later became Babylon, and the eventual supreme god; Nabu, the god of science (Marduk's son); Ninhursag (or Ninmah), the original 'Mother Earth', who helped Enki and Enlil with the creation of humanity; ...

The remains of the *Ziggurat of Sin*. Built over 4,000 years ago to worship the Sumerian Moon god, this ziggurat, or stepped pyramid, is thought by many to be the biblical *Tower of Babel*.

Humans have lived in the Middle East since about 100,000 BCE. They have only lived in Mesoamerica and the Andes since sometime between 10,000 and 35,000 BCE. Although the Aztecan religion appears to be a derivative of the Olmec (about 1100 BCE), and the Incan a derivative of the Tiahuanaco (about 600 CE), they can still legitimately be considered 'ancient religions'. Sumeria is much older, and likely "invented" towns (the earliest known towns being: Jarmal, Iraq; Catal Hüyük, Turkey; Ur, Iraq; and, Jericho, Israel. All of these date to as early as 9000 BCE, and certainly qualify Sumerian religion as 'ancient'.

Classical Religious Beliefs

But, what of "classic" religion? The English word *classic* comes directly from the Latin word *classicus*, and referred to the various classes of Roman (and Greek) society; in particular, it referred to the highest, or first class. Since the Romans invented the concept (and the word), it thus seems only fitting to consider Roman and Greek religion as classic. The *Paut Neteru* of the Egyptians also fits well into this category.

Hellenistic

What are Eoin, Seoc, Shawn, Ian, Jean, Ivan, and Juan? They are the Gaelic, Scots, Welsh, Irish, French, Russian and Spanish versions of the English name *John* (literally, "God is gracious"). Similarly, Inana, Ishtar, Rhea, Cybele, Baubo, Demeter and Allat are all versions of Hera (the "Mother Earth"). Care must be taken to recognize that having a lot of names does not make someone a lot of different individuals (either goddesses or Johns).

When the Hellenic peoples arrived in Greece, they found Hera (left) already being worshipped by the indigenous peoples. Usually, she was visualized as the supreme goddess, and had a younger consort (Pan) who died, was mourned, and then rose again. Pan was a god of vegetation or a god of the forest. The new Greeks (Hellenes) tamed Hera, and made her the goddess of wild nature — a virgin huntress. As such, she was then exported to Ephesus (as Artemis), Attica (as Brauron), and Cyprus (as Aphrodite). By the time she reached Corinth, her temple (high on the acropolis) was staffed by more than a thousand temple prostitutes (whose role was to shield her from the worshippers' baser desires by taking it upon themselves). Strabo (63 BCE – 23 CE), the Greek geographer and historian, once wrote that the prostitutes of Aphrodite's temple were "the city's chief attraction."

Archæologists know that the Mother Goddess had been around at least since Minoan (Crete) times (pre 2000 BCE). The invading Hellenes came south through the Balkans during the second millennium BCE — bringing the Indo-European sky god, *Dyaus*, with them. Dyaus, mispronounced *Zeus* by the native Greeks, had a wife: Dione. When they arrived in Greece, they "met" Pan and Hera. Initially, Zeus succumbed to Hera (dumping Dione, while Hera exiled Pan to the forest). Second to Hera, Zeus gradually became known as *Posis-Das* (literally, "husband of the Earth"). As later waves of Hellenes arrived, they were horrified at what their earlier kinfolk had allowed to happen to Dyaus. So, they literally pushed Posis-Das out to sea (where he became known as *Poseidon*, right), and reinstated the dignity and pre-eminence of Dyaus (Zeus). With Mother Earth (Hera) as his wife/consort and bedmate, the union of the Sky god and Earth goddess secured fertility for the agricultural Hellenes.

It seems natural that a sky god should be worshipped from a mountain, so Zeus [right] took Olympus, the highest local mountain, as the site for his palace. Around him, the Greeks did two things: they introduced a whole heavenly society filled with lesser gods; and, they took Hera and split her repeatedly into her various functions. Her name changed repeatedly as she was exported to other areas, and then imported back to Greece to serve in a variety of her functions. The result was a complex mythology peopled by numerous gods and goddesses exhibiting largely human traits.

In essence, the Greek pantheon looked something like this:
- *Zeus*, sky god, the supreme god
- *Poseidon*, god of the sea
- *Artemis*, goddess of wild nature
- *Demeter*, goddess of the harvest
- *Hermes*, god of the traveller
- *Hestia*, goddess of hearth & home
- *Hera*, goddess of marriage
- *Aphrodite*, goddess of love
- *Athene*, goddess of wisdom & skills
- *Apollo*, god of music & literature
- *Ares*, god of war
- *Hephæstrus*, god of smiths

et cetera

Jovian

In practice, the religion of Rome can be divided into 3 distinct phases. These phases represent fundamental changes in their concept of deity, and the responsibilities of the adherents. Chronologically, these can be referred to as:
- Etruscan
- Oscan
- Imperial

Etruscan

What is today the country of Italy was, prior to 509 BCE, a collection of tribal areas. That year marked the founding of the Roman Republic (later Empire), and the gradual inclusion or extinction of the other ethnic states — the people of these states known today by such names as Umbrians, Samnites, Oscans, Etruscans, Romans, *etc.*. There were also settlements of Greeks and Carthaginians (North Africans). Nobody really knows the origin of the Etruscan people prior to their migration into Italy, but it is likely that it was in Lydia (now part of Turkey). Religious rites, divination, and astrological practices all seem to support the idea that the Etruscans were originally Lydian emigrants. The timing is right, as the earliest reference to Lydia was in the 8th century BCE, and the Etruscan culture developed in the 6th and 7th centuries BCE.

In any case, the Etruscans had a distinctive early religion, and the smaller Roman tribe apparently followed their lead. The Etruscan religion recognized the existence of certain spiritual forces, or powers. These were not anthropomorphic deities (*i.e.* not assigned human forms, characteristics or relationships), although they were assigned names. These were *Numina* — forces with dominance over some specific natural operation, but have no existence separate from that function. Typically, Numina were associated with key events of life, such as childbirth, agriculture, *et cetera*.

Using childbirth as an example, *Alemona* protected the fœtus, while *Nona* and *Decima* (literally, "ninth" and "tenth") watched over the final two months of pregnancy. No, pregnancy did not take longer then; the 10 months of Etruscan pregnancy were lunar months. There were seemingly numina for everything; and, in the case of child birth, no less than 20 numina were involved in the period from conception to toddler. There were similar hordes of numina for the fields, home, hearth, forests, *et cetera*.

Two numinæ that are of particular interest are *Iuno* and *Genius*, since these were the numinæ that controlled procreation. Since these two numinæ that created the infant were believed to reside in the head of the mother, the later connection of genius with extreme intelligence became virtually inevitable.

Oscan

The Oscans were another of the early Italic tribes, and the Oscans generally lived much further south than either the Romans or Etruscans. In fact, the Oscans were the people responsible for originally building the city of Pompeii, at about the same time that Etruscans were establishing their culture to the north (*circa* 7th century BCE). Pompeii quickly fell to the Greek colonists who had founded nearby *Neapolis* (literally, Greek for "new city"; now known as Naples). The Greeks brought their Hellenistic, anthropomorphic deities with them, and gradually the Oscan numinæ began to acquire similarly anthropomorphic traits. There was frequent contact, and the Oscans may have been related to the Etruscans; as a result, these new anthropomorphic deities spread to the north.

Gradually, the *Numinæ* became *Numen* (which literally meant "nodding", and was related to the *Genius* concept — with all forces found in the head). These Numen had acquired male and female forms from the Greek contact, and the original Numinæ became merely the attributes of the new, anthropomorphic gods.

Apparently, the first great Roman god thus formed was *Mars*. Initially, he was the agricultural god (subsuming all of the agricultural Numinæ). Since agriculture was the life blood of the tribe, Mars gradually became their defender, and the god of war. When the Julian calendar was introduced by Julius Cæsar in 45 BCE, the first month was named in honor of Mars. This was the start of the Roman year, and marked the start of the agricultural season as well as the annual beginning of military campaigns; so, it was appropriate to name it after Mars. This carried into other languages as March (English), Mars (French), Marzo (Italian & Spanish), Março (Portuguese), Marzu (Maltese), Maart (Dutch), Μάρτιος (Greek), März (German), Març (Catalan), and Martxoa (Basque).

There were also other borrowings from the Greeks (and other neighbors of the emerging Roman nation): Dyaus, mispronounced in Greece as Zeus, was mispronounced in Rome as *Giove*. As this sky god was recognized as the supreme god, the father of all, he became known as Father Giove or, in Latin, *Giove Pater* (which came into English as *Jupiter*). The Numina of femininity and female procreation, *Iuno*, became *Juno*, his consort and queen. Other gods were either anthropomorphic versions of the Numinæ, or imported directly from the Greeks. The pantheon thus included:

- *Jupiter*, supreme god & creator
- *Mars*, god of war & agriculture
- *Minerva*, goddess of technical skill
- *Mercury*, god of merchants
- *Fortuna*, goddess of fertility
- *Juno*, Jupiter's consort–queen
- *Vesta*, goddess of the hearth
- *Hercules*, god of success
- *Apollo*, a healing god
- *Diana*, forest goddess

The Roman leadership ensured that the people observed the festivals, sacrifices, and rituals required to secure the *Pax Deorum* (a Latin term for "Peace of the Gods", or "Favor of the Gods"). Sacrifices were controlled by a group of *pontifices* (priests). The leader of this group, the *pontifex maximus*, thus carried a great deal of political power and prestige. Julius Cæsar, recognizing this as a key factor in political success, had himself declared the Pontifex Maximus. There were also numerous other priestly groups who had specific responsibilities, and equally specific taboos (*e.g.* the *Flamen Dialis*, the priest who was dedicated to Jupiter, was not allowed to ride a horse, see the military, take an oath, wear a ring, go without a cap, use iron to cut his hair or nails, walk under a vine, or touch a dog)

Imperial

Once Cæsar became Pontifex Maximus, the Roman religion entered a phase of radical change. Over a relatively short period of time, it essentially became a political religion. During the days of the Republic, the leaders manipulated the Sibylline books (a set of books that recorded the sayings and prophecies of Sibyl, an oracle or channeller of the gods). These were from Cumæ (the earliest Greek settlement, founded near Naples about 750 BCE. The Republic's leaders would alter the text of the books to introduce anything that was new or controversial so that it appeared to have the approval of the gods. This was actually relatively easy, as nobody but the priests could read the books (reflected in the actions of the pigs in George Orwell's *Animal Farm*).

The Roman citizens, however, quickly grew wary of the claims of the priests, and the religion began to lose popular appeal. Beginning in 29 BCE, this trend was effectively reversed by Cæsar Augustus. He restored 82 Jovian temples to their earlier splendor, and reinstated all of the pomp and ceremony that had once accompanied the religion.

Throughout this entire period, the Jovian religion shifted the mantle of divinity to the leaders (later, Emperors). The Romans were well aware that the Greeks and Macedonians had converted their Emperors into divine beings, and they quickly copied what they saw. Alexander the Great was declared divine by the Greek-Macedonian priests, so Pompey did the same in Rome. A little later, Cæsar Augustus took the title *Divi Filius* (*i.e.* "Son of God"). Later emperors went even further: Caligula, Nero and Domitian actually demanded worship as *Dominus et Deus*. This phrase literally meant "Lord and God". It is interesting to note that Emperor Domitian (81–96 CE) — one of the 3 megalomaniacs who insisted on being called *Dominus et Deus* — was on the throne when the Christian *Gospel of John* was being written. It was in John that Thomas is quoted as referring to Christ as χύριος and θεος (*kurios* and *theos*: the literal Greek translation of *Dominus et Deus*). It is highly probable that this usurpation of Domitian's (right) own title for Jesus by the upstart Christians contributed significantly to the fact that this was the very same emperor who most viciously persecuted the early church.

Kemetic

The earliest known version of the *Tree of Life* is known as the *Paut Neteru* (literally, "substance of the gods"). This came from ancient Egypt, and was apparently exported to Syria, Babylonia, and the Hebrews. This guided virtually every aspect and phase of Egyptian life: education, home, government, war, politics, religion, magic, medicine, …

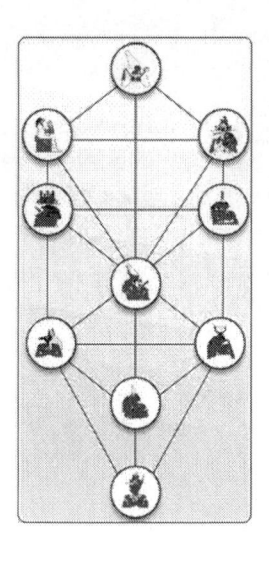

Basically, the Paut Neteru (left) was a graphic representation of Egyptian cosmology. The various nodes on this tree represented specific spiritual powers. Egyptian mystics and priests would go into trances for the primary purpose of awakening these spiritual powers. In this process, they would also seek to awaken the indwelling divinity they believed to be present in every person. They would try to reach the *divine presence within* (*i.e.* Osiris). Each node was personified as an anthropomorphic deity or *neter*. The worship of a deity was intended to bring forth their powers, and for the worshipper to personally become a living manifestation of that deity (*e.g.* to obtain romance, an Egyptian would worship the goddess Het-Heru, thus releasing her powers), and would then manifest the god(dess). In the case of Het-Heru, romantic happiness would be theirs as a natural consequence.

Although all of the neter were anthropomorphic in the sense of acting human-like, the physical features of these deities often comprised a mixture of both human and animal forms. The animals in these cases were generally symbolic of the natural attributes or powers of the god. For instance, *Anubis* was the god of the dead. As such, Anubis served as a guide for the recently deceased, as well as a guardian of the dead in general. Whenever bodies were buried in Egypt near the Nile River, they would not stay buried! When the Nile rose in the Spring, the ground water level would rise along with it. Anything hollow that was buried (such as a coffin, or even a body) would be forced upward by the ground water pressure until it popped out at the surface. This is the same reason why virtually all bodies interred in New Orleans were interred in above-ground mausoleums.

When bodies would reappear at the surface as a result of rising ground water, scavengers (primarily jackals) would show up to feast on the newly opened smorgasbord. Before long, Egyptians came to associate these jackals with the dead, and thus saw them as emissaries from the god of the dead. It was not a great leap, therefore, for them to visualize Anubis as a human with the head of a jackal (right); and, when painted, Anubis nearly always had black skin – reminiscent of the rich, black soil deposited each year by annual flooding, and representing growth and rebirth. Anubis was thus also a god of new life, and not just death.

This is typical of what is known as *theriomorphism* (assigning deities animal-like forms). Examples we find in Egyptian religion include: Osiris (often with the head of a ram); Horus, his son, as a falcon (the pharaoh was seen as the reincarnation of Horus for that era, and was often painted or sculpted with a falcon seated on his shoulder); Sekhmet, the goddess of war (with the head of a lioness); and, Ammut, the devourer of souls. Ammut is an interesting theriomorphic example: the hind quarters of a hippopotamus; the upper body of a lion; and, the head of a crocodile. All 3 of these were seen by Egyptians as deadly, with the hippopotamus and crocodile often seen as symbols of evil. Ammut was not nice; he was the god to whom Anubis delivered the souls of the damned. Being delivered to Ammut was the Egyptian equivalent of condemnation to hell. After someone died, the body was prepared (often mummified) in a process overseen by Anubis. Physically, this was done by a priest wearing an Anubis mask [right]. The deceased was taken by Anubis to be judged by Osiris in a process called the *Weighing of the Heart*. Anubis would balance the heart of the deceased with a *feather of truth*. If the scale balanced [left], Osiris would approve and Anubis would then escort the soul to eternal life; if, however, it was weighted down with sin so that the scale did not balance, Osiris would deny regeneration and eternal life, and the soul would be given to, and eaten by, the waiting Ammut.

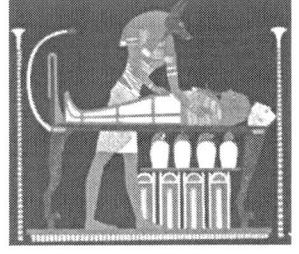

Summary

The examples given here of ancient religions show that they were not all the same. Similarly, the so-called classic religions also were often very different. One thing all of these had in common, however, was their value to their followers. In what must have been a very difficult and threatening existence, they helped their adherents "make sense of the world". Life was not random, subject to the vagaries of the weather, the environment, or other possible threats; it was controlled by God (or the gods), and the reverence and worship extended by the people ensured their protection.

As the religions practiced today appeared, they often borrowed extensively from these earlier faiths. They dropped what they thought was incorrect, or didn't reflect their understanding of deity; they retained what they believed was accurate; and, they built upon, and added to, this base. As such, these earlier faiths can be considered to be *background religions* with respect to modern faiths. They constituted the prevailing religious opinion at the time when modern faiths were being formulated, and what they believed often seeded what was to follow.

Section II
Judaism

The *Abrahamic* Religions

Judaism is the first of several religions to be covered which are most often grouped together into a category known as either the *Western Religions* or as the *Abrahamic Religions*. Western refers to their common, general area of origination at the western end of Asia; Abrahamic refers to their common descent from a single, historical figure from 4,000 years ago (*i.e.* Abraham). Although Abraham could be reviewed under any of the Abrahamic faiths, the one that is genetically and chronologically closest to him is Judaism. So, Abraham will be considered in the first chapter on this faith (Chapter 6).

For the purpose of this course, we consider Judaism, Christianity and Islam to be the major western religions. All three of these claim Abraham (or *Ibrahim* in Arabic) as their partiarch; they are therefore also known as *Abrahamic* or *Abramic* religions. The Mandæan and Baha'i religions also consider Abraham to be their patriarch; however, they are much smaller, and are usually simply ignored by most texts (not here).

These Abrahamic religions – frequently known as the *Western Religions* – derive that title from their origination points being further west than those of the other major religious groupings; it does not imply that they are regional in nature. When *western* is used, the group is frequently considered to also include Zoroastrianism and Platonism, which do not involve Abraham; however, many of the earliest beliefs of these Abrahamic faiths originated in one or the other of these background religions.

Chapter 6
Jewish Foundations

God longs to hear the prayer of the righteous.
                                              — *Talmud, Yebamot 64a*

I praise all good thoughts, good words, and good deeds through my thoughts, words, and deeds. I uphold all good thoughts, good words, and good deeds. I renounce all evil thoughts, evil words, and evil deeds. I dedicate unto you worship and praise, and with the very life of my own body through thoughts, words, and deeds, and with my conscience. I praise righteousness.   — *Khordeh Avesta, Khorshed Neyayesh*

Cradle of Western Religion

In the relatively small area known as the Middle East, all of the great Western religions were founded: Islam, Judaism, Christianity, Baha'i, Mandæanism, Manichæism, Zoroastrianism, Platonism, and Neo-Platonism. Although they were influenced by Egyptian, Greek, Roman, and Indic religious views — all of which were relatively nearby — this is without question the cradle of Western Religion. Any map of the early Middle East (*circa* 2500 BCE) also shows a different topography than that which exists today. When you compare an early map to a current map, you notice that on the modern map the 2 great rivers (the Euphrates and the Tigris) join and flow as one for about their final 150 miles to the Persian Gulf. On an earlier map, however, the two rivers never join, but enter the Persian Gulf as two separate rivers. Just as Louisiana gets bigger every year from the silt of the Mississippi River, the tip of the Gulf gradually filled in, became solid ground, and the rivers merged.

Wild wheat and barley grew in the area, and foraging tribes began to settle down in the region. About 8000 BCE, agriculture was "invented" in this area as these people not only collected the grain, but began to take an active role in the planting and harvesting of these grains. Weather was supportive, and the two great rivers provided plentiful water.

The results of agriculture were that: food became plentiful; populations rose; and, people began to live in closer proximity, forming towns. This required a social structure that led to further demand, and soon the area was criss–crossed with irrigation channels. Civilization was born. The primary architects of this new social structure were a group of people at the southern end of this fertile area — a group known to archæologists as *Ubaidians*. To most people, however, they are simply the "earliest *Sumerians*".

The Sumerians became rich, and their civilization flourished. In this part of the world, they are credited with having invented such fundamental items and concepts as irrigation, mathematics, writing, the boat, the wheel, roads, wheeled carts, and domesticated animals. Their religion was one where they attributed virtually everything they couldn't control to the gods — supernatural beings who behaved much like humans. They also believed that it was their duty and purpose in life to serve and please these gods.

The Sumerians left thousands of clay tablets that provide a remarkably detailed view into the everyday life of the people. They also left humanity one of its very earliest epics: *The Epic of Gilgamesh*. There were actually numerous story–poems about this early king of Uruk (a leading Sumerian town *circa* 2600 BCE). One of the oldest and best preserved versions of the epic was written by a scribe named Shin–eqi–unninni. It was unusual in those days for scribes to sign their work, but this one did.

Near the end of the epic, King Gilgamesh meets an old man named Utnapishtim. The old man tells him about a city, Shuruppak, which had once been located along the banks of the Euphrates River. He says it was at Shuruppak (modern Tell Fara in Iraq) that the gods met and discussed the state of the world; at one meeting, they decided to destroy the entire world in a great flood. All of the gods agreed not to let any of the humans know their plan; but, Ea (one of the gods) recognized Utnapishtim as a good man, and indirectly let him know what to do (by showing up and talking to the walls of his house). Utnapishtim overheard this conversation, and followed the implied instructions. He built a giant, multi-decked boat with a length equal to its breadth, to cover over the decks of the boat, and to bring "all living things" on board.

Utnapishtim did what he had heard, and loaded the boat with gold, silver, food, and all living things. He then got on board, closed up the door, and launched the boat. Soon, the skies became overcast and the rains came. The result was a flood like none that had ever been. The torrential rains lasted for seven days and seven nights, and then the sun broke through the cloud cover. Utnapishtim opened a window and saw water as far as he could see in every direction.

His boat finally came to rest on the top of Mount Nimush. After seven more days, Utnapishtim "released a dove from the boat. It flew off, but circled around and returned". He followed this by releasing a swallow; but, it did the same. Finally, he released a raven. By this time, the waters had receded somewhat, and the raven flew off — to be seen "nevermore" (apologies to Edgar Allen Poe, but it was impossible to resist). Realizing that, since it hadn't returned, the raven must have found dry ground, Utnapishtim ran the ship aground, opened the door and released all of the living things in the boat "in every direction". He closed his adventure by sacrificing a sheep where the boat had come to rest.

The story of Gilgamesh was one of the most popular stories in the world at the end of the third millennium BCE, and it was translated into a number of other languages. Numerous tablets with the story have been found from Turkey to India. It was from nearby Ur that Abraham emigrated, and this raises several questions. Was Noah another name for Utnapishtim (two versions of the same history)? Were both stories intended as parables? Were they two different men who had similar experiences when God flooded the world? *The Epic of Gilgamesh* is just one of several stories that has a close parallel in the Hebrew scriptures. The stories of the Garden of Eden, Adam and Eve, and Cain and Abel are just a few of those with earlier Sumerian counterparts.

Abraham is considered the patriarch of Judaism; and, Abraham came from Ur, one of the primary Sumerian cities. He is also called Ibrahim by followers of Islam; but, *Ibrahim* is simply the Arabic form of *Abraham.* Jesus, the focal point of Christianity, was born a Jew; and, the *Gospel of Matthew* goes into detail in the first 17 verses of chapter 1 to trace the lineage of Jesus directly — from Abraham!

The bottom line is that Judaism, Christianity, Islam and Zoroastrianism are all monotheistic, western religions founded in close proximity in this cradle of western religion. They share a great deal of common history and geography, occasionally share common prophets and patriarchs, and espouse overlapping beliefs.

Are they all branches from the same tree? No; but, they most certainly are all trees from the same forest. What is important is to explore where the overlaps exist, learn where differences reside, discover what these mean for people in today's world, determine exactly how and to what extent they are related, and appreciate how to live peacefully in a world where all of them are present and contribute to society.

Abraham

Abraham was not a Jew – at least not in the modern sense. Abraham was a man who lived in the city of Ur (on the banks of the Euphrates River in Sumeria). Genesis recounts that he was "called of God" to found a new nation in an undesignated land (later identified as Canaan), and left with his father (known to Jews as *Terah*); the Qur'an recounts that he was neither Jew nor Christian nor pagan, but a monotheist who left the home and idolatrous religious teachings of his father (known to Muslims as *Azar*) to strike out on his own. In either case, Abraham was a Sumerian who originally lived in Ur, but emigrated to Canaan. In fact, the stories may not even differ (Genesis says: Now Yahweh said unto Abram, "Get out of your country, and from your kindred, and from your father's house, and go unto a land that I will show you" – Genesis 12:1). The timing for this is difficult to safely ascertain, but probably fell sometime around 2050 BCE. If this date is accepted as a reference point, then the religious teachings of the area in which he lived were the pre–Zoroastrian beliefs of the Sumerian polytheistic system. The 3rd Dynasty of Ur had claimed the divine right of kings, and promoted Sin (the moon god) to status as the tribal, or local, god in their religious system.

Using the Biblical story as the base, and supplementing it with reliable texts which have come to light from Sumerian archæological work, there was a clan of Sumerians leaving Ur together. This tribal exodus was led by Abraham's father (according to Genesis), and also included several other biblically well–known people: Lot, Sarah, and Nahor. The *Encyclopædia Britannica*, using biblical and archæological sources, traces this caravan from Ur to Harran. Whatever the motivation for Abraham's departure from Ur, it was unlikely to have been to escape the religious views of his father, for his father was almost certainly leading the caravan (a caravan of this size would have been impossible without the blessings of the family patriarch). Also, the city of Harran (in modern Turkey, located in the Balikh valley between the Tigris and Euphrates) was a pilgrimage site in those days for the followers of Sin, and would have been a common destination for the citizens of Ur, who were faithful followers of this moon god. Thousands of stone tablets were found by archæologists when they discovered the palace at Mari (just south of Harran) which repeatedly refer to the *Hapiru**, and identify them (pre-1900 BCE) as being in Harran — at the Temple of Sin. There is no way of knowing Abraham's beliefs for certain; but, with the route of the caravan, it is fairly certain that Terah/Azar, his father, worshipped Sin.

The Bible recounts that Terah died at Harran at the age of 205. Abraham, aged 75, then took up the leadership of the caravan, and headed west to the Euphrates and the ford at Carchemish. The Mari tablets confirm this with references to them in Aleppo (on the banks of the river). It should be noted that Nayrab, near Aleppo, was also a center of the Sin cult. From there, they followed the fertile crescent (the shading on the map on the next page), which provided access to food and water for them and their animals while *en route*. Heading straight for the land of Canaan would have taken them directly across open desert, and would have most likely resulted in the death of the herds perhaps a third of the way across.

---

* *Hapiru* is an Akkadian term often translated as 'foreigner', referring to nomadic and semi-nomadic peoples who wandered the Middle East – often, as outlaws, vagabonds, social outcasts, or a military force. In Genesis 14, a union of local kings led by Chedorlaomer raided Sodom and captured Lot (Abraham's nephew). This was reported to "Abram the Hebrew", who is described in military terms as being "confederate" with several local leaders. Abraham then armed 318 servants, and pursued Chedorlaomer – using military maneuvers (dividing his forces and attacking at night) to defeat him. He then returned to the local king at Sodom with the spoils. Hapiru was apparently more of a social class than an ethnic designation, although it appears that, for one group of these militaristic social misfits, the term eventually took on ethnic connotations — and *Hapiru* (Sumerian *Habiru*; Egyptian *'prw*) evolved into *Hebrew*.

78   *An Introduction to* World Religions

After several other stops along the way, the caravan came to Bethel. This was a Canaanite holy city whose religion was centered on El, the Canaanite tribal god. In fact, Bethel is an Anglicization of *bet-El*, which translates into English as the "house of El". Archæologists believe they have found the original temple to El in Bethel, and radiocarbon dated it to before 1800 BCE. Biblical accounts report that Abraham and his clan took over this temple and rededicated it to YHWH (the tetragrammatron usually translated as either Yahweh or Jehovah), who might be described at this point as the Hebrew tribal god. This is disputed, however, by a majority of Jewish theological scholars who believe that YHWH was first revealed to Moses eight centuries later, and that the "Lord God Most High" which Abraham praises in his meeting with the king–priest Melchizidek was most likely El.

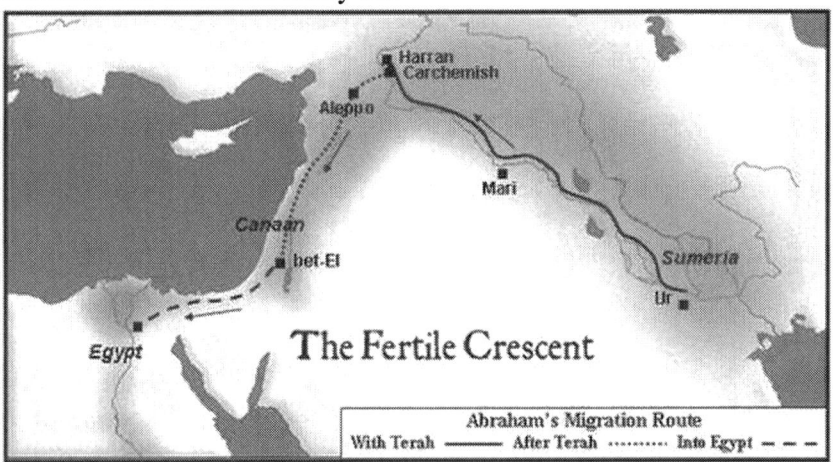

Note: at the time of Abraham, the Euphrates and Tigris rivers never met, but entered the Persian Gulf separately. The head of the Gulf then extended some 150 miles further northwest than shown on this map.

Joshua relates in the Tanakh (Jewish scriptures) that the patriarchs and forbears of the Hebrew people, when in Ur, had worshipped "other gods". Once in the land of Canaan, however, Abraham (according to the *Encyclopædia Britannica*) "met the Canaanite supreme god, El, and adopted him, but only partially and nominally, bestowing upon him qualities destined to distinguish him and to assure his preeminence over all other gods... This was not monotheism, but monolatry (the worship of one among many gods)... He was a personal god too, with direct relations with the individual, but also a family god and certainly still a tribal god."

Circumstances eventually led Abraham and his wife, Sarah, to continue on to Egypt. After returning to Canaan, Sarah gave birth to a son (Isaac). Isaac fathered twins – Esau and Jacob (later called Israel — Hebrew *Yisra'el*: "one who contends, or wrestles, with El"). Jacob fathered numerous children, but his 'favorite' was his next to youngest, Joseph. Jacob/Israel, considered by Jewish historians to be the 'father of the Hebrew people', lost Joseph when jealousy prompted his brothers to fake his death at the hands of wild animals (he was actually transported to Egypt and sold into slavery). Joseph eventually rose to power as the *Grand Vizier* (Prime Minister) during the reign of the Hyksos kings in Egypt —when Egypt was ruled by Asiatic "shepherd kings" most likely from Canaan or Syria. The Hyksos ruled from 1650 to 1550 BCE; so, if the 2000 BCE date of the departure from Ur is accurate, this could very well be accurate.

Alternate Historical Hypothesis

What follows is an alternative time line and account of this period. Although accepted (at least in principle, if not in detail) by some Judaic scholars, this is clearly not the accepted account. This is based primarily on the independent research of Egyptologists Ahmed Osman, Moustafa Gadalla, and Lisa Ann Bargeman

> Abraham and Sarah left Ur as described above, and eventually entered Egypt. As Genesis recounts, Abraham had Sarah say she was his sister rather than his wife in order to ensure he would not be murdered so that his widow would be 'available' to Pharaoh. This was only partially untrue, since — according to Genesis.— his wife was also his half-sister. As feared, Pharaoh was attracted to Sarah and took her for his wife — paying Abraham (her 'older brother') a generous bridewealth for her hand. Later, when he discovered that she was actually Abraham's wife, he furiously expelled them both from Egypt. After they arrived back in Canaan, Sarah discovered that she was pregnant — with the child of Pharaoh Tuthmosis III. According to the Jewish Talmud, the birth of Isaac brought great humiliation to Abraham, for the child was clearly partially Egyptian. Isaac's birth-right (as a prince of Egypt) would have transferred — first to his son, Jacob, and then to his grandson, Joseph.

When Joseph interpreted Pharaoh's dream (as described in Genesis), he was recognized for who he was by Pharaoh Tuthmosis IV, and was appointed *Grand Vizier* (Prime Minister). When Tuthmosis IV died, his young son (about 12), Amenhotep III, became the pharaoh. Joseph (known as *Yuya* — compare that to the modern Arabic equivalent for Joseph, *Yusuf*) became a virtual father figure to Amenhotep. Although Amenhotep married his sister (Egyptian practice if he wanted to be Pharaoh, as the throne passed through the eldest daughter), he also married Tiye (Yuya's daughter, with whom he had grown up); and, it was Tiye that he made 'Queen of Egypt' (technically, his "great royal wife").

A son of Amenhotep III and Queen Tiye eventually became king of Egypt as Pharaoh Amenhotep IV. Later known as Akhenaten, he fostered a growing monotheistic religion in Egypt; and, it has even been claimed (by Osman) that Akhenaten and Moses were, in fact, the same person!

One piece of evidence Osman thinks supports his claim is the mummy of *Yuya* [left]. A 1905 discovery in a tomb in the Valley of Kings, this near-perfect mummy shows hand positions, unpierced ears, and physical features not consistent with an Egyptian. Osman claims this enhances the likelihood that Yuya was Joseph.

It is interesting to note that the stories of Gilgamesh and other Sumerian myths bear such strong resemblance to the corresponding stories in Genesis in the Hebrew Pentateuch (the first five books of Jewish scripture) — particularly since this was the area from which Abraham, the founding patriarch, had emigrated. These stories provide insight into the environment into which Judaism was born.

Zoroastrianism

Why introduce Zoroastrianism in a discussion of Judaism? What relevance does it have to Jewish foundations? Somewhat surprisingly to many, it is highly relevant. The Zoroastrian faith was prominent in the area in which Judaism was born and grew, and there were repeated contacts between the two — contacts that resulted in a number of shared beliefs and concepts.

Zoroastrianism was the religion of Persia, and is named after the founder, Zoroaster [right]. Known as Parsis (pahr'-seez) in India, there are about 150,000 adherents in the world today* — a population which makes Zoroastrianism one of the smaller religions. Zoroaster (known as *Zarathushtra* in Persian, and *Zarthosht* in Hindi and Farsi) is an historical challenge to researchers, as there is no agreement as to exactly when he lived. Conservative Zoroastrians believe that it was about 6,000 BCE; more liberal adherents estimate it to have been about 1800 BCE; anthropologists and other non-believers often assign a date of about 600 BCE. The 1800 BCE date is based largely on *paleography* (analysis of the writing he employed), which provides no reason to dispute the traditional date of 26 March 1767 BCE. In reality, however, this is not critical to understanding the religion, for this is not a faith that gains its credibility from an historical presence. The date serves little purpose other than to establish bragging rights regarding which faith is earlier.

Although small in number today, the Zoroastrian faith made numerous contributions to other theologies (such as Judaism, Islam, and Christianity). Beliefs thus "borrowed" include those involving God and Satan, the human soul, heaven and hell, a savior, resurrection, a final judgment day, and others.

Zoroaster was born and lived in ancient Persia (modern Iran). Legends recount how his birth was foretold, and that several attempts were made by "forces of evil" to kill him as a child. However, he survived to preach a dualistic monotheism — in a land that was fiercely polytheistic. At the time of Zoroaster's life, this part of the world was practicing an Aryan religion that might be described as *proto-Hinduism*. His ideas gained support, however, and his teachings became the state religion of the Persian Empires until the 7th century CE. In 644 CE, Arabic Muslims under Caliph Umar conquered coastal Persia and began forced conversions. The people were essentially given a choice: convert to Islam; defy the invaders, practice their religion, and be executed for it; or, flee the country. Most converted; many died; but, some managed to flee before the influx of the invading army.

---

* Some sources place the number of Zoroastrians at 2 to 3 million, but this is highly questionable.

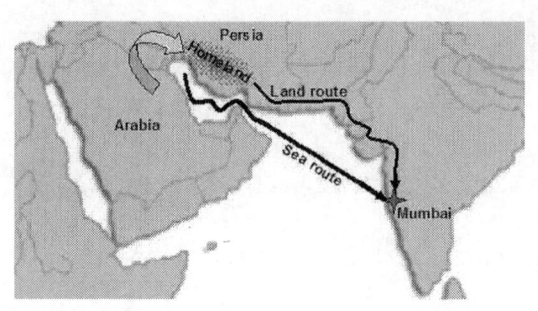

Notice on the map (left) that a sea route of escape from the Persian Gulf leads directly to the west coast of India. A land route has a similar effect, as the mountains force travelers to remain close to the coast. By either route, the fleeing Zoroastrians arrived at *Mumbai* (formerly known as *Bombay*), India.

Indians regarded religion as nearly synonymous with ethnicity. Therefore, when Zoroastrian refugees arrived in India, they were known to the native Indians as *Parsis* (literally, "Persian"). This Zoroastrian, or Parsi, community flourished in India, and a majority of adherents in the world today live within a 50 mile radius of Mumbai, India.

Beliefs

Zoroaster taught that there is a single God, called *Ahura Mazda*. This God is supreme, eternal; in fact, most scholars recognize Zoroastrianism as the world's first truly monotheistic religion. Ahura Mazda, however, is not easy for humans to understand or comprehend. So, communication between Ahura Mazda and humans is accomplished through His attributes, known as *Amesha Spentas*. One translation of this is "Holy Immortals". Although they are sometimes personified as human–like spiritual beings, they are more often seen within the Zoroastrian scriptures simply as concepts — ways of viewing God.

The faith is dualist in that, while Zoroastrians recognize that Ahura Mazda (God) is the only Deity, they also acknowledge the existence of *Angra Mainyu* (an "evil spirit of violence and death", *i.e.* the Devil). They envision the conflict between this pair as played out in the universe as the ultimate battle between good and evil, and humanity must choose which side they will follow (humans can not just sit on the sidelines and observe). Although they see this battle as real (some see it as a battle of spiritual entities involving humans, while others see it as an ethical battle fought in the human consciousness), the outcome is already pre-determined. At the "end of time", Good will conquer *Ahriman* (another name for Angra Mainyu, or Evil), and Good will be All-in-All.

Asha is a righteous, all-encompassing, natural law. This is of Ahura Mazda's creating, and everything is governed by it. Following death, the human soul (*urvan*) is given three days to reflect on its past life. After three days, it is judged by three of the Amesha Spentas, and is either brought to heaven or condemned to hell.

Zoroastrians see the universe as spanning three phases: Creation (entirely good, as made by Ahura Mazda); the current world, where good and evil battle it out; and, a final phase once Good triumphs, the souls damned to Hell are released, and all is purified and returned to its original, natural state of perfection.

An interesting Zoroastrian myth regards the *Saoshyant*. This is a savior who will be born to a virgin, of the lineage of Zoroaster, will perform miracles, raise the dead, and will judge everyone at the "end of time" in a Final Judgment Day.

Practices

At a Zoroastrian temple (right), worship includes prayers to Ahura Mazda as well as a number of symbolic ceremonies. These all occur before a *sacred fire* (the reason these houses of worship are called *Fire Temples*). Although not literally worshipping the fire, they do see it as a symbol of their God.

Children, generally between the ages of 8 and 12, are formally confirmed into the faith by use of the Navjote ritual. This ritual involves the tying of a sacred string around the child to serve as a constant reminder of duties and responsibilities to God. The weaving of this *sacred thread* is a high honor, and is usually done by a close relative. Conversion to Zoroastrianism is hotly debated. Traditionally, their marriages were all endogamous (*i.e.* they did not marry outside of their faith community). In those rare instances where this was not what happened, the children of such a marriage were not considered true Zoroastrians, and were limited in their access to the temple and its rituals. In recent years, many believers are pointing out that nothing Zoroaster ever wrote forbade new converts; and, as a result, some Zoroastrian temples (especially in the West) are now willing to accept converts; others do not.

The Zoroastrian scriptures are a collection of books known as the *Avesta*. This includes a series of five hymns (known as the *Gathas*) written by Zoroaster. A relatively abstract sacred poetry directed to Ahura Mazda, these relate core theology for the faith. They deal specifically with human understanding of righteousness, the cosmic order of things, social justice, free will, and good and evil. They are universal (*i.e.* not ethnic) in perspective, and this is often used by those who accept converts to imply Zoroaster's implicit approval. Later writers added additional parts of the Avesta that deal specifically with rituals, practices and matters of faith.

To non-believers, one of the more bothersome Zoroastrian practices is their handling of death. They consider the Aristotelian elements (earth, air, fire, water) as symbolic of God's creation (*i.e.* sacred). Since they regard fire as sacred, they can not cremate the body without defiling the sacred symbolism of the fire; with earth seen as sacred, they can't bury the dead for the same reason; the sanctity of water precludes burial at sea; and, leaving it out to rot would defile the air. What to do with the body? Their answer is the Zoroastrian *Tower of Silence*. The body is washed, covered with flower petals, and placed on a platform that is raised to the sky (to Ahura Mazda) for disposal. Ahura Mazda then sends his emissaries to retrieve it. In practice, buzzards (these emissaries) completely remove the body in minutes. This so offends Indian Hindus that the Fire Temple in Mumbai has planted tall trees all around it to shield this process from their neighbors.

Concepts

Zoroastrian religion can be summed up in what is referred to as the *three fold path*: **Humata, Hukhta, Huvarshta** (*good thoughts, good words, good deeds*).

Ahura Mazda   Literally, Ahura means "Lord Creator", and Mazda means "Supremely Wise." So, *Ahura Mazda* literally translates into English as "the Supremely Wise Lord Creator."

Free Will   As human beings, Ahura Mazda has given us the right to choose. However, due to the *Law of Cause and Effect*, we are responsible for our choices and the consequences.

Ch 6 – Jewish Foundations

Dualism Although there is only one God, our universe works on the basis of moral dualism: *Spenta Mainyu* ("good spirit") and *Angra Mainyu* ("evil spirit"). Zoroaster pleaded for humanity to think clearly before choosing, and to choose good to bring about beneficial consequences. He said *Ahura Mazda* would neither make the choice, nor compel humanity to choose a particular way. In other words, having given us free will, God allows us to make our own choices: if we choose good, we will bring about good; and, if we choose evil, we will cause evil. This, said Zoroaster, is how the moral universe operates.

Ahriman (Devil) Based on this dualism, humans are the ultimate cause of all the good and evil in the moral universe. Simply put, Zoroaster did not believe in a devil — other than the one created by bad choices. His followers, however, later personified *Angra Mainyu* (evil) as *Ahriman*.

Life's Purpose To be with those who are renewing the world, and to make the world progress toward perfection is life's purpose. In modern terms, it is "to be part of the solution rather than part of the problem".

Happiness Happiness is seen as a by-product of the choices made and the life chosen; Zoroaster saw it as belonging solely to those who work for the happiness of others.

Amesha Spentas The Amesha Spentas are seen as the personified attributes of Ahura Mazda. They are six in number: *Vohu Mano* (the spirit of the 'Good Mind'); *Asha* ('Truth and Right'); *Khshatra* ('Holy Sovereignty'); *Spenta Amaiti* ('Benevolent Devotion and Love'); *Haurvatat* ('Perfection and Well Being'); and, *Ameretat* ('Immortality').

Angels Although Zoroaster never preached angels, later followers personified the Amesha Spentas as angelic beings, and then also reintroduced some of the pre-Zoroastrian gods into Zoroastrianism as angels (much as early European and British people did in Christianity).

Cosmology Zoroaster had an interesting perspective on the universe. First, Ahura Mazda created Vohu Mano (Good Mind), through which He made a plan (a "blueprint") for the universe. Part of this blueprint was to incorporate an operating mode and operating laws. This was Asha, Truth and Right (sometimes known as the "universal software"). This was then followed by the actual, physical creation —

an act that required specific actions and manifestations (Khshatra, or Holy Sovereignty).

These manifestations were actualized through Spenta Amaiti (Benevolent Devotion, Faith and Love). Finally, the universe is created in the spirit of Perfection (Haurvatat) and Immortality (Ameretat).

Microcosm Each person is a microcosm of creation, and carries the divine essence within them. It is the duty of everyone to recognize this, and act accordingly. Based on Zoroaster's teachings, humanity can (and should) act like Ahura Mazda: thinking through every choice to be made, choosing based on the 'good mind', respecting the natural and moral laws and operating mode of the universe, and acting diligently with love and faith. The result will then (inevitably) be perfect and timeless choices, fulfilling our purpose in life to aid in renewing the world.

Partners Humans are co-workers and co-creators with God — here to fulfill the Divine Plan, neither as obedient slaves nor helpless children of God. This is the reason for free will — to choose between coöperating with God's plan and working against it. The reason for evil in the world is because there are some who have chosen (unwisely) to obstruct the Divine Plan.

Heaven / Hell Zoroaster taught that the human soul will, based on what choices it makes in its mortal life, either go to the *House of Songs* (a *Realm of Light*), or to the *House of Separation* (a *Realm of Darkness*). Zoroaster said these are not physical places, but eternal states of consciousness — either a state of oneness with Ahura Mazda or of separation from Him. Later followers mythologized these states of consciousness into physical locations, and then "loaned" this view to Judaism (and later, Christianity and Islam).

Consequences Since humanity is endowed with Divine Essence, humans are good and divine. Therefore, it is not humans that are evil, but their choices, actions and deeds that may be evil. The only way to fight darkness is to spread light. The only way to fight evil is to spread goodness. The only way to eliminate hatred and enmity is to spread love.

The Faravahar (also known as the Farohar) is the best known symbol of the Zoroastrian faith (right). The name is derived from the Old Persian word *Fravashi*, which is best described as a *guardian angel*. The winged disk dates to the Bronze Age in the Near East (ca. 3300 – 1200 BCE), with the figure added around 500 BCE. This probably got added during the reign of King Darius I, and the figure is supposedly of him. The symbol reminds followers of their purpose in life – *frasho-kereti* (ultimate union) with Ahura Mazda.

Impact

The impact of Zoroaster and his theological developments can not be overestimated: the faith he founded was likely the first to preach a monotheistic theology (*i.e.* one God), teach that this life will be judged and result in either Heaven or Hell, believe in the existence of angels, and define a dualistic (*i.e.* good and evil) view of existence. Today, Judaism, Christianity and Islam accept and preach these very same views.

But, did Zoroastrianism precede Judaism, or did it follow Judaism (and, perhaps, adopt these views from them)? This is widely debated, and there is no conclusive proof which came first; but, it is more likely, paleographically, that Zoroastrianism came first.

Modern Judaism is often thought to have had its first formulation in the time of Moses (*circa* 1200 BCE); so, if Zoroaster is dated to 600 BCE, Moses (and, therefore, Judaism) preceded him by 600 years. If, however, Zoroaster is dated to 1767 BCE (the traditional date), then he preceded Moses by nearly 600 years. It really doesn't matter except to devotees of one of the two faiths.

But, a related question that can be asked is whether or not modern Judaism should really be dated to the time of Moses. The story of Moses is recounted in the books of Exodus and Deuteronomy; and, a number of events, miracles, and actions are atributed to Moses (either happening *to* him, or being brought about *by* him).

He is regarded as a saint, prophet, or messenger by Jews, Muslims, Christians, and Baha'is. He is mentioned more than 500 times in the Islamic Qur'an, and nearly all of the stories about him in the Jewish scripture are also recounted in the Qur'an (plus one that only occurs in the Qur'an).

Among the many miraculous events associated with Moses is his receiving of the Ten Commandments on Mount Sinai. At the start of this account (presented in both Exodus and Deuteronomy), it states:

> You shall have no other gods before me. You shall not make for yourself a carved image, or any likeness of anything that is in heaven above, or that is in the earth beneath, or that is in the water under the earth. You shall not bow down to them or serve them, for I the LORD your God am a jealous God.
> [Exodus 20:3-5; Deuteronomy 5:7-9]

Many religious scholars see this as implying that Moses recognized (and God confirmed) the existence of "other gods", and told the faithful not to "bow down to them or serve them" because God is "a jealous God". If this implies monolatry (rather than monotheism), then modern Judaism should probably be dated to the time of Isaiah rather than Moses; and, that clearly came after the time of Zoroaster.

Chapter 7
Historical Development

The Holy Spirit rests on him only who has a joyous heart.
— *Jerusalem Talmud, Sukkat 5.1*

Make a joyful noise to the Lord, all the lands! Serve the Lord with gladness! Come into his presence with singing! Know that the Lord is God! It is he that made us, and we are his; we are his people, and the sheep of his pasture. Enter his gates with thanksgiving, and his courts with praise! Give thanks to him, bless his name! For the Lord is good; his steadfast love endures forever, and his faithfulness to all generations. — *Psalm 100*

According to the historical account in Genesis, Jacob and his descendents were welcomed by Joseph (his long lost son) to settle in Goshen, an area at the 'edge of Egypt' in the eastern Nile delta region. First moving there during a period of drought and famine, they reportedly remained there until their numbers had grown to where the Egyptians feared them as a possible threat to Egyptian sovereignty, and stripped them of any rights (reducing them to the status of slaves). This was their status for the next 4 generations* until they were led out of captivity by Moses (*Moshe*) – the next great figure in Judaic history; so, the descendents of Jacob would have lived in Egypt from 100 to 400 years (*ca.* 1650 – 1250 BCE). This Egyptian exile is one of the longest, as well as most important, periods in Hebraic history which remains essentially unattested in any non–religious text (there is no written record outside the Tanakh). However, this does not disprove it, since Egyptians rarely kept records on this type of captivity. It was common for them to take captives to work in their households and on their lands, and the source of those captives was generally of little interest to them.

---

* Known in Judaism as the "Egyptian captivity", this was reported to have lasted for 4 generations according to Exodus 6 and 1st Chronicles 6, which would be about 70-100 years; and, Genesis 15:16 specifically states that it will be "in the fourth generation". But, according to Genesis 15:13, it was 400 years (although this was a prophecy, and could be interpreted as approximate); and, Exodus 12:40,41 states explicitly that is was 430 years.

What is of most importance to Judaism was the Egyptian religious scene — which was clearly polytheistic; but, which was as close to being monotheistic as possible during the reign of Akhenaton (called Amenhotep IV prior to his monotheistic religious conversion). This occurred *circa* 1350–1334 BCE, at the height of the Hebrew captivity. Moses, as an ethical and legal leader of the Hebrew people, may very well have been influenced in some way by this shift to monotheism which occurred under Akhenaton, and by the turbulent return back to polytheism which took place under the XIXth dynasty as he was preparing his people to flee Egypt. Much of the book of Exodus is devoted to the events as the Hebrews prepared to flee Egypt, and the events that occurred during their 40 years of exile wandering in the deserts of what is today the Sinai, Arabia and Jordan. Moses died before the close of this journey, and it was his successor, Joshua, who finally led the Hebrews (by this time, generally referred to as Israelites, or "sons of Israel") across the Jordan River and back into Canaan – the area they had left 100 to 400 years earlier.

The Golden Age

The *Golden Age* for the Israelites came after they had conquered the local tribal leaders in Canaan and consolidated their control as 12 federated tribal states. Collectively referred to as Israel (after their common ancestor), the area was divided into twelve semi-independent states ruled by tribal leaders and judges; each state was effectively a clan holding.

This arrangement held for nearly 200 years, with each of these clans claiming descent from one of the 12 sons of Israel*. True greatness for the Israelites, however, came after they adopted a government system closer to that of their neighbors rather than the loosely confederated theocracy they first established. To accom-

---

* This is true with just 2 exceptions: 10 tribal lands were granted to the descendents of Reuben, Simeon, Judah, Dan, Naphtali, Gad, Asher, Issachar, Zebulun, and Benjamin; Joseph was dead and did not take part in the Exodus; but, his two sons (Manasseh and Ephraim) were treated as half-tribes, and tribal lands were granted to their descendents. The descendents of Levi served as the common priesthood for everyone, lived amongst all of the tribes, and were granted no exclusive tribal lands.

plish this, they chose Saul (of the tribe of Benjamin) to become the first king of their unified nation-state.

Saul reigned from *ca.* 1049 BCE to 1007 BCE (42 years). He was an effective ruler, and it was during his reign that Israel truly "came into its own". The Israelites had initially been divided as to who should become their king, as the smaller tribes were fearful of someone from one of the larger tribes (such as that of Judah), fearing they would effectively lose their sovereignty to that tribe. The larger tribes apparently thought it logical that one of theirs should become king. Saul was a perfect compromise. He had an established reputation as a military leader (having led an army over the Ammonites – 1 Samuel 11); and, he was from the smallest tribe[#].

Saul and his wife (Ahinoam) had 4 sons and 2 daughters. His younger daughter (Michal) was given in marriage to David following his defeat of Goliath. At the age of 72, in a battle with the Philistines (the *Battle of Mount Gilboa*), Saul and his 3 oldest sons were killed (Saul falling on his sword as defeat became inevitable). His youngest son, Ish-baal (literally, "man of Ba'al"), was declared king on the battlefield by Saul's military captain. The tribe of Judah, however, believed it should have been David to replace him, and they seceded from the unified kingdom. War soon developed between Judah (under David) and Israel (under Ish-baal). David succeeded in defeating his brother-in-law, and reunited the kingdom (with him replacing Ish-baal as Saul's successor). Ish-baal's reign was short – just 2 years. At the end, Ish-baal was murdered by two of his own military leaders. The assassins had expected David to reward them handsomely; but, he had them stoned to death for high treason. Due to the shameful way in which Ish-baal died, the scriptures often refer to him by the name Ish-bosheth (literally, "man of shame").

[#] Earlier, a group of thugs from the tribe of Benjamin had raped a Levite woman to death. When the Levites demanded that they be turned over to them, the Benjamites refused. This so incensed the other tribes that they gathered an army and systematically slaughtered the Benjamites – men, women, and children – at the *Battle of Gilbeah*. Only very few survived, and tribal strength never returned – leaving them "the smallest tribe in Israel".

David had ruled Judah from 1010 BCE (in defiance of Saul), and reigned over a reunited Israel from 1003 BCE (following the death of Ish-bosheth). Jewish history portrays him as righteous (although not without a few serious character faults); they also note his status as a great warrior, musician, and poet (crediting him with both the words and music for many of the Psalms). Under David, Israel grew in reputation and internal cohesiveness, and the capital (both religious and political) was established at Jerusalem.

Following David's death in 970 BCE, he was replaced as king by his son, Solomon (Arabic: *Sulaiman*). Solomon was wealthy, wise, and powerful; but, he is also accused of having easily fallen into idolatry. He succeeded David largely as a result of involvement by his mother, Bathsheba. She got David to declare Solomon his co-regent, and Solomon ruled jointly with his father for 3 years before David died at the age of 70.

That was very old for that time, and David became weak and bedridden; he could not get warm. In addition to needing Solomon to co-rule with him, his family arranged for the young and beautiful Abishag to lie next to him to keep him warm.

(*The 1879 painting, David and Abishag is by Brazilian artist Pedro Américo.*)

It was Solomon who had the first temple built in Jerusalem, but he also fell under the influence of his many foreign wives (scriptural accounts credit him with 700 wives and 300 concubines). He also built temples to foreign gods, and drifted from strict Jewish religious constraints. To maintain his wealth and power, he implemented oppressive taxes as well as forced labor. When he died (*ca.* 931 BCE), his son Rehoboam assumed the kingship, and continued his father's repressive policies. The result was that the northern ten tribal areas seceded from the kingdom. This left two separate states: Israel in the north (comprising the 10 secessionist clans, with their capital at Shechem (*i.e.* Nablus, in the West Bank); and, Judæa (comprising Judah and Benjamin) to the south.

This marked the end of the Golden Age, as Israel and Judæa fought seemingly endless battles with each other. Although few were decisive[*], the result was a general crippling of both kingdoms – making both more vulnerable to attack from outside. Between 740 and 722 BCE, Israel was slowly defeated by the Assyrians (successors to the Sumerians), and tens of thousands of captives were exiled to northern Assyria. They were never heard from again, and are often referred to as the "ten lost tribes of Israel".

Exile and Captivity

The next major step in the development of modern Judaism resulted from the exile and captivity of the southern kingdom of Judæa by Babylonia. On March 16, 597 BCE, Jerusalem fell to the Babylonians, who had laid siege to it months earlier. Jehoiakim (who had been enthroned by Egypt in 609 BCE) was taken captive and sent to Babylon along with many of the people. In his place, Babylon crowned Zedekiah. In 588, Jerusalem was destroyed, and still more Jews were exiled to Babylon. Zedekiah was deposed the next year (587); four years later (583), Judæa ceased to exist, and the third and last deportation to Babylon occurred. Less than 50 years later (in October 539 BCE), Cyrus, the king of Persia, conquered Babylon. That same year, the exiled Jews began a repatriation to their homeland. Their exile in Babylon had lasted nearly 5 decades, and their benefactor became the Zoroastrian Cyrus. It is believed by biblical scholars that it was most likely during the exile that scribes committed oral traditions to print — as the Torah[#].

---

[*] The exception was *ca.* 913 BCE, when Abijah (king of Judæa) and Jeroboam (king of Israel) fought a major battle in the mountains of Ephraim. Abijah fielded 400,000 men, while Jeroboam fielded nearly 800,000. Abijah won the battle despite the odds when he thwarted Jeroboam's pincer movement, and killed more than 500,000 of Jeroboam's troops. As a result, Israel lost several towns and cities in their south to the kingdom of Judæa.

[#] Torah (Hebrew: "teaching") is the Jewish term for the first 5 books of scripture (Genesis, Exodus, Leviticus, Deuteronomy and Numbers). These same books are known as the Pentateuch (Greek: "five books") to Christians, and as Tawrat (Arabic: "law") to Muslims.

Sometime during the fifth century BCE, Ezra and Nehemiah arrived in Jerusalem from Persia. Although exact dates are nearly impossible to determine, the most commonly accepted date is that Ezra arrived about 458 BCE; he is called a "priest and scribe" who had been sent "to teach in Israel statutes and ordinances". The Persian king at the time, Artaxerxes II, had evidently sent him. Ezra taught numerous laws and teachings to the Hebrews, not the least of which was a ban on taking foreign women as wives. This had been a common practice among the Jews, but was a clear violation of Zoroastrian teachings. Ezra was probably a Zoroastrian priest, for it would have been foolish for a Zoroastrian king to send a Jewish priest to the Jews to teach them Jewish law, but perfect sense to send a Zoroastrian priest to teach the Jews Zoroastrian law.

Nehemiah arrived from Persia as the *oinochoos* of the Persian king. This is the Greek term for a "cup bearer"; and, was nearly always a young, but highly trusted, favorite of the king. Often, the cup bearer, whose function was the king's wine taster, was the only person that stood between the king and assassination. When Artaxerxes sent Nehemiah to Jerusalem, he was sending a very junior diplomat, but one he clearly trusted. From 445 to 433 BCE, Nehemiah oversaw the rebuilding of Jerusalem's walls as their governor (they had been broken down during the exile). He also re-enforced Ezra's Zoroastrian teachings in Jerusalem. Again, the idea that Artaxerxes would have had a Jewish *oinochoos* is absurd, as no king would have entrusted his very life to a member of a captive people.

This was also when their theology changed in tone. Prior to this, God was seen in tribal terms. The Jews had been monolatrist (worshipping one god of many), and often referenced "other gods".

Compare: You shall have no other god to set against me. ... You shall not bow down to them or worship them; for I, the Lord your god, am a jealous god. (Exodus 20:3, 5)

to: My witnesses, says the Lord, are you, my servants, you whom I have chosen to know me and put your faith in me and understand that I am He. Before me there was no god fashioned nor ever shall be after me (Isaiah 43:10)

It would appear that Judaism had transitioned from the earlier monolatry to Zoroastrian monotheism.

Ancient Divisions

It was about this same time (as Ezra and Nehemiah) that the seeds were sown for the development of divisions within Judaism which were described by the historian Flavius Josephus as their "three schools of philosophy": Pharisees, Sadducees, and Essenes. The actual teachings of these groups (particularly the Pharisees) is clouded in history, for Pharisees and Sadducees frequently served together, and the differences appear to have been more philosophical than confrontational. As a result, only a few major differences were recorded by observers such as Josephus. First, consider the two primary lines of thought today.

Traditional Theory

Jewish historians and scholars view the Sadducees as purists who only followed the rules and guidelines of the Torah (which, at that time, had only recently been committed to writing). They often were wealthy, politically powerful people. The Pharisees, too, followed the Torah, but also followed oral traditions. The Essenes were unique in that they followed a communal life style based on an ascetic, pure reading of Jewish law (recognized for their communalism, celibacy, and purity). The English word Pharisee was brought into English from the Greek *pharisaios*, which in turn is thought to have come from the Hebrew *pârushim*. This derivation might make the Pharisees a separatist organization, since *pârash* meant "to separate", and *pârushim* "separate ones" (the problem is that they were not separate, but were in the middle of everything).

The derivation of the term Sadducee is traditionally more controversial. Some place it as a derivative of the Hebrew *tzaddikim*, meaning "righteous ones", while others derive it from "followers of Zadok" (the high priest under David and Solomon). In practice, it could be either (as 'followers of Zadok' were seen as righteous).

Alternative Theory

Where this becomes less certain and more controversial is with the alternative derivation for Pharisee proposed by some modern Zoroastrian historians. These scholars believe the word Pharisee is a minor corruption of *pharsee*, a 'person from Persia'. These scholars have proposed that the Pharisees were the religious group following the teachings of Ezra (who, according to them, was a Pharsee). Etymologically, this may not be as much of a stretch as it first appears; there are precedents (consider that *Wales* is just west of England, and the Scots *Wallace* clan lived just north of England; *Waleis* is the Old English term for "foreigner", and both *Wales* and *Wallace* (or *Wallis*) are derivatives of it). It is not illogical to suppose that *pârushim*, a Hebrew term meaning 'separate ones', could similarly apply to foreigners to the east (*Pharsees*), from whom they were separated. Therefore, consider what is known about the teachings of these two groups (Pharisees and Sadducees).

Teachings

The Sadducees believed:
- o in the free will of man to the exclusion of fate;
- o that God did not pass judgment on man on the basis of his actions in this world;
- o there would be no future resurrection of man; and,
- o there was no life after death.

By contrast, the Pharisees:
- o accepted free will as well as fate;
- o expected that there would be a *Final Judgment Day*;
- o believed in the future resurrection of humanity; and,
- o accepted that there was, in fact, a life after death.

The etymology of Pharisee as a derivative of Pharsee may be offensive to some modern Jews, but the known teachings of the Pharisees are in close harmony with those of the Zoroastrians, whereas those of the Sadducees are not. They may be wrong, but the Zoroastrians have proposed a scenario that is plausible, and which does account for the differences between the groups.

Other ancient divisions within Judaism included:
- o Essenes — a group of fairly isolated purists;
- o Zealots — actively opposed Roman occupation and control;
- o Herodians — saw Herod's rule as supportive of an eventual return to a truly Jewish theocratic state;
- o Sicarii — literally, *dagger men*, a terrorist wing of the Zealots;
- o Karaites — accepted only the authority of the Tanakh (scripture);
- o Ananites — ascetics who followed Anan ben David;
- o Beta Israel — Ethiopian Jews dating back to Solomon and the Queen of Sheba – they still exist, although most now live in Israel.

Mandæanism

Most people have never encountered, and are unaware of, Mandæanism. Despite its significant age, this religion has never been a world presence. Today, it is mostly in Iraq and Iran, where they have managed to preserve their unique language (Mandaic, apparently a West Aramaic dialect), a complex baptismal ritual, and their religious structure — *for at least 2,000 years*.

Mandæanism is an ancient monotheistic religion, and believes in an almighty God that was created from and by Himself (*aseity*: "Self-existence"). Their name for God is *Haii* (meaning "Eternal Life"), and He is considered the Creator and Source of the entire universe. In addition, they recognize the existence of a World of Light *(Nhura)*, and a World of Darkness *(Hshuka)* – *i.e.* the presence of God, and the absence of God. These two worlds are seen as being in constant hostility to one another. Haii also serves as the *King of Light* — *i.e.* the leader of the forces of good.

Constant conflict between the World of Light and the World of Darkness led to the creation of this earthly world — essentially an evil creation in which the King of Light has injected goodness to "tilt the balance in its favor". They view the peak of creation as the creation of the first human (*Adam*). Adam's material body (including his desires and instincts) was made from elements of the evil, earthly world (and thus contains its essence); but, his soul or consciousness (*Nishimtha*) descended from the World of Light on the orders of Haii, and manifests goodness as its essence.

History

Mandæan history is both speculative and controversial. What follows is the view of the Mandæan people – a view broadly supported by early Mandæan, Dead Sea and Islamic texts.

At the time of the Hebrew revolt against Rome (*ca.* 70 CE), the three major groupings of Jews were the Pharisees, the Sadducees, and the Essenes. Pharisees and Sadducees have already been outlined; but, the Essenes were not. Of these three, the Essenes were the more *mystical* branch of the faith. Often living in communes, they built temples outside the main cities (even those living in the city kept largely to themselves — *e.g.* in Jerusalem, the Essene

Quarter was isolated at the southwest corner of the walled city). Each morning, they welcomed the dawn with prayers and a ritual baptism — a "spiritual cleansing" in the moving waters of a nearby river. Mandæans believe that John the Baptist was, in all likelihood, an Essene.

The Romans crushed that 1st century rebellion, and capped this with the destruction of the Jerusalem Temple. The last group of rebels took refuge in the former stronghold of Herod the Great, *Masada* (Hebrew: "fortress"). This fort was located atop a cliff overlooking the Dead Sea; the sheer east face dropping 1400 feet to the water. It took the Romans 3 years to breach the walls and conquer the fort — only to have the rebels burn it to the ground before committing mass suicide. Well over a thousand died. Once Roman control was assured, they began to execute or disperse anyone they suspected of being subversive. Since the rebels had been led by Zealots (a radical religio-political group possibly affiliated with the Essenes), that would have included any of the secretive religious groups (such as the Essenes). They also destroyed any scrolls written by these suspected seditionists.

A small group at Qumran (probably Essenes) hid scrolls in hand hewn caves, and then fled the area. It isn't recorded where they went; but, there are indications. Ebionites (which translates as "poor men" – coincidentally, the name the Essenes used for themselves) fled Judæa into the desert to escape Roman persecution; also known as Sabæans, these were probably the remnant of an Essene community — most likely those from Qumran.

A family-based Essene group on Mount Carmel also fled Roman persecution. Historical references show that they went east into the desert toward Damascus, eventually finding refuge in Mesopotamia. Also known as *Nasorai, Nasoræans*, or *Nazarenes*, these are the spiritual (and possibly biological) ancestors of the modern Mandæans.

Beliefs

As a mystical branch of Judaism which "marched to a different drummer", the Mandæans have several key beliefs-practices:

- o *Sahdutha* strict monotheism;
- o *Masbuta* frequent (daily) baptism;
- o *Brakha* intense prayer;
- o *Suma* fasting — either a "Great Fast", abstaining from anything impeding man's relationship with God, or a "Small Fast", abstaining from meat, fish, or animal products; and,
- o *Zidqa* giving of alms — both moral and material.

The daily baptism ritual must be performed in running water, known as *yardna* in Mandaic (also Aramaic for "Jordan River"). They also share scriptures in common with modern Judaism, but often interpret them differently. There appears to be significant Persian aspects to their beliefs (*e.g.* an emphasis on angels and demons). The Mandæan *Book of Saint John* (John the Baptist, not John the disciple of Jesus) is remarkably similar to the *Genesis Apocryphon* found in the Dead Sea Scrolls; and, the *Ginza Rba* shares ~85% with *Genesis*. The Mandaeans have a Eucharist ceremony that predates Christianity, and was marked by taking *pehta* ("a bit of bread") and sanctified water — their "new wine".

Scriptures

The Mandæans have a number of books which they consider sacred — historical, mythological and theological. These include:
- o *Ginza Rba* the oldest text, also called the *Book of Adam*;
- o *Book of Saint John* telling the message & activities of John the Baptist;
- o *Book of the Zodiac* a collection of ritual, magic and astrology; and,
- o *Baptism of Abel the Brilliant* describing purification of a heavenly savior.

Cosmology

Mandaean cosmology consists of a more gnostic[*] interpretation of traditional Jewish mythology. This is not surprising, since they emigrated to an area that was primarily gnostic in its beliefs. God is the *King of Light*, and dwells in the uppermost world, or heaven; the earth is home to a female spirit, *Ruha*. Earth is seen as a dark

---

[*] Gnosticism is not exclusively a Christian heresy, as it is so often portrayed. Derived from the Greek word *gnosis* (meaning "knowledge"), it is the belief that an individual can attain spiritual knowledge and insight through personal action or revelation. As such, it is extremely difficult to organize along dogmatic lines, since different individuals may have experienced different truths. This system of personal religious knowledge found adherents not only among Christians, but also among Jews, Hindus, Muslims, and others. Their beliefs are not proscribed, but are more statistically or demographically identified.

place created out of Ruha's black waters — the solid land forming only after mixing with a little light from above (*conf* Genesis 1).

In Genesis, *Ruach* is the Hebrew term for the "breath of God", and serves as the basis for the Christian *Holy Spirit*. Ruach is a feminine noun, and Ruha is its translation from Hebrew into Aramaic. They view the body as a tomb, and the physical world as a prison which keeps the human soul from reunion with the supreme God. For this reason, the physical world is seen as corrupt, and doomed to ultimate destruction. However, the righteous can save their souls by being moral, practicing the ritual observances, and acquiring true knowledge. Following death, the souls of those who led a good life pass into the *world of light*, while others undergo torture. Even the most evil, however, will be purified in a "great baptism" at the end of the world — equivalent to the Essene and Zoroastrian 'baptism with fire' on the *Day of Vengeance*.

Mandæans consider Jesus to have been a fraud, and view John the Baptist as having been the legitimate savior. They believe Jesus was an attempted usurper of this role, and consider him to have been a younger, ambitious member of an Essene community at Mount Carmel. Two of the featured characters in the Mandaean *Book of Saint John* are Zachariah and his wife, Enishbai (a Mandaic version of Elizabeth). Christians generally accuse the Mandæans of having "lifted" this from the first chapter of *Luke*; but, Luke was quite possibly reflecting a small part of Essene history. If so, then both books would be drawing on the same history.

John had reportedly been baptizing people, and had periodically performed healings. Rivalry began to occur between the followers of each. This was recorded in the biblical *Gospel of Luke* when it recounts that "the people were in expectation, and all men mused in their hearts of John, whether he were the Christ, or not." [Luke 3:15] By the fourth century, church father Clementine reported (in *Clementine Recognitions* 1:60) that the disciples of John claimed that he had been greater than Jesus and was the true Messiah.

Whether or not the Mandæans can be considered derivative of an ancient Jewish sect depends upon whether or not one accepts that they are the modern descendents of the Essenes. This is widely debated; but, they claim they are.

Chapter 8
Scripture, Concepts, Practices & Holidays

Whosoever labors in the Torah for its own sake merits many things; and not only so, but the whole world is indebted to him: he is called friend, beloved, a lover of the All-present, a lover of mankind; it clothes him in meekness and reverence; it fits him to become just, pious, upright, and faithful; it keeps him far from sin, and brings him near to virtue.
— Mishnah, Abot 6.1

Scripture

Jewish scripture is referred to as the TaNaKh, and is composed of three primary divisions: *Torah* ("teachings"); *Nevi'im* ("prophets"); and, *Ketuvim* ("writings"). Tanakh is thus an acronym for the three sections that comprise the entire scripture.

This was studied and analyzed, and the reflections that arose were recorded in what is known as the *Talmud*, and which recounts discussions of ethics, law, philosophy, customs, and history. This is, in turn, composed of the *Mishnah* (an accounting of oral traditions that accompanied the written word), and the *Gemara* (which expands on the Mishnah, and which gives broad interpretations of the Tanakh).

Jewish tradition maintains that the Tanakh was codified in its current form no later than 450 BCE, and comprises 24 books.

Torah
- *Bereshit* (Genesis)
- *Shemot* (Exodus)
- *Vayikra* (Leviticus)
- *Bemidbar* (Numbers)
- *Devarim* (Deuteronomy)

Nevi'im
- *Yehoshuah* (Joshua)
- *Shophtim* (Judges)
- *Shemuel* (Samuel)
- *M'lakhim* (Kings)
- *Yesha'ayahu* (Isaiah)
- *Yirmeyah* (Jeremiah)
- *Yehezqel* (Ezekial)
- The Twelve Prophets

Ketuvim
- *Tehillim* (Psalms)
- *Mishlei* (Proverbs)
- *Iyyobh* (Job)
- *Shir Hashirim* (Song of Songs)
- *Ruth* (Ruth)
- *Eikhah* (Lamentations)
- *Qohelet*h (Ecclesiastes)
- *Ester* (Esther)
- *Daniel* (Daniel)
- *Ezra v'Nechemia* (Ezra-Nehemiah)
- *Divrei Hayamim* (Chronicles)

The Tanakh counts 24 books where the Protestant Christian Old Testament counts 39 — the divisions are different (*i.e.* considering the Twelve Prophets, Chronicles, Ezra-Nehemiah, Samuel, and Kings as single books), and that accounts for the different count while being identical in content.

Holidays and Rituals

Most festivals and holidays are either unique to Judaism, or are not widespread in other faiths. One of the reasons for these unique religious holidays (*i.e.* holy days) is that Judaism is largely an *historical religion*. This refers to any religion where, if absolute, incontrovertible proof that historical claims made by the faith were shown to be fictional, fabricated, or grossly divergent from historical reality, the faith itself would suffer irreparable damage. In other words, one where the historical veracity of their claims is foundational to the modern practice of the faith. No faith is purely historical*; but, Judaism comes closer than most. As the various holidays of Judaism are reviewed, notice the frequency with which they are related to an historical event in Jewish history.

o **Shabbat**

Shabbat, the Sabbath, is set aside as a day of worship, when Jews recall and reflect on the Creation of the universe. Genesis recounts that God created everything in six days, and then rested on the seventh day. It tends to be a festive day, when Jews are released from the normal day-to-day burdens of life. Worldly cares are put to rest on Friday in time to be able to bathe and put on clean clothes for the Sabbath, which is observed starting minutes prior to sundown on Friday evening.

The Shabbat celebration begins with the lighting of two candles by the mother of the family 18 to 40 minutes prior to

---

* In addition to *historical religions* (as described), other "classes" of faith would include *theological religions* (where historical veracity is immaterial, and the faith is based entirely on ethical, moral, or theological teachings), and *mythical religions* (where historical veracity is either inconsistent or debatable, and the "historical stories" told in the faith are primarily important as a way of illustrating or teaching the values of the faith, but their existence as actual, historical events is not particularly important).

sundown, followed by a special prayer welcoming the Sabbath. This is usually followed by two songs: one welcoming the *Shabbat angels* to the house; and, the second thanking the mother of the home for all of her work for the family over the prior week. A blessing is then offered over the wine and *challah* (a braided, egg bread), and a special meal is served. Typically, there are three family meals celebrated on the Shabbat. The remaining two are on Saturday at lunch and then in the late afternoon.

Public Shabbat worship services are held at the synagogue on Friday evening, Saturday morning, and late Saturday afternoon – featuring singing, chanting, and the reading of scriptural selections. The day is brought to a close when three stars can be seen in the sky on Saturday evening.

Jewish law (*halakha*) acknowledges a total of 39 categories of "work" that are not allowed on the Sabbath. These categories are known as *melakhot*. Observant Orthodox and Conservative Jews (covered in the next chapter) refrain from performing any of these prohibited activities. These restricted activities are:

- Reaping
- Ploughing
- Sowing
- Threshing
- Winnowing
- Binding sheaves
- Selecting
- Grinding
- Sifting
- Kneading
- Baking
- Shearing wool
- Washing wool
- Kindling a fire
- Extinguishing a fire
- Finishing an object
- Transporting an object
- Making 2 loops
- Weaving 2 threads
- Separating 2 threads
- Writing 2+ letters
- Erasing 2+ letters
- Sewing stitches
- Ripping stitches
- Trapping
- Cutting hides to shape
- Flaying
- Tanning
- Scraping hides
- Marking hides
- Slaughtering
- Tying
- Untying
- Building
- Demolishing
- Beating wool
- Dyeing wool
- Spinning
- Weaving

Among the most observant Orthodox Jews, there is some debate as to whether modern activities are *melakhah* or not: using your car is generally restricted (you start a fire, transport yourself and others, and extinguish the fire); throwing an electric switch is debated (is the tiny spark generated in an electrical switch technically a fire?). To ensure that they do not inadvertently violate the *melakhot*, the strictest Orthodox Jews employ a *shabbas goy* (*i.e.*, a *Sabbath gentile*).

The difficulty with the *melakhot* is that these are categories, not activities. As an example, winnowing not only refers to separating the chaff from wheat, but might also be pulling the husk from an ear of corn, separating small bones from a piece of fish, or picking lint off your clothes. So, if all of this is restricted, what does Judaism encourage the faithful to do on the Sabbath?

All of the Jewish sects encourage the faithful to:
- o read, study, or discuss the Torah and Jewish commentaries on it;
- o extend hospitality to friends, family and guests at Sabbath meals;
- o attend synagogue services for prayer;
- o sing religious songs (known as *zemirot*) at Sabbath meals;
- o enjoy marital relations (*i.e.* sex) between a husband and wife; and,
- o sleep.

High Holy Days

The term *High Holy Days* refers to *Rosh Hashana* and *Yom Kippur*. Also known as "Days of Awe" (*Yamim Nora'im*), they are based on the Jewish lunar calendar and usually fall during, or close to, the month of September

o **Rosh Hashana**

Rosh Hashana is the Jewish New Year, and is observed in memory of God's creation of the world. This is followed by 10 days of repentance. It gets a little confusing when discussing the New Year, because there is both a *Jewish New Year* and a *Hebrew New Year*. The *civil year* (often called the *ecclesiastical year*) begins on the Hebrew date of 1 Tishri (in the Fall). This is used for numbering years[*],

---

[*] For example, year 5773 began at sundown on September 16, 2012. This may be called '5773 of the Hebrew era', or 5773 AM (*Anno Mundi*).

and for secular activities. However, Exodus 12:12 (attributed to Moses) declares that 1 Nisan "shall be unto you the beginning of months". This was clearly explained by Josephus (in his *Antiquities* 1.81) as:

> Moses ... appointed Nisan...as the first month for the festivals ... the commencement of the year for everything relating to divine worship, but for selling and buying and other ordinary affairs he preserved the ancient order (*i.e.* the year beginning with Tishri).

So, *Rosh Hashana*, the "Jewish New Year" falls on 1 Tishri – the seventh month of the religious calendar!

o **Yom Kippur**

Yom Kippur immediately follows the days of repentance, and is the *Day of Atonement*. It is, without question, the holiest and most solemn day of the year. Featuring atonement and repentance, it is usually observed with a 25-hour period of fasting and prayer. Devout Jews may spend most (or even all) of the day at services. In fact, the High Holy Days are the only religious holidays typically honored by secular Jews (a classification of *ethnoreligious* Jews that follow Jewish customs and culture, but typically do not follow religious edicts). As a result, synagogue attendance often skyrockets on Yom Kippur, when Jews of virtually all persuasions (even the non-religious and marginally religious) attend services.

o **Pesach**

> *And this day shall become a memorial for you, and you shall observe it as festival for the Lord, for your generations, as an eternal decree shall you observe it. For seven days you shall eat unleavened bread, but on the first day you shall remove the leaven from your homes ... you shall guard the unleavened bread, because on this very day I will take you out of the land of Egypt; you shall observe this day for your generations as an eternal decree. — Exodus 12:14-17*

Passover (Hebrew: *Pesach*) is a remembrance of the Jews' flight from Egypt, and the "passing over" of the Israelite firstborn children by God as he put a plague on the Egyptians. This week-long celebration uses special foods to remind the Jews of hardships endured by their ancestors in their flight from Egypt. It also marks the beginning of the agricultural year in the Middle East, but this aspect of the holiday is rarely even noticed, and certainly not celebrated.

Passover "rules" are strictly followed. As a result, no leavening whatsoever must be in the home, and nothing that has come in contact with it is kept (to avoid any possible cross-contamination). Even pets and livestock in the home can not be fed anything with leaven, and thus held to the same rules. Anything that has come in contact with a leavening agent must either be disposed of, given, or sold to a non-Jew. This sometimes leads to the strange practice of giving (or selling) the family dog or cat to a non-Jewish neighbor, and then buying it back after the holiday is over!

A special meal (known as the *Seder*) is held on the first two nights of Passover (first night only in Israel). It is a ritual-dense meal during which prayers, songs, toasts, blessings, ritual acts, and specific discussions are pre-defined. Work of any kind is strictly forbidden on both the first two days (first in Israel) and last two days (last in Israel); work is permitted on intermediate days. The entire holiday extends over eight days (seven in Israel).

This is an important holiday on the Jewish calendar (some would say the most important holiday), and is often even observed by those who observe none of the other holidays or traditions. A survey conducted[*] in 2000-2001 found that, while just 46% of American Jews attend synagogue services, 67% routinely either attend or host a Seder.

o **Shavu'ot**

Shavu'ot is now celebrated as the giving of the Ten Commandments to Moses on Mount Sinai; however, it origin-

---

[*] Published as the *National Jewish Population Survey*, this was conducted under the auspices of *The Jewish Federations of North America*, the *Roper Center for Public Opinion Research*, and the *University of Connecticut's Center for Judaic Studies and Contemporary Jewish Life*.

ated as a harvest festival similar to the pagan *Lughnasadh*. As such, it was a festival of "first fruits". The holiday lasts 2 days, and begins on the 50th day when one starts counting on the second day of Passover. The holiday is also known as the *Festival of Weeks* (since it is 7 weeks plus a day after Passover), and sometimes *Pentecost*. No work is performed during the two days of Shavu'ot.

o **Sukkot**

Just as pagans had a second harvest festival, another Jewish harvest festival is *Sukkot*, during which they give thanks to God for His bountiful harvest of fruits and vegetables that year. The celebration begins the fifth day following Yom Kippur. As such, a remarkable transition occurs over those 5 days: Yom Kippur is the most solemn day on the Jewish calendar; but, Sukkot is an unrestrained celebration of joy (Hebrew: *Z'man Simchateinu*, or "Season of Rejoicing").

This seven day festival is a way to commemorate the forty years that Jews wandered in the desert after the escape from Egypt. During that time, Jews lived in temporary shelters constructed in the desert (singular *Sukkah*, plural *Sukkot*). Many observant Jews construct a temporary shelter (often in their yard), and live in it rather than the house this week.

The two days that immediately follow Sukkot are both observed as holidays on their own, although they are often seen as a sort of extension of Sukkot. These holidays are *Shemini Atzeret* and *Simchat Torah*.

o **Purim**

Purim is a "minor holiday" that comes during the winter months, and is in honor of when the Israelites in Persia were saved from persecution by Queen Esther (as recounted in the biblical book of that name). It is often described as being the holiday that is the most "fun".

Mordecai was a good man, and was Esther's uncle. Haman was an advisor to the local king, and was a deceitful and vicious man. Haman planned on exterminating the Jews in Persia, but was thwarted by Esther's intervention with the king (at the suggestion of Mordecai). Jews are instructed that, on this day, they should "eat, drink, and be merry". The Talmud has the specific instruction that they should drink until they can no longer tell the difference between "cursed by Haman" and "blessed be Mordecai" (modern Jewish scholars are divided as to just how drunk that is). In addition, the tradition is to make gifts to charity, and to give gifts to others of food or drink.

o **Chanukkah**

Chanukkah is probably one of the best known Jewish holidays among Christians. Although technically another "minor holiday", it falls at roughly the same time as Christmas, and has "grown" to compete with the Christian celebration for the hearts and minds of children. This is a commemoration of the 165 BCE rededication of the Jerusalem Temple.

When the Temple was restored, there was only enough oil not desecrated by the Greeks to burn for one day; but, the oil lamps were supposed to burn continuously throughout day and night. As they worked to prepare a new supply of oil, the oil they had remarkably burned for eight days and nights. To commemorate this (and the rededication), *Chanukkah* is an eight day celebration. Ironically, the holiday celebrates a rejection of Jewish assimilation into secular Greek society and the repression of the Jewish faith. This is ironic because Chanukkah is the most secular holiday on the Jewish calendar, and many of the traditions associated with the holiday (*e.g.* decorations, music, gifts, *etc.*) resulted from assimilation into the surrounding Christian society.

o **Yom HaShoa**

This holiday was created by a 1953 decree by Israeli President Yitzhak Ben-Zvi and Prime Minister David Ben-Gurion. Yom HaShoa (English: *Holocaust Memorial Day*) remembers the nearly 6 million Jews exterminated by the Nazis from the late 1930s through 1945. Although it falls in April / May for Jewish communities, other governments and political entities (such as the UN) have also adopted the holiday, but celebrate it on other dates (*e.g.* UN - January 17; France - July 16; Netherlands - May 4).

- o **Yom Ha'atzmaut**

    Another modern holiday, this is Israeli Independence Day. Commemorating Israel's modern indendence (May 14, 1948), the celebration is based on the Jewish calendar and varies from year to year.

In addition to the holidays, there are also ceremonies and rituals that are of significance:

- o **Shiva** – after a death, first-degree relatives* are identified as mourners. They gather in a single house (usually that of the deceased), and "sit shiva" for seven days (*shiva* is Hebrew for "seven"). It is considered a very positive act to pay a respectful visit to the shiva house during this period. Greetings are not exchanged upon arrival, and any conversation should be started by a mourner, not the guest.

- o **Brit Milah** – eight days after birth, male babies are circumcised (the foreskin of the penis is removed) in a ceremony conducted by a *mohel* (pronounced moy'el), and known in Yiddish as a **Bris.**

- o **Bar Mitzvah / Bat Mitzvah** – a Jewish boy is considered responsible for his actions once he reaches the age of 13. This is recognized at a gathering where the boy presents a learned presentation on the Torah, and is blessed by the Rabbi (thus becoming a *bar mitzvah*, or "son of the covenant"). This officially welcomes him into the adult Jewish community, and makes him eligible to do whatever adult Jewish males may do (read from the scriptures, be part of a quorum of adults for a prayer service, *etc.*). In most Jewish divisions, girls celebrate a similar process known as a *bat mitzvah* ("daughter of the covenant"). Orthodox Judaism is the most resistant to this ceremony, but it is becoming more common even amongst traditional Orthodox communities.

---

* First-degree relatives comprise the deceased's father, mother, son, daughter, brother, sister, and spouse.

Practices

Jewish communities have a number of traditional practices that mark them as Jewish. Some of these are as follows:

- **Diet** – Jews follow a dietary regimen known as *kashrut* (foods that are acceptable under this system are known as *kosher*, or "fit"). These rules are part of those spelled out in Leviticus and Deuteronomy, and place a number of restrictions on what can and can not be eaten. For example, the following are forbidden:
    - carnivores;
    - mammals that neither chew their cud nor have cloven hooves (*e.g.* pigs, camels, hares);
    - birds of prey;
    - scavengers;
    - reptiles;
    - amphibians;
    - insects; and,
    - water animals that don't have both fins and scales.

  In addition, meat and dairy products may not be consumed at the same meal, and may not be prepared or stored using the same utensils.

- **Spelling** – Jews do not write out the name of God, the word God, or any euphemism for it. Instead, they will substitute a hyphen for one of the letters (*e.g.* G-d, L-rd, *etc.*). This originated because it was considered disrespectful to erase or discard a reference to God. If you can't erase it or throw it away, how do you dispose of it? You can't. To avoid this dilemma, they substitute *G-d* rather than write out *God*.

- **Fringes** – known in Hebrew as *Tsitsit*, these are fringes or tassels attached to the corners of a garment, and intended to remind the faithful of the mitzvot, or commandments. Jewish clothing with these tassels can not be sold or given to a non-Jew without first removing the tassels. It is based on the following scriptural injunction:

  > Speak to the people of Israel, and bid them that they make them fringes in the borders of their garments throughout their generations, and that they put upon the fringe of the borders a thread of blue; And it shall

> *be to you for a fringe, that you may look upon it, and remember all the commandments of the Lord, and do them.*   *– Numbers 15:38-39*

- o **Yarmulke** – also known as a **kippah**, a *yarmulke* is a hemispherical, brimless cap worn (predominantly by males) as a head covering. Jewish law, or *halakha*, requires that a Jewish man cover his head during prayer. Wearing it at other times became a widely accepted custom, and is explained by saying we are always in the presence of God.*

- o **Tefillin** – are small, black, leather boxes worn by observant Jews during weekday morning prayers. They contain small pieces of parchment inscribed with verses from the Torah, and are also known by the Greek term *phylacteries*. They are worn (attached by a strap) either on the upper arm or at the top of the forehead.

- o **Mezuzah** – Deuteronomy 6:9 instructs the Jews to inscribe the words of the *Shema* "on the doorposts of your house." This is accomplished by attaching a small, decorative box that contains a parchment inscribed with the *Shema Yisrael* (a Jewish prayer that begins with the words "Hear, O Israel, the Lord is our God, the Lord is One."). Orthodox tradition holds that the Shema should be recited aloud twice a day at times, and in locations, that are respectful and exhibit reverence.

- o **Naming** – Jewish parents usually name their children by the tradition of naming the first two boys born after their two grandfathers, and the first two girls born after their grandmothers. Among the Ashkenazic Jews (essentially of northern European heritage), that ancestor must have already passed on, and the naming also serves as a way of keeping their spirit alive in the family and community. Among the Sephardic Jews (essentially North African and Iberian heritage), the grandparents may be either alive or deceased when the naming occurs.

---

* Rabbi Hunah Ben Joshua stated that he always wore the covering because "the Divine Presence is always over my head."

Chapter 9
Modern Divergence

The days of our years are threescore years and ten; and if by reason of strength they be fourscore years, yet is their strength labour and sorrow; for it is soon cut off, and we fly away. ... So teach us to number our days, that we may apply our hearts unto wisdom. — *Bible, Psalm 90:10, 12*

Modern Divisions

Today, there are basically two ways in which modern Judaism is broken into divisions: either based on ritual practice (movements, or sects), or on national origin. In general, theology does not vary much from group to group — all believed to be modern descendents of the earlier Pharisees. The 2 major groupings based on regional origin are the *Ashkenazic* and the *Sephardic*.

Ashkenazic

Ashkenazic is from the Hebrew word for Germany, and this branch primarily includes Jews from Germany, Russia and the countries of Eastern Europe (most American Jews trace their ancestry to this group). The name is derived from the biblical *Ashkenaz*, a son of Gomer, grandson of Japheth, and great-grandson of Noah. According to Rabbinic literature, the kingdom of Ashkenaz was first described as being in Scythia (northeastern Iran today), and then later in Eastern Europe (in the Slavic regions); finally, starting about the 11th century, it was situated in Northern Europe and Germany. Mediæval European Jews associated with this heritage, and referred to themselves as *Ashkenazim* (literally, "Jews of Ashkenaz"). Since the main Jewish learning centers were located in Germany, the term was gradually adopted by Western, Central, and Eastern European Jews, as well.

Historically, there was strain between the Ashkenazic Jewish communities and the non–Jewish populations among whom they lived; and, this often resulted in the establishment of *ghettos*. The term *ghetto* was originally from Venetan (the pre-Italian language of Venice), and was probably a shortened form of *borghetto*, the

Venetan diminutive of *borgo* (meaning a borough, or city section); as such, it loosely translates into English as "neighborhood".

These Jewish ghettos spread to other cities all across Europe, and were often rigidly restricted. Typcially, there was a large wall that surrounded the ghetto, and the gates in these walls would be closed and locked (from the inside) at night and during times of communal stress in order to provide protection to the Jewish community. The Jews were seen as alien and anti-Christian, however; and, these same gates were frequently locked from the outside during major religious festivals (Christmas, Easter, and Passover). On several occasions, fires broke out during the night, and a refusal by the Christian community to have the gates unlocked for fire fighters (for fear that the Jews might "get out") resulted in large numbers of ghetto residents dying in the uncontrolled flames.

Yiddish became the *lingua franca* (common language) of the Ashkenazic Jews. This evolved from a blending of High German, German dialects, Hebrew, Aramaic, the Slavic languages (*e.g.* Polish, Russian, Czech), and even some Romance languages (*e.g.* Italian, French, Romanian), all written using the Hebrew alphabet. There are numerous words in fairly common use in English which are, in fact, Yiddish words. For example:

- Bagel
- Blintz
- Chutzpah
- Drek
- Farfel
- Glitzy
- Kibitz
- Kibosh
- Klutz
- Link
- Nit
- Nosh
- Nudnick
- Pastrami
- Schmaltz
- Schmooze
- Schmuck
- Tochus

There are well over a hundred more that routinely show up in English writings and conversations, although perhaps two of the more "famous" are *schlemiel* and *schlimazel*, which both occurred in the *Laverne and Shirley* sitcom theme song from 1976 to 1983. The song is a Yiddish-English hopscotch song. These two terms (describing the two stars of the show) are both Yiddish, and generally unknown to an American audience: *schlemiel* is a bungler, a dolt; and, *schlimazel* is an extremely unlucky or inept person. In this Milwaukee-based sitcom, that described the two female leads, who supposedly worked in a brewery (a principal business for immigrant Ashkenazic Jews in America).

Sephardic

Sephardic is from Hebrew for Spain; and, this branch of Judaism developed in the Moorish lands of Spain, Portugal, North Africa and the Middle East. Since this branch of Judaism is prevalent in Israel, it is the Sephardic pronunciation of Hebrew that is gradually being adopted today — even in Ashkenazic areas. The Sephardic Jews rarely had strain with their non–Jewish neighbors; there were no closed ghettos; they were relatively well integrated into the larger society; and, consequently, there are virtually no divisions within Sephardic Judaism.

Traditional foods, service melodies, holiday customs, and prayer services exhibit minor differences between the two groups; but, there are few substantial theological differences (between Ashkenazic and Sephardic) that separate them.

Other

There are also other Jewish groups; however, these are all quite small in number, and are rarely seen and little known in America. Aong these would be:

- Beta Israel (Ethiopia – *a.k.a.* Falashas);;
- Temani (Yemen);
- Kaifeng (Henan Province, China);
- Bene Israel (Pakistan & India);
- Conversos (Northern New Mexico);
- Lembo (Bantu-speaking from South Africa); and,
- Isro'il or Yahudi (Uzbekistan – *a.k.a.* Bukharan).

Ashkenazic Movements

The modern movements of Judaism are based essentially on differences in ritual practice, and occasional, minor differences in interpretation of *Halakha* (Judaic Law). And, they all exist within the Ashkenazic Jewish tradition.

Orthodox

The modern orthodox Jews believe in being integrated into modern society while still maintaining observance of the Jewish Law, or *halakha*. They believe that:

- o God gave Moses the *Torah* on Mount Sinai (comprising the written Pentateuch, the first five books of scripture, as well as an oral tradition which interprets and explains the written Pentateuch);
- o the Torah is true and has come to modern Jews intact and unchanged; and,
- o the Torah contains a total of 613 commandments which are binding on Jews, but not on non–Jews.

Chasidism

The followers of this movement are known in America as Hasidic Jews. Chasidism, or Hasidism, developed in the late 1700s in Ukraine and then spread across Eastern Europe and Western Russia. The founder is considered to have been Israel ben Eliezer Baal Shem Tov. It is a fairly ascetic sect in some ways, but very worldly in others. Chasidic Jews believe that emphasis should always be on the positive side of life; and, that the highest form of communion with God is through social relations, which must therefore be kept optimistic and joyful. Underlying Chasidic theology is a metaphysics which sees God as the only reality — filling all existence. What is humanly perceived as reality is seen as the "veil of the divine light". This monism comes very close to denying the very existence of the material world with respect to the divine. Followers of Chasidism are often considered an Orthodox subset.

Reform

Reformists do not accept that the Torah was written by God. They tend to accept modern critical views of Biblical authorship — *i.e.* written by different sources and humanly assembled. Although Reform Judaaism retains many of the values and ethical beliefs of Judaism as well as some of the practices and culture, they don't observe the commandments *per se* — since they do not automatically accept that God said "Thou shalt not …". This is the primary branch of what is usually called the *liberal wing* of Judaism.

Conservative

As can be imagined, there was a huge level of tension between the Reform and Orthodox groups. In Germany of the 1850s, there was a conservative reaction to the liberal theology of Reform Judaism. The term *Conservative Judaism* referred to their desire to "conserve" Jewish tradition, rather than "reform" it. This came to a head in America in 1883 when a Reform congregation hosted a dinner (the *Trefa Banquet*) in Mount Adams (a section of Cincinnati) to honor the first graduating class at Hebrew Union College. At the banquet, they served shrimp and other shellfish, considering the *kashrut* tradition to be anachronistic. This outraged some of the more traditional Reform rabbis at the dinner, and a schism developed that resulted in a formal organization of the more traditional members of the Reform Movement. Although Conservative Judaism typically believes that the *halakha* should change and adapt to time and circumstances, they also accept that it is binding on Jews. Since the movement was largely reactive, it tends to vary widely across congregations. Except for their more frequent use of Hebrew, some Conservative congregations are difficult to distinguish from Reformists, while others are nearly Orthodox in their practices (except for seating men and women together at services).

Reconstructionist

This group, an off–shoot of the Conservatives, believes that Judaism is an evolving religious civilization. They neither accept a personified God who has been active in history nor espouse the claim that the Hebrews are "God's chosen people". They follow Jewish Law not because it is theologically binding on them, but because they see it as a valuable cultural remnant.

Humanist

Humanisit Judaism is really a rejection of Judaism as religion. They view Judaism as the historical and cultural experience of the Hebrew people. In addition, they are non-theistic (*i.e.* typically agnostic or atheist). They encourage Jews to celebrate and embrace Jewish ritual, holidays, and life events (*e.g.* bar mitzvot, weddings, *etc.*), but with cultural services rather than as dictated "by God".

Most of the differences between the various Judaic divisions are differences of practice or ritual, and theological differences between the various divisions and movements of Judaism are minimal (with the obvious exception of Humanist Judaism). In fact, most Jews do not have any serious objection to praying or worshipping in the synagogues of other congregations. Nevertheless, liberal services are not usually religious enough for Orthodox adherents, and Orthodox services are often unintelligible to the liberal sects (mostly due to their heavy reliance on Hebrew).

Anti-Semitism

Anyone who learns anything about Jewish history quickly realizes that the Jewish faithful have been isolated, marginalized, persecuted, and victimized repeatedly throughout their history. And yet, many people to this day feel "justified" in what has occurred. It has to be asked how this could possibly be justified, and ensure that future generations don't fall into similar traps, either with Judaism or any other religious community.

Genetics & Social Darwinism

In the early 20th century, a new science was evolving; this science became known as *genetics*. Gregor Mendel, an Austrian botanist, had developed the mathematical foundation for genetics in the late 1800s; and, by the early 1900s, scientists were experimenting to determine in which fields this new science could be applied. Psychology was also just evolving (Freud published his first work in 1895), and a merger of genetics and psychology led to what became known as *Social Darwinism*. This was the idea that social and psychological factors were just as heritable (and mathematically predictable) as the color of one's eyes. Using what were assumed to be sound scientific methods at the time, research was done to determine the genetic basis for intelligence, inventiveness, laziness, criminality, morality, *etc.*

Eugenics

Realizing that if parents are carefully selected, a child could be predisposed to have blue eyes, blond hair, *etc.*, it seemed logical to these scientists that parents could also be selected to preclude the likelihood of undesirable social traits such as prostitution, criminality, laziness, stupidity, *etc.* This "selective breeding" to enhance the human species was known as *eugenics*. The leading American eugenicist was Charles Davenport, who wrote that it was "the science of the improvement of the human race by better breeding." To determine who was desirable, he needed to know who contributed to the gene pool in a positive manner, as well as who didn't.

In 1917, just prior to World War I, Dr. Robert Yerkes (a Harvard psychologist and colleague of Davenport) convinced the US Army to administer a general social profile assessment to nearly 2 million Army inductees. The results clearly showed that certain ethnic and/or religious groups were more prone: to commit crimes; to be unable to hold a steady job; to become social transients; or, to be stupid! As a result, Yerkes claimed he could identify entire ethnic and racial groups that were genetically predisposed to socially undesirable traits. Those tests, printed only in English, had been administered to many inductees who neither read nor wrote in English; and, they weren't allowed help that might "bias" results.

Yerkes came to the conclusion that the "darker peoples of southern Europe and the Slavs of eastern Europe are less intelligent than the fair peoples of western and northern Europe." Even further down, at the bottom of Yerkes' scale, were Gypsies, Jews and Africans. A peer of Yerkes was researcher Henry Goddard, who maintained that "immigrants from southern and eastern Europe, especially Jews, were racially so different from, and genetically so inferior to, the current American population that any racial mixture would be deleterious." It never occurred to them the reason for those test results might be that they hadn't been able to read them!

Legal Consequences

Consequences of these "scientific findings" appeared in many quarters; one of the most dangerous of these was US law. The US Federal Government, on May 19, 1921, seriously curtailed immigration from all of the areas the eugenicists had identified as producing inferior human stock. This was codified into 1924 US law as the *Immigration Restriction Act* (*a.k.a.* the *Johnson Act*). This law limited the number of "inferior peoples" allowed to immigrate into the US. Although revised numerous times since then, current immigration laws are still significantly based on the Johnson Act.

This limited "new" inferior peoples; but, what of the inferior element already legally in the United States? Eugenicists pushed for sterilization laws that would allow the states to sterilize anyone determined "socially disabled or stupid". By 1934, 25 states had sterilization laws on the books. These laws allowed states to sterilize mental patients, convicts, moral degenerates, epileptics, and anyone who scored too low on a Binet IQ test! You might expect a challenge to these laws in court; and, there was. The Virginia law was challenged all the way to the US Supreme Court; and, on an 8 to 1 vote (with the majority opinion written by legendary jurist Oliver Wendell Holmes), it was upheld!

Moral Consequences

As a consequence of the global acceptance of eugenics as scientifically valid, the Nazis* felt fully justified in their persecution and program of execution of Gypsies, Jews and the disabled; and, as a result of the immigration quotas in the US, thousands of fleeing Jews were turned away from the US during the 1930s. Jews who could read the handwriting on the wall, and were attempting to get out of Nazi Germany, were not allowed entry into the United States; ships were stopped at sea by the US Coast Guard and turned back. That is one reason why so many US Jews trace a part of their history through Argentina. That became a half-way point on the road to the US. Ironically, it was loose Argentinian immigration laws that also made it a haven for former Nazi officers after Germany's defeat in 1945. Knowing they were not welcome in the US forced many Jews to remain in Europe — to their detriment.

In Retrospect

In retrospect, there were numerous problems with this "scientific evidence". To start with, Yerkes' test (administered by the Army) was given in war time — to a largely uneducated, recently immigrated population. The northern Europeans who took the test were more likely to share cultural and linguistic backgrounds with their new American homeland; the southern Europeans, Jews and Africans were more likely to have come from significantly different cultural settings, and frequently unable to read or write English. But, that didn't excuse them from taking the test — without help.

---

* The *Nationalsozialistische Deutsche Arbeiterpartei* (NSDAP), or National Socialist German Worker's Party — the German political party founded by Anton Drexler and headed by Adolf Hitler.

It should have surprised nobody that they scored poorly on a test they couldn't read; but, that did not occur to them.

British eugenicists instituted the English *eleven plus* test that is still used to this day to determine who gets to continue on to University; German eugenicists became key members of Hitler's ruling cadre. As the world learned what Hitler was doing, the American eugenics movement fell into disfavor, and leading American eugenicists had to find other work. One of Yerkes' chief lieutenants was a Princeton psychologist, Dr. Carl Brigham, who chaired the College Entrance Examination Board from 1923 to 1926 — developing the SAT (Scholastic Aptitude Test).

The Holocaust

The holocaust was justified by German eugenicists as a means to rid Germany of what they perceived as an alien, lower class, inferior specie. They initially applied this approach to physically disabled Europeans; then, to the semi-nomadic European Gypsies; and finally, they turned it on the nearly 11 million European Jews. Before the German defeat put an end to the ethnic cleansing of Europe, the Nazi eugenics program had executed 50,000 Gypsies, 5,000 physically or mentally disabled children, and approximately 6,000,000 Jews.

What can be learned from the Holocaust is two-fold:

- o first, the remarkable ability of the Jewish people to endure the trials to which they were subjected as a result of bigotry, fear and misunderstanding; and

- o second, that even so-called scientific evidence can not legitimately, in retrospect, justify inhuman, immoral, and unethical behavior. That is every bit as true today as it was 50 to 100 years ago.

Summary

The commonality between Zoroastrianism and the Pharasaic form of Judaism is notable, although theologians are often reluctant to suggest a reason. It was clear, however, that there was a great deal of contact between the two religions both during and after the Hebrew captivity in Babylon. It is reported in the Bible how Nehemiah served two terms as governor of Judah for Artaxerxes (the Babylonian king), and how Ezra was dispatched from Babylon to "bring the law" to the Jews. It was also Ezra who convinced the Jews of the 5th century BCE to divorce their foreign wives, pledge to only marry within the faith, honor the sabbath, and to implement numerous other revisions that were all practices espoused and already faithfully put into practice by the followers of Zoroaster. It was also at this time that Heaven, Hell, Final Judgment, a Savior, life after death, fate, and a final divine resurrection of humanity (all Zoroastrian beliefs) became part of Judaism. Interestingly, it is also at this time that the earliest references to the group that became known as the Pharisees are found. None of this, however, should detract from the Jewish religion. No major world religion was established or grew in a vacuum; they all came about in the presence of some *background religion* — a common historical religion of the people among whom they lived. It was inevitable that a new religion — whatever it was — would be highly influenced by this background religion. In the case of Judaism, the predominant background religion was Zoroastrianism. This process will be seen repeatedly as other major religions are reviewed in the sections to follow.

In 70 CE, the Hebrew revolt against Roman rule climaxed in the Roman capture and destruction of Jerusalem by the Roman Emperor Titus, and the scattering of the Jews of Palestine. The rabbinical movement within Judaism was largely influenced by the views of the earlier Pharisees, and this is the movement that has comprised Judaic leadership from then to the present. In fact, "During the rabbinic era, the dualistic view of human nature [*i.e.* Zoroastrian] replaced biblical monism as an expression of the strong spiritual bias of the rabbinic sages"*. Virtually all of the major Jewish Movements today have branched off of this tree; and, although they may not be a totally cohesive religious structure, they are not nearly as divisive as the many organizational labels (*i.e.* Orthodox, Reform, Conservative, *etc.*) might indicate.

---

* Ariel, David S (1995) What Do Jews Believe? New York: Schocken Books

Section III
Christianity

Christianity started out in Palestine as a fellowship;
it moved to Greece and became a philosophy;
it moved to Italy and became an institution;
it moved to Europe and became a culture;
it came to America and became an enterprise.
— Rev. Sam Pascoe

In terms of the number of adherents, Christianity is the largest religious grouping in the world. It has to be called that (*i.e.* a religious grouping) rather than a religion, as the internal theological diversity in Christianity is as great (or greater) than it is within virtually any other faith except Hinduism. The epigrapha above is from an Episcopal priest, the Reverend Sam Pascoe, and is actually reasonably accurate. Christianity, as will be seen in the following 4 chapters, consists of followers of an individual 2,000 years ago known as 'Jesus of Nazareth' (commonly known as the *Christ*). This Christ was born and raised Jewish, and the earliest groups of followers essentially comprised a fellowship within the Jewish religion. They can be seen, not as a reform or rejection of Judaism, but an attempt to identify Christ as the Messiah that traditional Judaism was (and still is) awaiting.

Within a generation, the leading evangelists had spread his message beyond the region of the Middle East, and it took its place alongside the philosophies of Socrates, Plato, and Aristotle in Greece. When followers were organized in Rome, the capital of the Roman Empire, the growing faith was effectively institutionalized as a "church". From there, riding on Roman power and authority, the faith thoroughly permeated the cultures of Europe (effectively forming the underlying culture of the entire continent).

Finally, Christianity came to the Americas. Reverend Pascoe sees its domination of modern America as a pseudo-enterprise, with Christianity becoming a major economic and electoral force in the United States. Although this is certainly a somewhat critical perspective, there can be little doubt that Christian ownership of businesses, electoral clout in local, regional and national politics, and active participation in the electoral process has had a profound effect upon the United States.

Chapter 10
Christian Foundations

Jesus said to them, "Truly, truly, I say to you, before Abraham was, I am. — John 8:58

But you, O Bethlehem Ephrathah, who are little to be among the clans of Judah, from you shall come forth for me one who is to be ruler in Israel, whose origin is from of old, from ancient days. — Micah 5:2

Environment

At the start of the Common Era*, the Middle East was a thriving cosmopolitan area with numerous peoples and cultures. At the eastern end of the Roman Empire, there were numerous Roman residents and significant financial ties to Rome. However, it was also at the heart of *Hellenization* (*i.e.* Greek being the preferred language of the educated, there were also many ties to Greece). Egypt had been a neighboring powerhouse; so had Babylon. The Roman presence in the area was only about 60 years old, and tales of Parthian, Syrian and Macedonian domination were well known. The Parthians, in fact, had controlled the area within the lifetime of many of the residents. So, the area that now comprises Israel and Lebanon had effectively come to serve the role of a cosmopolitan "buffer zone" between several wealthy, influential world powers.

Most of the major world religions at the time were also represented — at least to some degree. Only the teachings of Lao–tse (Taoism), Kung Fu–tse (Confucius) and Mahavira (Jainism) were apparently not represented. The rest, however, mixed in a vibrant, competetive environment for the hearts and minds of the people.

The idea that this was strictly a Jewish area is greatly overstated. Although Judaism was the predominant religion, there are two qualifiers: first, it was not the exclusive religion of the area;

---

* Dates are given as CE (Common Era) and BCE (Before Common Era). This system was devised to avoid the religious connections associated with using AD (*Anno Domini* – Christian), AM (*Anno Mundi* – Jewish), or AH (*Anno Hegira* – Muslim).

and second, there were several different varieties of Judaism. At times, it even appears that there might have been more animosity and competitiveness amongst Jews than there was between Jews and non–Jews.

At this time, there were three primary Jewish groups, sects or *philosophical schools*: the Pharisees, the Sadducees, and the Essenes. In addition, there were numerous smaller movements. For example: there was an anti-taxation group under the leadership of a man known as *Judas the Galilean*; and, there were the followers of *Theudas*, *Honi the Circlemaker*, *Haninah ben Dosa*, and numerous small bands of people who followed self-styled kings, prophets, and messiahs — the aggregate sometimes referred to collectively as *charismatic Judaism*. There were also the *Diaspora Jews* and the Samaritans. This all begs the question: why so much variety? One explanation often offered is that "the many popular movements in this period resulted from social unrest, a failure of the ruling class, and Roman maladministration."*

Charismatic Judaism

Theudas was a charismatic leader described by the historian Flavius Josephus. Theudas evidently persuaded a large number of people to pack up all of their belongings and follow him — to the River Jordan. He purported to be a prophet of God, and claimed to be prepared to repeat Moses' miracle of parting the waters by making the River Jordan part for his followers. The only parting that occurred, however, was when Fadus (the governor of Judæa) had Theudas intercepted, and parted his head from his body.

Hezekiah led a band of followers operating along the frontier with Syria. Before becoming king, Herod was a military general under his father in the region known as Galilee. Herod took it upon himself in 55 BCE to hunt down and kill the leader of this group. Hezekiah, however, had a son named Judas [see the next entry].

---

* Freedman, David Noel [sr. ed.] (1992) The Anchor Bible Dictionary [6 volumes] New York: Doubleday

Judas the Galilean (Hezekiah's son and, consequently, someone who hated Herod and his family) was from a village in what is now known as the Golan Heights. He was a leader in the anti-tax movement that arose to protest an attempt by the Romans to conduct a census to determine the maximal tax that could safely be extracted from Judæa. His group, commonly known to Biblical scholars today as the *Fourth Philosophy*, was a revolutionary movement that openly resisted the inept leadership of the local Roman governors. Philosophically, they appear to have been aligned with the Essenes — diverging only in their revolutionary zeal for freedom and independence from the Roman yoke. Whereas most seemed to think Roman rule would be a long burden, and chose to wait it out, the followers of Judas the Galilean chose to actively resist. The most extreme of the group were known as *Sicarii* (meaning "hidden daggers") — a terrorist arm of the anti-tax group. The tax census in question finally occurred in 6 CE, and Judas was crucified that same year by Antipater, the son of Herod (maintaining a family tradition: father killed father; son killed son). Although the taxation took place and Judas was killed, the Sicarii (as a branch of the Zealots) kept fighting for Jewish independence.

Honi the Circlemaker was another personality with a following. He was a highly righteous Jew widely known to history as the Circle-maker or Circle-drawer. This started when a drought so parched the land that he drew a circle on the ground in Jerusalem and vowed not to leave it until God made it rain (it did).

Honi was stoned to death by Jews outside the walls of Jerusalem as a witch, and great winds destroyed much of the local crop soon thereafter; these were believed by many to be punishment from God for having killed Honi. It was said at the time that Honi performed miraculous healings through prayer, and that he was the "son of God".

Haninah ben Dosa was a rabbi who was widely revered as a sage and teacher. A highly righteous man, he steadfastly denied being a prophet, and most likely lived an ascetic life. He was a renowned miracle worker, and widely recognized for healing.

He had a loyal following, and was regarded by many as having been 'chosen by God'.

Diaspora

Diaspora is a dispersion of a previously homogeneous people. In the case of the Jews, this usually refers to either those scattered following the Babylonian captivity or those living outside of what was then Palestine (modern day Israel). There were large Jewish populations as far away as Rome to the west, and India to the east, with the largest centers in Rome, Alexandria, Asia Minor, and Cochin (southwest India). In fact, Judaism often accounted for as much as 10 percent of the total population in some cities (25% in Alexandria). It was conceivably evolving into a successor to the Roman state religion of the time. There were obstacles to this, however: the tribalism and exclusivity tendencies of Judæan Jews; and, their endogamy (*i.e.* only marrying within the faith). The spread of *Judaism* was hampered by both.

Samaritans

It might be concluded from reading the New Testament (with Jesus' parable of the *Good Samaritan*) that Samaritans were foreigners with beliefs antagonistic to Judaism. In fact, the Samaritans were Jews. The biggest difference between them and the prevailing Judaism was identification of the location of certain sites. Whereas the predominant Jewish group recognized Jerusalem as the center of Judaism, the Samaritans believed it was on the high ground between Palestine's two largest mountains (about 40 miles north of Jerusalem); and, this alone was enough to cause serious friction between the Palestinian Jews and the Samaritans. Historically, the Samaritans had some claims to being correct, since this had been the center of Judaic worship prior to the Temple cult in Jerusalem gaining precedence. The temple in this area had been built during the reign of Alexander the Great, but was destroyed about 100 BCE There were also Samaritan Jewish communities as far away as Rome — a sort of Samaritan Diaspora.

Others

- o   Large numbers of Zoroastrians lived throughout the area;
- o   Roman soldiers adopted Mithraism (a Zoroastrian branch);

- o Ancient coins and tablets from the Indus River civilization have shown there was an active Hindu presence; and,
- o the Indian king Ashoka had established a thriving Theravada Buddhist mission at Alexandria, with similar centers in Greece, Turkey and Syria.

In summary, the social, political, linguistic and economic environment in Israel at the beginning of the Common Era was a rich mosaic. The people were trying to bring control to their lives, and there was a wide variety of paths from which they could choose.

Jesus

Birth

Into this diverse environment, a child was born. Tradition claims that he was born on December 25, 1 CE. Tradition is almost certainly wrong. The accounts of his birth in the Christian Bible would place his birth more likely in the late Summer or early Fall; and, the team led by Christoph Clavius (a Jesuit astronomer & mathematician working for Pope Gregory) made miscalculations in developing the Gregorian calendar that result in a more likely birth date 3 to 6 years earlier. Several hundred years ago, Johannes Keppler decided from historical and astronomical events that the calendar was off by exactly 4 years, and that Jesus was therefore born on December 25, 4 BCE. This quickly became the accepted view for nearly all Christians. But, this was challenged in a 1978 book by Dr. Ernest L. Martin, a theologian who also held astronomical and meteorological degrees.

Dr. Martin's assessment can be summarized as follows::
- o Flavius Josephus wrote that King Herod died shortly after a lunar eclipse.
- o Suitable eclipses which fell at the right time were:
  5 BCE (March 23 & September 15);
  4 BCE (March 13); and,
  1 BCE (January 10).
- o Josephus also lists what transpired in Herod's final days between the eclipse and Passover (according to the Gospel account). Experts estimate this to have been about 12 weeks of activity.

- A physically ill Herod, resting in Jericho (which Josephus reports), could not have done all those things in the few days between the eclipse and Passover if the eclipse was only days prior to Passover. This is the case for March 23, 5 BCE and March 13, 4 BCE; so, Dr. Martin eliminated them.
- September 15, 5 BCE eclipse is discounted because there is no reason a seriously ill Herod would have been in Jericho on that date (often over 130°F in September – a virtual furnace at 800 feet below sea level). It would also have left 4 months for which Josephus did not account.
- So, the only eclipse that meets the requirements well is January 10, 1 BCE; but, Jesus must have been born less than two years prior to that, since Herod ordered that all male children under the age of 2 be executed.
- Since there is no record at that time of a tax census being done; and, since Quirinius would not become the Roman governor for several more years, some historians question Biblical accuracy. But, Dr. Martin points out that Luke does not use the term *governor* when referring to Quirinius, but *governing*. This is important for the following reason: Augustus Cæsar was to receive the prestigious title of *Pater Patriæ* on February 5, 2 BCE, and all of the Roman officials were expected to be in Rome for the festivities.
- As a Roman safety measure, sailing the Mediterranean was halted each year about November 1, and did not resume until the following Spring. To be in Rome the first week of February, Varus (the governor) would have had to leave the previous Fall. He couldn't be gone 6 or 7 months without leaving anyone in charge, so he would need someone to govern for him in his absence; and, the ranking Roman official nearby at that time was Quirinius, who had just finished a military campaign against the Homonadenses.
- So, beginning around the start of September 3 BCE, Quirinius would have been *governing* the region —as the 'acting governor' in Varus' absence.

Ch 10 – Christian Foundations

- o As for the census, Roman records show that, although there was no tax census at that time, a census was taken in 3 BCE in which all subjects were required to return to their origins to register for an oath of allegiance to Augustus. This was documented by historians Orosius and Moses of Khorene, and was also recorded on tablets from Paphlagonia, Turkey.
- o Jesus was therefore born in the Fall of 3 BCE during this registration. Traditional historians, having Herod die in 4 BCE, rejected Martin's claims; however, Martin provided answers for each of their objections (too lengthy for here).

But, what of the shepherds, wise men, and the Star of Bethlehem? Martin explains:

- o There was a spectacular astrononomical event on the evening of June 17, 2 BCE. Venus appeared to collide with Jupiter, appearing as a single star (not 2) in the western sky (over Palestine for people from 'the east'). This conjunction had not occurred for hundreds of years, nor again for several hundred more. To Zoroastrian astrologers in Parthia (known as *magi*), Jupiter was the father star and Venus the mother star. Their "union" was therefore an obvious portent of things to come.
- o Then, on September 3rd, Jupiter went into conjunction with Regulus, the king star of the constellation Leo (which represented Palestine in Parthian astrology). In Hebrew, Jupiter was *sedeq* (*i.e.* "righteous").
- o On September 11 came the new moon (Jewish New Year, *Rosh Hashana*). By this time, Jupiter entered *Virgo* (the virgin). Dr. Martin claimed the magi would have astrologically identified September 11, 3 BCE as the birth date of Jesus (actually, in the early evening, about 7 PM)

These astrological events would have been of great importance to Zoroastrian priests (professional astrologers by training and profession). There were, however, a few loose ends to tie up.

- o Shepherds in Israel are out in the fields with their flocks at night only in the Spring and early Fall. It is too cold for them to remain out at night in December.

- o The planetary paths of Earth and Jupiter are such that it appears that Jupiter stops in its track across the sky, reverses direction, stops again, and then goes on. This is known in astronomy as a *retrograde loop*. Jupiter stopped for the second time on December 25, 2 BCE. At that time, Jesus would have been just a little more than 15 months old; and, Herod ordered all children under 2 killed.
- o Dr. Martin proposed December 25, 2 BCE as the visit of the Magi to the toddler, and points out that this was Chanukkah that year — and, the Magi brought gifts.

Is Martin correct? It is impossible to be certain; but, within 20 years of publication, more than 600 planetariums altered Christmas programs to reflect Martin's research.

Regardless of the actual date, however (December 25th or September 11th), it is the story of this child that underpins Christian beliefs and theology. *Yeshua bin Yosef*, the child in question, is more often known to Christians by the Latin form of his name: as *Jesus of Nazareth* or *Jesus the Christ*.

The Birth Story   An angel appeared to a young girl named Mary in the village of Nazareth, and told her that she would give birth to a son, and that she should call him Jesus. Mary objected on the grounds that she was a virgin, and was engaged to be married to Joseph. Mary and Joseph came to accept the message, however, and made plans for the baby. As a result of a census (registration), both Mary and Joseph were required to travel to Bethlehem (90 miles south) about the time Mary was due. When they arrived in Bethlehem, there was no place for them to stay, so they made arrangements to stay in the stable of a local inn. That evening, in the stable, Jesus was born. Shepherds from the surrounding fields were told by angels to go and witness the birth. The birth had also been heralded by the appearance of a star in the sky which had been seen and interpreted by the *magi* (Parthian priests).

It may come as a surprise to most Christians, but the claim of a virgin birth are neither exclusive nor original to Christianity. Examples of divine or virgin conceptions include:
- o *Perseus* (Greek) – after Zeus sent a rain of gold over Diana;
- o *Hercules* – the son of a mortal woman and Zeus;

- *Plato* – the son of a mortal mother, Perictione, and Apollo;
- *Alexander the Great* – conceived by Olympius when she was impregnated by a clap of thunder the night before she was to consummate her marriage to Philip;
- *Jupiter* – impregnated numerous mortal women;
- *Siddhartha Gautama* (*Buddha*) – a divine birth to a mortal woman;
- God told the shepherd Pamyles to declare to all that a great king was born – the Egyptian *Osiris*, born to a virgin, and then raised by Pamyles until he "became a god";
- *Krishna* (Hindu) was a miraculous, divine birth; and,
- Zoroastrianism maintained that the birth of the *Saoshyant* (savior) would be of the seed of Zoroaster, but by a virgin.

Some of these are mythological; others are historical. Many Christians accept the virgin birth of Jesus, but denounce these other births as superstition. What have Christian theologians had to say about this apparent double standard?

- We Christians are not the only persons who have recourse to miraculous narratives of this kind. — *Origen (2nd century)*
- How does the historian respond to that story? Are there any who take it literally? ... That divergence raises an ethical problem for me. Either all such divine conceptions, from Alexander to Augustus and from the Christ to the Buddha, should be accepted literally and miraculously, or all of them should be accepted metaphorically and theologically. It is not morally acceptable to say ... our story is truth, but yours is myth; ours is history, but yours is a lie. It is even less morally acceptable to say that indirectly and covertly by manufacturing defensive or protective strategies that apply only to one's own story.
  — *John Dominic Crosssan*

Crossan, author of that last quote, is often recognized as one of the leading historical Jesus scholars in the world today. Professor Emeritus of Religious Studies at DePaul University, he has written more than 20 books on the historical Jesus and early Christianity. He holds a DD (Doctor of Divinity) from Maynooth College in Ireland (a Jesuit college), was ordained a Roman Catholic priest, and is the leading Roman Catholic historical theologian today.

There are few stories of Jesus up to the age of twelve, and then nothing is recorded until he appears at about the age of thirty. At that age he appears to his 2nd cousin, a holy man baptizing people into a life of God's approving. This cousin, known today as John the Baptist, baptized Jesus in the Jordan River, and marked the start of Jesus' ministry. Mandæans, and many scholars, accept that John was an Essene; it is much more debatable and controversial to believe that Jesus was (although there are some who do).

For one to three years*, Jesus wandered the immediate area teaching and performing miracles – both of which astounded his followers. He gathered a large group of followers to his message, as well as a small, inner group of twelve who were closest to him personally. His teachings so stirred up the religious and political powers that they conspired to have him silenced. Through a combination of religious and Roman judicial law, he was sentenced to be crucified: that is, to be nailed to a cross until dead. He was executed by this means on a Friday, and the body was placed in a cave used as a tomb. On the following Sunday, the "third day", he arose from the dead in a physical resurrection, and appeared to his closest followers. He lived with them for forty days, teaching and leading them in what they needed to know to carry his message to the world, after which he ascended to heaven. He is thus considered to be one person or aspect of God, who is viewed as a triune godhead: God the Father (an omnipotent creator god), God the Son (as seen in the deity of Jesus), and God the Holy Spirit, or Holy Ghost (God's immanent and active presence).

Following his ascension to heaven, his followers began to teach and practice what he had taught them, and Christianity was born. It was not, however, a uniform, smooth transition. There were periodic differences of opinion that led to syncretism, division, and even conflict. Historically, there were: (a) a few centuries of winnowing and consolidation; (b) two distinct divisive reform movements; and, (c) a more recent burst of 'second-generation' Christian movements (spawned by and within traditional Christianity, but often theologically divergent on one or more central tenets). These occurred primarily during: (a) the 1st to 4th centuries CE; (b) the 11th and 16th centuries; and, (c) the 19th century.

---

* The *Gospel of John* explicitly describes his ministry as just shy of 3 years; the synoptic gospels (Matthew, Mark and Luke) imply the shorter 1 year.

Chapter 11
Historical Development

A man ran up and knelt before him, and asked him, "Good Teacher, what must I do to inherit eternal life?" And Jesus said to him, "Why do you call me good? No one is good but God alone. — Mark 10:17-18

Growth (Early Years)

Apostolic Christianity

The original companions of Jesus are referred to as *apostles*, and early groupings of their followers are thus often referred to as apostolic Christians. Biblical scholars, however, often refer to these earliest followers today as the *Jesus movements*.

During the life, and for a number of years after the death, of Jesus, there actually was a broad diversity within the various Jesus movements. Although ignored for centuries by Christian historians, these *Jesus movements* were, in fact, the very earliest forms of Christianity. Today, it is generally considered reliable that James, biblically described as "the brother of Jesus", was the leader of the Jerusalem–based Jesus sect. This group considered Jesus to be a great prophet and leader; but, they did not consider him to be God incarnate — at least, there is no evidence that they considered him anything other than human. These were charismatic Jews who had accepted the teachings of Jesus, and were attempting to follow his example after the crucifixion.

Pauline Christianity

Early in the years after the crucifixion of Jesus, the view of just what Jesus was began to be reviewed. A leader in this process was *Saul of Tarsus*. Following a dramatic religious experience and subsequent conversion from persecutor to follower, Saul took the name of Paul. However, whether it was Paul personally, or simply that Paul was representative of a theological shift at that time, the nature of the Jesus Movements changed dramatically during his lifetime. The letters and instructions of Paul are heavily imbued with references to the *Christ*. There were numerous messiahs (leaders) active in the area at the time of Jesus. The concept of *the* Messiah (as opposed to *a* messiah) was something that was much more prevalent in some sects of Zoroastrianism than in the Charismatic Judaism of the time. The Latin term *christos* meant anointed, and Jesus was viewed by Paul as having been anointed by God to be *the* Savior of humanity. This resulted in the term *Jesus the Christ* (*i.e.* "Jesus, the anointed") being used repeatedly by Paul. This concept was more salable to the Romans (many of whom had already adopted the faith of Mithraism, with its strong messianic message); and, this conversion of Jesus from the itinerant teaching sage of the Jesus Movement of James to the risen Christ and Savior of humankind has been described as the *Romanization* of the Jesus Movement. This is also often called *Pauline Christianity* (to distinguish it from *Apostolic Christianity*).

Syncretism is "the attempt or tendency to combine or reconcile differing beliefs in philosophy or religion." Syncretic reactions often occur when different theological traditions come into close and frequent contact with one another. True syncretic behavior occurs when, as a result of this contact, one (or both) restructures itself to incorporate parts of the other. Sometimes these changes are exact (such as adopting a specific ritual or deity); however, partial modifications are more common.

In practice, syncretism is a fairly common occurrence. It may be the growth of a tradition into a fuller expression; the creation of a new, amalgamated tradition; or, the confusion of an established tradition through the addition of incongruent rituals and practices. What happened to the Jesus Movement when it encountered Mithraism in Rome?

> Many years ago in the Middle East, God visited a young girl — a virgin — and she experienced what is best described as *immaculate conception*. Nine months later, as foretold by the Magi, the 'Son of God' was delivered on that date which, on the Gregorian calendar, would be December 25th. The birth took place in a humble grotto, attended by shepherds from the fields. This young girl was later accorded the title 'Mother of God'.
>
> Upon adulthood, this 'Son of God' began to teach his followers — teaching the basics to all who would listen, but teaching the innermost secrets only to an inner circle of his closest dis-

ciples. His followers referred to Him as "the Light of the World", and viewed Him as the Mediator for humanity between heaven and earth. As such, He is viewed as one part of the Holy Trinity. He remained celibate throughout his life, and taught renunciation and resistance to sensuality among his followers. Following death, this leader demonstrated his Divine Sonship through the greatest of all possible miracles: resurrection from the dead. In fact, He was placed in a cave by having a boulder rolled into the entrance, and emerged only after having been 'born anew'.

His followers held beliefs in a celestial heaven and an infernal hell. They accepted, however, that God would sympathize with their suffering and grant eternal salvation in the world to come. They looked forward to a final Day of Judgment on which the dead would be resurrected and all who had believed on the Saviour would be redeemed. They also foresaw a final conflict between good and evil which would end the existing worldly order and bring about the final triumph of light over darkness.

Following His ascension, a more formal religion grew up around his teachings. Despite an injunction to 'call no man Father but God', the priests of this new religion came to be called Father, and the head of the priesthood took the title of The Holy Father. An intermediate level of priesthood, known as bishops, adopted the miter as a sign of their office; the Holy Father adopted a red cap and garment, an official ring, and carried a shepherd's staff. Priests of the new religion adopted robes that featured a cross, and initiated the *mass* as their religious service.

Purification in this new religion came through baptism, and Sundays were set aside as sacred. After His earthly mission was completed, He held a Last Supper with his followers where bread and water were eaten as symbolic of His body and blood. Later, followers of the new religion regularly celebrated this Last Supper, using symbolic bread and wine.

Familiar? This is the story of Mithra, and is a compilation from academic web sources on the practice of the Mithraic faith in early pre-Christian Rome[*]. This faith was especially popular with

---

[*] This is a composite account derived from material found at:
The Cult of Mithra (1996) at http://marlowe.wimsey/gnosis/mithra.html
Mithraic Mysteries (1996) at http://www.bioch.ox.ac/mithra/intro.html
Mithraism (1996) at http://www.lglobal.com/~hermes3/mithras/html

the Roman military, and a leading center of Mithraism at the time of Jesus was the Roman legionnaires' camp at Tarsus — the home of Saul.

Coincidence? Perhaps. But, consider other, later examples:

Easter

Although buried in antiquity (and therefore not known by the typical layman), the name of Easter was taken from *Œstre* (also spelled *Eostre*), the Germanic goddess of fertility that ruled over springtime festivities. Baby chicks, eggs, and the bunny are all pagan symbols of fertility brought along with Œstre. The *hot cross bun* eaten at Easter time is also taken from pagan ritual. The ancients would sacrifice an ox (Anglo-Saxon: *boun*) when planting new crops in the Spring in honor of the fertility goddess. After the ritual, they would eat small cakes decorated with a topping that resembled the horns of the ox they had just sacrificed. Early Christians did not want to participate, but feared being blamed for a bad harvest (by not taking part, and alienating the gods). Not wanting to support the pagan practice, they took the ox-horn pattern as a stylized cross, and ate their *hot cross bun* while their neighbours were devouring their identical *cécel eac boun*.

Easter comes at the close of Lent, a period of 40 days of fasting and solemnity that starts on Ash Wednesday. The day before Ash Wednesday is known to many as *Mardi Gras* (French: "Fat Tuesday"). This is a feast day held prior to the fast, and is also of pagan origin. The early Romans always partied the last day prior to a religious fast and, in France, a fatted ox was paraded through the streets of Paris. Another name for this day is *Carnival*, which is derived from the Latin *carnevalēm*, which meant "to remove meat" (from the diet) — marking the start of the fast.

Christmas

The date of *December 25* was selected to coincide with the Saturnalia, and to be coincidental with the Mithraic birth mass. It brought unwanted attention if Christians didn't celebrate; and, choosing this date precluded Romans from knowing what Christians were really celebrating (thus keeping them from being killed for it). The *Christmas tree* was an Ásatrú (*i.e.* Viking) pagan tradition in Germany and Scandinavia that was adopted by Christianity when Saint Boniface converted them to Christianity. The *Star tree topper* is Zoroastrian (a new star foretells a great happening). *Presents*, or gifts, are taken from the Mithraic Feast of the *Sol Invictus* (literally, "the invincible sun").

The traditional *Yule log* is an Ásatrú tradition in honor of Thor, an ancient Norse god. In fact, the word Yule is an anglicized version of *Juul*, an Old Norse word for a large, oak log; therefore, a *Yule log* is – literally – a "log log". The Russians honored their patron saint (an attendee at the Council of Nicæa) with a feast day and gift giving. This spread to areas of early Russian influence, such as Belgium and The Netherlands. Dutch settlers to the US brought this feast day (December 6th) and their *Santa Niklaus* with them. Gradually, Americans and other Europeans merged the gifts and feast on December 6th with the similar feast and gifts on December 25th, and made the Russian saint a part of the Christmas tradition. In the process, his name was anglicized from *Santa Niklaus* to *Santa N'Klaus* and eventually to *Santa Claus*.

All Saints Day

The first of November is celebrated in many Christian denominations as *All Saints' Day*. This is, according to Roman Catholic history, a day set aside to honor all departed Christian saints. Originally celebrated on May 13th, it was moved to November 1st when Pope Gregory III dedicated a chapel in Saint Peter's basilica to "all saints" on that date in 740 CE; it was moved permanently to that date by Gregory IV in 837. Celebration of this day, though, was something that was widespread well beyond Christianity. The Aztecs of ancient México, the peoples of China, and many of the peoples of Africa have similar holidays that predate All Saints Day. Mexicans still celebrate *Dia de los muertas* on November 1st and 2nd each year (the "Day of the Dead" is of Aztec origin, and predates introduction of Christianity to México). Halloween was not created to undermine Christianity; All Saints Day was moved for a chapel dedication and, in part, to undermine pagan festivities.

Whether any of this really detracts from Christianity depends on the viewpoint of the adherent. Those who believe Christ was *God Incarnate*, and Mary to have been the virgin *Mother of God* may have real problems with Mithraism. Those who believe the teachings and demonstrations of Jesus are what matter probably have little or no problem with Mithra. They typically see the syncretic effects on Christianity to be the result of a power struggle for the hearts and minds of the people of Rome and the Middle East. These do not detract from what Jesus taught his disciples nor from the demonstration of those teachings to 'those who had ears to hear'

Eventually, the Christian religion spread from the Middle East to Rome; and, once the Roman Emperor was converted to the new religion, it became the official state religion of the Roman Empire. As a result of Roman military power, the Pauline version of Christianity was spread throughout the Empire – through what is now Germany and northern Europe and even into Celtic England.

Establishing Orthodoxy

Orthodoxy

The *orthodox church* is what grew from Pauline Christianity. Celsus was a great pagan thinker of the late 2nd century, and sarcastically described Christianity as the "great church". This great church, which initially began as democratic and open branches of the Jesus Movement, evolved into a rigid, orthodox, hierarchical structure based on a three–tiered leadership: bishops, priests and deacons. These layers were later supplemented with the addition of sub–deacons, exorcists and acolytes. Conflicting teachings and gospels came out of the gnostic tradition at an alarming rate, and there were numerous leaders claiming divine inspiration or revelation. As a result, many of the church leaders saw the need to regulate this to ensure that Christianity did not devolve into countless warring factions. There may have been theological issues at stake; but, in retrospect, it would appear that self preservation may have been the greatest factor in organizing the structural hierarchy that ultimately became the orthodox church.

The development of the orthodox church followed in close step with developments in the political leadership of the Empire; but, there were several areas which had to be resolved before a truly orthodox position could be defined.

The Trinity

Flavius Valerius Constantius [285–337 CE] gradually gained control of the entire Roman Empire after his father's death in 306 CE. Known as Constantine the Great, he was ruler when the so-called *Arian heresy* surfaced. Basically, Arius (a Libyan lay theologian) espoused the belief that Christ was *created* by God; Athanasius (later Bishop of Alexandria) disagreed, and maintained that God and Christ were coeval and co-eternal. People in those days fought wars over issues such as this, and Constantine began to be concerned that his Empire would be torn apart by internal warfare if this disagreement were not resolved. He pressured the church to resolve its internal disagreements before it affected his Empire; but, the leading bishops of the church were themselves divided and were unable to effect a peaceful solution.

Finally, Constantine took matters into his own hands and called an ecclesiastical council at Nicæa in 325 CE to resolve it. Travel was not easy 1700 years ago, so only 318 Christian bishops (less than a fifth of the total) attended. All but a handful of the attendees were from the Eastern portion of Constantine's Empire (those who were the closest); and these were more easily manipulated by the Emperor. Constantine dictated doctrinal positions to the bishops; murdered a son, a nephew, and one of his wives; retained his status as *High Priest* of the local pagan religion until his death; and, was not baptized until he was on his deathbed. Nevertheless, he is known to history as the *Christian Emperor*.

Constantine forced the attending bishops' to support Athanasius. A denial of this ignores the facts: nearly two–thirds of the pro–Arius bishops left the council before the voting for their own safety; Arius was condemned and exiled from Constantine's empire; the two bishops who did stay and vote for his position were also exiled; the Emperor ordered all of Arius' writings burned; anyone caught in possession of his writings was subject to the death penalty; and, the council issued what is known as the *Nicene Creed*. This creed stated, in part, a belief "in one God: the Father Almighty, maker of heaven and earth, and of all things visible and invisible; and in one Lord Jesus Christ, the only begotten Son of God: begotten of his Father before all worlds, God of God, Light of Light, very God of very God, begotten, not made, being of one substance with the Father, through whom all things were made."

It appears that the early Apostolic church was predominantly what we now call *Unitarian*; and, despite Constantine's deception and power, and despite the Nicæan creed (or statement of faith), the Arian position slowly regained control of a majority of the church. Constantine again exhibited that political realities were more critical to him than ecclesiastical, and "changed sides" — exiling Athanasius, ending the exile of Arius and the two Arian bishops, and being baptized on his deathbed by an Arian bishop!

Following Constantine's death, his sons became co–Emperors and divided the Empire. Eventually, Constans I (an Athanasian Christian) ruled the western empire, and Constantius II (an Arian Christian) ruled the east. Constantius II instated Arian Christianity as the state religion, reinstated all Arian bishops to full power, outlawed paganism, condemned the Athanasians, and actually drove Athanasius into hiding.

Roughly 50 years later, a valiant military officer, Theodosius, took the crown; again, the tide shifted (Theodosius was Trinitarian). Trinitarianism was not actually the Athanasian position, but the suppressed pagan religions were Trinitarian, and most of the "foreign religions" with which the Empire interfaced regularly were at least Trinitarian on the surface (*e.g.* Hinduism, Kemetic, Zoroastrian, *etc.*). It appears that Theodosius thought that making Christianity trinitarian would lessen internal frictions within his Empire. The Athanasian bishops apparently saw this as a boon to conversion efforts among pagan and foreign religions, so many agreed. Theodosius called a new council in 381 CE in Constantinople, and was even more astute than his predecessor — only inviting bishops who agreed with him. A total of 150 bishops (this time, less than a tenth of the total) attended the council; to no surprise, they amended the original Nicæan Creed to include the Holy Ghost as part of the Godhead. Trinitarianism became official church and state policy, and all opposing bishops were defrocked (*i.e.* dis-ordained), excommunicated (*i.e.* booted out), and replaced.

This new creed was periodically amended with minor changes until it was finalized around the middle of the next century as the

Athanasian Creed. Athanasius was long dead, but his name was used to honor the original protagonist of this position. This creed reads in part: "We worship one God in Trinity . . . The Father is God, the Son is God, and the Holy Ghost is God; and yet they are not three gods, but one God." Trinitarianism was now church doctrine; but, only Eastern church doctrine. It was not accepted by the Christian church in Spain, France, and Germany (*i.e.* the Holy Roman Empire) *until the ninth century*!

Original Sin

Another major issue resolved about this same time was original sin. Pelagius, an ascetic from the British Isles, maintained that humanity is born good and pure (as it states in Genesis 1), while Augustine (who, prior to his conversion to Christianity, was raised by a Manichæan gnostic father in North Africa) maintained that man had inherited the sins of Adam (as described in Genesis 2; and, a Manichæan position) and was born depraved and sinful. This argument raged throughout the Roman Empire until the orthodox church finally accepted the Augustinian position. John Calvin summarized this more than a thousand years later, by writing:

> Original sin ... may be defined a hereditary corruption and depravity of our nature, extending to all the parts of the soul, which makes us obnoxious to the wrath of God. ... Hence, even infants bring their condemnation with them from their mother's womb, suffer not for another's, but for their own defect. For although they have not yet produced the fruits of their own unrighteousness, they have the seed implanted in them. Nay, their whole nature is, as it were, a seed-bed of sin, and therefore cannot but be odious and abominable to God.

This position was accepted by the orthodox church, and Pelagius was banished. This was typical of the years in which the orthodox branch of Christianity was being formed: all those who disagreed (*e.g.* Pelagians, Arians, Gnostics, Montanists, Docetics, *et cetera*) were killed, dispersed or banished by the Roman military.

Other Early Issues

Two other developments occurred that permeated the orthodox movement, and which had a lasting impact on Christianity as we know it today: Latinization and what is often called Mariolatry.

Latinization

The books of the New Testament of the Bible were originally written in Greek, as Greek was considered the language of philosophy and learning in the western world at that time (Christian worship was also usually conducted in Greek). Today, people often assume that, from the very beginning, the missions to Rome created a church that spoke Latin, the language of Rome. But, Paul would have spoken Greek when dealing with issues of education and philosophy, although he may have been able to speak Latin as a vulgar language (the language of common, everyday life).

Late in the 4th century (nearly 400 years after Christ, and about 50 years after Constantine died), the Roman bishop Damasus I began to wean the western church from Greek to Latin. The Arian movement still remained a theological sore point. The Arian belief that God is Supreme, and nothing – not even Christ – is His equal, apparently gave the Arian church an air of superiority and grandeur that was attractive to many. Bishop of Rome (Pope) Damasus I moved to change this. He started papal patronage, a move which eventually led to financial and military power for the church, and ultimately provided a lot of the force behind the Renaissance. He began building huge, ornate churches; and, it was under Damasus that Jerome was sent to Jerusalem to translate the Greek Bible into proper Latin (there were already inferior Latin texts in circulation). Latin, being the vulgar (common) language of the people, led to this new version of the Bible becoming known as the *Vulgate*. The Pope made this new Latin Bible obligatory for services, and thus *Latinized* the mass. He also changed the mass significantly at this time. The traditions of the Jesus Movement of the 1st century had determined much of the content and style of the mass, including readings from the Bible, a sermon, and the eucharist. Damasus lengthened the readings, lengthened the entire service, added a sense of grandeur to the mass, and inserted prayers at fixed intervals into the now much longer scriptural readings.

Clearly, one of the primary motivations of Damasus (and those who followed him) was to supplant the pomp and ceremony of the pagan rituals which surrounded them, as well as undermine the apparently higher theological ground held by the Arians. The church took an active role in promoting the magnificence of orthodox belief, and there was an ostentatious explosion of pageantry and splendor in the church: the wall hangings and priestly vestments became more colorful; gold, silver and marble ornamentation was used throughout the churches; silver canopies were introduced over altars; and, incense and candles were used in abundance. Their use was a sign of wealth and opulence in Rome, and their extensive use in churches gave orthodox Christianity an air of wealth and grandeur that impressed both the pagans and Arians.

Mariolatry

Mariolatry served another purpose. Although *Mariolatry* is etymologically sound, the word is generally considered derogatory and is usually used disparagingly. Technically, it means the worship of Mary, and accompanied the recognition of Mary as *Theotokos* ("God-bearer") by the Orthodox, but *Christotokos* ("Christ-bearer") by the followers of Archbishop Nestorius. The Bible says very little about Mary* except that she was the mother of Jesus, and an entire mythology around Mary had begun to develop by the 4th century. Primary beliefs about Mary were:
- o her Immaculate Conception (born without sin);
- o the Virgin Birth (of Jesus); and,
- o her Assumption (taken into heaven without death).

Augustine had introduced original sin into Christianity at about the same time as Latinization and Mariolatry. Mary would never have been selected by God to be the mother of Christ if she had possessed original sin; so, Mary must have been an *Immaculate Conception*: (*i.e.* she was conceived and born without original sin). Introduced in the 4th century, this did not become dogma (church doctrine) until 1854.

The Virgin Birth was an extrapolation of the story in the New Testament. The Bible reports that Mary was a *virgin* at the time of Jesus' conception (although there are many scholars who reject this view, since the Greek word translated as virgin – *parthenos* – can be translated equally well as "young girl"). The Bible stories

---

* Mary actually appears (is referenced) more often in the Islamic Qur'an than she is in the Christian Bible.

(introduced much later) do not discuss the idea that Mary had remained a virgin – after conception, during pregnancy, and, even after delivery.

The third belief is that Mary, not possessing original sin, would not need to pass through death as other mortals do. This led to the concept of *assumption*, whereby Mary ascended directly into heaven; *i.e.* she was *assumed* bodily into heaven. This, of necessity, would have occurred after Jesus ascended, since Jesus must take precedence over all others. This was not immediately accepted as a matter of faith, but did become Roman church dogma in 1950.

These disagreements within the orthodox church may appear to be minor when viewed by modern observers; however, the differences could be quite severe. One example should serve to illustrate the differences that could occur, and the seriousness with which they were viewed. As the Roman Empire was approaching collapse, numerous attacks and insurrections began to occur across the Empire. The attackers varied depending on the area of the Empire: Vandals in North Africa, Visigoths in Spain and southern France, Ostrogoths in Italy, *et cetera*. These "pagan barbarians", as they were described by the Roman government and the orthodox church, were not pagans (*i.e.* rural people following a pre–Christian religion of the area). Modern people assume the worst about these attackers of the Roman Empire based on this vilification and defamation in what has come down to us from the Romans. But, what was so barbaric about these invaders? *They were Arian Christians!*

Modern Divisions

*Orthodoxy: Western Liturgy**

Strain had steadily increased between the church at Rome and the eastern churches; and, this fully surfaced in 1054 CE. The increasing power of the Bishop at Rome and the strong ties of the church at Rome to the political power struggles in western Europe combined to bring the rift in the orthodox church to a full split. The eastern view was that all of the bishops were equal in authority, and that the church was run by councils, as had been done in the past; the Roman view was that the Bishop at Rome, by virtue of

---

* Liturgy refers to the rituals and observances of a tradition.

his location at the heart of the Empire and his 'descent from Peter' (as the first Bishop of Rome), had a more centralized role to play than the other bishops. Eventually, this came to a head when the Bishop at Rome formally instituted the papacy with the excommunication of the Bishop at Constantinople; but, the Bishop at Constantinople immediately excommunicated the Bishop at Rome! Theologically, there was very little difference between these two at that time. The largest gulf was the Roman view that the Holy Spirit, or third Person of the Trinity, emanates from the Father and the Son (using the Latin *filioque*). In fact, that term, designating an emanation, was even inserted into church prayers and statements — to the consternation and dismay of the Eastern churches.

Another difference that drove a wedge between the two groups was the use of icons. The eastern orthodox churches relied on the use of icons to represent God Incarnate, Mary as the Mother of God, and the role of many of the Saints. Western Christians often viewed the use of icons as idol worship; and, in 725 CE, Pope Leo III instituted the *iconoclastic movement* (*i.e.* the total destruction of all religious images). Leo was reacting primarily to the heavy use of icons in the Eastern churches, and the growing influence of Islam in western Europe (a faith that rejects all forms of idols and icons). This difference in approach caused strain between the eastern bishops and the Bishop of Rome, but was all for nought — as Leo's precepts were ultimately rejected in the western church as well, and iconography today is widespread in both the eastern and western liturgical groupings.

Modern Eastern Orthodox icons from the Russian Orthodox Church.

Following the split, the western church grew and flourished, gradually adopting the designation *catholic* (Latin: "universal"). But, many other branches of Christianity also considered themselves to be the universal (*i.e.* catholic) church, so this division added the localized adjective *Roman* to distinguish which universal church they were. This resulted in the somewhat oxymoronic expression *Roman Catholic* (*i.e.* the "local universal" church). They accept seven sacraments, or sacred rituals: baptism, holy orders (ordination), eucharist (communion), unction (anointing the sick), marriage, confirmation and penance (confession). They also use creeds, and a belief in Apostolic succession (starting with Peter[*]).

St. Peter's Basilica in Vatican City (a sovereign state within the city of Rome).

Orthodox: Eastern Liturgy

At the time of the split between Western and Eastern churches, the Eastern churches established themselves in a common communion (*i.e.* they honor, accept and respect each other's practices) with

---

[*] The idea that St Peter was the 'first Pope', or Bishop of Rome, is a long Catholic tradition. The New Testament never mentions either the presence or martyrdom (64 CE) of Peter in Rome. *Saint Peter's Basilica*, the largest church in the world (60,000 people, photo above) was built directly above his alleged burial spot. In 1950, Pope Pius XII announced they had discovered his bones in a tomb below the altar. The church, however, was built on land that served as an ancient Roman cemetery for hundreds of years; and, it is impossible to prove whether the bones they found were truly those of Peter.

no centralized authority. Each region, or church, is governed by a Patriarch, each of whom is equal to his peers and who are in communion with each other. Although priests need not remain celibate (provided they are married prior to their ordination), they may not aspire to the role of Bishop (or Patriarch). Monks, who do maintain celibacy, are the only eastern liturgical leaders who may attain the office of bishop. They refuse to accept Papal authority (*i.e.* the Bishop at Rome), and they deny the concept of *filioque*.

Compared to other Christian branches, there is greater emphasis within the Eastern churches on monasticism and the mystical union of man with God. Following the split with the western (*i.e.* Roman) church, the eastern orthodox churches evolved toward regionalization: *i.e.* Greek Orthodox, Russian Orthodox, Romanian Orthodox, Albanian Orthodox, Bulgarian Orthodox, Ukrainian Orthodox, *et cetera*. Although many of these were suppressed under communism, they all expanded once the official atheist position of their respective governments was removed.

Protestant

Although technically inaccurate, the term Protestant is often broadly used to describe those Christians who are neither Roman Catholic nor Eastern Orthodox; but, the breadth of the term Protestant often depends upon who is using it. Roman Catholics use the term very broadly, and use it to identify those western Christians they believe have "strayed from the path" — a broad collection of beliefs which are all, in some way, erroneous or heretical. Mainstream Protestants (those belonging to one of the larger denominations) also use the term rather broadly, but without the disparaging implications. Denominations[*] which do not trace their roots to the Reformation of the 16th century tend to use the term Protestant much more narrowly, and often do not include themselves within that grouping. A common term used by Religious Anthropologists to define these groups is *Revelatory Churches*.

After the 1054 CE split, the ecumenical councils of the eastern churches ceased to have an impact on the western orthodox church;

---

[*] Denomination is from Latin *denominationem*, meaning to be given a group name or nickname. In religion, it refers to a subgroup of a larger entity.

and, the Roman church became much more involved in political and military events in Europe. This involvement with these activities was one of several factors that led to eventual corruption and decay within the church, and planted seeds for the Reformation. As an example, consider the situation with *indulgences*.

The Roman church had developed a more complex view of the afterlife than the earliest Christians espoused. There was: *heaven*, a place of eternal goodness and love; *hell*, its antithesis, a place of eternal fire and damnation; and, *purgatory*, an intermediate place where one could 'serve time' to pay off debts and earn entrance to heaven. It was necessary, however, to know what would force someone into purgatory or hell so that one could take appropriate steps to ensure a future in heaven. This led to the classification of sins as *mortal sins* and *venial sins*. Mortal sins included offenses such as murder, adultery, or missing Sunday mass. Venial sins were of a less severe nature, and included lying, theft, harsh words to another, swearing, *etc.*. If a Roman church member died in a state of mortal sin, they were headed for hell. Confessed mortal sins and all venial sins (confessed or not) resulted in temporal punishment: *i.e.* spending time in purgatory. In general, this time was reduced or mitigated through confession of the sin or willingness to do *penance* to earn forgiveness. Penances had evolved to where they could be very complex, elaborate and time consuming. Many of them even included activities which were publicly humiliating.

Through World War I in the United States, if you were drafted into the military, you were allowed to hire someone else to serve in your place. By the seventh century, a similar situation had evolved with respect to penance for the church: penance was defined by a priest after having heard a confession, but the penitent could then pay someone else to do their penance for them. It seemed logical that acts of penance done by a monk or priest would be more effective than if done by a sinner; so, it became common to hire monks to perform penance. But, this put financial temptation before these monks, who had made a vow of poverty. Eventually, the church removed this temptation and cut out the middle man – having penitents make payment directly to the church, which would then assign a monk the task.

A common Roman belief was that Jesus, Mary and the Saints of the church had earned more merit in the eyes of God than they needed to ensure entrance into heaven. This excess merit was viewed as a commodity. The church, as God's agent on earth, felt authorized to dispense these *indulgences* (as these units of excess merit were called). Those assigned to dispense them were known as *quaestores* (Latin: "pardoners"). Since the application of an indulgence either mitigated, reduced or eliminated the need for penance, paying for penance on your behalf and the selling of indulgences merged into a single practice: selling *plenary* (*i.e.* complete) *indulgences*; and, this became an alternate form of financial capital to the church. For example, knights who went to fight in the Crusades (and others, who financially supported the Crusades) were offered either plenary indulgences or a reduction of penance as a reward for their service. This practice seemed to be a way to buy your way into heaven to the laity who couldn't afford the cost. This offended them as well as some of the priests, and became one of the better known issues which Martin Luther addressed in his attempt to reform the church.

Other issues included the fact that the Bible was forbidden to be translated into any of the vernacular languages. Even though Latin had ceased being a vernacular language by the 7th century, only Latin Bibles were allowed. This kept the common people from reading it, and required them to have priests read and explain the Bible to them. Hymns were also kept in Latin in a very soothing, but strict, musical format now known as Gregorian chants. Started under Pope Gregory the Great (590 –604 CE), these chants were actually based on earlier Hebrew psalmody. They were later collected and systematized (9th century). As beautiful as they may be, most people could neither understand them nor sing them.

Starting in the 14th century, some of the priests and deacons began to make unauthorized changes. Gerhard Groote, a Dutch deacon, objected to the practice of *simony* (the selling of church ordination, offices, or indulgences) and taught what he considered a more Apostolic vision of Christ. The church forbade him from preaching these radical ideas (at that time, only the church could give you a license to preach – if you preached without a license, you went to jail); so, he withdrew from public society and formed a Christian lay community known as the *Brethren of the Common Life*. The members of his community took vows of poverty, chastity, obedience (to God), helping the poor, *et cetera*. Although the actual text is usually credited to either Thomas à Kempis or Florens Radewijns, Groote's community schools led indirectly to the writing of *The Imitation of Christ*, which is what Groote preached: living a life in imitation of Christ.

Later in the 14th century, John Wyclif and his followers (known as *Lollards*) began to translate the Latin Bible into English — for which he was excommunicated. Other reformers also appeared throughout Europe. Savonarola was a famous Italian preacher who managed to reform many of the problems in Florence for a while; however, when he finally became too much of an irritation to Pope Alexander VI, he was hanged and burned – simultaneously!

The invention of a printing press with movable type led to the production of the Gutenberg Bible, and removed one of the major impediments to the common people having access to the Bible; but, the other offenses only got more severe. In 1517, this came to a head. Martin Luther had been a monk in the Augustinian order, had been ordained a priest, and held his doctorate in theology from the University of Wittenberg (Germany). The Roman church at that time believed that the workings of the church and its ritualistic and sacramental observances could actually mount an "attack on heaven" to ensure a future heavenly abode for its supporters. But, Luther thought that forgiveness of sin only came from the grace of God, and that salvation only came from faith in God. Unfortunately for him, this view was in total opposition to the church position.

In 1517, Luther locked the doors of *Schlosskirche* (the Wittenberg parish church), and nailed *95 Theses* (his concerns) to the wooden doors (brass doors have replaced the originals, lost in a 1760 fire; photo, below). Although seen today as a founder of the Protestant Reformation, Luther was not trying to form an alternative to the church at Rome; he was attempting to reform what he saw as problems in the Roman church. This was not to be, however; and, an irrevocable split occurred between Rome and reform-minded leaders such as Martin Luther of Germany [below, left] and Jean Chauvain (*i.e.,* John Calvin) of France/Switzerland [below, right]. The church attempted to avert the split in 1529 at the Diet of Speyer, and the leaders of the various groups (organized under princes, along national lines) protested what they saw as a very heavy-handed response: issuing a document disputing the church's actions, and setting forth their goals. From this paper (written in Latin, and beginning *Protestantum*, or "we protest"), the Roman church began using the term Protestant as a disparaging name for followers of these 'heretics'.

Revelatory

The idea of a separate Christian division known as *Revelatory* is simply ignored by the Roman church and the larger Protestant bodies. This is also often the case in comparative religion texts, where Quakers, Christian Scientists, Jehovah's Witnesses, 7th Day Adventists, Mormons, and others are either rejected as heretics, marginalized as radical Protestants, or lumped together as New Age. In truth, they are none of these; they are Revelatory.

From the perspective of the Roman Catholic or Eastern Orthodox churches, calling them Protestant seems logical. There is one major difference, however, between these groups and true Protestant groups: *i.e.* they neither formed at the time of the Protestant Reformation nor are they direct descendants of any of the churches that did. Lutherans and the Reformed Church both resulted from the Reformation; Baptists are Protestants because they evolved from the Reformed Church. Mormons, however, resulted from the personal revelation of Joseph Smith Jr. more than 300 years after the Reformation. Including any church based on his revelation under the heading Protestant not only diminishes the validity of his revelation, it detracts from Protestantism by making it the proverbial "all other" category. All of the churches listed here as Revelatory evolved either from *independent revelation* by some individual, or a split unrelated to the 'German' Reformation of the 16th century.

Common Divisions (Denominations) ## *and* ## *Examples (not a complete list)*

Western Orthodox	Eastern Orthodox	Revelatory	Protestant
Roman Catholic	Greek Orthodox	Christian Science	Anabaptist
Polish National	Serbian Orthodox	Unitarian	*Hutterite*
Maronite	Russian Orthodox	Divine Science	*Mennonite*
Melkite Greek	Romanian Orthodox	LDS (Mormon)	*Brethren*
	Albanian Orthodox	7th Day Adventist	*Amish*
	Bulgarian Orthodox	Friends (Quaker)	Lutheran
	Ukrainian Orthodox	Iglesia ni Cristo	Reformed
	Coptic Orthodox	Unity	Baptist
	Polish Orthodox	Jehovah's Witness	*General B*
	Georgian Orthodox	Anglican	*7th Day B*
	Church of Cyprus	*Moravians*	*Regular B*
	Czech & Slovak Orth.	*'High' Episcopal*	Presbyterian
		'Low' Episcopal	
		Methodist	
		Methodist Episcopal	
		African Methodist	

Chapter 12
Scripture, Concepts, Practices & Holidays

But, as for you, continue in what you have learned and have firmly believed, knowing from whom you learned it and how from childhood you have been acquainted with the sacred writings which are able to instruct you for salvation through faith in Christ Jesus. All scripture is inspired by God and profitable for teaching, for reproof, for correction, and for training in righteousness, that the man of God may be complete, equipped for every good work .— 2 Timothy 3:14-17

Scripture

Christianity is a scriptural religion — *i.e.* it is based nearly entirely on what is conveyed by the Christian scriptures. The problem is that there are not only numerous interpretations of these writings, there are even alternative collections, differing in language, emphasis, and even content.

The Holy Bible Bible is an English word that was derived from βιβλία, the Greek term for a collection of books; so, in essence, the Bible can be thought of as a "library". Organizationally, there are two distinct divisions within this collection: the so-called *Old Testament*, and a corresponding *New Testament*.

Old Testament The Christian Old Testament is a collection of writings that were extant at the time of Christ. In fact, it is virtually certain that Jesus was personally well acquainted with these writings. Jesus — growing up as a young Jewish boy — would have known these texts as the Jewish scriptures (the *Tanakh* discussed earlier). The collection consists of Jewish law, histories, wisdom books, and books of prophecy. In general, Christians see Jesus as the fulfillment of many of these prophecies.

New Testament The Christian New Testament is a collection of writings that deal specifically with Jesus and his followers. This collection begins with 4 gospels. The word *gospel* evolved in Middle English (*ca* 1200s) from the earlier Old English *gōdspell* (literally, a "story of God"). Contrary to popular myth, it does not mean "good news" (according to no less of an etymologist than Wordsworth's Walter Skeat). So, the 4 gospels tell the story of Christ (seen by most Christians as being *God Incarnate*). This is followed by the story of his closest followers in the years that immediately followed his crucifixion, and then by a number of letters (*epistles*) written to: the faith at large; individuals; and, various congregations by several of these early leaders of the Christian movement. It closes with a book of prophecy which recounts the religious experience of a follower writing as 'John of Patmos' (few biblical experts today believe that it was written by John the Disciple).

Canonization Officially acknowledging that certain texts are *canonical* (Greek: that they "measure up") is a process that virtually all scriptures must go through; the Bible was no exception. The problem is that different Christian leaders canonized different collections of texts; *e.g.* it was not until about 400 CE that there was any real agreement on what should be included in the New Testament. As a result, there are several different "bibles" (or libraries) in use. What is included (and, what is not) is almost entirely a function of which branch of Christianity is using it. Differences occur in both the Old and New Testaments. For example:

- *Protestant* 66 books (39 Old Testament – identical to the Jewish Tanakh, but divided differently; 27 New Testament).
- *Roman Catholic* 73 books (all of the Protestant Old Testament, but with 7 additional books: Judith, Tobit, 1 & 2 Maccabees, Wisdom of Solomon, Ecclesiasticus, and Baruch plus some additional material).
- *Syriac Orthodox* 61 books (identical to Protestant OT, but lacking 2nd and 3rd John, 2nd Peter, Jude, and Revelation in the NT).
- *Luther Bible* 62 books (Luther dropped Hebrews, James, Jude, and Revelation from the NT, but followers usually included them anyway. To this day, they are sequenced last in the German language *Luther Bible*.)
- *Greek Orthodox* 77 books (the Roman Catholic Old Testament plus Psalm 151, 1 Esdras, 3 & 4 Maccabees, and the Prayer of Manasseh).
- *Armenian Apostolic* 79 books (adding the *Testaments of the Twelve Patriarchs* and 3rd Corinthians to the Greek Orthodox OT and NT canon).
- *Coptic Church* 79 books (adding 1st & 2nd Clement to the NT)
- *Ethiopian Church* 81 books (adding Jubilees, Enoch, 1st & 2nd Esdras, and 3rd Maccabees to the Septuagint OT).
- *Latter Day Saints* 81 books (traditional Protestant canon plus 15 books of the Book of Mormon).

Add the tremendous variations in translation and interpretation to the numerous variations in content – plus variations in source texts* – and it becomes easier to understand the more than 2,000 Christian sects today. The problem is that nearly all 2,000 sects ultimately base their legitimacy on — the Bible. The problem is: "which Bible?".

Evolution

The following is an abbreviated (very abbreviated) look at how the English language Bible evolved into what it is today. Translations ... soooo many translations!

Probable Date	Version	Primary Language	Historical Sources
before 400 BCE	Old Testament	Hebrew	*the original books*
250 – 50 BCE	Septuagint OT	Greek	*earliest available texts*

This translation was done for non-Hebrew speaking Jews at Alexandria, and was popular throughout the Roman Empire. This was the version known to many of the early Christians.

| 6 BC – 40 CE | New Testament | — | *actual events* |

This is when the events depicted actually took place.

| 50 – 150 CE | New Testament | Greek | *original books & letters* |

Although often bearing the names of disciples, most Bible scholars believe that a better interpretation is that a book or letter was written *"in the style of ..."* rather than by the actual person named. The one major exception is that Paul most likely was the author of at least 6, and possibly 8, of the 13 letters attributed to him.

| ~150 CE | Massora OT | Hebrew | *earliest available texts* |

An authoritative Hebrew text prepared by early Jewish scholars, and the primary vehicle that preserved the original texts. Early Hebrew was written only in consonants, and this work "stabilized" the text with a system of vowel sounds and accent marks — although speculation was still inevitable.

| ~190 CE | Peshitta | Syriac | *earliest available texts* |

Syriac translations of the Massoric Old Testament and Greek New Testament. Parts were in circulation in the 2nd century.

---

* Two different bibles may include the same book, but use sources that were written a thousand miles or 300 years apart – often leading to significant differences in content.

200 – 250 CE   **Coptic Versions**   **Coptic**   *earliest available texts*
Egyptians had the Old Testament by 200 CE, and a New Testament by 250 CE (the Old Testament was a translation of the Septuagint). Two versions existed in Sahadic and Bohairic – the southern and northern Coptic dialects, respectively.

~340 CE   **Carthage Bible**   **Old Latin**   *earliest available texts*
The first known Latin version, and was written in Old Latin. In circulation around Carthage early in the 4th century, it was supplanted at the end of the century by the Vulgate (below).

360 – 400 CE   **Armenian Versions**   **Armenian**   *earliest available texts*
The Septuagint (OT) and Syriac (NT) were translated into Old Armenian and in wide circulation by 400 AD.

382 – 404 CE   **The Vulgate**   **Latin**   *Septuagint & earliest NT*
Pope Damasus I sent his secretary, Saint Jerome (left), to the Holy Lands to develop a proper Latin translation of the Bible at the end of the 4th century. Although Jerome could read & write Hebrew as well, he used the Greek language Septuagint and the earliest Greek New Testament works available. His end product was the standard for more than a thousand years.

735 CE   **Bede's Bible**   **Old English**   *Latin Vulgate*
The Venerable Bede [673 – 735] lived in England, and is the individual who defined time as before (BC) or after (AD) the birth of Christ. He undertook to translate the Bible into Old English, and had translated through John before he died.

1382 CE   **Wycliffe**   **Middle English**   *Latin Vulgate*
John Wycliffe (left) led a group of heretical priests (the Lollards) who preached in the vernacular. Aided by Nicholas of Hereford (who did parts of the Old Testament), he translated the Latin Vulgate into the English of his day (1382). Shortly after his death, a revision appeared (1388) as a result of the efforts of his friend, John Purvey. Wycliffe was a respected Oxford scholar, and was hounded (not harmed) for his work. After his death, however, his body was exhumed, burned and thrown into a river on orders from Rome "to the damnation and destruction of his memory".

1528 CE   **Pagninus**   *Latin*   *originals*
Pagninus was a monk in Italy. In 1516, he went to Rome, and Pope Leo X sponsored his translation. Published in 1528, it was the first new Latin version since Jerome's Vulgate. Done in a modern, scholarly Latin, it proved immensely helpful to later translators (the Vulgate was in a Latin not in common use for over a thousand years). This was the first Bible to break Chapters into numbered verses.

Ch 12 – Scripture, Concepts, Practices & Holidays

1530 CE **Tyndale**   **Middle English**   *early German texts*
When William Tyndale (left) started his translation work, he was forced to flee England, and completed his translation of the New Testament in Hamburg (Germany). This was printed at Worms in 1526, and was the first Bible printed (not hand copied); the printed copies had to be smuggled into England. Over 15,000 copies reached England within 4 years; the king (Henry VIII) and the clergy hunted them down and burned those they found. Tyndale translated the Pentateuch and Jonah and revised his New Testament from 1530 to 1534. Betrayed by enemies, he was simultaneously strangled and burned at the stake as a heretic for his blasphemy.

1534 CE **Luther**   **Old High German**   *earliest available texts*
Martin Luther translated the New Testament into German in 1522 and the Old Testament in 1534. Widely used in Europe (up to the present) among Protestants, this was so influential that it even influenced development of the German language.

1537 CE **Coverdale**   **Middle English**   ***Pagninus***
Luther's and Tyndale's translations were so popular that a petition was presented to King Henry VIII in 1534 to have an English translation by scholars appointed by the King. The following year, Miles Coverdale completed his translation. Publication occurred in 1537.

1537 CE **Matthew's**   **Middle English**   ***Greek NT & Coverdale***
Attributed to Thomas Matthew, this was a pseudonym of John Rogers. His work, along with Coverdale's, is one of two simultaneously accepted versions of the Bible in English — *accepted* (often called "licensed") by King Henry VIII.

1539 CE **Great Bible Middle English**   ***Matthew's Bible***
A revision, the name was derived from the large size of the finished product. It was produced under the direction of Miles Coverdale at the request of Thomas Cromwell (Vicar General under King Henry VIII). As such, this is the first English version officially authorized by King Henry VIII. It was approved for use in every parish church in England.

1556 CE **Beza's (NT only)**   **Latin**   *earliest available texts*
Beza (Théodore de Bèze) was a French theologian, successor to John Calvin, a degreed lawyer, and professor of classical Greek. Beza completed a Latin translation of the New Testament from the ancient Greek manuscripts he possessed (5th century texts later donated by him to Cambridge University as the *Codex Bezæ*). His translation became a major source document for later translators — for both the Geneva Bible (below) and the later King James Version (also below).

1560 CE   Geneva   Middle English   *Great Bible & Beza's NT*
The Puritans went into self-imposed exile in Geneva during the reign of Mary Tudor. This group produced the 1st English translation divided into numbered verses. The New Testament is a combination of Beza's and a revision of Tyndale's. It was published in 1557. The Old Testament was a revision of the Great Bible. The complete Bible wasn't published until 1560. Calvin made extensive marginal notes to ensure that average, uneducated priests would understand what they were reading.

1568 CE   Bishop's   Elizabethan English   *Great Bible*
A revision of the Great Bible was conducted during the reign of Elizabeth I. The name is from the ecclesiastical rank of many of the translators, and leadership fell to Matthew Parker.

1610 CE   Douai–Rheims   Elizabethan English   *Vulgate*
Just as Puritans had fled to the continent during the reign of Mary Tudor, Roman Catholics fled there during the reign of Elizabeth I. It was while in France at the English College in Douai, Flanders that an "English Roman Catholic translation" based on the Latin Vulgate was undertaken. The New Testament was published at nearby Rheims in 1582; and, the Old Testament was published in Douai in 1610.

1611 CE   King James   Elizabethan English   *earliest texts*
King James I (left) tried to unite his kingdoms (Scotland & England) with this, known as the Authorized Version in Britain. In 1604, James called a conference to hear complaints about existing versions from his people. He then commissioned 47 experts to do a new translation acceptable to both Puritan and Anglican factions. It was first published in 1611.

1750 CE   Challoner Bible   English   Douai–Rheims
At the age of 39, Richard Challoner was sent by the Roman Catholic Church to London. While in London, he completed a revision of the Douai–Rheims. His intent was to make it more readable, and to correct some errors in it. It became the most used Roman Catholic version in the US for nearly 200 years.

1851–56 CE   Benisch   English   *earliest available texts*
Renowned Biblical scholar Abraham Benisch was an English Jew. He conducted the first complete Jewish translation of the Old Testament into English, published from 1851 to 1856.

1853 CE   Leeser   American English   *earliest available texts*
About the same time Benisch was doing a Jewish translation in Britain, Isaac Leeser was doing an American translation. Published in 1853, it was widely used in the United States.

Ch 12 – Scripture, Concepts, Practices & Holidays   161

1885 CE   **Revised Version   English   *earliest & King James***
A four year translation effort designed to update the English, it incorporated linguistic & archæolgical advances for a more accurate translation. Initiated in 1870 by the Convocation of Canterbury (Anglican), it included scholars from other denominations. One team, over 10 years, translated the New Testament (1881), while another team translated the Old Testament over 14 years (1885). It was unique in that it was printed in prose poetry as opposed to verses.

1901 CE   **Standard Version   American English   *Revised Version***
An *Americanized* Revised Version and based wholly upon it.

1903 CE   **Weymouth   American English   *Revised Version***
Done by Richard F. Weymouth, and also known as the New Testament in Modern Speech, he maintained it was a new translation from Greek and Hebrew texts; but, most scholars believe it is drawn from the Revised Version,.

1903 CE   **Modern English   English   *earliest available texts***
This translation of the Bible was done by Fenton Ferrar as a new translation of the early Greek and Hebrew texts in 1903.

1917 CE   **JPS   American English   *earliest available texts***
Following the work of Benisch and Leeser, the Jewish Publication Society (JPS) spent twenty five years on this project.

1922 CE   **Moffatt   English   *earliest available texts***
James Moffatt produced a "modern language" translation of the original New Testament texts in 1913, and completed the entire Bible translation in 1922.

1924 CE   **Centenary American English   *earliest available texts***
A New Testament translation by Helen Barrett Montgomery.

1927–31 CE   **Goodspeed American English   *earliest available texts***
Edgar Johnson Goodspeed, a professor at the University of Chicago, produced an idiomatic translation of the New Testament in 1923. He then joined J.M.P. Smith to produce a new translation of the entire Bible in 1927. It is also commonly known as the *Smith–Goodspeed Bible.*

1941 CE   **Confraternity   English   *Latin Vulgate***
The Confraternity of Christian Doctrine (through its Episcopal Committee) produced a new Roman Catholic translation based on the Vulgate, but influenced by earlier Greek translations.

1949 CE   **Basic English   American English   *Standard Version***
Linguist Charles Kay Ogden created the artificial language *Basic English.* Essentially a "stripped down" English, *Basic*

English was touted similar to Esperanto — as a potential universal language. His Bible translation is a translated version of the Revised Version, and technically is not an English version, but a *Basic English* version.

1949 CE   **Knox**   **English**   *Challoner & Vulgate*
Ronald Knox was chaplain of Trinity College. He converted from Anglican to Roman Catholic and was appointed chaplain at Oxford. He completed an independent translation of the *Vulgate* and the *Challoner Bible*; the New Testament was published in 1945; and, the Old Testament was published four years later, in 1949. His translation became an "authorized" version for use in the Roman Catholic tradition.

1952 CE   **Plain English**   **American English**   *Standard Version*
This was an independent revision of the American Standard Version by Charles K. Williams.

1952 CE   **Revised Std**   **American English**   *Standard Version*
The New Testament was published in 1946 with the complete Bible in 1952. The New Testament was revised in 1971.

1957 CE   **J.B. Phillips**   **English**   *earliest available texts*
Originally, J.B. Phillips translated the New Testament in 1957, and this was updated and revised in 1972.

1959 CE   **Berkeley**   **English**   *earliest available texts*
The New Testament was published in 1945, with the complete Bible in 1959. Updates were incorporated in a 1969 revision.

1964–present   **Anchor Bible**   **American English**   *earliest available texts*
An exhaustive translation and commentary being published in multiple volumes (the 1st volume in 1964, and on–going). Currently, over 80 volumes have been published, and the work is reportedly nearly complete.

1966 CE   **Cath. Rev Std**   **American English**   *Revised Standard*
This was a Roman Catholic edition of the Protestant Revised Standard Version incorporating some changes requested by Roman Catholic scholars.

1966 CE   **Cushing**   **American English**   *Revised Standard*
Publication of the complete Revised Standard Version with Roman Catholic preferences added as footnotes (rather than altering the translation). It was published under the direction of Roman Catholic Cardinal Richard Cushing of Boston.

1966 CE   **Jerusalem**   **American English**   *earliest available texts*
A new "critical" translation based on the originals and inspired by the French *Bible de Jérusalem* (published in 1954).

Ch 12 – Scripture, Concepts, Practices & Holidays 163

| 1969 CE | **Barclay**   **English**   *earliest available texts* |

A 1969 New Testament translation by William Barclay.

| 1970 CE | **New English**   **English**   *earliest available texts* |

Translated by scholars from leading Protestant denominations in Britain (NT published in 1961, and the full Bible in 1970).

| 1970 CE | **Today's English**   **English**   *earliest available texts* |

A translation by the American Bible Society that they said "does not conform to traditional vocabulary or style".

| 1970 CE | **New American**   **American English**   *earliest available texts* |

The Old Testament is from the originals, while the New Testament is a revision of the 1941 Confraternity translation. It has become the predominant modern Roman Catholic version.

| 1971 CE | **Living Bible**   **American English**   *paraphrased* |

A paraphrase of earlier texts (NT published in 1967 and the entire Bible published in 1971).

| 1978 CE | **NIV**   **American English**   *earliest available texts* |

The New International Version (NIV) is the most commonly used version in evangelical denominations (NT in 1973, and the complete Bible in 1978).

| 1979 CE | **Good News**   **American English**   *earliest available texts* |

Originally, the New Testament was published in 1966 and then followed by the complete Bible – known as *Today's English Version* until it was renamed in 2001.

| 1982 CE | **New King James**   **English**   *King James Version* |

An extensive modern language revision of the King James Version. The New Testament was published first, in 1979, and the entire Bible followed in 1982.

| 1982 CE | **JPS**   **American English**   *earliest available texts* |

The Jewish Publication Society said in 1961 that they were undertaking a new translation of the Old Testament. This was more than an update of the 1917 version, with new translation of the Torah in 1962, Prophets in 1978, and Writings in 1982.

| 1990 CE | **New Rev Std**   **American English**   *earliest texts; RSV* |

This is a revision of the 1952 Revised Standard incorporating later knowledge and discoveries regarding the original texts.

| 1993 CE | **Five Gospels**   **English**   *earliest available texts* |

Presented as a new translation with critical analysis of five Gospels (including the apocryphal Gospel of Thomas) by the fellows of *The Jesus Seminar*, led by Robert Funk and Roy Hoover. Presented in the context of "what Jesus really said."

1995 CE	Contemporary	English	*earliest available texts*

A recent translation relying on current knowledge of the original texts (NT published in 1991; the entire Bible in 1995).

1996 CE	New Living Trans	English	*earliest available texts*

A gender inclusive update of the 1971 paraphrase.

2001 CE	New English	English	*earliest available texts*

The NET is an impressive translation done primarily by Dallas Theological Seminary, including extensive translator notes and explanations. It is available free on the internet.

2002 CE	The Message	English	*earliest available texts*

A contemporary translation by Rev. Eugene Peterson.

2006 CE	Today's NIV	English	*New International Version*

This is a 21st century update of the NIV, originally published in 1978 and previously updated in 1984.

The above listing is not even close to complete. The list is far more extensive. If you would like to see some of what is missing, this website will give more detail: *www.bible-researcher.com*

Concepts

Identifying underlying concepts in Christianity is not a simple task. Some are drawn from Jewish texts (the Old Testament), some from early Christian texts (the New Testament), some from biblical exegesis (critical analysis of the scriptures), some from historical tradition, and some from theologically based philosophical treatises. Some of these are universal (*i.e.* all Christians worldwide agree); some are general (*i.e.* most Christians around the world would agree), and some are denominationally specific (*i.e.* views held by specific sub-groups of Christians that are widely held, but do not rise to the level of a general belief). *Denomination* is a "designation for a class of things"; in the case of religion, it is a group of people who concur on nearly all major points, and are thus "counted together". With a few thousand Christian denominations, the possibility of finding many universal concepts is limited, while the probability of identifying denominationally specific concepts is quite high.

Consider the following *Christian Concepts*:

1) The *Holy Bible* is the divinely inspired Word of God (*i.e.* albeit God did not "dictate it", it is in complete concurrence with God through revelation to prophets). Written by humans, it is authoritative in that the writing was inspired by the Holy Spirit;

2) God is the Ultimate Creator of the universe, and can be described as possessing various attributes. Among these are: aseity (self-existent, self-sufficient beingness), eternal (timeless, not temporal), holy (separate and untouched by sin), immanent (accessible, and can be dynamically experienced), immutable (unchanging), incorporeal (not physically constituted), omniagape (all loving), omnibenevolent (all good), omnipotent (all power), omnipresent (everywhere), omniscient (all knowing), transcendent (over and above all), and veracity (Truth).

3) There is only One God (*i.e.* monotheism).

4) God exists in three *persons* of one substance (*i.e.* the Trinity).

5) Jesus was both "fully human" and "fully divine". The title of *Christ* was applied to indicate his status as *anointed of God.*

6) The Virgin Birth – his mother, Mary, had not had sex.

7) Jesus was God Incarnate (literally, "God in the flesh").

8) Jesus performed numerous physical miracles (healing the lame, sight to the blind, hearing to the deaf, curing both mental and physical illnesses, *et cetera*);

9) Jesus was crucified* by the Romans after one to three years of preaching, teaching, and performing miracles;

---

* Crucifixion was a penalty reserved by the Romans for those they most despised (most often, treason or threat to the Empire). The person to be crucified was attached (with either ropes or nails) to a large wooden cross, and left there until dead. Crucified totally naked (to increase discomfort and shame), death was nearly always by asphyxiation (suffocation) – brought about by the weight of the body crushing the lungs. Death typically took several days to as much as two weeks to occur.

10) Three days after the crucifixion, Jesus was physically resurrected (brought back to life) and spent time with his former followers – demonstrating his authority over even life and death; and,

11) Heaven and Hell are alternate states of existence following death for humans. Purgatory may be an intermediate stage used for purification to enable entrance into heaven.

Do all Christians accept all of these concepts? No. Of these, only 4 might be considered universal (2,3,8 and 9). Some of the others come close – definitely general, but not universal. Some are barely general (*i.e.* more than half, but just slightly). In addition, there are others that are accepted only by certain, specific denominations; and, these are usually alternatives to one of the concepts listed above (*e.g.* the Unitarian-Universalist denomination denies a Triune God, and declares that "God is One").

Holidays

Holy days (holidays) can be divided into two general categories: major holidays (with significant importance, and nearly universal acceptance), and minor holidays (with lesser significance, and accepted by only certain denominations or groups of denominations). The major holidays are relatively easy to identify and enumerate; the minor holidays are far too numerous to cover here (so, we'll only list a few as examples).

Major Holidays

Christmas *Cristesmæsse* (Anglo-Saxon: "Christ's mass"), or Christmas, is an annual celebration of the birth of Jesus Christ. Generally, it is celebrated on December 25th; however, there are a few exceptions. Originally, the Eastern churches observed Christmas on January 6th; but, the only one that still does is the Armenian Apostolic Church. In addition, areas that still use a Julian calendar for religious celebrations (*e.g.* Russia, Ukraine, Serbia, Moldova, Macedonia, and Ethiopia) currently observe it on January 7th.

Common customs associated with the day include giving gifts, singing related music (caroling), a feast, church services, and decorations. Residential decorations can become quite large, and often include an evergreen tree (brought inside and décorated with lights, ornaments, *etc.*), garlands, wreaths, mistletoe, holly, poinsettias, nativity scenes, and exterior lights. Many (probably most) of these traditions are actually pre-Christian, pagan practices *adopted* by Christianity and *Christianized*.

There is disagreement over exactly when Jesus was born, but it was not on December 25th. That date was almost certainly adopted so early Christians would not stand out in Roman lands by not celebrating the winter solstice. Romans (and most other pagans) celebrated the *Saturnalia* (winter solstice, the shortest day of the year) over 5 days, culminating in a feast on the 5th day – December 25th.

Good Friday Good Friday was neither good nor Friday! The term *Good* is used in the sense that the day is considered holy; it has been assumed that it was a Friday because the New Testament account of the crucifixion says Jesus was crucified on the day prior to the Sabbath (which, for Jews, is Saturday). The day is thus a commemoration of the crucifixion and sacrifice of Jesus. The difficulty in accepting Friday for this reason is that the same accounts say that Jesus was in the tomb three days and three nights; and, that the tomb was found empty before dawn on the first day of the week (for Jews, Sunday). The two accounts can not be reconciled unless the gospels were either: (a) referring to a Sabbath other than the weekly Sabbath; or, (b) the first day of the week was not Sunday that week. Logic dictates it must be (a), regardless of how hard it is to explain.

In all probability, the Sabbath that the gospels are referencing was the first day of *Pesach* (Passover). That is also considered a Sabbath, and can occur on any day of the week (with timing based on a lunar cycle). If that fell on a Thursday, the crucifixion would have occurred on Wednesday, and Jesus would have been in the tomb all night on Wednesday, Thursday, and Friday, and all day Thursday, Friday, and Saturday – being resurrected during Saturday evening or night. So, Christianity should probably be celebrating *Good Wednesday* rather than *Good Friday*.

Easter Easter is a commemoration of resurrection. Jesus was crucified by the Romans, but rose bodily from the dead pre-dawn on the first day of the week (Sunday). This is commonly observed by Christians as a day of celebration. The actual date is again debated by the various denominations. The *First Council of Nicea* (325 CE) set the date of Easter as the first Sunday after the first Full Moon after the Vernal Equinox (the first day of Spring); as such, Easter can fall on any day between March 22 and April 25. Today, the Eastern churches, using the Julian calendar and tying it to *Pesach*, celebrate it between April 4 and May 8.

Eostre was actually the name of an Anglo-Saxon pagan goddess. She was associated with the arrival of Spring, and the old Anglo-Saxon calendar had the springtime month of *Eosturmonath*. This lent her name to the Christian celebration, along with a number of Spring and fertility related symbology (eggs, bunny rabbits, new clothes, flowers, *etc.*).

Lent Lent is the 40 day period that runs from *Ash Wednesday*[+] through *Maundy Thursday*[*] (the day before *Good Friday*). The purpose of Lent is one of pre-

---

[+] Ash Wednesday is the first day of Lent, 46 days before Easter. The Bible recounts that Jesus fasted and spent 40 days in the wilderness before beginning his public ministry. Christians take Ash Wednesday as a public affirmation of their willingness to follow in Christ's footsteps by emulating his actions.

[*] Maundy Thursday is derived from *Mandatum novum do vobis ut diligatis invicem sicut dilexi vos* (Latin: "A new commandment I give unto you, that ye love one another, as I have loved you.")

paration of the Christian believer – through prayer, penance, repentance, and self-denial. It is usually observed by limited fasting, or giving up specific luxuries (the most common today being chocolate and soft drinks). Many cultures participate in a raucous celebration immediately before Ash Wednesday (essentially, to "get it out of their systems"). These feasts are known by names such as *Mardi Gras* (French: "Fat Tuesday") and *Carnival* (Latin: *carnevālem*, "to remove meat" – which is given up during Lent).

Minor Holidays

Pentecost   *Pentecost* (Greek: "fiftieth day") is seven weeks after Easter, and commemorates the pouring forth of the Holy Spirit on the disciples and followers as recounted in the New Testament biblical book of *Acts of the Apostles* [2:1-31]. Commonly known in the UK as *Whitsun* or *Whit Sunday*, it is seen by many as the unofficial birthday of the Christian church.

All Saints Day   In the Western churches (Roman Catholic, Protestant, and others), this is celebrated on November 1st. In Eastern churches, it falls on the first Sunday after Pentecost. Traditionally, in Roman Catholicism, it refers to all those who have died and attained heaven. Protestants have a broader concept, with it referring to all Christians, both past and present.

It appears that Pope Boniface IV consecrated the Pantheon in Rome to Mary and all of the Christian martyrs. This was May 13, 609 CE. More than a hundred years later, Pope Gregory III, making a dedication at St. Peter's, moved the date from May 13th to November 1st. After that, the May celebration was suppressed, and the November celebration was emphasized.

The pagan celebration of *Samhain* (*i.e.* Halloween) was <u>not</u> created to undermine *All Saints Day* (as some religious leaders claim), but was celebrated long before Christianity moved All Saints Day to November.

All Souls Day This is the day immediately following All Saints Day (*i.e.* November 2nd), and is observed in solemn recognition of those who have passed and not yet attained heaven. It is believed by many that prayers for these souls may aid in their purification, and result in a more speedy attainment of heaven.

Palm Sunday One week prior to Easter, Palm Sunday recalls the triumphal entry of Jesus into Jerusalem. It is often celebrated by churches distributing palm fronds to the faithful in memory of those reportedly thrown before Jesus as he entered the city in defiance of Jewish and Roman rejection of his message.

Chapter 13
Modern Divergence

The physical healing of Christian Science results now, as in Jesus' time, from the operation of Divine Principle, before which sin and disease lose their reality in human consciousness and disappear as naturally and as necessarily as darkness gives place to light and sin to reformation. Now, as then, these mighty works are not supernatural, but supremely natural. They are the sign of Immanuel, or "God with us" — a divine influence ever present in human consciousness.
— Science and Health with Key to the Scriptures, xi.

All bloody principles and practices we do utterly deny, with all outward wars, and strife, and fightings with outward weapons, for any end, or under any pretence whatsoever, and this is our testimony to the whole world. That spirit of Christ by which we are guided is not changeable, so as once to command us from a thing as evil and again to move unto it; and we do certainly know, and so testify to the world, that the spirit of Christ, which leads us into all Truth, will never move us to fight and war against any man with outward weapons, neither for the kingdom of Christ, nor for the kingdoms of this world.
.— Friends Peace Testimony (Margaret Fell, 1660)

And behold, I tell you these things that ye may learn wisdom; that ye may learn that when ye are in the service of your fellow beings ye are only in the service of your God.
.— Mosiah 2:17, The Book of Mormon

"YOU are my witnesses," is the utterance of Jehovah, "even my servant whom I have chosen, in order that YOU may know and have faith in me, and that YOU may understand that I am the same One. Before me there was no God formed, and after me there continued to be none. I – I am Jehovah, and besides me there is no savior. — Isaiah 43:10, 11

There are literally thousands of Christian denominations in existence today; but, so-called *mainstream denominations* often deny that some of these others are truly Christian. Usually, the disagreement arises over the rejection of one or more of the several common Christian concepts. Those most often the source of this disagreement are: the Trinity, Jesus as God Incarnate, the Virgin Birth, the physical resurrection, miraculous occurrences, and the nature (or existence) of Heaven and Hell.

These other groups, however, certainly consider themselves to be Christian — their definition of Christian essentially being that "a Christian is anyone who follows the life, teachings, example, and person of Christ to the best of their understanding and ability." Four well known examples of these groups follow, with very brief overviews of their core beliefs. This is followed by a summary of where they agree or disagree with the mainstream denominations.

Christian Science

History

Mary Baker Eddy

The Church of Christ, Scientist (*i.e.* Christian Science) was founded in 1879 by Mary Baker Eddy [1821-1910]. Born into a strict Calvinist family in Bow, New Hampshire, Mrs. Eddy (left) suffered from severe, chronic, physical problems as well as a string of misfortunes. As a result, Mrs. Eddy spent the better part of her life searching for meaning and solutions in life. This came to a head in 1866 when she fell on ice, and was "written off" by the doctor. This forced her to intensify her search for Truth; and, inspired by the biblical accounts of Jesus' healings, she was instantaneously healed. Ultimately, the culmination of her search was the 1870 completion of her book, *Science and Health with key to the Scriptures* (published in 1875). This led to the founding in Boston of the *First Church of Christ, Scientist* four years later. Her book became an all-time best seller, and has never been out of print since it first went into publication.

Mrs. Eddy went on to: write numerous books; found several magazines; establish a major, awared-winning newspaper; serve as pastor of her church; establish and direct the *Massachusetts Metaphysical College* (the only college ever granted a charter to issue medical degrees for spiritual healing); and, take an active role in the denomination until her death at 89.

Beliefs

Although the church does not classify itself as an Idealist faith, Christian Science is nonetheless one of the strictest Metaphysical

Idealist faiths in existence. This is not easy to summarize, but there are several significant beliefs that "stand out":

- God is All;
- God is "incorporeal, divine, supreme, infinite Mind, Spirit, Soul, Principle, Life, Truth, Love";
- the universe, including man, is the manifestation of that perfect God, and therefore is also perfect and good. In fact, "all reality is in God and His creation, harmonious and eternal. That which He creates is good, and He makes all that is made. Therefore the only reality of sin, sickness, or death is the awful fact that unrealities seem real to human, erring belief, until God strips off their disguise. They are not true, because they are not of God.";
- awareness, understanding and acceptance of the realities of God and His relationship with His creation will directly and inevitably transform the apparent, physical world to conform with this Reality;
- there is no Devil; the apparent problems in the world result from our mortal, erroneous thinking, not some malevolent spiritual being;
- absolute acceptance of the virgin birth, crucifixion and resurrection;
- acceptance of the Trinity (although defining it such that they are essentially Unitarian rather than Trinitarian — defining the deific Trinity as Life, Truth and Love – rather than Father, Son, and Holy Ghost).
- seeing Jesus as a human who understood humanity's relationship with God better than anyone else ever has, resulting in him possessing the *Christ Consciousness* (*i.e.* a consciousness "anointed of God") — He was not, however, uniquely "God incarnate" any more than we all are;
- acknowledging Jesus' healings and other miracles not as being miracles in the traditional sense of the word, but as divinely natural events resulting from Jesus' *demonstration* of his understanding of God and his relationship with Him; and,
- declaring all humans to have the potential to similarly demonstrate God's perfection if they can lift thought to a level approaching that of Jesus.

Practices

It seems to be the practices of Christian Science, rather than its beliefs, that have made it one of the more controversial faiths:

- The most notable feature of the faith is their reliance on *spiritual healing* instead of medical treatment. Although there is no church requirement to forego medical treatment, most adherents prefer to engage the services of a *Christian Science Practitioner* (a member who works and prays with the adherent to come to a personal realization of the Truth, and thereby experience a physical healing) rather than a medical doctor.
- The Christian Science movement pioneered spiritual healing, and special exemptions have been written into state law in all 50 states to enable the

practice of their faith without running afoul of the law. Many health insurance companies recognize, and will pay for, Christian Science *treatment* in lieu of a doctor. The church emphasizes that this is *spiritual healing*, and clearly differentiates that from *faith healing*. Their position is that the latter comes from blind faith and may just be auto-hypnosis, while the former is based on theological and scriptural understanding and analysis put into practice.

- A *Christian Science Reading Room* is a combination bookstore – library. They sell Bibles, religious books, reference books, the writings of Mary Baker Eddy, and magazines and the newspaper produced by the church. In addition to a sales area, there is a separate room set aside to read or study any of these materials without purchasing them; and, most of the materials can be borrowed at no charge.

- There is no ordained clergy, and the service is conducted by two *Readers* elected by the membership. The original church in Boston is known as *The Mother Church*, and all others are referred to as *branch churches*. Only worship services are conducted in the church; it is never used for weddings, funerals, social events, *et cetera*. The original Boston church (foreground) is a hewn stone church, and seats about 1,200. The Extension (background) is a connecting, domed, granite and marble structure that seats in excess of 5,000 attendees.

- Sunday services are simple, and churches are typically rather austere. There is no altar, and there are no paintings, statues, crosses or other symbols in the church. The service consists of hymns sung by the congregation, a solo, scriptural readings, and a *Lesson-Sermon* consisting of excerpts taken from the *Bible* (King James Version in English speaking countries) and *Science and Health*. The Lesson-Sermon excerpts are selected in Boston at The Mother Church and sent to all branches world wide; so, the core of the service on any given Sunday is word for word identical in every branch church in the world.

- Wednesday evening meetings are held during which members and guests are invited to recount instances of Christian Science healing.

- Members may apply to undertake intensive religious training offered by the Massachusetts Metaphysical College (now subsumed into the church hierarchy), and are awarded the right to place *C.S.* after their names. A second, higher degree (*C.S.B.*) enables them to teach for the college.

- *Christian Science Practitioners* must have the C.S. degree, must have documented evidence of proficiency, and are officially recognized and listed by The Mother Church in one of their publications.

- The church has a *Publishing Society* which publishes:
  - the writings of Mrs. Eddy;
  - other books, articles and pamphlets;
  - children's books, films and materials;
  - *The Christian Science Monitor* (a 7-time Pulitzer Prize winning secular weekly newspaper);
  - *The Christian Science Sentinel* (a weekly religious magazine);
  - *The Journal of Christian Science* (a monthly magazine which also lists churches, organizations, and officially recognized practitioners around the world); and,
  - *The Herald of Christian Science* (a monthly/quarterly magazine similar to the Journal in over a dozen non-English languages).
  - They regularly publish documented testimonies of healings that occurred as a result of the practice of Christian Science.

Summary

Periodically, the church has had to defend spiritual healing in court. This becomes a contentious and inflammatory issue if the death of a child is involved when parents relied on spiritual healing rather than medicine; and, in a few cases (approximately 50 in nearly 140 years), they have been charged with child abuse, manslaughter, or murder. As of 2013, 38 states have laws shielding them from this type of prosecution (based on the *Free Exercise Clause* of the First Amendment); 48 states allow Christian Science parents an exemption from compulsory vaccinations. The Mother Church also participates actively in seminars, conventions and academic studies of spiritual healing conducted by Harvard Medical School, Johns Hopkins, and several other academic institutions.

Latter Day Saints

History

The *Church of Jesus Christ of Latter-day Saints*, also known colloquially as either *LDS* or *Mormons*, was founded in western New York in 1830 by Joseph Smith, Jr. (right), born in Sharon, Vermont. As a child, his parents moved from one tenant farm to another in Vermont and New York. Just 14, Smith had a religious experience when he saw the images of God and Jesus. He recounted later that they had told him not to join any of the established churches, since "all their creeds [were] abomination" to God. Three years later,

Smith was visited by the angel *Moroni*, who told him to go to Cumorah Hill, near Palmyra, New York. Moroni told him that he would find a collection of gold plates on which he would find the history of early America as well as the complete Christian gospel.

Smith went to Palmyra, as told, and found gold sheaves and a translation key; but, Moroni had instructed him not to touch them for 4 years. He left them until 1827, after which he began dictating the translation to 3 scribes that worked with him. After completion (known as the *Book of Mormon*), Moroni retrieved the plates.

In 1830, Smith and 5 supporters founded the *Church of Jesus Christ of Latter-Day Saints* at Fayette, New York. The group grew quickly, but also faced ridicule and abuse; so, Smith and the group left New York for Kirtland, Ohio. This didn't last, and they moved on to Independece, Missouri. Smith's polygamy and abolitionist ideas resulted in violence against them; and, this time, they headed for Illinois, where they established their own town of Nauvoo, Illinois. In Nauvoo, some left the group and accused Smith (falsely) of gross immorality. When Smith and the City Council destroyed the newspaper facilities, his opponents went to the governor and Smith and the other leaders were arrested. Smith appealed this to the Illinois governor, but was remanded to prison in the interim. A mob later stormed the jail at Carthage, and Smith was killed in a gunfight trying to fend off the attack.

After a divisive struggle over succession (since he was just 38, no thought had been given to who would succeed Smith), most supported Brigham Young [1801-1877; left]. Young took his followers and left Nauvoo for the American southwest. Although settling by the Great Salt Lake in what is now Utah, the group was hounded by the US federal government, who objected to the official church policy condoning (even encouraging) polygamy.

Many of the Mormons (as they were derisively called) had to flee across the border into México, eventually returning to Salt Lake City after church bylaws were amended to forbid polygamy after a later revelation. Salt Lake City remains the world headquarters of the church, and is home to Temple Square — housing a

Mormon Temple, the Tabernacle (world known for its massive pipe organ), an Assembly Hall, and 2 visitor centers.

Beliefs

Traditional Mormon beliefs include the following:
- God, the Eternal Father, was once a mortal who became God.
- Final judgment will be based on good works, not the "grace of God".
- *The Book of Mormon* constitutes divine revelation, a third testament of the Bible — equal in authority with the Old and New Testaments.
- Redemption and forgiveness of sin is attained through obedience to all of the scriptures with a life of good works.
- Although all humanity will be resurrected, only the Mormon faithful will have a place in the third (*i.e.* highest) heaven.
- The Mormon church is the Kingdom of God on earth.
- Baptism is essential to return into the presence of God; therefore, *proxy baptisms* are held so that the deceased may also be reunited with God.
- Marriage can survive death, and can continue for eternity.
- Before Jesus returns to earth to rule for 1,000 years (as is foretold in Biblical prophecy), two conditions must be met: Mormons must be gathered together; and, the Jews must have returned to Jerusalem.
- Mormons espouse the Trinity, but describe Father, Son and Holy Ghost as being "one in purpose, but separate in being".
- Revelation is not restricted to one people, one area, or one time; Divine revelation continues today as it has, and will, throughout history

Practices

Although polygamy has not been sanctioned by the church since the 1890s, it continues to plague the church. Other practices include:
- tithing (Mormons are very faithful about donating one-tenth of their income to the church);
- eating meat only in moderation, and fasting at least one day each month;
- avoidance of all stimulants, including tobacco, alcohol, coffee, tea, and caffeine containing beverages;
- holding a weekly *Family Home Evening*, where the entire family remains home to sing, play games, discuss family relationships, and pray;
- supporting youth and recreational programs for their young people;
- dedicating 2 years to full time missionary work (often in their late teens or early twenties; and, entirely at their own expense);
- there are over 10,000 Mormon chapels and temples in the US alone;

- Chapels are used primarily for worship services, which are:
  - held on Sunday;
  - presided over by a *Bishop*, and conducted by one of two *Bishop's Counselors* (all priesthood positions are non-professional, unpaid lay positions); and,
  - called *Sacrament Meetings*, consisting of hymns, prayers, a sermon, and Communion (Eucharist) consisting of bread with water; the prayers are led, and the sermon is given, by a lay member of the church.
- Temples are used primarily for weddings, and other sacred ordinances, and are usually open every day except Sunday and Monday.

Summary

The Church of Jesus Christ of Latter-Day Saints is often accused of being non-Christian for three primary reasons:

- it does not interpret the Trinity in precisely the same manner as Roman Catholic and mainstream Protestant denominations;
- it accepts the scriptural validity of
  - the *Holy Bible*,
  - the *Book of Mormon*,
  - the *Pearl of Great Price*, and
  - the *Doctrine of Covenants*; and,
- it believes that Divine Revelation is still being communicated from God in the present day.

Despite the controversies that have occasionally surrounded the church, the Church of Jesus Christ of Latter Day Saints is one of the fastest growing Christian denominations in the world, and currently numbers approximately fourteen million members.

Jehovah's Witnesses

History

The foundation of the group known today as *Jehovah's Witnesses* began with the teaching of Charles Taze Russell (1852-1916). Russell (left), a former Presbyterian, Congregationalist, and Adventist organized a Bible study group in Pennsylvania in 1870. Their reviews of the Bible caused them to reject many of the more traditional teachings, such as the nature of God and the immortality of the human soul.

Within 10 years, the original group had grown to 30 congregations across 7 states. Russell decided that a more formal structure was needed, and the *Zion's Watch Tower Bible and Tract Society* was incorporated in 1884. When Russell died in 1916, the leadership of the rapidly growing group fell to Judge Joseph Rutherford. Under his leadership, the group became even more centrally controlled, and the growth rate continued to increase dramatically.

As the US entered World War I, the Society officially recommended that members abstain from entering the armed forces. If required to serve, they were advised to serve in non-combative roles. One group of members —the *Steadfasters* — opposed all support of the war; and, this later became the official position of the whole Society.

As other Bible study groups formed across the US during the early 20th century, confusion often set in. As a result, in 1931, the Society changed its public name to *Jehovah's Witnesses*. When Rutherford died in 1942, the Society presidency went to Nathan Homer Knorr. Knorr's focus was on publication, and the group greatly increased its publication efforts — including a 1961 translation of the Bible (the *New World Translation*) that is used almost exclusively by the JWs (Jehovah's Witnesses).

Their objection to the war was not solely in the US, and JW members in other countries suffered severely for their faith-based refusal to participate. The most reliable sources from Nazi Germany estimate that 90% of Jehovah's Witnesses in Germany were exterminated during the Holocaust for refusing to fight. When Canada entered World War II, it promptly banned the JW religion: children were expelled from school; parents were declared unfit, and their children placed in foster homes; adult members were imprisoned; and, those who refused to go into the armed services were sent to work camps. There are many countries where JW are still heavily persecuted, and a number of nations where their religion is illegal. Between 1938 and 1955, they brought a remarkable 45 religious discrimination suits to the US Supreme Court — winning 80% (36) of them.

From their international headquarters, they provide coördination and direction to millions of active followers in nearly 100,000 congregations from about 235 countries and autonomous regions. Headquarters is often referred to as *Bethel* by the members, and all of the officers and administrative posts of the Society are volunteer (*i.e.* unpaid, although a very small stipend is paid to defer costs).

As a measure of their total strength, attendance at the *Lord's Evening Meal* service held at Passover in 2011 numbered nearly 19½ million participants. During that same year, about 7¾ million Jehovah's Witnesses spent roughly 1¾ billion hours in various evangelistic activities around the world — including the distribution of over 800 million pieces of printed material in over 500 languages, and tens of thousands of audio and video cassettes. They also baptized more than a quarter of a million new members.

Beliefs

Many of the Jehovah's Witness beliefs are fairly typical of most fundamentalist Christian groups. Among these are that:
- the Bible is the inerrant Word of God;
- the birth of Jesus was a physical virgin birth;
- Jesus gave his life as a ransom for past and future humanity;
- divorce is not acceptable in the eyes of God;
- homosexuality is a sin against God;
- pre-marital sex is a sin;
- abortion is murder; and,
- Satan is a powerful opponent to God who must be defeated.

There are, however, numerous instances where JW disagrees with "conventional" Christian fundamentalistm. For example:
- they adhere to a strict unitarianism, and deny the Trinity (Jehovah is Supreme; Jesus is the son of God — a created being who took human form and, after his death, was resurrected as an invisible, non-material spirit being; the Holy Ghost is not a separate "person", but the force of God's interaction with the world);
- the *Heavenly Kingdom* took effect in 1914 with the invisible enthronement of Christ as king;
- this kingdom was populated by about 135,400 souls (all selected after Christ's ascension at Pentecost, and during subsequent centuries);
- selection of the remaining 8,600 (bringing the total to the 144,000 prophesied in the biblical *Book of Revelation*) was completed in 1935;
- rejection of the traditional symbol of Christianity (the cross) as being of pagan origin (translating the Greek *stauros* as "torture stake"), and maintaining that Jesus was crucified on a single upright wooden stake;
- Christ's *Second Coming* is not a physical return to earth, but an invisible event in 1914 in which Christ and Satan engaged in a heavenly battle

Ch 13 – Modern Divergence

(Christ has since ruled as *King of Kings*, and Satan was expelled to earth — World War I being a visible sign of Satan's earthly presence and the start of the worst to come);
- in the near future, the battle of Armageddon will begin (Jesus leading the forces of God — Satan leading the forces of evil; after massive suffering and extermination, the world will be purified and *God's Kingdom* will be established on earth for 1,000 years);
- following this thousand year reign, Satan and his followers will be released for a short time, after which they will be destroyed;
- all those who die before Armageddon simply cease to exist (they die, the body deteriorates, and they return to dust; but, at the time of resurrection, God will create a new body for them);
- *Hell* is just the "common grave of mankind" — people are not conscious there, and unbelievers simply cease to exist at death;
- *Salvation* requires that a person —
  - accept biblical doctrine as interpreted by the JW Governing Body;
  - be baptized as a Christian (*i.e.* Jehovah's Witness); and,
  - follow the program of works laid out by the Governing Body.

Practices

The Jehovah's Witnesses are a major publishing house. In fact, measured in the number of pieces of literature produced annually, they are the largest publishing house on earth. They produce:
- *WatchTower*, a magazine published every 2 weeks in over 200 languages, alternately printing 14 and 45 million (*i.e.* 700 million magazines a year);
- *Awake*, another semi-monthly magazine — it has a circulation of about 43 million in over 100 different languages (*i.e.* 1.12 billion per year);
- *Kingdom Ministry*, a magazine for use within the organization that is produced monthly (printing is most likely about 75 million per year);
- *Jehovah's Witnesses – Proclaimers of God's Kingdom* — a video which addresses outside criticism of their past failed predictions;
- *Should you Believe in the Trinity?* — a video which denies the traditional Christian concept of the Trinity; and,
- *Jehovah's Witnesses, The Organization Behind the Name* — a video that depicts life inside their head office.

All told, they produce about 2 billion publications each year. Nobody else even comes close! (*Time* magazine publishes about 175 million magazines per year; and, the largest newspaper, *USA Today*, publishes a little over 500 million papers a year — about a fourth of the JW output). In addition to these central publishing activities, local Jehovah's Witnesses have a total of 5 meetings each week (although not having a specific sabbath day — considering all days as holy). The typical weekly meetings are:

- *Public Talk*, typically Sunday, by an Elder on a specific subject;
- *Watchtower Study*, following the public talk, is usually a lesson based on a study article from the current *Watchtower* magazine;
- *Theocratic Ministry School* typically occurs on a weekday evening, where speakers practice giving talks and witnessing their faith;
- *Service Meeting* usually follows the Theocratic Ministry School, and includes training for specific ministry activities; and,
- *Book Study* is held sometime during the week when a portion of a *Watchtower* publication is studied in depth.

Jehovah's Witnesses are encouraged to set a goal of reading the entire Bible cover to cover once each year. Either because they believe the source of something to be pagan (marked here with a P), under the control of Satan (S), or explicitly biblically stated (B), Jehovah's Witnesses:
- do not run for public office (S);
- do not vote (S);
- do not salute the flag or pledge allegiance (S);
- do not serve in the armed forces (S);
- do not celebrate birthdays (P);
- do not use any of the traditional Christian symbols (P);
- do not celebrate any of the traditional Christian holidays (P);
- do not allow blood transfusions (B); and,
- may disfellowship (*i.e.* excommunicate) members found celebrating the 'worldly holidays' of Christmas, Thanksgiving, Independence Day, Halloween, Valentine's Day, *et cetera* (P).

No discussion of JW practices would be complete without reviewing their evangelical fervor. JWs are, literally, *Witnesses*. As such, they consider it their religious duty to proselytize the faith to all who will listen. Typically, this is done either on street corners or door to door. There is a 6 step process to spread the word that they are attempting to initiate. It goes in the following sequence:
- *Initial Contact* introduces the Witnesses and leaves literature to read;
- *Back Call* is the second call to those who accept literature. The goal is to determine the reaction to the literature, and to try to arrange a Home Study Group;
- *Home Study Group* is when friends join together in studying some of the literature in one of their homes;
- *Kingdom Hall* is the name for a JW church and, following Home Study, an invitation to a local Kingdom Hall is extended to further study and make further contacts;
- *Visiting* is attendance at the mid-week lectures and training sessions on how to become a JW evangelist; and finally,
- *Baptism* completes the process of becoming a Jehovah's Witness.

Religious Society of Friends

History

At the age of 19, a nonconformist English religious reformer, George Fox [1624-1691; right], left home on a four year search, seeking answers to questions which had troubled him from childhood. Fox searched out many of the country's spiritual leaders, but gradually became disillusioned with both the leaders and the existing Christian denominations. At the age of 23, he heard a voice, saying "there is one, even Christ Jesus, who can speak to thy condition". He interpreted this as a direct call from God to become an itinerant preacher, and to promote the concept of the *Inner Light* — preaching a divine essence within every person's soul, (*i.e.* "the seed of Christ"). It follows that everyone has an innate capacity to comprehend the *Word of God* and to express opinions on spiritual matters. The consequences of this are:
- that every man and woman has direct access to God;
- no priestly class or "*steeple house*" (as Fox called churches) is needed;
- that every person — male or female, slave or free — is of equal worth;
- that there is no need in one's religious life for elaborate ceremonies, rituals, gowns, creeds, dogma, or other "*empty forms*"; and,
- that following the inner light leads toward individual perfection through spiritual development.

Fox taught his followers to worship in silence — to speak only when they felt moved by the Holy Spirit. He promoted simple living, and the prohibition of alcohol. He spoke against holidays, sports, theater, wigs, jewelry, *et cetera*. Considering themselves friends of Jesus, they often called themselves the *Friends of Truth* (John 15:15). Also known as *Seekers* (after Truth), or simply *Friends*, their official label is the *Religious Society of Friends*.

The movement came into conflict over a number of points both with Cromwell's Puritan government and the restored monarchy of Charles II: they refused to pay tithes to the state Church; to take oaths in court; to practice *hat honor* (tipping their hats to persons in positions of power); or to go to war. They developed an intense concern for the disadvantaged, including slaves, prisoners and asylum inmates. They agitated for abolition, improvements in penitentiary living conditions, and treatment in mental institutions.

Fox was greatly persecuted during his lifetime and imprisoned many times. When he didn't remove his hat for a judge, he was asked if he was not fearful of what the judge could do to him; he said that he "quaked" at the thought, but that the judge should "tremble at the word of the Lord". The judge referred to Fox as a *Quaker*; the term stuck, and has become the popular name for the *Religious Society of Friends*. During the late 1600s, over 3,000 Quakers spent time in English jails for their religious beliefs; several hundred died there.

About 1660, a group of congregations were established called *preparative meetings*. Monthly, these groups gathered to hold a *monthly meeting*. Four times a year, these latter groups would hold a *quarterly meeting*. Finally, all of the quarters gathered annually for a *yearly meeting*.

In America, the Quakers were seen as dangerous heretics in many of the colonies, and were often deported, imprisoned or hanged. Four Quakers (including a 12 year old girl) were hanged on Boston Common in 1660; and, 30 years later, a Quaker family in Salem (Massachusetts) had their children sold into slavery to pay fines the town had levied for not attending the Puritan church (the author is descended from the daughter). Fortunately, they were bought by another Quaker family, and later granted their freedom.

Eventually, the Quakers found sanctuary in the Rhode Island colony (founded on the principle of religious tolerance), and in the Pennsylvania colony of William Penn (1644-1718). In fact, early Quakers played a major role in the creation of the colonies of West Jersey (1675) and Pennsylvania (1682), and these colonies became noted for their toleration of minority religious groups such as Jews, Mennonites, Amish, Muslims and Quakers.

In 1688, a group of *Friends* in Germantown, Pennsylvania took a public stand against slavery that is thought to be the first instance within any religious organization of the abolitionist movement in America. Initial opposition toward the Quakers faded after the *Toleration Act* of 1689, and Quakers became accepted as a denomination — with many colonial constitutions even exempting them from giving oaths in court. Quakers distanced themselves from the larger society through their simple clothing and plain language (*e.g.*

the use of "thee" and "thou" in place of "you"); and, they were collectively respected for industriousness and moral character.

In the years leading up to the Revolution, tensions between Britain and the colonies increased. The Quakers tried to remain neutral; but, during the war, most refused either to pay military taxes or to fight. This resulted in their being intensely disliked; and, some were even killed or exiled from their communities.

After the war, a number of Quaker organizations were formed to promote social change in the areas of slavery, prison conditions, poverty, Native American affairs, *et cetera.* Quakers later had a major role in conducting the *Underground Railroad*, helping runaway southern slaves escape to freedom in Canada.

Early in the 19th century, Elias Hicks began preaching the primacy of the *Christ within* and the relative unimportance of the virgin birth, the crucifixion, resurrection, and other fundamental Biblical beliefs. In time, the movement split over this into *Hicksite* and *Orthodox* factions. A second split occurred in the 1840's in the Orthodox group. The Philadelphia Yearly Meeting remained Orthodox, but the remaining Orthodox Meetings split between the evangelical *Gurneyites,* and conservative *Wilburites*. By the early 20th century, the movement was divided into four primary groups:

- *Hicksites*: the liberal wing, mostly in the east, emphasizing social reform;
- *Gurneyites*: the progressive, evangelical wing that retains pastors, and are Bible centered;
- *Wilburites*: traditionalists devoted to individual spiritual inspiration who retain traditional Quaker speech and dress; and,
- *Orthodox*: the *Philadelphia Yearly Meeting*, a Christocentric group.

The first and second World Wars created a crisis for the movement. Until that time, the Society was a pacifist organization, and Quakers who became soldiers were ejected from the community. However, in the two World Wars, many men got caught up in the nationalistic fervor, and entered the armed forces. All four branches joined during World War I to create the *American Friends Service Committee* to allow Quaker conscientious objectors to avoid military service while helping to alleviate suffering.

There are about 300,000 members worldwide, including a large group in Kenya. In fact, the greatest concentration of Quakers in the world lives in Kenya, where they follow an evangelical interpretation of Quakerism. There are 125,000 in North America. In the United States, they are concentrated in the Northeast and Midwest. Although many had settled in the South early in the 19th century, almost all later left in protest over slavery.

Beliefs

As with larger denominations, individual Quakers are highly diverse. Their beliefs range from evangelical (conservative) to liberal. The following, however, are common to most Quakers:

- A belief that there is an element of God's spirit in every human soul;
- That all persons have inherent worth, independent of their gender, race, age, nationality, religion, and sexual orientation (their opposition to sexism, racism, religious intolerance, warfare and the death penalty comes from this belief);
- simplicity, pacifism, and inner revelation are long standing Quaker beliefs (their religion does not consist of accepting specific beliefs or of engaging in certain practices; it involves each person's direct experience of God);
- there is a strong mystical component to Quaker belief. In the words of one devout Quaker, *"in Meeting for Worship, God is there. God is probably always there, but in Meeting, I am able to slow down enough to see God. The Light becomes tangible for me, a blanket of love, a hope made living."*
- Without a specific creed, several coördinating groups have created statements of faith. That of the largest group, the *Friends United Meeting* includes belief in:
  o true religion as a personal encounter with God — not ritual and ceremony;
  o individual worth before God;
  o worship as an act of seeking;
  o the virtues of moral purity, integrity, honesty, simplicity and humility;
  o Christian love and goodness;
  o concern for the suffering and unfortunate; and,
  o continuing revelation through the Holy Spirit.

As a result of being a highly socially-engaged Christian denomination, the Friends often found themselves actively involved in many of the more high profile social issues. As a result:

- they were leaders in the abolitionist movement to eliminate slavery in the United States (including such leaders as John Woolman, Elias Hicks, and John Greenleaf Whittier) – establishing the *Underground Railway*;

- they were leaders in the suffragette movement to acquire the right to vote for women (including such leaders as Susan B Anthony, Alice Paul, Elizabeth Cady Stanton and Lucretia Mott);

- they were active in the leadership of the Temperance (anti-liquor) Movement (with leaders such as Daisey Barr, Hannah Bailey, Edward Stabler and William Martin) — today, Quaker Meeting Houses are frequently home to the local meetings of Alcoholics Anonymous, Narcotics Anonymous, and Gamblers Anonymous;

- they led Prison Reform in the US and Britain – seeking to convert prisons into penitentiaries for the reform, not punishment, of convicted prisoners;

- they led mental hospital reform in the US – seeking to have people treated rather than just "locked away";

- they served as intermediaries in negotiations between Native Americans and the US government, since the natives only trusted the Quakers to look out after their interests;

- they were responsible for changes to the "swearing in" in US courts (no longer required to "swear on a Bible"), establishing Conscientious Objector rights (for non-arms bearing, alternate service), and many others.

Many Quakers do not regard the Bible as the only source of belief and conduct. They rely upon their *Inner Light* to resolve what they perceive as biblical contradictions. They also take advantage of scientific and philosophical advances from other sources.

- Although individual Quakers hold diverse views concerning life after death, few believe in the eternal punishment of individuals in a Hell.

- All aspects of life are sacramental; and, they do not differentiate between the secular and the religious. No one day or one place or one activity is any more spiritual than any other.

- Quakers have a long tradition of opposing war, and follow the lead of the early Christian movement (early Christians even refused to bring charges against others if there was a possibility of a death penalty being imposed). Together with the Amish, Brethren, 7th Day Adventists, and Mennonites, Quakers lobbied for the right to be conscientious objectors.

Practices

Most faith groups have specific beliefs that their members are expected to follow. Sometimes, as in the case of the Roman Catholic church, these requirements are numerous. The *Religious Society of Friends* is close to the opposite end of the religious spectrum on this, and rely upon spiritual searching by individual members, individual congregations and meetings (regional assemblies). This makes the *Quakers* difficult to describe. The intent here is to show mainstream Quaker practice, but Quaker meetings at both liberal and evangelical ends of the spectrum may differ from this.

Quakers have probably contributed more *per capita* to the promotion of tolerance, peace and justice than any other Christian denomination. They have been influential far beyond their numbers in many areas: promotion of world peace, abolition of slavery, fair treatment of Native Americans, universal suffrage, prison reform, improvement in mental hospitals, *et cetera*.

Many believe that Quakers simply seek a consensus; this is not true. They seek the will of God – following His leading to resolve differences. One of their documents states: "In all our meetings for church affairs we need to listen together to the Holy Spirit. We do not seek consensus; we are seeking the will of God. The unity of the meeting lies more in the unity of the search than in the decision which is reached. We must not be distressed if our listening involves waiting, perhaps in confusion, until we feel clear what it is God wants done."

Most meetings are unprogrammed: *i.e.* they are held in silence; and, attendees only speak when moved to do so. Some have programmed worship, usually led by a pastor. Typically, the congregation is facing each other, so that everyone is aware of everyone else, yet no one appears above another in status. Programmed services are often composed of prayer, Bible readings, a sermon, hymn singing, music, and "free worship based upon silent waiting," Rather than churches, services are held in a *Meeting House*.

Summary

Throughout their history, Quakers have refused to take oaths. Their belief is that one should tell the truth at all times; and, that taking an oath implies that there are two types of truthfulness — one for ordinary life and another for special occasions.

The common names of the days of the week and of the months of the year were originally either from Pagan deities or numbered using a Pagan Roman notation (*e.g.* Wednesday is from Woden's Day; Monday was Moon Day; January was named after the Ro-

Ch 13 – Modern Divergence   189

man god Janus; and, December was originally the Tenth Month). Early Quakers replaced the names with numbers, so that Sunday became First Day, Saturday Seventh Day, January First Month, and December Twelfth Month. About a hundred years ago, however, they began to revert to the common names — feeling that the public had long forgotten their Pagan origin.

Individual, autonomous congregations are still referred to as *Meetings*, and there are a number of geographically defined Yearly Meetings in North America (in Europe, a Yearly Meeting may be all of the congregations within a country). The largest Quaker associations in North America are:

- *Friends United Meeting* which coordinates 14 yearly meetings and includes about 60,000 members in North America, and 140,000 worldwide. They are an outgrowth of the Orthodox group, and publish the periodical *Quaker Life*;
- *Friends General Conference* links together about 500 meetings and worship groups with some 35,000 members. They follow the original unprogrammed style of worship service, are largely an outgrowth of the Hicksite movement, and publish the *FGC Quarterly*; and,
- *Evangelical Friends International* is composed of almost 300 conservative Quaker churches in North America, involving over 30,000 members. Worldwide, their membership is about 100,000.

In Review

Listed below (next page) are eight primary tenets/beliefs often associated with Christianity. Clearly, these denominations do not adhere to all of them, but they do follow "the life, teachings, example, and person of Christ to the best of their ability and understanding.". Isn't that what all Christian denominations try to do?

Are these groups Christian denominations? They each agree with a majority of the major beliefs of traditional sects; but, there are others where they do not agree. To strict, traditionalist Christians, this is sufficient to define them as heretical non-Christians. To more liberal Christians, this consitutes a difference of understanding within a larger religious context, and does not preclude acknowledging them as fellow Christians.

An Introduction to World Religions

Tenet/Belief	Traditional Christianity	Christian Science	LDS (Mormon)	Friends (Quakers)	Jehovah's Witnesses
Jesus was a Virgin Birth	■	■	(5)	(9)	■
Jesus Christ was God Incarnate	■	(1)	(6)		
Death by Crucifixion	■	■	■	■	■
Physical Resurrection	■	■	■	(9)	(10)
Monotheistic (One God)	■	■	■	■	■
Trinitarian	■	(2)	(7)		
Man Subject to Original Sin	■	(3)	(8)	(9)	■
Actual, Eternal Heaven & Hell	■	(4)	■		

1. Although Jesus is not seen as the incarnation of God, he is seen as one who was more thoroughly imbued with the *Christ Consciousness* than anyone else to have ever lived. As such, he is the *Divine Exemplar* for humanity.

2. Although Christian Science claims to be *Trinitarian*, they define the Trinity as the three primary attributes of God: Life, Truth, and Love.

3. Christian Science believes a Perfect God could create a perfect universe (including humanity); therefore, they deny original sin. They also point out that the term *sin* was originally an archaic Anglo-Saxon archery term that meant "to miss the mark"; and, the solution for missing the mark is not punishment, but to improve one's skill until the mark is hit. The third Tenet of their Faith states: *"We acknowledge God's forgiveness of sin in the destruction of sin and the spiritual understanding that casts out evil as unreal. But the belief in sin is punished so long as the belief lasts."*

4. Christian Science sees heaven and hell as states of being, not actual places.

5. Maybe Jesus was a virgin birth; maybe not. It is not explicitly stated.

6. Jesus was not God Incarnate, but was the 'eldest spiritual son' of God.

7. Father, Son, and Holy Ghost are three separate and distinct entities.

8. Children are not born with original sin from the fall of Adam, as Christ's sacrifice absolves humanity of that inheritance.

9. Quaker beliefs on several points are individual, not denominational.

10. Jehovah's Witnesses believe that Jesus was resurrected in a *Spirit Body*, not physically.

Section IV
Islam

Despair not of the Mercy of Allah, Who forgiveth all sins. Lo! He is the Forgiving, the Merciful. — *Qur'an 39.53*

Whosoever keepeth his duty to Allah, Allah will appoint a way out for him. And will provide for him from whence he hath no expectation.. And whosoever putteth his trust in Allah, He will suffice him. Lo! Allah bringeth His command to pass. Allah hath set a measure for all things. — *Qur'an 65.2-3*

Islam was formulated as a religious institution in the Arab world, and therefore most of the terms used are in, or from, Arabic. This needs to be worded this way because Islam does not view itself as having been founded as much as explained. The reason for this can be seen in the very term *Islam*, which means "submission to the will of God". Obviously, both God and submission to His will existed long before oral teachings of the prophet Muhammad were recorded as the Qur'an (the Islamic scriptures).

The Arabic root of the word *Islam* (*s-l-m*) means "peace", and is closely related to the Hebrew word from the same root that is usually rendered in English as *shalom*. This comes from the peace and social stability that is seen to inevitably arise from submission to the will of God. It is also the source for several other related terms. It is the selection and placement of vowels (for verbal pronunciation) that determine the precise meaning.

- Shalom – peace
- Salem – place of peace
- Solomon – man of peace
- Salome – woman of peace
- Absalom – father of peace
- Islam – submission to the will of God
- Muslim – one who submits to the will of God

- Shelem – a peace offering
- Shalam – a covenant of peace

Chapter 14
Islamic Foundations

Let there be no compulsion in religion. Truth stands out clearly from error; whoever rejects evil and has faith in God has grasped the most trustworthy, unfailing handhold. And God hears and knows all things. — *Quran 2:256*

I like Muhammad a lot, because he's like us more than anybody else. Jesus is just so exalted, and Buddha is just so exalted, it's almost beyond our reach. — *Dr. Deepak Chopra*

Life of Muhammad

Muhammad was born in 570 CE in the town of Mecca. At the time, Mecca was a small mountain town in the high desert plateau of western Arabia. His name is derived from *Hamada* (an Arabic verb: "to praise"); and, he was the first and only son of Abd Allah bin Al-Muttalib and his wife, Amina bint Wahb. Abd Allah died before Muhammad's birth, and he was raised by his mother. Initially, he was cared for by a wet nurse from a local, nomadic tribe named Halima; and, he grew up in this hill country, learning to speak (but not read or write) their pure Arabic.

At about five, Muhammad's mother took him to Yathrib, an oasis town a few hundred miles north of Mecca. They went to visit his father's grave, and stayed with relatives while there. On their way home, Amina fell sick and died. She was buried in the village of Abwa on the Mecca-Yathrib Road. Halima, as his nurse, brought the new orphan back to Mecca, and left him with his paternal grandfather, Abdul Al-Muttalib. Mecca was Arabia's most important pilgrimage center (home of the *Kaaba*, a granite cuboid building ~40 ft along each edge; right), and Abdul Al-Muttalib was its most respected leader. It was from his grandfather that Muhammad was first exposed to the essentials of leadership he would use in later life. Abdul controlled important pilgrimage concessions and frequently presided over Mecca's 'Council of Elders'.

Just two years later, Muhammad's grandfather died; so, now eight years old, Muhammad passed to his father's brother, Abu Talib. Muhammad grew up in this uncle's home, and enjoyed his protection for many years. Islamic historians often emphasize Muhammad's broken, disrupted childhood. Even the Qur'an states: "Did God not find you an orphan and give you shelter and care? And He found you wandering, and gave you guidance. And he found you in need, and made you independent" (93:6-8).

His uncle, Abu Talib, was not a wealthy man; and, the added care of raising his nephew undoubtedly put strain on his modest resources. So, as a young boy, Muhammad worked as a shepherd to help pay his keep. Like his father, Abu Talib was a merchant, and often accompanied caravans to trade centers (in Arabia, and as far as Egypt, Yemen, and India). As a teenager, Muhammad often went with him on these trips. The older merchants recognized his character, and nicknamed him *El–Amin* ("the one you can trust").

In his early twenties, Muhammad went to work for a distant cousin, a wealthy widow by the name of Khadija bint Khuwaylid. Unusual for the time, she ran a caravan trade that largely operated between Mecca and the areas to the north (*i.e.* Syria). Muhammad often made these runs, and always returned with a profit. Impressed by Muhammad's honesty, success and character, Khadija eventually proposed marriage; and, they were married in 595 CE. At the time, he was twenty-five; she was nearly forty. Muhammad continued to manage Khadija's business, and their years together were pleasant and prosperous. They had six children: two sons (both died as infants), and four daughters. During this period, Mecca also grew, becoming a wealthy trading center controlled by an elite group of clan leaders.

Traditionally, the area's religious views had been highly idolatrous. With new wealth and materialism, the moral and ethical character of the town deteriorated rapidly; and, this deeply disturbed Muhammad. He began to take long retreats in a mountain cave outside town, where he would fast and meditate. On one occasion, after a number of vague experiences, Muhammad was visited by a "presence" that he came to recognize as the angel *Jibra'il* (Arabic for "Gabriel", the archangel who also appears in Jewish,

Christian, and Baha'i scriptures). Gabriel instructed Muhammad, and had him recite this back to him. These 'messages from God' shook Muhammad to the core, and it was several years before he dared to talk about it outside his immediate family.

After several similar experiences, Muhammad finally began to reveal the messages he was receiving to his tribe. (These were later gathered and written down, and became the *Qur'an*, Arabic for "recitations", the Islamic scripture). Over the following years, Muhammad and his followers were initially ridiculed, then persecuted, and finally physically attacked for renouncing the traditional tribal faith. Muhammad's message was monotheistic, and the tribal faith was polytheistic. For several years, the Quraysh (a dominant tribe in Mecca) levied a ban on trade with Muhammad's people. The result was near famine conditions. Late that decade (619 CE), both Khadija and Abu Talib died; without their protection, the Quraysh tried to assassinate Muhammad.

With this new vulnerability and renewed hostility, Muhammad and his few hundred followers emigrated from Mecca to Yathrib (the town where his father was buried). The local leaders there were engaged in a vicious civil war, and they welcomed this 'outsider' known for his wisdom to act as mediator. Yathrib soon became known as Medina ("City of the Prophet"). Muhammad remained here for the next six years, building the first Muslim community and gradually gathering more and more followers.

The Quraysh in Mecca did not take Muhammad's new success lightly, and launched three major battles over the next three years. Of these, the Muslims won the first (the *Battle of Badr*, in March, 624 CE), lost the second (the *Battle of Uhud*, in March, 625 CE), and outlasted the third (the *Battle of the Trench* and the *Siege of Medina*, in April, 627). Finally, in March, 628 CE, a treaty was signed which recognized the Muslims as a community, and gave them the freedom to move unmolested throughout Arabia. However, allies of Mecca breached the treaty only a year later.

By this time, power had shifted toward Medina; and, in January, 630 CE, they launched a counter-offensive against Mecca. As they marched the 210 miles (more if they didn't go in a straight line), they were joined by tribe after tribe. By the time they reached

Mecca, they had swelled to a massive force, and the local people of Mecca acquiesced — without bloodshed. Muhammad then returned to live in Medina. In just three years, he unified most of the Arabian Peninsula under Islam; and, in March, 632 CE, he returned to Mecca one last time in a pilgrimage. Tens of thousands of Muslims joined him. After the pilgrimage, he returned to Medina; and, following a brief illness, he died there (June 8, 632 CE). He is buried on the grounds of the mosque in Medina.

A frequent criticism from non-Muslims is Muhammad's polygamy; so this needs to be addressed. The best records available indicate that Muhammad had 12 or 13 wives (Arabic: *Ummahat ul-Mu'minin* – Arabic for "Mothers of the Believers"). These were:

- Khadija bint Khuwaylid — his first and, while she was alive, only wife;
- Sawda bint Zam'a — a widow married after Khadija had died;
- Aisha bint Abi Bakr — aged ~6 at the marriage, Aisha was the daughter of Abu Bakr, and married Muhammad at his request[*];
- Hafsa bint Umar — widowed when her husband died in battle;
- Zaynab bint Khuzayma — widowed when her husband died in battle;
- Hind bint Abi Umayya — a widow with young children, a devout Muslim, and whose husband had died in battle fighting for Islam;
- Zaynab bint Jahsh — a widow, and Muhammad's cousin;
- Rayhana bint Zayd ibn Amr — a slave captured after a major battle, historians dispute whether she was his wife or concubine;
- Juwayriyya bint al-Harith — a widow and daughter of a defeated chief;
- Ramlah bint Abi Sufyam — the widowed daughter of the Quraysh leader, after a treaty was signed between them;
- Safiyah bint Huyeyy — a widowed noblewoman from a local Jewish tribe;
- Maymuna bint al-Harith — the sister-in-law of a longtime ally.
- Maria al-Qibtiyya — an Egyptian Christian slave sent to Muhammad as a gift by a Byzantine official; and,

Note that, while Khadija was alive, she was Muhammad's only wife. After she died, he was polygamous; however, these were either (a) proposed by the wife; (b) requested by the girl's father; or, (c) a widow with no other means of support. In some cases, it was

---

[*] According to all accounts, Aisha remained in her parents' home until she was 9 or 10, at which time the marriage was consummated (most likely after her 1st menstrual cycle, making her a woman, not a child).

actually a combination of these. Most were older than Muhammad, and pre-deceased him. All factors considered, the multiple marriages appear to be reasonably noble in purpose, and hardly a reason to criticize either him or the faith.

Foundations and Growth

After Muhammad's death, Abu Bakr (his father-in-law), and Umar* devised a system which maintained Islam's stability. Accepting the title caliph (Arabic *kaliphar*: "deputy of the Prophet"), Abu Bakr began to militarily enforce his authority over the Arabian followers of Muhammad; however, Abu-Bakr died just two years after replacing Muhammad. Umar followed him as the second caliph, and quickly began a highly successful campaign against the neighboring empires. By the year 637 CE, Umar's forces occupied the capital of Persia, Ctesiphon.

The following year, Umar's forces defeated the Romans at the *Battle of Yarmouk* – giving the Muslims control over Palestine. Before entering Jerusalem, however, Caliph Umar entered into a covenant with the Jewish population pledging protection of their religious freedom. With no Jewish resistance, he moved north and gained control over Syria, Lebanon, and Iraq by 641 CE.

It was about this time that Islam spread west into Egypt. The Christian Archbishop invited the Muslims to help free Egypt from their Roman oppressors, and illustrates the early alliances that were formed with Christians and Jews – largely due to Muslim guarantees of religious freedom for them (which they upheld).

Umar died in 644 CE, and was replaced by Caliph Uthman˙. Uthman was a member of the Umayyad clan, and protests arose in support of making Ali the third Caliph instead of Uthman. Ali was both a cousin and son-in-law of Muhammad, and many believed that Muhammad had wanted Ali to assume control after his death

---

* Umar ibn al-Khattab [579 – 644] was a companion and follower of Muhammad. He was the second leader of Islam after Muhammad, and was known as a brilliant military and political leader: spreading Islam by conquering the Persian Empire as well as about ⅔ of the Byzantine (Eastern Roman) Empire. Commonly known to Muslims as *al-Faruq* ("he who knows truth from falsehood"), he was assassinated by a captive Persian servant.

♦ Uthman ibn Affan [579 – 656], Third Caliph, followed Abu Bakr and Umar.

(they had accepted Abu Bakr and Umar, but a Umayyad was too much for them to bear). The supporters of Ali formed a separate party (Arabic: *shi'ah*) in support of Ali and his sons, and this became the source of the modern division of *Shi'ite Islam*. Uthman was the first caliph from the Umayyad clan (a division of the larger Quraysh tribe that had originally fought Muhammad); and (after 5 years of rule by Ali*), it was leaders from the Umayyad clan that served as Caliph for nearly the next hundred years.

By 654 CE, Islam had spread across all of North Africa, and two years later Caliph Uthman was murdered. The leadership fell to Ali, the son-in-law of Muhammad, but he was described by contemporaries as 'short, fat, late fifties, and politically and militarily inexperienced'. Conflicts arose, and Ali was murdered (probably by Uthman's followers) in 661 CE.

Through some complicated and obscure processes, the next Caliph – who would essentially establish the caliphate as hereditary (the *Umayyad Dynasty*) – was Mu'awiyah. He was not, however, what most non-Muslims would recognize as an Islamic leader, as both his chief financial advisor and his wife were Christian. He had previously been the Islamic governor of Syria, and his reign there had been both stable and peaceful (largely as a result of his acceptance of participation by Jews and Christians). It was reported that Muslims and Christians even met and prayed together in Syria during his reign. Under this Dynasty, Islam spread to become one of the largest empires in history (left): from the Atlantic in the west to India in the east.

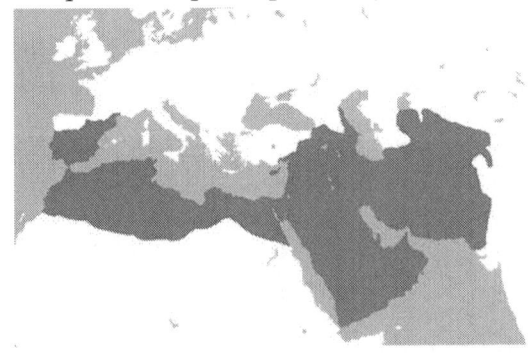

---

* After Uthman was assassinated, there were 3 main contenders to replace him. With internal dissension, all three declined the caliphate. They all met in the Mosque at Medina on June 18, 656 CE; and, under strong pressure from both rebels and companions of Muhammad, Ali finally accepted.

By the start of the 8th century (700 CE), mysticism had become a factor in Islamic theology. Known as *Sufism*, this mysticism can be identified by an individual's effort to form an intimate relationship with Allah (*i.e.* God). Their objective was to promote spiritual harmony with the physical life – resulting in a *mystical union* of the spiritual and material. Sufism blossomed in the 8th century CE.

Under the Umayyad Dynasty, Tariq ibn Malik (a military commander) crossed the narrow Straits of Gibraltar and invaded what is now Spain. In only 8 years, he had conquered nearly all of the Iberian Peninsula (*i.e.* Spain, Portugal, and even parts of southern France). Although they would lose those areas in France, Muslims ruled Spain and Portugal for more than 500 years, and continued to rule southeastern Spain for another 250 years after that.

Throughout areas under Islamic control, education and knowledge were held in the highest respect*. Writings of early Greek philosophers, mathematicians, and scientists were translated into Arabic and preserved (while European governments were burning them). Rhazes, a mediæval Islamic physician considered the greatest mediæval doctor in the world, discovered the difference between measles and smallpox (865 CE). Less than a hundred years later, Al-Farabi was considered the greatest Muslim philosopher (Arabic: *faylasuf*), and was teaching that an enlightened individual could perfect his life through intellect and philosophy without being corrupted by common public beliefs.

Internal divisions and disagreements combined with military losses (*e.g.* to Spanish, Persian, Mongol, and the Crusades) to weaken and fracture the once powerful and unified Umayyad Dynasty. European influence came to an end when Ferdinand of Aragon and Isabella of Castile♦ finally forced the Muslims to abandon the Iberian Peninsula.

---

* The three earliest Christian degree-granting universities were University of Bologna (1088), the University of Paris (1150), and Oxford University (1167). By comparison, the earliest comparable Muslim schools were al-Karaouine University (founded by a woman, Fatima al-Fihri) in Morocco (859), al-Azhar University in Egypt (950), and a string of medical schools across northern Africa and Spain during the mid to late 800s.

♦ The same two who sponsored Christopher Columbus' voyages.

Since then, the spread of Islam has largely been divorced from politics (although many of those states who attained majority Muslim populations established themselves as Islamic republics). The largest Islamic country in the world today is Indonesia, converted largely by traders and Sufi mystics. In fact, the Constitution of Indonesia was designed to illustrate that same tolerance shown by Mu'awiyah more than 1300 years earlier, a national policy enshrined in what is known as *Panchashila* (the "five principles"), which are:

- belief in one, and only one, God;
- just and civilized humanity;
- unity in diversity of Indonesia;
- democracy guided by inner wisdom; and,
- social justice for all of the people of Indonesia.

These were implemented by establishing the following:

- a requirement for all citizens to carry a national ID card which, along with other things, identifies the religion of the holder;
- a requirement to select from one of 6 recognized religions, which are:
  + Muslim (roughly 200 million followers);
  + Christian (*i.e.* Protestant, at about 20 million);
  + Hindu (comprising 90% of the island of Bali with approximately 10 million adherents);
  + Catholic (distinguished from Christian, with about 8 million);
  + Buddhist (with approximatelty 4 million; and,
  + Confucian (recognized in 2006, and with 1 to 2 million adherents).

Atheism is not recognized as a legitimate national option; and, marriages must be between partners of the same faith (if not, one of them must convert to make them the same).

Chapter 15
Historical Development

Conduct yourself in this world as if you are here to stay forever, and yet prepare for eternity as if you are to die tomorrow. — Muhammad

It is better to sit alone than in company with the bad, and it is better still to sit with the good than alone. It is better to speak to a seeker of knowledge than to remain silent, but silence is better than idle words. — Muhammad

Growth

Islam began as an institutional religion during the lifetime of Muhammad, and has been growing ever since — more rapidly, in fact, than any other religious faith on earth. It has been calculated that the average annual growth rate of Islam over the first nearly 1400 years of its organizational existence has been 1.51%; and, that growth rate has been even higher in the time period that began with the 21st century (1.84%). This modern growth rate is higher than that of Hinduism (1.52%), Christianity (1.32%), and world population as a whole (1.12%). This means that, not only is Islam increasing its *market share* (*i.e.* the % of the world that is Muslim), but it is also gaining ground on what has been the largest religion in the world for more than a thousand years (Christianity).

The remarkable growth of Islam has occurred mostly as a consequence of growth over the past century. There are conflicting opinions as to what the future is likely to hold; however, one of the most respected sources on religion in the world* has projected continued rapid growth followed by a leveling out of the growth rate during the latter part of the 21st century.

Divisions and Movements

There were no divisions within Islam while Muhammad was alive; but, they began to appear almost as soon as he passed. Muhammad foresaw them, but not as a positive development.

---

* The Pew Research Center's Forum on Religion and Public Life.

Early Forms of Islam

Kharajis

One of the first apparent divisions to appear within Islam was that of the *Kharajis*. This group rebelled from the conventional views of the early Muslims and what they perceived as the misrule of the third caliph (Uthman). They were active supporters of a narrow interpretation of the concept of *jihad* (in this sense, either holy wars or militancy), and this led to frequent outbursts of violence. The result of being so militant was that they were virtually exterminated during the first two hundred years of Islam.

Mu'talizahs

The *Mu'talizahs* (Arabic: "seceders") viewed the Qur'an as temporal, not divine, and believed that human reason was all that was required to distinguish good from evil (divine revelation not being necessary). Allah was seen as a pure and indescribable essence with no specific external attributes. This sect became popular and, by the ninth century, was effectively the official branch of Islam (whatever that is). It was reaction to the Mu'talizahs that led to what is considered to be modern "orthodox" Islam.

Modern Forms of Islam

Sunni

The *Sunnah al-jamaah*, or Sunni division, is the largest of all current Islamic groupings, and includes roughly 85% of all Muslims world wide. By definition, *sunnah* means "well trod path" in Arabic. The other term, *al-jamaah*, is a "consolidated majority". Taken together, *sunnah al-jamaah* thus translates from Arabic into English as the "well trod path of the consolidated majority". As the principle division of Islam, it includes all adherents who subscribe to the generally accepted (*i.e.* majority) interpretation of Muhammad's teachings. Another phrase sometimes suggested as a possible source for the name Sunni — *ahl as-sunnah* — comes into English as the "people of the path".

Interestingly, the Sunnis do not generally adopt an attitude of exclusivity or superiority with regard to other sects of Islam. It has been widely ascribed to Muhammad as having once told his followers that "differences of opinion among my community are a blessing"; and, it is difficult to condemn those who bring a blessing upon your own faith. This has generally led the Sunni to adopt a stance of tolerance and accommodation that is unusual in most religious bodies. This is not to say that they see the adherents of the other divisions as correct; they don't. Muhammad reportedly foresaw an eventual 73 divisions within Islam; but, he also expected the followers of 72 of them to end up in Hell. Followers of these sects are unprotected by God; however, it is not seen as man's place to condemn or shun them. In order to condemn certain schisms while tolerating others, Sunni Islam has adopted a number of non–Qur'anic historical customs. Among these are their view that the earthly, temporal states are a political reality which they must accept so long as it accommodates the proper practice of Islam.

Wahhabism

Wahhabism is named for, and follows the teachings of, Muhammad ibn Abd-al-Wahhab [1703 – 1792]. In agreement with most Sunni positions, Wahhabism has been described as "one of the most conservative forms of Islam". It is fiercely monotheistic, and classifies a number of practices as "polytheistic innovations" (*e.g.* listening to hymns in praise of Muhammad, celebrating his birthday, *et cetera*). It has become the prevailing form of Islam in Saudi Arabia, Kuwait, and Qatar. Many consider Wahhabism to be supportive of violence, but this is most often derived from guilt by association (since Ossama bin Laden was a Wahhabist).

Shi'i

The other major form of Islam today is Shi'i Islam. Late in Islam's 1st century, a political division led to the creation of the Shi'ite sect. Over time, the *Shi'ah* (adherents of *Shi'i Islam*) evolved theological differences with the Sunni majority branch of Islam. Relying heavily on inspiration and revelation (through an *imam*, a divinely guided individual) to reveal the truth of the Qur'an, the Shi'ah tend to be more mystical than their Sunni counterparts. They have a strong belief in jihad as an appropriate means to spread Islamic truth and values, and are commonly viewed by non-Muslims as being the equivalent of Muslim fundamentalists.

Today comprising nearly 15% of the global Muslim population, that has been projected to drop to about 10% between 2030 and 2040. This projection is largely the result of two related facts: Iran is the largest national population of Shi'ah Islam, and has one of the lowest fertility rates (*i.e.* birth rates) in the Muslim world.

All Muslims accept Muhammad as the final prophet of Allah. However, Sunni Muslims maintain that he never designated his successors (*i.e.* Caliphs), while Shi'ite Muslims believe that he explicitly designated his son-in-law, Ali. Both groups acknowledge Abu Bakr, Muhammad's father-in-law, as the first leader of the faithful following Muhammad's death in 632 CE.

Sunni Muslims selected Caliphs by consensus, and his authority was strictly temporal, not spiritual. Spiritual leadership is granted solely to the Qur'an and the example left to us by Muhammad. Caliphs thus could not declare new divine decrees, and could only enforce those already existing (*i.e.* revealed through Muhammad).*

Shi'ites believe that society is in need of continued spiritual, as well as temporal, leadership. This leadership is provided by an *imam*. Although *Nubuwwah* (essentially, "prophethood") ended with Muhammad, Shi'ites believe this was then followed temporally by *Imamah* (*i.e.* leadership through Muhammad-designated imams). This follows from Ali through his direct descendents – believed to have direct contact with Allah, which makes their judgment infallible (investing them with the knowledge and authority required to interpret the Qur'an).

Since Shi'ites believe only imams had the right to be Caliphs, and Sunnis chose Caliphs by consensus (rejecting the idea of spiritual infallibility), all Caliphs who were not imams are considered usurpers of the Caliphate by faithful Shi'ites.

Sufi
The Sufi movement arose as a reaction to the worldliness of the early Muslims. Adhering to an ascetic lifestyle, the Sufis directed religious zeal to missionary efforts, and converted much of India,

---

* The final Caliphate was under the authority of the Republic of Turkey, which did away with the office on March 3, 1924.

Central Asia, Turkey and sub-Saharan Africa without resorting to jihad. Sufis try to attain divine love and knowledge through a direct, personal, religious experience. In pursuit of this goal, the Sufi relies on mysticism to ascertain the nature of God and man, and then uses this to facilitate the process of experiencing the presence of divine love and wisdom in the world.

Ahmadiyya

Although not mentioned in the Qur'an, the *Mahda* concept is widely (although not universally) accepted in Islam. The *Mahdi* (Arabic: "guided one") is seen as a future redeemer, converting the world into a perfect and just society prior to the Day of Resurrection. With no specific reference to this in the Qur'an, different Islamic cultures have widely divergent views of the Mahdi.

Late in the 19th century in the Punjab (northern India), Mirza Ghulam Ahmad [1835 – 1908] developed quite a group of followers. Ahmad [right] claimed the *Mahdi*, the coming *Messiah*, and the *Second Coming of Christ* are, in fact, all referring to the same event; and, Ahmad claimed to be that individual. As such, he believed that he was here to reinvigorate Islam, and to begin a virtual Islamic renaissance. Ahmadis (followers) consider themselves to be true Muslims, and base all spiritual authority in the Qur'an and Hadith (collections of the words and deeds of Muhammad). Most Muslims are highly skeptical of Ahmad's claims, and question whether or not his claims conflict with the finality of prophethood with Muhammad. As a result, most Muslims refuse to accept Ahmadiyya as a true Islamic expression, and consider Ahmadis to be either non-Muslims or Islamic heretics.

Druze

Druze is perhaps the only religion in the world named for an enemy of their faith! The name is derived from *Nashtakin ad-Darazi*; adherents to the secretive faith refer to themselves as *ahl al-Tawhid* (literally, "people of One God"). The history of the group is shrouded in the mists of time, but it is safe to assume that they began as Muslims isolated in the mountains of Syria and Lebanon. They later experienced significant influence by the *Ismailis*, a small Shi-ite sub-sect. They also incorporate beliefs believed to come from Gnostic, neo-Platonic, or Pythagorean philosophies.

Often referred to as an Islamic sect (which is why this is placed here in this review), they are also often considered a separate religious entity (granted their own religious court systems in Lebanon, Syria, and Israel). Israeli Druze are considered a distinct ethnic community, work well with the Jewish government, serve in the Israeli military, and comprise a significant portion of the Israeli Border Patrol. The basic tenets of their faith are secret, and they do not accept converts. Nevertheless, it is known that they:
- are strictly monotheistic, and accept the unity of God;
- believe God interacts with the world with Divine emanations;
- accept reincarnation (human-only);
- reject smoking and alcohol;
- refrain from eating pork products; and,
- practice monogamy in their marriages.

Chapter 16
Scripture, Concepts, Practices & Holidays

And Allah endows those who avail themselves of [His] guidance with an ever-deeper consciousness of the right way; and good deeds, the fruit whereof endures forever, are, in thy Sustainer's sight, of far greater merit [than any worldly goods], and yield far better returns. — *Qur'an 19:76*

Scripture

Islam is another scriptural religion. In this case, the scripture is a collection of transmissions from Allah (Arabic: "the God") to humanity — *via* the angel Gabriel to the Prophet Muhammad. This collection is known as the *Qur'an*.

Qur'an is an Arabic term that literally means "recitations". Alternatively known in English as Qur'an, Quran, Alcoran, and Koran, it is the collection of revelations brought by Gabriel over a period of nearly 23 years, and which Muhammad then recited to his followers. Muslims consider it to be the final revelation of God to humanity. In some ways, the Qur'an [right] is almost mythical in nature —rarely offering detailed accounts of historical events, and typically emphasizing moral significance rather than historicity.

The Qur'an consists of 114 *suras* (chapters) that vary widely in length, and comprise a total of 6,236 verses. It is organized and presented in roughly reverse chronological order — the later (and typically longer) revelations at the beginning of the collection, and the earlier (typically shorter) revelations nearer the end.

According to Shi'i, Sufi and Sunni scholars, Ali compiled a complete version of the Quran immediately after Muhammad's death. The order of this text differed from that compiled later, during Uthman's era. Despite this, and although Ali retained his own collection, he had no objection or resistance to the new, standardized version.

After seventy reciters* were killed in the *Battle of Yamama*, the first caliph (Abu Bakr) decided to collect the different chapters and verses into a single volume. He selected a group of reciters, collected chapters and verses, and produced several hand-written copies of the complete new book.

In about 650, as Islam expanded beyond Arabia into Persia, the Middle East, and North Africa, the third caliph (Uthman ibn Affan) ordered the preparation of an official, standardized version, to preserve the sanctity of the text (he may have had political motives as well, as this provided a 'universal' version of the revelations for the growing empire). Earlier copies in the hands of Muslims in outlying areas were collected and sent to Medina where, on orders of the Caliph, they were destroyed either by burning or boiling. This later compilation remains the authoritative Qur'anic text to this day. The Quran, in its present form, is generally considered by academic scholars to record the words spoken by Muhammad because searches have found no differences of real significance.

The Quran speaks highly of the relationship it has with former religious books (*i.e.* the Torah and the Gospel), and explains similarities by saying all of them were revealed by the one true God.

Although the details are often somewhat different, the Qur'an tells the stories of many of the people and events also told in Jewish and Christian scriptures. Prophets mentioned in the Qur'an who also appear in these other scriptures include Adam, Enoch, Noah, Eber, Shelah, Abraham, Lot, Ishmael, Isaac, Jacob, Joseph, Job, Jethro, David, Solomon, Elijah, Elisha, Jonah, Aaron, Moses, Zechariah, John the Baptist, and Jesus. The one that is mentioned the most frequently is Moses; Jesus is actually mentioned more often than Muhammad; and, Mary is mentioned more often in the

---

* The term *reciter* refers to an individual companion of Muhammad who had completely memorized the text of the revelations.
♦ After Muhammad died in June 632, several local tribes revolted against Medina leadership; Abu Bakr organized 11 corps to battle the rebels, and a major battle occurred near Yamama in December of that year; 70 of the companions of Muhammad who had memorized the revelations were killed in that battle.

Qur'an than she is in the Christian New Testament. Muslims acknowledge that the revelations in these other scriptures (*i.e.* the Torah and Gospels) are, in fact, divine revelations from God.

Although Muslims maintain that the Qur'an has remained unchanged (and faithful to the original revelation) throughout history, there are academic doubters. The earliest known copy of the text is kept at the Manuscript House of Sana'a (the capital of Yemen), and has been carbon-14 dated to about 795 CE. This early version has a number of areas that differ from the modern texts:

- unusual verse sequencing;
- rare styles of spelling;
- artistic embellishments;
- parts written in a rare, early script; and,
- minor content variations.

Although traditionally considered one of the first texts written in modern Arabic (and thus a primary source for language style), many scholars believe that the initial collection would have been written in what was then the spoken language of the area: a form of Syro-Aramaic; and,it does seem logical that one would most likely write something in the same language one spoke.

Arabic, like all languages, does not "map" directly into other languages — grammar, vocabulary, tenses, cases, and other complexities of a language mean that a translator can not just do a 'word for word' translation. They must decide how to phrase something in the target language that accurately reflects the original meaning. This was further complicated by the fact that the years immediately following Muhammad's life saw rapid and dramatic changes in the Arabic language – rendering many original wordings nearly unintelligible for modern readers. For this reason, any translation must be considered an interpretation; and, even reading it in the original Arabic may not leave the reader with a full understanding of the original intent.

The Qur'an has been translated into many languages (including English); but, these translations are considered to be *glosses* for personal use or study, and are never consulted in serious religious discussion. The first translation recorded was into Persian by Salman al-Farisi during the 7th century. Although born a Zoroastrian, having converted to Christianity as an adolescent, and having been owned as a slave by a Jew, Salman met Muhammad in Medina and converted – becoming one of his most devoted and loyal followers.

The first western translation (Latin; 1143 CE) was by Robert of Ketton, and the initial English translation was in 1649 by Alexander Ross. Several other, more scholarly translations appeared over the years; but, all were by non-Muslims. One of the earliest, most popular, English translations was by Maulana Muhammad Ali.

Within the Shi'a community, the only valid scriptural text is the Qur'an. Since they accept the spiritual leadership and guidance of imams, there is no need for them to conduct an exegesis of the Qur'an to understand its meaning — an imam can explain it.

Within the Sunni community, however, there are no contemporary spritual guides. Therefore, understanding the context in which a Quranic verse might have occurred became very important. Originally, this was transmitted verbally. Older followers who had known, and travelled with, Muhammad would explain to new adherents the circumstances under which a verse might be better understood. These verbal traditions would have died along with the adherents who remembered them if they had not been transmitted from teacher to student, and eventually committed to writing: collected traditions of the words and deeds of Muhammad known as the *Hadith*. They carry no weight in Shi'ite circles, but are invaluable to Sunni Muslims as both clarifying the Qur'an, and as appropriate guides when there is no specific Quranic instruction.

Concepts

The Qur'an is the basis for virtually all aspects of Islamic life: religious, social, legal, *et cetera*; and, the importance of the Qur'an to the Muslim faithful cannot be overstated. The basic tenets of Islam are referred to in Islamic law as *ibadat*, or religious duties (commonly called the *five pillars*). They consist of:
- *shahada* – witnessing to God, His Oneness, and the status of Muhammad;
- *salat* – five daily prayers to God (at set times, in a prescribed manner);
- *sawm* – fasting for the Islamic month of Ramadan;
- *zakat* – annual donation of a portion of one's income to the work of God (not spontaneous charity, which is to be practiced continuously); and,
- *hajj* – a pilgrimage to Mecca at least once in one's life.

Ch 16 – Scripture, Concepts, Practices & Holidays

Although not one of the five pillars, the Islamic concept that stands out most with non–Muslims is their total avoidance of, and objection to, graven images (which is why no portrait of Muhammad is included here). This results in a lack of statuary and iconography in mosques that is rare in other major religions. When tourists enter the Court Chamber of the US Supreme Court in Washington, DC, they see the judicial bench in front of them. On the north wall of the courtroom is a marble frieze that depicts 18 of the "great lawgivers" of history:

- Menes
- Solomon
- Draco
- William Blackstone
- Hugo Grotius
- Charlemagne
- Hammurabi
- Lycurgus
- Confucius
- John Marshall
- Saint Louis
- Muhammad
- Moses
- Solon
- Augustus
- Napoleon
- King John
- Justinian.

But, having a statue or carving of Muhammad on public display has generally been considered blasphemous by devout Muslims (historically, there have been very limited exceptions to this in Turkish and Persian cultures). Following renovations, *Karamah* (Muslim Women Lawyers for Human Rights) approached the court administrators to explain their objection to the frieze. Although the court offered to change wording in brochures and papers sold with tourist-quality miniatures, they refused to alter the original work by sculptor Adolph Weinman.

Islam is fiercely monotheistic, and Muslims are seen as an undivided community with a common faith — despite what appear to be rather obvious divisions to non–Islamic observers. The scriptural *Qur'an* is regarded as the word of God, and Muhammad as the last of a series of messengers of God. Others in this series include Abraham, Moses, Buddha and Jesus; all of these messengers are seen as human, not divine. Muhammad is seen as the most nearly perfect of these godly messengers, but still entirely human.

God (Arabic: *Allah*), is omnipotent, omniscient and merciful. A Muslim accepts the verbal *Shahada* as a complete and accurate statement of belief: "There is no God but Allah, and Muhammad is the prophet of Allah." Along with this, there are *five articles of faith*. These are a belief in:

- one God;
- a coming Day of Judgment;
- prophets
- revealed books, or scriptures.
- angels

The articles of faith can be seen in what is expected of a practicing Muslim. Note that, just as Judaism and Christianity were influenced by Zoroastrianism, Islam (directly or indirectly) was similarly influenced (by Judaism, Christianity, and Zoroatrianism) — specifically, the beliefs in angels and a Day of Judgment.

Islam accepts that the laws of a temporal state should reflect and incorporate God's law and the theological views of the people. *Shari'ah* (Arabic: "the law") thus embraces the total life of typical Muslims. This includes everything commanded by God — either explicitly or implicitly. Both legal theory, doctrine, and actual daily practice are included. It would be considered ludicrous for a person to try to separate their material, physical, political life from their religious life. Therefore, "separation of church and state" is, in effect, a denial of faith, and is certainly not a goal to be pursued.

Holidays

Islam uses a lunar calendar for all religious purposes (Saudi Arabia also uses it for commercial purposes). A lunar calendar of 12 months is shorter than the solar calendar, so the solar dates of holidays calculated using the lunar calendar "drift" through the seasons (falling 11 or 12 days earlier on the solar calendar each year). The Islamic calendar is known as the *Hijri Qamari*, and dates are often written as 1434AH*. Years are counted beginning with the emigration of Muhammad from Mecca in 622 CE.

Milad un Nabi is Muhammad's birthday. Many Muslims consider this to be inappropriate, and regard it as a later innovation. This is a joyful holiday among those who do celebrate, and is usually observed by parents telling children stories of the life of Muhammad. Focus is on the character of Muhammad, his teachings, sufferings, and how he forgave even his most bitter enemies. The actual date is in doubt: Shi'ites observe the birth 5 days later than Sunnis.

Eid al-Fitr is a celebratory observance of the end of Ramadan. Muslims are not only celebrating the end of a month of fasting, but also thanking Allah for the help and support

---

* AH stands for the Latin *Anno Hegiræ*. 1434AH closely aligns with 2013CE.

offered throughout the preceding month in helping them maintain their self-control. Traditions include new clothes, home decorations, special services, street processions, and a major feast.

Eid al-Adha is a 4 day holiday commemorating Abraham's willingness to follow Allah's instruction (to sacrifice his son), and reflect on their own submission to Allah (and their willingness to sacrifice anything to God's wishes).

Ramadan is the ninth month of the Islamic calendar, and is a month of sacrifice and self-control. For the entire month, Muslims fast throughout the daylight hours. Anything that might distract a person from unity with God is removed – no water, food, smoking, sex, *et cetera* from dawn to dusk for the entire month. Many Muslims also use this month to try to break bad habits or tendencies.

This month-long holiday is based on several factors: the gates to Heaven are open; the gates to Hell are closed (and the devils are in chains); and, this was the month in which the Qur'an was first revealed (see Lailat ul Qadr, below). Mosques recite Qur'anic passages each day with a plan to read the entire scripture over the course of the month.

Lailat ul Qadr a holiday in the month of Ramadan during the night of which the Qur'an was actually revealed for the first time. It is said that to stand in prayer on this one night is better than to spend a thousand months in worship.

Al-Hijra is the first day of the month of Muharram, and marks the day of the emigration to Medina. As such, it is the date that marks Islam as being a community, and is celebrated as the Muslim New Year. Other than making New Year's Resolutions, this is usually a low-key holiday.

Ashura is generally a very solemn holiday. The Sunni community fasts on this day, and uses it to mark the day Noah disembarked from the Ark and the day Moses was saved from Pharoah's army by Allah. The Shi'a community observes the day to mark the martyrdom of Hussein (the son of Ali, and grandson of Muhammad).

Jumu'ah is the weekly *gathering day*. In the same manner as Judaism, Islam considers a day to begin at sundown on the prior evening. They also consider Saturday the Sabbath, although they do not observe it the way that Jews do. Friday, the day prior to the Sabbath, is known as *Jumu'ah*. A *muezzin* (who "calls the faithful to prayer") calls out to the faithful from one of the minarets of the mosque just prior to the five daily prayers. The most important of these is the Friday noon prayer (*i.e.* on *Jumu'ah*) at the mosque. Majority Muslim countries frequently have their weekends include Friday to make this more convenient (much as Christian countries include Sundays in their weekends).

Most Islamic countries conduct the weekend on Friday and Saturday, while a few (*e.g.* Saudi Arabia, Qatar, and Afghanistan) continue to observe the weekend on the more traditional Thursday and Friday.

Practices

Many common Islamic practices actually pre-date Islam itself. Many of the people that became active Muslims already followed customs associated with the other Abrahamic faiths (Christianity and Judaism) at the time; minor cultural changes may have occurred, but the fundamental practices were largely retained.

Name of God It is a common practice to pronounce the name of Allah before eating or drinking (*conf.* "saying grace").

Eat Right Handed Eating or drinking is done with the right hand only. Muslims do this because the Qur'an states that, on the Day of Judgment, the faithful will receive a record of their deeds in their right hands (while the doomed receive theirs in their left hand).

Adhaan The Adhaan is the Islamic call to prayer, and the words are an affirmation of a Muslim's total submission to the will of God. It is traditional to whisper the Adhaan into the right ear of a newborn.

Personal Cleanliness Muslims are expected to trim their moustaches (bushy, untrimmed moustaches are seen as a sign of arrogance); remove all body hair from their armpits and pubic area; keep their nails neatly trimmed; keep their nose, mouth, and teeth clean; and, circumcise their male children.

Menstruation As directed in Leviticus, Muslims refrain from all sexual contact during a woman's menstrual cycle.

Men & Women Contrary to what many in the west believe, Islam instructs that women are to be treated equally under the law. They must be treated with respect, and are not to be exploited in any way. Their sexuality is not to be an issue with anyone other than their husband.

Pre-Islamic traditions and cultures often put severe restrictions on their women, but these are localized cultural traditions and not an Islamic teaching.

Clothing Islam requires that clothing be appropriate, modest, and clean for both men and women. Women usually wear the *hijab* (head scarf) when in public; in private (with other women or male relatives), she may remove outer garments and beautify herself in any way she wants.

Cultures may interpret "modesty" in the extreme – resulting in veils, *burkas*, and the like. These are cultural interpretations of modesty, and are not required by Islam.

Eye Contact Muslims are taught to lower their eyes when talking with others (out of respect), although this may be misinterpreted in societies where eye contact is seen as a sign of sincerity.

Chapter 17
Modern Divergence

The first problem with "Islamic-related movements" is that Islam recognizes no such animal. What are being described here as related movements are, to nearly all Muslims, heretical groups that are <u>not</u> Islamic movements. Nevertheless, these are all groups that either: (a) trace their history to Islam (*e.g.* Baha'i); (b) bear a significant geographical, historical, or theological alignment with Islam (*e.g.* Sikh); or, (c) maintain that their *raison d'être* ("reason for being") is in support or defense of Islam (*e.g.* al Qaeda).

Baha'i
In truth, knowledge is a veritable treasure for man, and a source of glory, of bounty, of joy, of exaltation, of cheer and gladness unto him. Happy the man that cleaveth unto it, and woe betide the heedless.
— Epistle to the Son of the Wolf (v49), Bahá'u'lláh

Baha'i is a religion founded in Persia (Iran) during the middle of the 19th century. With steady and impressive growth, it now numbers nearly seven million across more than 200 countries. Religious growth is seen by Baha'is as a gradual, evolving educational process that is periodically spurred on by the presence of divine messengers, or *manifestations of God*.

In 1844, Siyyid Ali-Muhammad declared that he was the *Bab* (*i.e.* "gate"). This was based on a Shi'ite concept, and the local clergy saw him as a real threat to their faith. As a result, The Bab and his followers were ruthlessly persecuted, and often forced to choose either renunciation or death. The Bab himself was caught, jailed, and finally executed in 1850. A shrine to the Bab was built on Mount Carmel near Haifa, Israel, and is now a popular Baha'i pilgrimmage site. This did not end the movement, however. The Bab had promoted the religious concept of a future savior, or messiah – a concept found in Christianity, Islam, Judaism, Buddhism, Hinduism, and numerous others. He saw himself as the gate leading to that salvation. Thirteen years after his execution, Mirzá Husayn Ali (an early follower) declared that he was that savior – Bahá'u'lláh [right].

For the next 30 years, he did whatever he could to continue to spread a message of hope, peace, and unity. This was difficult, as he was repeatedly exiled from area after area – eventually living out his life under house arrest in a prison colony in Palestine. By the time of his death in 1892, there were followers in 13 Asian and African countries – especially within the Ottoman and Persian empires; and, he left a huge volume of writings. Among these writings, the four most theologically significant are:

- *Hidden Works*
- *Seven Valleys*
- *Kitáb-i-Aqdas* (The Most Holy Book)
- *Kitáb-i-Íqán* (The Book of Certitude)

Prior to his death, Bahá'u'lláh designated Abdu'l-Bahá (his son) to succeed him and serve as official interpreter of his writings; and, under his tireless leadership, the faith gained a strong foothold in Europe and the Americas as well as Asia and Africa. By the time of his death (1921), there was a strong, cohesive religious community with elected councils, appointed leaders, and a world headquarters on the outskirts of what is now Haifa, Israel (the location of the Bab's tomb).

Beliefs

The Baha'i faith is a worldly functional faith, and asceticism and monasticism were both specifically prohibited by Bahá'u'lláh. He considered the successful performance of ordinary tasks to be the only legitimate way of proving the legitimacy of one's faith. He carried this one step further by declaring that one's service to humanity was – in the eyes of God – equal in value and worthiness to both prayer and worship.

Bahá'ís are strictly monotheistic, and believe that God is the Creator of all things. God is seen as eternal, personal, unknowable, inaccessible, the source of all Revelation, omniscient, omnipresent and almighty. Although inaccessible, God is understood as conscious of His creation, and having periodically intervened on behalf of creation by sending *manifestations* to the world. These manifestations invariably result in religions that address a global need in a manner that is appropriate for the world at that time.

This idea that religions address the needs of humanity in terms appropriate for the world at that time invariably leads Baha'i to accept the legitimacy of nearly all world religions. Their founders are seen as *manifestations of God*, and their teachings are seen as expressions of the ability of a culture at that point to accept divine intervention and guidance. World history is thus seen as an evolutionary progression where each new manifestation brings a more advanced revelation to light – one that was right for the time and place where it was expressed. Baha'is do not see this as a finite process with an end point, and expect it to continue indefinitely (although they do not believe that a manifestation to enhance Bahá'u'lláh's message will be needed for a thousand years).

Baha'i teaches that the human soul becomes closer to God by recognition of God through one or more of His messengers (manifestations), conformity to their teachings, regular prayer, spiritual practices, and service to humanity. They believe that, at death, the spiritual development of the soul is evaluated and judged. As a result of this evaluation, the soul then either proceeds to evolve in the spiritual realm, or is assigned an eternity of nearness (Heaven) or distance (Hell) from the presence of God.

Baha'i emphasizes the equality of all human beings, and thus encourages the elimination of all forms of prejudice. Human diversity – ethnic, racial, sexual, physical, national, social, *et cetera* – is treated as worthy of tolerance and even appreciation; unity is the ultimate goal of all humanity.

Social Principles

Derived from Bahá'u'lláh's thousands of letters and other writings, and compounded by the even greater number of writings and talks by Abdu'l-Bahá, it is possible to extract a summary listing of the social principles and teachings to which all faithful adherents of Baha'i are expected to adhere. These would be:
- Unity of God (rejecting Trinitarian and polymorphic views of God);
- Unity of Religion (all faiths being true expressions of God for their time);
- Unity of Humanity (regardless of how it may appear);
- Gender equality;
- Elimination of bias and prejudice (in all forms);
- World peace (*i.e.* a world without conflict);
- Religion-Science harmony (with religion expressing the wholistic view of that which science sees in the particular);
- Independent investigation of truth (each pursuing God in their own way);
- Universal compulsory education (a "no human left behind" approach);

- Universal auxiliary language (to facilitate cross-cultural communication);
- Universal obedience to temporal governments (Baha'i does not encourage any form of civil disobedience);
- Avoidance of partisan politics (*i.e.* choosing sides, and pursuing specific individual programs as opposed to general group goals); and,
- Financial leveling (eliminating all extremes of wealth and poverty).

Abdu'l-Bahá (the son of Bahá'u'lláh) designated his grandson, Shogi Effendi, to serve as his successor and interpreter. When he passed in 1921, this took place as he had instructed. Shogi, however was the last living descendent of Bahá'u'lláh, so following his death in 1957, the faith organized the *Universal House of Justice*, as Bahá'u'lláh had originally devised. Once formed and staffed, this assumed permanent guidance of the faith, and is home to the governing council which directs and manages the faith.

Scripture

Scripture is a somewhat problematic concept for Baha'i. Reasons for this are several, and generally involve the number of writings that could become canonized. For this reason, Baha'i prefers to use the term *authoritative writings* rather than *scripture*.

In broad terms, *authoritative writings* include any of the works of the Bab, Bahá'u'lláh, Abdu'l-Bahá, Shoghi Effendi, and the Universal House of Justice. Since the House of Justice is still in a position to author writings, any list this broad is inherently incomplete. Because the Bab and Bahá'u'lláh are both considered to have been divine messengers, or manifestations of God, their writings take on a significance that the others do not have. Their writings may be considered *Holy Writ* (what other faiths would consider *scripture*) since they are effectively "the Word of God". In fact, although all of the writings are considered authoritative, Shogi Effendi made it clear that he considered the writings of the Bab, Bahá'u'lláh, and Abdu'l-Bahá as *scripture*, while not including either his own or House of Justice writings as such. There is a massive amount of material thus included as either authoritative or scriptural. Scriptural writings comprise roughly 15,000 works by Bahá'u'lláh, 27,000 works by Abdu'l-Bahá, and a massive (but as yet uncounted) number of writings by the Bab. Authoritative writings include 17,000 works by Shogi Effendi, and a comparable number (to date) by the House of Justice.

Despite the fact that this places totals at around 50,000 scriptural writings plus 35,000 authoritative writings, there also exists a so-called *semi-canonical* body of scripture: transcripts of talks and explanations provided, but never personally verified for accuracy by the speaker; notes taken by pilgrims to Haifa or other sites referencing what was said by one of the Manifestations; and, a biographical account of the life of the Bab and his disciples written by Nabil-i-Zarandi (later edited and translated by Shogi Effendi).

Sikhism

Some call on the Lord, "Rama," some cry, "Khuda," Some bow to Him as Gosain, some as Allah; He is called the Ground of Grounds and also the Bountiful, The Compassionate One and Gracious. Hindus bathe in holy water for His sake; Muslims make the pilgrimage to Mecca. The Hindus perform puja; others bow their heads in namaz. There are those who read the Vedas and others — Christians, Jews and Muslims — who read the Semitic scriptures. Some wear blue, some white robes, Some call themselves Muslims, others Hindus. Some aspire to bahishat, *some to* swarga. *Says Nanak, Whoever realizes the will of the Lord, he will find out the Lord's secrets!*
— Adi Granth

Sikhism is often viewed as the syncretic result of merging mediæval Hinduism and Islam. The only group willing to accept this description, however, would likely be Hinduism. Islam considers itself pure and undivided; and, a syncretic mesh with another tradition would be considered a heresy. The Sikhs themselves see their religion as a natural occurrence which, logically, exhibits many of the beliefs and traits of other great religions — but, they maintain that this hardly would classify it as a spawned religion.

The Sikh faith was founded roughly 500 years ago by Guru Nanak (1469-1539). Nanak (right) reported a religious experience at about the age of 38. Soon thereafter, he began teaching that *true religion* was being ever conscious of God, meditating on the name of God, and reflecting God in all activities of secular daily life. While wandering throughout Sri Lanka, India, Tibet, and as far west as Iraq, he spread a message that condemned superstition, dismissed ritual, and brought God to the forefront of life. Having come from northern India, Nanak's native language was Punjabi; and, the name *Sikh* is based on the Punjabi word for disciple, *shishya* (the Punjabi verb "to know").

Following Nanak, other Gurus (*i.e.* teachers, leaders) followed: 9 more, to be precise. As Guru Gobind Singh, the tenth Guru, was approaching the end of his life, he ordained the *Adi Granth* (a collection of hymns and verses collected or written by the ten gurus) as his successor. Ever since, the *Adi Granth* has also been known as the *Guru Granth Sahib*. His intention was to help the community avoid a succession dispute (since it was not automatically hereditary). Ordaining the Sikh scripture accomplished this.

The 11 gurus of the Sikh religion are thus:

Name	Lifetime	Served as Sikh Guru
Guru Nanak	1469 – 1539	1507 - 1539
Guru Angad	1504 – 1552	1539 – 1552
Guru Amar Das	1479 – 1574	1552 – 1574
Guru Ram Das	1534 – 1581	1574 – 1581
Guru Arjan	1563 – 1606	1581 – 1606
Guru Hargobind	1595 – 1644	1606 – 1644
Guru Har Rai	1630 – 1661	1644 – 1661
Guru Har Krishan	1656 – 1664	1661 – 1664
Guru Tegh Bahadur	1621 – 1675	1664 – 1675
Guru Gobind Singh	1666 – 1708	1675 – 1708
Guru Granth Sahib	(scripture)	1708 - present

Hinduism accepts *yoga* (meaning "union" or "process") as aiding humanity in several ways in its quest for spirituality: *karma yoga* (union through good works), *bhakti yoga* (union through devotion) and *jnana yoga* (union through knowledge). In a similar manner, Sikhs emphasize *bhakti marg* ("path of devotion"), but also accept *karma marg* ("path of good works") and *gian marg* ("path of knowledge") as viable paths to God. Another means to union with God is to constantly be thinking and meditating on His name – constantly reminding oneself of the power and attributes of God, and inculcating an expectancy of good in the follower. This path of dwelling on the name of God is known as *Nam marg*.

In western terms, Sikhism is a very upbeat religion. Sikhs believe unquestioningly in *Chardi Kala*, or 'optimism and progress' as applied to the *khalsa* (the Sikh community, considered sanctified by God). Individual Sikhs donate one tenth of their income (*i.e.* tithing) to support a system of community kitchens known as *deg*. This ensures that all Sikhs are supported in the bare necessities by the community at large, and this support is seen as emanating from God through His community.

Teg, or strength, is seen as an attribute of God, and Sikhs have often been warriors in Indian society. This role has almost always been as protectors, defenders or soldiers — never as barbarians or thugs. Sikhs consider themselves to be servants of the *Sangat* (congregation), and consider it essential that they always display *garibi* (humility) and discipline. Humanity is seen as fundamentally good. Humankind is not seen as born in sin, but as having the ability to reform and attain godliness regardless of how depraved the prior time might have been. This change, or conversion, comes through understanding and acceptance of God's grace.

Sikhism, unlike some of its better known Indian neighbours, is not a monastic religion. The active, practicing Sikh is encouraged to be an active, lively, social individual within the larger community. Isolation and monasticism are seen as negative traits, and not something to be emulated or sought after. Rather than reject the material world, Sikhs attempt to live a life of example: being a better farmer, better engineer, better entrepreneur, *et cetera* than their non-Sikh neighbour. Each Sikh is expected to be self sufficient, to earn their living, and to not become a burden to the community. This is exemplified in the *Adi Granth*, which says that "Salvation is not incompatible with laughing, eating, playing and dressing well" (page 522).

Sikhism is one of the first, if not *the* first, religion to grant women equal status, religious freedom and social equality. They participate in the community and receive *amrit* (*conf.* baptism) on equal terms with men. Surrounded by a society where widows historically martyred themselves on the funeral pyres of their departed husbands, Sikhs encourage widow remarriage. At times of crisis, Sikh women have borne arms and become a second line of defense protecting the homeland (*e.g.* the 1971 India-Pakistan war).

God, to the Sikhs, is both personal and transcendent. They consider it incomprehensible that God should be believed to take human form (incarnation), since God is not subject to any of the material limitations of space and time. This makes Jesus (Christian) and Krishna (Hindu) incomprehensible to them. Also, there is no God for nations or tribes to call upon in war, since there is no Muslim God, Hindu God or Jewish God: there is the "Only One God." Sikhs refer to God as *Waheguru* ("Wonderful Lord", or "Wonderful Enlightener"), but do not see God as "their" God.

The *Adi Granth*, or *Guru Granth Sahib*, is a collection of devotional compositions. This includes articles, essays and verses written by the various gurus as well as hymns by both Hindu and Muslim religious leaders. As a result, the scriptures are multi-lingual. Just as the Christian Bible was written in Hebrew, Aramaic and Greek, the Adi Granth is written in Punjabi, Sanskrit, Persian, Marathi, Arabic, and Hindi (plus several others). In addition, there is the *Rihat Maryada* (their "Code of Conduct"), published in 1945 by the leadership, that regulates individual and societal Sikh life.

Beliefs

The Adi Granth opens with the *Mool Mantra*, an effective summary of Sikh beliefs:

> *There is One God.*
> *He is Supreme Truth, without fear, not vindictive, Timeless, Eternal, not born, so He does not die to be reborn. Self illumined, by Guru's grace He is revealed to the human soul.*
> *Truth was in the beginning, and throughout the ages, Truth is now and ever will be.*

Since Sikhs consider time cyclical rather than linear, they have no eschatalogical beliefs (*i.e.* no "end times"). They do believe in reincarnation, and consider *haumai* (literally, "self-centeredness") the end result of greed, lust, pride, anger, and attachment to the transient values of earthly existence. Thus *haumai* is the 'source of all evil'; and, it is a person's inclination to, and desire for, this evil that produces the *karma* that results in the endless rebirths. God is seen as All-Pervading, the Source of All Life. Human life constitutes the opportunity to be reunited with God, to merge with Ultimate Reality as a raindrop merges with the ocean. This is from the

Grace of God, and not as a result of one's human merit. Salvation is therefore accomplished by enlightenment, not redemption.

Practices

Worship
- The Sikh place of worship is known as a *gurdwar*.

Names
- Newborn children are named in a "naming ceremony" in the *gurdwar*.
- Given names do not indicate gender, so men use the surname *Singh* ("lion"), and women the surname *Kaur* ("princess").
- Guru Gobind Singh instructed his followers to drop their family names (which in India indicate caste), and to only use Singh and Kaur.

Ceremonies
- Marriages are conducted in a *gurdwar*.
- Funeral services are held in a *gurdwar*, after which the body is cremated; monuments of any kind are forbidden as not displaying family humility.
- Upon reaching adulthood, a Sikh (male or female) is admitted to the *Khalsa* (religious community) in the *Amrit* ceremony. In this uniting ceremony, the initiate vows to follow the Sikh 'code of conduct'.

Lifestyle
- Asceticism is rejected.
- Participation in family life, society and the "working world" is encouraged.
- The caste system is rejected, and women have equal authority with men.
- Racism, ethnocentrism, religious bias and social classes are all rejected.
- At the *Amrit* ceremony, new Sikh community members vow to:
  + abstain from alcohol, tobacco and other intoxicants;
  + never cut the hair on any part of the body;
  + not to eat meat from animals killed in a religious or sacrificial manner;
  + refrain from all sexual activity or contact outside of marriage; and,
  + to wear these *five symbols*:

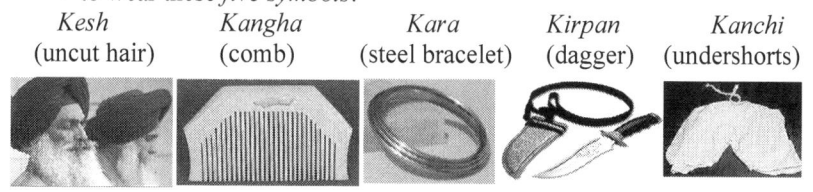

Kesh	*Kangha*	*Kara*	*Kirpan*	*Kanchi*
(uncut hair)	(comb)	(steel bracelet)	(dagger)	(undershorts)

Based on the Punjabi words (all of which begin with the same sound), these are most often known as "the five *k*'s").

One final observation on Sikh beliefs is their view of Truth. If there were a Sikh lexicon, Truth would have three basic meanings:

1) **Truth is God.** It is not seen as something which can be observed humanly, possessing some 'truth value'. Truth is seen as synonymous with God; Truth *is* God; God *is* Truth.

2) **Truth is virtue.** As such, it is honesty, righteousness, justice, detachment, compassion, humility, *et cetera*.

3) **Truth is discipleship.** It is granted by God to the devotée. To earn this gift, however, the devotée must display actions appropriate for the gift to be warranted. There must be acts of charity and altruism, and submission entirely to God. It is said that the Sikh must speak the Truth, act the Truth, and think the Truth. A 'life of Truth' is considered to be greater than Truth itself. A superior character implies compassion, humility, meditation, and a desire to serve and guide others. Such a life will lead the devotée to earn the gift of Truth, and to ultimately merge with God like a rain drop which merges with the sea.

The most famous of all Sikh gurdwars is the *Harimandar Sahib* (above). Although known as "the Golden Temple" for hundreds of years (even listed by the United Nations under this name), Sikhs consider it demeaning and asked the UN to stop using this colloquialism (which they did). Built in 1588 beside (and over) a body of water known to locals as the *pool of nectar*, it is revered for many accounts of spontaneous healings in its waters (much like Lourdes, in France). The sanctuary building (center) is coated entirely in hammered 24 karat gold leaf.

In closing — a Sikh prayer

> You are the Creator of all. You give the soul, the body, and life. We are meritless, without virtue. Bless us, O Merciful Lord. ... You create the Universe and then reveal Yourself to us and in us. You make Yourself manifest. — Aid Granth

al Qaeda

It would be foolish in an American course on World Religions to discuss Islam without addressing what happened on September 11, 2001. A group of 19 *terrorists* successfully hijacked 4 commercial jetliners, and turned them into missiles (delivering warheads consisting of thousands of gallons of JP4 aviation fuel). Italicizing the word *terrorist* was done deliberately because it is a commonly used word today that may or may not always be appropriate when used. Although this is one of the more blatant examples of it, there are still people who would argue that this was not what they were. Another issue commonly misunderstood is why they did it; and, what connection (if any) it had to Islam.

Although virtually all Muslims (especially Wahhabists) seem to understand why it happened, "The vast majority of Muslims in the Middle East were as shocked and horrified as any American by what they saw happening on their TV screens. And they are frightened of being lumped together in the popular American imagination with the perpetrators of the attack."* They were concerned that Americans would equate all Muslims with what Osama bin Laden and his *al Qaeda* network had done 'in the name of Islam'. Videos of Muslims cheering and dancing in the streets as they learned of the attack (widely shown on American television) were actually highly localized and quite rare.

Jihad is a "striving or struggling in the way of God" — a central Islamic concept requiring adherents to strive to know (and do) the will of God. Often, this is separated into the *greater jihad* and the *lesser jihad*. In the *greater jihad*, a Muslim struggles internally to know and do what is right; and, it is human pride, selfishness and sinfulness with which the faithful must wrestle within themselves. By contrast, the *lesser jihad* is the external defense of Islam against those that would attack the faith. Nearly all Muslims reject the violence of September 11, and there is only a very small percentage who make any attempt to justify it as a legitimate form of *lesser jihad*.

---

* Ford, Peter The Christian Science Monitor *Why do they hate us?* September 27, 2001.

Dr. Martin Marty, a well known scholar on religious fundamentalism, has identified some of the common factors he believes are found in virtually all forms of fundamentalism:
- a belief that there was, at one point, a more perfect expression of the faith — an ideal state, if you will;
- a reaction (often violent) to any perceived threat to restoration of this ideal (even if it actually never existed); and,
- a unique, often very literal, interpretation of relevant scripture.

In the case of Islam, some Islamic groups see an increasing presence of US and other western nation powers as being a pollutant to Islamic culture, and coincident with the decline of Islamic authority in traditionally Muslim nations. In the case of *al Qaeda*, the result was suicide bombers. Interestingly, there is only one verse in the Qur'an that even comes close to mentioning suicide:

> *O ye who believe! Squander not your wealth among yourselves in vanity, except it be a trade by mutual consent, and kill not one another. Lo! Allah is ever Merciful unto you..* — *Qur'an 4:29*

However, in the *Hadith*, or 'sayings of Muhammad', there are a number of references that seem to refer directly to suicide:
- condemning anyone who "throws himself off a mountain";
- rejecting anyone who "drinks poison"; and,
- declaring that anyone who "kills himself with a sharp instrument" will be damned to the fires of hell.

Muslims accept that it is God, not you, who has final authority over the length of your life — even in cases of excruciating pain or terminal illness. Extremists commonly classify suicide-type events as *martyrdom* rather than *suicide* to "get around" the condemnation of suicide within the faith, for the Qur'an promises paradise for those who "are slain in the way of Allah." (2:154) Seeing these missions in this light makes the perpetrators martyrs rather than suicide victims; but, the vast majority of Mulsims view this as a misinterpretation. They also point out that the taking of innocent, or non-combatant, life — even in war — is specifically forbidden by the Qur'an.

So, who or what was the source of the September 11th attack if it wasn't Islam? Most believe the answer to have been *Osama bin Laden*. But, why did he hate the United States so?

Bin Laden left his engineering education and the family business (the largest family owned construction company in the world) and headed for Afghanistan shortly after military forces of the Soviet Union invaded in 1979. Once there, he used his personal fortune and charismatic personality to organize, arm, and lead a loose coalition of Muslim rebels (known as the *Mujahideen*) who eventually were successful in forcing the Soviet forces to give up and go home.

Once the Soviets had been defeated, he shifted his focus to getting what he considered to be destructive Western influences (especially the US) out of the Middle East and other Islamic countries. This gradually escalated until it included what are generally categorized as *terrorist activities* by the mid 1990s. The CIA defines terrorism as "acts against non-combatant civilians primarily to apply political pressure through fear and worry of the general populace". After the Soviet defeat, the foreign allies of the Mujahideen began to filter home to the countries from which they had been recruited. Seeing his influence starting to wane, bin Laden worked to convince many of them to stay and follow his lead in this new, expanded mission. In doing this, he shifted the focus of their resentment from the Soviets to the West. This was the basis for what we now know as *al Qaeda* (literally, "the base").

Bottom line

There is simply no way that Osama bin Laden or *al Qaeda* can legitimately claim Islamic teachings as justification for their terrorist paramilitary actions. Their views are on the extreme periphery of accepted Islamic beliefs, and are even extreme for the very conservative Wahhabist teachings that bin Laden claimed to follow. They are comparably representative of Islam as the racist, paramilitary *Aryan Nations* and *Ku Klux Klan* are representative of Christianity. All of these groups may quote passages selectively from their respective scriptures, but their actions are clearly outside traditional, accepted and reasonable interpretations of their faiths.

Considering them to be legitimate expressions of their respective faith is a disservice to both the teachings and beliefs of those faiths.

Section V
Hinduism

Life without goodness, good thoughts, good actions, and good words is like the sky in the night without the moon or stars. It is like a wheel without a hub or spokes! No one can push a boulder away while standing on it; you can not be free from anxiety while all the entrances through which it sneaks in are open. — *Atharva Veda*

Hinduism, Jainism and Buddhism (and, in the minds of some academics, even Sikhism) can reasonably be grouped together as *Vedic religions.* This springs from the fact that Buddhism, Sikhism and Jainism evolved on the Indian subcontinent alongside the predominant Indian religious systems of Hinduism. To many Hindus, these religions are essentially wayward branches of Hinduism. Buddhists would disagree; Sikhs would strongly disagree; and, most Jains would claim that Jainism actually predates Hinduism (a fact widely accepted by the Jain faithful, but unprovable to non-believers in today's highly skeptical world). It should be noted that, where Hinduism appears to have evolved directly from Vedism, these others may be seen more accurately as negative reactions to, or denials of, all or part of Vedism. For this reason, many experts refuse to categorize anything but Hinduism as truly being Vedic.

There is also disagreement over how to categorize Hinduism itself. Whereas most texts consider it to be a religion, some insist that it is more of a cultural 'way of life' than it is a religion. In addition, the derivation of the term Hindu even makes it clear that there is no requirement for the various branches of the faith to have any shared theological beliefs.

Hindu is actually an externally applied label that followers have only relatively recently begun to use (perhaps for a few hundred years out of a history that goes back at least 3,500 years). As Persian, Mongol, and European invaders encountered the Indian sub-continent, they usually invaded through the northwest (the east and west are coastal; the north boundary is the Himalayas); so, invading armies attacked through the lowlands of the northwest.

Entering from the northwest, the first impressive natural feature an army would encounter was the massive river system that drained the valleys in the western Himalayas down to the Sea. This system comprised seven principal rivers*, and was known in Sanskrit as the *Šapta Šindhu* (Sanskrit: "seven rivers"; the *Š* designating an "aspirated S"). The Persians, with no aspirated S sound in their language, substituted their only aspirated consonant (H), and pronounced this as *Hapta Hindu*. Finally, when the armies of Alexander the Great reached this area, they (speaking Greek) had no aspirated consonants at all, and pronounced it *Apta Indu*. It is from these western mispronounciations that we get *Hindu* (the religion), *Hindi* (the predominant language of the area), *India* (the western name of the country), and *Indus* (the name of the predominant river of the area. *Hindu* thus became a geographical description indicating the religion(s) of the people from that region in the northwest of the sub-continent and all of the areas beyond.

It is primarily for this reason that Hinduism is more appropriately a "family of related religions" than a unique faith. Just as the three primary faiths that make up Abrahamic Religion (Judaism, Islam, and Christianity) are related and share some similar beliefs and features, the various faiths found on the Indian sub-continent were also related with similar features. They weren't all the same faith, but they were related.

---

* Compare this to the Mississippi River system, which is a water shed for most of central North America – from the Rockies to the Appalachians. It consists of the Mississippi, Ohio, Illinois, Arkansas, Red, Missouri, and Tennessee and other tributaries. The Indian system includes the Kabul, Satluj, Beas, Chenab, Ravi, Jhelum, and Indus – 7 rivers, with the Indus being the largest.

Chapter 18
Hindu Foundations

Veda (pronounced *Vay'-duh*) is a Sanskrit term meaning "true knowledge". As such, *veda* is a compilation of truth and knowledge accumulated over thousands of years. Many historians believe that sometime around 2000 to 2500 BCE, Aryans entered what is now Pakistan. Tradition long held that they were a warlike people who came roaring in on horses and chariots — killing everyone in their path. That theory has now been largely discredited, and modern DNA studies cast doubt on how many of these new folk actually arrived.

If the traditional story is true, these Aryans were essentially farmers; but, they had migrated down from Turkey through Iran to the Indus River valley. Arable land was critical to these people; and, the fact that it was much more readily available in their new surroundings didn't alter the political structure that had evolved to support a land-hungry society. Their structure consisted predominantly of what could be called 'clans with warlords' or 'gangs with leaders'. They were warlike — more often against each other than outsiders. In fact, the ancient Sanskrit term for "enemy" is the same as the word for "cousin". This Aryan society settled in this new land, and their beliefs became integrated with those of the natives who were already there.

An alternate history, proposed by Hindu academics, maintains that the Vedic faith was already present; and, any arriving Aryans were simply absorbed into this environment. In either case, it was a naturalist theology: the gods and goddesses (it was definitely polytheistic) were virtually indistinguishable from the forces of nature which were their domain (*e.g.* moon, sun, thunder, sky, *etc*). One of their gods — *Dyaus*, the "sky god" — evolved into *Zeus* when Aryans migrated into Greece, *Giove Pater* (Jupiter) when they migrated into Italy, *Tinia* to the Etruscans, and perhaps *Thor* to the Scandinavians. In India, this deity is known in the Ṛg Veda as *Indra*. 250 of the hymns in this collection are to Indra, and he was at that time recognized as the highest of the gods.

Religious practices of these people are not too well known, and have largely been reconstructed from the stories that got passed into modern Hinduism. We do know that there was a reliance on a fire temple which likely was the origin of the Fire Temple that the Zoroastrians adopted from the Aryan tribes that dominated Persia at the time of Zoroaster.

Sometime between 1200 and 1500 BCE, the Vedic oral traditions were transcribed into print. The earliest of these is known today as the *Ṛg Veda* (often written *Rig Veda* in English). Also including information regarding traditional rituals, this is predominantly a hymnal. The three other ancient Vedic collections are the *Yajur Veda*, the *Sama Veda*, and the *Atharva Veda*. Each of these Vedic texts consists of verses or hymns (*samhita*), explanations or interpretations of these verses (*brahmana*), mystical writings associated with them (*upanishad*), and esoteric teachings based on the verses (*aranyaka*).

It is believed that the caste system in India traces its roots back into Vedic theology more than 4000 years ago. It is known that the ancients saw virtually everything in threes. Thus, their society was divided into three: the priests and educated caste (*brahman*), royalty and warriors (*kshatriya*), and commoners (*vaishya*). As Aryan and Dravidic cultures merged in India, the native Dravidians, not belonging to any of these 3 groups, were added as a fourth group (*shudra*). This was derived from *dasyu* (meaning "slave").

The Vedic liturgy is seen most clearly in the mantra* portion of the four Vedas, which were compiled in Sanskrit. The religious practices relied on a member of the clergy administering rites; and, this mode of worship is largely unchanged today within Hinduism. Texts dating to this period (all composed in Sanskrit) are mainly the four Vedic Samhitas (listed above). The Vedas record

---

* A *mantra* is a sound, symbol, or phrase considered capable of generating a spiritual transformation in the individual. Beginning in the Vedic tradition, mantras are common in modern Hinduism, Jainism, Buddhism, Sikhism, and several other faiths. Although the term *mantra* is not generally used, the practice can also be found in faiths not indigenous to the Indian sub-continent.

the liturgy connected with the rituals and sacrifices typically performed by 16 or 17 priests and pandits (*pandit* and *purohita* are Sanskrit terms often used synonymously, and generally refer to 'family priests'). Traditionally, the hymns of the Ṛg Veda and other Vedic hymns were divinely revealed to the rishis (*i.e.* those who "hear" these divine messages, rather than those who "author" them). The Vedas are described as *apaurashaya*, a Sanskrit term meaning "uncreated by man" – which further reveals their divine, eternal, non-changing status.

Vedic worship focused on the elements (*e.g.* fire and rivers), worship of heroic gods (*e.g.* Indra), chanting of hymns, and performance of sacrifices. The priests performed the solemn rituals for the kshatriya, and some of the more wealthy vaishya. Typical goals for the people were an abundance of children, rain, cattle, a long life, and an afterlife in heaven with their ancestors. Similarities to modern Hinduism can be seen today in priestly prayers for prosperity, wealth and general well-being.

Most religious scholars consider the Vedic period to have ended around 500 BCE, Vedic religion having gradually transitioned into the various schools of Hinduism. Some (a few) aspects of the earlier Vedic religion have managed to survive to the present in the more remote corners of India (*e.g.* Kerala, where *Nambudiri Brahmins* perform ancient rituals considered extinct in most of India).

There are numerous rituals, rites, and practices spelled out in the Vedas that were conducted by Vedic priests and pandits.

- **Soma** is extensively mentioned in the Ṛg Veda (with the *Soma Mandala* section including 114 hymns in honor of it), and is described as a ritual drink made from the Soma plant. It also features in the Zoroastrian Avesta as *Haoma*, where it has a similar role in their tradition. The Soma plant, from which this drink is made, is not known for certain today; but, most western scholars believe it to have been *Ephedra sinica* (also known as *Ma-huang*, or "yellow cannabis"). Ephedra extracts are amphetamines, and classified as a psychoactive drug (often used medicinally as a stimulant, decongestant, or anti-depressant).

- ***Yajna*** can be translated into English in many different ways (*e.g.* worship, prayer, sacrifice, praise, or offering), but most often is used to refer to a sacrificial rite. These are typically conducted by casting offerings into a fire, where the smoke transports the essence of the sacrifice directly to the gods.

- ***Agni*** was the Vedic god of fire, and was one of the primary gods in the Vedic pantheon. He served as a messenger between earth and heaven, between humans and deities, and transported sacrifices from the yajna to the appropriate deity.

- ***Ashvamedha*** was the "horse sacrifice", a year-long ritual at the close of which a stallion (at least 24) was slaughtered. It was only performed by, and for, royalty to acquire power and glory, general prosperity of the kingdom, and to ensure sovereignty over neighbouring provinces and areas. This closely parallels rituals in mediæval Ireland, Central and Eastern Asia, and ancient Rome (the *October Horse*, the right horse of the winning team in a chariot race, sacrificed to *Mars* at the *Campus Martius* on the ides of October [Oct 15]).

- ***Cremation*** – the *Ṛg Veda* specifically mentions cremation of the dead, a practice that appears to pre-date the Vedas.

- ***Other*** – rituals described in the *Atharva Veda* are predominantly concerned with medicine, healing, and magic.

Pantheon

The Vedic *pantheon* (literally, "all the gods") is similar to its Greek and Germanic counterparts – comprising both anthropomorphic deities (*i.e.* with human-like forms) and deified natural phenomena (*e.g.* fire, storms, rivers, *etc.*). These deities were divided into two distinct classes: *Devas* and *Asuras*.

The *Devas* (typically benevolent deities) are deities of cosmic and social order, and included:
- *Bhaga* — the patron deity of wealth and love;
- *Indra* — King of the Gods, and patron deity of storms, war, and rainfall;
- *Mitra* — the patron deity of friendship, honesty, contracts, and meetings;
- *Prajapati* — the god of creation and life;
- *Rudra* — the god of wind, storms, and the hunt;
- *Surya* — the sun god; and,
- *Varuna* — the patron deity of sky, water, law, and the underworld;

The *Asuras* (typically power-seeking, often sinful and materialistic) are deities who often are a cause of chaos and disorder (often seen as the "in-laws" of the Devas), and included:
- *Andhaka* — a malevolent demon;
- *Holika* — a demoness burnt to death with the help of Prajapati (above);
- *Mahabali* — a benevolent Asura king;
- *Rahu* — the decapitated head of an asura who swallows the sun or moon (causing an eclipse);
- *Sunda* — one of two brothers whose goal was world domination; and,
- *Upasunda* — Sunda's brother, the world was saved when they killed each other fighting over Tilottama (an *apsara*, or "celestial nymph", sent by Brahma to cause dissension and distract them from their goal).

Despite the many gods (both Devas and Asuras), there are obvious indications in the *Ṛg Veda* to monotheistic tendencies (which would blossom as Vedism evolved into modern Hinduism).

Indraṃ mitraṃ varuṇamaghnimāhuratho divyaḥ sa suparṇo gharutmān, ekaṃ sad viprā bahudhā vadantyaghniṃ yamaṃ mātariśvānamāhuḥ

They call him Indra, Mitra, Varuṇa, Agni, and he is heavenly nobly-winged Garutmān. To what is One, sages give many a title they call it Agni, Yama, Mātariśvan. — Ṛg Veda 1.164.46

Hinduism evolved from this Vedism of the proto-historic civilization of the Indus River valley (in what is now Pakistan and northwest India). The earliest archæological evidence in the area indicates a belief in a mother goddess. The Great Mother, or Goddess, has been common in many areas of the world — apparently dating back to about 30,000 BCE, shortly after the appearance of Cro-Magnon people. It is likely that this was reinforced by the extreme importance of fertility with respect to crops, domesticated and wild animals, and the people themselves. The female life bestowing aspect was a mystery to these people, and often considered to be divine. The introduction of Aryan theology to the Indus Valley (with their predominantly male gods — and phallic representation of fertility) led to a syncretic development which likely either led to, or reinforced, much of Hinduism's mythology. This was not unusual: similar events and syncretic development also occurred in other areas when male gods met an indigenous Great Goddess.

Chapter 19
Historical Development

Deities and Paths

There are a great many scholars (albeit not many great scholars) who refuse to classify Hinduism as a religion. The wide diversity of teachings and the lack of a consistent theological basis (by Western standards) occasionally result in Hinduism being classified as a philosophy rather than a religion. However, in the context of its sociological impact, this makes Hinduism more influential rather than less. Hinduism is a complex collection of social, cultural and religious beliefs and practices which evolved over thousands of years — growing out of the earlier Vedic beliefs. Although flourishing in many areas of the world (*e.g.* Indonesia, the US, and the Caribbean), practice remains overwhelmingly Indian (having primarily developed there). There are numerous Hindu temples in the US, including: an impressive ISKCON temple in Pittsburgh, a Saivite temple in Orlando, and a magnificent Iraivan (Tamil for "He who is worshipped") temple on Kauai, Hawaii.

In the most traditional examples of Hindu influence, society is marked by the caste system and an outlook which tends to view all forms and theories as aspects of one eternal being and truth. Generally, Hindus subscribe to a belief in repeated rebirths; and, it is widely accepted that adherence to one of four primary ways can serve as a means to release the individual adherent from this perpetual cycle of births and deaths. These are the way of works (*karma yoga*), the way of knowledge (*jnana yoga*), the way of devotion (*bhakti yoga*), and the way of meditation (*raja yoga*).

Traditionally, the Hindu pantheon contains three hundred and thirty million gods (*i.e.* 33 *crore* in the Indian numbering system). Nevertheless, virtually all educated Hindus would say that Hinduism is monotheistic. This apparent paradox arises from the fact that *god* means something altogether different to a Hindu than to a Christian or Muslim. There is no direct, corresponding Western concept; however, Hindu gods may be seen as being somewhat analogous to Western angels, saints, elven, or færies. The monotheism of Hinduism which underlies these millions of gods is expressed quite clearly in the *Artharva Veda*: "Great indeed are the Gods who have sprung out of Brahman."

Brahman is the Hindu name for "God" – the One, Singular, Divine Essence. Since Brahman exists simultaneously both as *Parabrahman* (absolute, transcendent, omniscient) and *Purusha* (individual, personal —the Primal Soul), it is comparable to Judaic concepts for God: being both personal and transcendent. God is seen as the original Soul who creates and emanates innumerable individual souls — human, non-human and spiritual. Hinduism sees humanity as individual soul 'beings' (as is God). Consciousness exists within humanity without beginning or end, essentially making humanity an expression or manifestation of God. Humanity also displays *Satchidananda*. This is the superconscious mind of the Soul — the mind of God, Brahman. It is, in Western terms, the *very presence of God* — taking some major liberties, it could even be seen as analogous to the Christian concept of the Holy Ghost.

Hinduism is so diverse and multifaceted that it exhibits remarkable degrees of both syncretic and devotional acceptance. This devotional acceptance is displayed in the fact that while one Hindu may be worshipping Ganesha (a Hindu *Mahadeva*, one of the spiritual entities closest to God — so close, in fact, that they function in perfect accord with God's wisdom, intent and action) while another Hindu might be worshipping Şiva (Shiva). There is remarkable tolerance and acceptance of this difference of choices, and the individual Hindu exhibits extreme tolerance toward alternate modes of worship, expression, devotion, and god to guide one through life.

In general, most Hindus view all reality as a unity — the entire universe as one divine entity. To the Westerner, this appears at first to be pantheistic: God and the universe being one (thus denying God's transcendence and personality). However, the common Hindu view of the material world is *maya* (illusory), so God is viewed as both pantheistic *and* transcendent. The primary aspects or persons of God are: *Brahma* (a Creator from Whom spring the many souls of humanity); *Vişnu* (the Preserver, the source of eternal order, righteousness, law and duty); and *Şiva*, the Destroyer (who appears either compassionate or destructive at various times). The result is that Hinduism is often misunderstood, since it can be labeled monotheistic (Brahman), Trinitarian (Brahma, Viṣnu, Şiva – in total harmony), or Polytheistic (with all 330 million gods) — depending entirely on the perspective and bias of the observer.

As stated above, the Hindu godhead is generally viewed as a triad of 3 principle manifestations. *Şiva* (pronounced, and occasionally written in English, as Shiva) is a Sanskrit word that means "friendly and auspicious". A personalized *Şiva* is frequently pictured in Hindu art as a dancing male with 4 arms (illustrating omnipotence). An excellent example of this is a bronze statue dating from the 11th century in the collection of the Victoria and Albert Museum [right].

The second member of the Hindu *Trimurti* is *Viṣnu*. This is the manifestation of Universal Spirit which has appeared to mankind in the form of ten different *avatars*. An avatar is an incarnation or embodiment of a concept or philosophy. In the case of Hindus, it is generally seen as the incarnation of a deity in earthly form. *Viṣnu*, as the preserver manifestation of *Brahman*, is the source of these incarnations. Ten generally recognized avatars of *Viṣnu* are a fish, tortoise, boar, dwarf, Rama-with-the-Ax, man-lion, King Rama, Krishna, Buddha and Kalkin. That tenth avatar (Kalkin) has not yet come, but is expected to be in the form of a man on a white horse with a flaming sword in his hand. The most widely worshipped and revered avatar of Viṣnu is *Kṛṣna* [Krishna, right], the 8th avatar, whose story is recounted in the *Bhagavad Gita*. Contrary to common Western expectations, not all Deific incarnations are pastoral and beneficent. The most recent historical incarnation of *Viṣnu* is Buddha; and, most Hindu theologians view Buddha as a way for *Viṣnu* to delude the wicked, lead them away from Hinduism, and ensure their eternal damnation. Krishna is always depicted with blue skin (representing purity and nobility), and is often playing the flute.

The third and final member of the Hindu trimurti is *Brahma* [left] Often a more abstract concept to the Hindu believer, the name *Brahma* literally translates from Sanskrit as "prayer". The fact that Brahma is more abstract does not, however, preclude the existence of Hindu sacred art depicting Brahma as a key aspect of the Hindu Trimurti, and He is often portrayed with 4 distinct faces, each facing a different direction. Temples to Brahma are not common, and there are only two major examples in all of India.

Much of the material that is available with respect to these personifications of the godhead arises from a series of voluminous texts known generally as the *Puranas*. Traditionally, there are 18 Puranas. Each text is devoted to one of the forms or manifestations of the godhead. They deal, as an encyclopædia would, with the traits, character and surrounding myths of their subject. The influence of these texts has been strong over the centuries; however, they're rarely quoted. An exception to this is the *Bhagavata-Purana*, a popular text on the worship of Viṣnu through His Krishna incarnation. ISKCON (the International Society for Krishna Consciousness) is a modern development which focuses on the deific incarnation of Krishna, and has become popular in many Western countries (with adherents often derisively referred to as *Hare Krishnas* – from a prayer they commonly recite*).

Hindu mythology often provides explicit descriptions of some of their better known gods and goddesses. These include:

- *Ganesha*, with the head of an elephant and body of a human (bringing good fortune and removing obstacles);
- *Hanuman*, the Commander of a troop of monkeys who aided Rama by rescuing Sita (his wife) from the demon, Ravana;
- *Durga*, the wife of Şiva (mother of *Lakshmi* and *Sarasvati*);
- *Lakshmi*, the wife of Viṣnu and goddess of wealth; and,
- *Sarasvati*, Brahma's wife; goddess of wisdom and the arts.

---

* Calling ISKCON members "Hare Krishnas" would be analogous to calling Roman Catholics "Hail Marys".

Americans often think Hindus worship cows; not true. Jesus was portrayed in the Christian Bible as a shepherd, and sheep became symbolic in Christianity. The cross is also used as a symbol of Christianity; however, Christians worship neither the cross nor sheep. Similarly, Krishna was a cowherder (a bull was also considered to have been the companion of Şiva). Hindus consider the cow sacred (as Christians do the cross), but they are not worshipped: they represent Krishna, Şiva, and the bounty of creation. Şiva's vehicle and companion was a male bovine known as *Nandi*. There are statues of Nandi [below; on Chamundi Hills, Mysuru, India] as well as temples built to honor Nandi, but these are to venerate and show respect for the bovine role in society. They are never slaughtered nor eaten; and, as opposed to America (where they are seen as walking hamburgers), bulls and cows are respected and venerated. They wander the streets of Indian cities, and go pretty much wherever they want. Despite the fact that India only accounts for 2.4% of the world's land area, it is reported that 30% of all of the cows and bulls in the world live in India.

Another development in the evolutionary theology of Hinduism is the Tantric tradition. *Tantras* are texts that, in the same manner as the Puranas, promote and extol the virtues of a particular manifestation of God. They tend to be more practical, less philosophical and more widely followed by the masses than the *Puranas*. The basic Tantra consists of some philosophy, concentration techniques (rooted in yogic training), ritual and practice. Concentration is developed to enable the adherent to gain spiritual release through the repetition of certain sounds or syllables with symbolic meaning (*mantras*), visual assimilation of symbolic drawings (*mandalas*) or practice of special rituals (*tantras*). The three classes of the Tantras do not align perfectly with those of the Puranas — the three forms of Brahman being *Şiva*, *Vişnu*, and *Sakti*. *Sakti* developed within Hindu teaching at about the time of the fifth century; and, Saktism is the worship of the active power of God. Although closely related theologically to the creative role of *Brahma*, *Sakti* is perceived as feminine, and often represented by one of the goddesses.

There are two primary means of differentiating different groupings within Hinduism: theological schools, and functional sects.

Theological Schools

There are six "orthodox" (Sanskrit: *āstika*) schools of Hindu thought, and these are all focused on the same goal: liberation from the constraints of this world, and release from the cycle of rebirth. These six schools are:

- ***Samkhya*** is a dualistic, atheistic view of existence (mind & matter, but not spirit) – credited to a Vedic era sage by the name of Kapila;

- ***Yoga*** is closely related to Samkhya, but emphasizes development of the mind to experience reality – the earliest presentation of Yoga (specifically, *Raja Yoga*) was in the *Yoga Sutras* of Patañjali, most likely about 300 BCE;

- ***Nyaya*** is essentially a system of logic that allows the practitioner to analyze information to determine a logical revelation of God. Nyaya takes great care to distinguish valid sources of knowledge from speculation and opinion, and is thus more than logic – being a mixture of both logic and epistemology – based on the *Nyaya Sutras* of the 2nd century CE written by Aksapada Gautama;

- ***Vaisheshika*** is closely related to Nyaya, but reduces all existence to atoms (differing from the modern atomic theory in that these atoms are assumed to act by the will of God) – initially developed by the sage Kanāda, who lived in the 2nd or 3rd century BCE (prior to the related Nyaya school);

- ***Mimamsa*** is based largely on the earlier parts of the Vedas, and is focused on ritual, anti-asceticism, and anti-mysticism. Sometimes called *Purva Mimamsa*, the primary goal is liberation through an understanding of *dharma* (universal law), and is not overtly concerned with the existence or nature of God. Therefore, there are both theistic and atheistic followers of Mimamsa;

- ***Vedanta*** is Sanskrit for "the end of the Vedas", or "the goal of the Vedas". This school of thought was systematized in the *Vedanta Sutra* about 200 BCE by Badarāyana. The problem is that the sutra was written in short, often cryptic, aphorisms that lead to multiple possible interpretations. The result is that there are currently five "sub-schools" of Vedanta:

- *Dvaita* was developed by Madhwāchārya, and identified God with Brahman (specifically, Viṣnu or His incarnations). It is dualist (*Dvaita* is Sanskrit for "two"), and considers Brahman, individual souls, and matter to all be separate and distinct.

- *Advaita* was expounded most convincingly by Adi Shankara and his 'grand-teacher', Gaudapada. Brahman is seen as being the only reality; with the material world being illusory. Brahman is said to be impersonal (without attributes), and possesses the power of *maya*, which brings forth the illusion. It is believed it is ignorance of this that causes all suffering, and knowledge of this that results in liberation.

- *Vishishtdvaita* (propounded by Ramanuja) sees individual souls as part of Brahman – similar, but distinct. Brahman is worshipped as Viṣnu, has attributes, and *maya* is seen as His creative power.

- *Dvaitādvaita* appears to be an attempt to have it both ways: it defines three categories of existence (Brahman, soul, and matter). Soul and matter differ from Brahman in their attributes and capabilities, and are mutually dependent. Brahman exists independently. This perspective can be summarized as "Brahman controls; the soul enjoys; and, matter is enjoyed". It is a much younger school, and was first proposed by Nimbarka in the 13th century CE.

- *Shuddhādvaita* is the youngest (newest) of the six orthodox schools, and was founded by Vallabhacharya [1479-1531]. It is described as a "purified non-dualism", where it agrees with Advaita on most points, but not all (believing individual souls are 'not Brahman', but 'part of Brahman').

In addition to the six *āstika* (orthodox) schools of thought, there are also three primary *nāstika* (heterodox) schools These are

Hindu philosophical movements that essentially reject the divine supremacy of the Vedas, and are:

- **Buddhism**, as founded by Siddhartha Gautama (the *Buddha*), and which will be covered in depth in Section VI;

- **Jainism**, as established by Vardhamana Jnatrputra (the *Mahavira*), and which will be covered in Chapter 21; and,

- **Cārvāka**, an atheistic, materialist philosophy that minimalizes God, exhibits religious indifference, and employs philosophical skepticism. As an organized philosophical school, it grew out of *Lokāyata*, and was apparently named *Cārvāka* in an attempt to disparage it (since Cārvāka was the name of a villain in the epic *Mahabharata*). They did not believe in a life after death, thought that everything occurs as a result of natural (*i.e.* physical) causes (not as an action of a deity or Supreme Being), accepted sensual indulgence as the only enjoyment worthy of pursuit, and considered all religion as man-made and having no divine authority (referring to priests and the authors of the Vedas as "buffoons").

Hindu Sects

The overwhelming majority of Hindus participate in one of 4 'major' sects (out of many, many more). These are:

- **Vaishnavism**, the sect consisting of those who worship Viṣnu as the Supreme Being (effectively as Brahman perceived with attributes). They may worship Him either directly or through one of His incarnations (avatars). Some of the subgroups of this sect are:
    - **ISKCON** (International Society of Krishna Consciousness) was founded by A.C. Bhaktivedanta Swami Prabhupada in 1966 in New York City. Commonly known (derisively) as *Hare Krishnas*, the group espouses four regulative principles and four crucial aspects of dharma. The four principles are
        - lacto-vegetrianism (no meat, fish, or eggs; dairy being OK);
        - no illicit sex;
        - no gambling; and,
        - no intoxication (alcohol, drugs, caffeine, or tobacco).

The four crucial aspects of dharma are:
- *Daya* (mercy);
- *Tapas* (self-control);
- *Satyam* (truth); and,
- *Śaucam* (cleanliness of body and mind).

- **Krishnaism** is a loose collection of groups that worship Viṣnu through Krishna, and who make their central text, or scripture, the *Bhagavad-Gita* (the "Celestial Song", a 700 verse section of the epic *Mahabharata*).

- **Ekasarana** is a simplified religious system that rejects most rituals, and maintains a connection to Brahman through repetition of the 'name of God' (which they call *Narayana*). This branch is very tightly aligned with the Advaita philosophical school, and practices constant devotion (*bhakti*).

- **Ramanandi** is a group that worships Viṣnu through His seventh avatar, Rama. They often also worship Hanuman as part of this structure.

- **Śaivism** is the sect (second in size to Vaisnavism) consisting of those Hindus who consider Śiva the Supreme Being. Some of the sub-groups of this sect are:

  - **Paśupata** is the oldest of the Śaivite traditions, and dates to Vedic times, when Śiva was referred to as *Rudra*. Literally, *Paśupati* means "Lord of the animals", and was a common Vedic epithet for Śiva/Rudra.

  - **Śaiva Siddhanta** is a modern continuation of the Paśupati. Perhaps the best known Śaiva Siddhanta group is the monastic community on Kauai in Hawai'i (a branch of the Śaiva Siddhanta Church founded in Sri Lanka in 1949) that publishes *Hinduism Today*.

  - **Lingayat** was a 12th century CE Śaivite reform movement that sought to eliminate caste restrictions and distinctions.

  - **Aghori** are Saivite advaitins who espouse the unity of all existence in the person of Śiva. As such, there is nothing that exists that is not perfect, for to deny the perfection of anything would be to deny the sacredness of life as well as to deny the perfection of Şiva. To demonstrate that all is Şiva, and all is perfect, the Aghori often flaunt what can only be called social taboos. They claim an illusory nature for all conventional categories, demonstrating this by partaking of *tamasic* practices (Sanskrit: "darkness"): eating meat; drinking alcohol; consuming food with opiates, cannabis, and other psychotropic drugs as ingredients; cannibalism; living on cremation grounds; smoking banned substances; drinking urine; eating feces; and, engaging in proscribed sexual practices.

- **Nagas** are Saivite ascetics that often go naked on their travels The term originally referred to nature spirits, and may still be used that way; however, it has come to refer to these Saivite *sadhus* (ascetics) who have renounced all material support (including clothing).

- **Shaktism** is the worship of Brahman through the feminine aspects of deity. Known as either Shakti or Devi, worship may be focused on specific goddess forms of this feminine deity, such as Parvati (the "gentle" aspect of Sakti), Durga (the embodiment of feminine force, often pictured with 18 arms, riding a lion or tiger, bearing weapons, but carrying a flower), or Kali (the manifestation of empowerment and feminine authority, She appears alternatively as a loving Mother Goddess and the fearsome goddess of time and death).

- **Smarta Tradition** is a sect that believes that, since all of the Hindu gods are manifestations of the one True Source, it really doesn't matter which form you choose to worship. Therefore, Smarta temples have statuary representing several different Hindu gods/goddesses (Şiva, Vişnu, Devi, Ganesh, Surya, and Skanda*).

---

* *Skanda* is much more popular in Tamil Nadu and throughout southern India than elsewhere, and is known by a number of names (including, most commonly, *Murugan*). He is seen as being the elder son of Şiva, and therefore the older brother of Ganesh.

These variations of Hinduism are not as diverse as the average non-Hindu may at first suspect. Brahmanism*, Vaiṣnavism and Ṣaivism are all formed to worship the Hindu godhead, but vary in their understanding and belief as to which aspect of the triune godhead best serves as representative of the supreme God. Tantrism and Saktism are often more esoteric and magical than other forms of Hinduism, and also tend to stress more devotional aspects of their faith than the groups from which they evolved.

The true nature of humanity and its relationship with God is treated somewhat differently by the various groupings within Hinduism. Man is often seen as being an indispensable part of creation. The universe, known as the *sat* [Sanskrit: "universe"], is seen as being a real, structured entity which is naturally governed by *ṛta* [Sanskrit: "order and truth"]. This balance is always in jeopardy of being disrupted by *asat* [Sanskrit: "chaos"]. Traditionally, *enas* [Sanskrit: "sin"] and *papman* [Sanskrit: "evil"] are often put on a par with illness, enmity, distress and malediction. The cause of all of the *asat* (chaos) is thus accepted as a kind of pollution. As such, it is thought that it can be removed or neutralized through strict adherence to religious practices. Total purity is expected to result in a world where harm and danger are unknown. This state is believed to include prosperity, tranquillity, and a realization of the *atman* [Sanskrit: " the individual Self"] in the body.

Despite the fact that various sects may worship different gods or avatars, God is definitely perceived monotheistically. Brahman (God) is viewed as the sole Creator and Cause of humanity, the universe, and Himself. He is omnipotent, omniscient, omnipresent, the source of all positive qualities and the logical goal toward which all religious practice should be directed.

---

* Brahmanism views Brahma as the Supreme Manifestation of Brahman, but was not reviewed here, as it is numerically very small.

Chapter 20
Concepts, Scripture & Holidays

If God is infinite, the ways that lead to him must be infinite.... Why discuss or debate? What matters is to find God at all costs and not to torture oneself over the choice of the best road to take. Rigid adherence to certain dogmas is not indispensable; at times it can be harmful. — Sri Ramakrishna*

Concepts

There are several beliefs and practices which are fundamental to Hindu practice. These practices define, even better than some abstract philosophical description, the nature of a Hindu society.

- *Ahimsa* [Sanskrit: "noninjury"] is central. It is the doctrine of refraining from harming or injuring others: in addition to the taking of life, it is often seen to apply to non-human life as well. Although there are individual exceptions, the result is generally a rather benign, gentle and nonviolent existence. When fully applied, it frequently results in pacifism or vegetarianism (or both♦).

- *Karma* [Sanskrit: "work"] is seen as the force generated by a person's actions. It is held to be the motive power behind the round of rebirths and deaths endured by an individual, and remains in force until spiritual liberation is attained. Westerners marginally acquainted with the concept may see it as Deific reward or punishment; but, the Hindu view of *karma* is somewhat more esoteric: it is not reward/punishment, but is the actual motive force which propels the true identity of the individual from one birth to the next – a sort of cosmic law of cause and effect.

- *Dharma* [Sanskrit: "that which is established"] constitutes the total body of cosmic principles or laws by which existence is

---

* Sri Ramakrishna (1836 – 1886) was known as the *Madman of God*. Known also by the title *Paramahansa* ("the greatest swan"), he was the guru (teacher) of world famous Swami Vivekananda

♦ Mahatma Gandhi was a well-known, widely-respected pacifist & vegetarian.

created and governed (essentially encompassing the "rules of Deity").

- *Samsara* [Sanskrit: "passing through"] is the constantly temporal, finite, changing existence in which we find ourselves.
- *Nirvana* [Sanskrit: "extinguish"] is that state which all Hindus wish to cultivate and develop — freedom from *karma*. Often associated with the Western concept of heaven, there are distinct differences. Whereas heaven is often viewed as a place or state where man is rewarded for a life of good — a place where all human desires and passions are fulfilled, *Nirvana*, by contrast, is the extinction of all desire, passion, illusion and the empirical self. It is the attainment of rest, truth, and unchanging being.
- *Moksha* [Sanskrit: "release"] is release from karmic effects and the samsara experience — *i.e.* the attainment of *nirvana*.

Hindus believe that there are four primary methods of gaining this *moksha* (release): meditation, good works, knowledge, and devotion. These constitute the ways of salvation — the means of attaining release from an otherwise continuous round of rebirths.

- *Bhakti-marga* is the path (*marg*) of religious devotion or love for a deity as the expression and manifestation of Brahman, God. The devotée who practices this devotion is known as a *bhakta* [Sanskrit: "belonging to"]. The extreme depth of this devotion can be seen in the Sanskrit words used to describe the process [*bhakti* and *bhakta*]. The devotée literally commits to 'belonging to God', and the devotion itself becomes a portion or share of what actually constitutes God.
- *Karma-marga* is a second path of escape from this continual cycle of reincarnation. This is an attempt to attain salvation through the practice of good works and the deliberate positive directing of *karma* (that motive force which results in rebirth). A typical means of practicing *karma–marga* is to adhere strictly to the social and cultural duties expected of them. This often includes caste regulations, religious restrictions, and organized rituals. It is believed that, by being responsive to one's duty, no negative *karma* will result.

- *Jnana-marga* [Sanskrit: "path of knowledge"] is the third path to salvation. This was initially developed in the *Upanishads* (a collection of very early Hindu writings). Later, it was expanded by the various philosophical systems that followed (e.g. *Sakhya* and *Vedanta*); and, it was the *Upanishads* that developed the modern Hindu philosophy of a Universal Soul with which individual souls are ultimately reunited. *Jnana-marga* involves the individual in a rigorous mental and ascetic self discipline, often done in conjunction with a *guru*. When a *guru* is working with a student of Hinduism, the *guru* is not so much a teacher as a fellow traveller and companion on the road of *jnana-marga*. The *guru* is simply one who has progressed further along this road.

- *Raja-marga* [Sanskrit: "royal path"] is a complex system which features meditation and bodily activities to control mental and physical perception. It is seen as enabling the practitioner to 'rise above' this illusory, material existence.

- *Maya* [Sanskrit: "the illusion of time and space"] is used to describe the physical universe, which is seen as an obstacle to union with God. It is not, however, seen as being real, so much as it is our perception of the physical universe

- *Yoga* [Sanskrit: "union"], which is often misundersood in the West, is a state of union where the individual self is brought into harmony with the Universal Spirit. *Yoga* is derived from the same Indo-European root as *yoke* (a tool to bind oxen together), and is a means to unite with, to be tied to, God. The physical form of *yoga*, along with the breathing and postures which accompany it, is but one approach to facilitate this union. This form of *yoga* is properly known as *hatha yoga*. *Yoga* is often used interchangeably with *marga* to indicate the method by which union is being sought: *bhakti-yoga, karma-yoga, jnana-yoga, hatha-yoga,* or *raja-yoga*.

Scripture

Hinduism is a mythological (or mythical) religion. In other words, the beliefs, the practices, and the ethics of the faith are largely communicated through lessons learned by the faithful in the stories of the many Hindu deities. As a result, there is a huge collection of material that is involved which can be considered as scriptural. In fact, one could argue that Hinduism has the largest collection of scriptures of any religion on earth (perhaps not as many as Baha'i, but definitely longer). Not everyone would agree with any listing of Hindu scripture, and there is no ultimate authority in Hinduism that can simply decree it so. As a result, there are varying ideas of what should probably be classified as scriptural. Among these writings are the following.

Vedas The *Vedas* are a huge collection of early writings that originally began as oral traditions sometime between the 2nd and 6th millennium BCE). *Veda* [Sanskrit: "true knowledge"] comes from the root *vid*, meaning "to know", and are classified as *shruti* ["that which is heard"]. This is derived from a belief that the Vedas constitute authoritative revelations from Brahman that were heard by wise and spiritual leaders of the past.

Ṛg Veda The oldest of the vedic texts, this is essentially a hymnal combined with other religious material. It is generally dated to have been first written down between 1500 and 1700 BCE, which makes it the oldest existing written religious text in the world. Based on the food and animals mentioned in it (and those which are apparently unknown to it), experts usually conclude that it was first composed in what is today the northern Indian state of the Punjab.

Sama Veda Second only to the Ṛg Veda in terms of reverence and sanctity, this is essentially a guidebook for priests. It consists mainly of hymns, poems, and verses – many shared with the Ṛg Veda – arranged to support specific priestly rituals and functions.

Atharva Veda Sometimes referred to as the text of mystical science, the Artharva Veda is unusually symbolic; and, it is often the most disliked Hindu scripture by apostates (those who have left the faith, *e.g.* Jains and Buddhists).

Yajur Veda The name of this collection means "knowledge of the sacrifices". It provides the liturgy (forms of public worship) required to correctly perform the rituals and sacrifices of the early Vedic (proto-Hindu) faith. It delves into numerical and scientific studies that are the first known introduction to the world of numbers as great as a trillion, and provides the world's first discussion of *puma* (a mathematical concept known in English as *infinity*).

Upanishads The Upanishads are technically part of the Vedas, and concern themselves with discussion of the nature of God, and the philosophical and meditational aspects of faith. Considered mystical contemplations of the Vedas, they form their culmination and essence. For this reason, they are often referred to as *Vedanta* (literally, "the end of the Vedas" or "the goal of the Vedas").

Agamas Just as the Vedas are *shruti* (that which is heard), the Agamas are *smriti* (that which is remembered), and refer to a vast collection of early Sanskrit writings that recall the teachings of ancient spiritual leaders. Where *shruti* is considered to have come from God, *smriti* is considered to be of human creation. Each sect of Hinduism has its own Agama collection, and there is wide disagreement over what should be included.

Puranas The Puranas are an encyclopædic collection of mythology, history, philosophy, and ritual. Originally transmitted orally, they have now been written. There are 18 "great Puranas", and these all date in written form from sometime during the 1st millennium CE. The range of topics included is immense, and ranges from an entirely spiritual and philosophical reflection on the gods to appropriate forms of architecture, ritual, and even veterinary medicine.

Mahabharata This is the grand-daddy of all religious texts – 74,000 verses (180,000 lines; 1.8 million words – roughly 2½ times the length of the Christian Bible). It is a poem that tells the story of the Pandava brothers (the heroes) and their struggles with their cousins, the Kauravas (the demons), for control of the Bharata Kingdom (*i.e.* India). The Pandavas are seen as blessed, advised and aided by the gods, or even as gods themselves; the Kauravas are seen as demons, rejecting the gods. As a result, the Mahabharata serves as a tremendous metaphor for the struggle between good and evil, right and wrong.

Bhagavad Gita   *Bhagavad Gita* literally means the "Song of God", and refers to roughly 700 verses in the Mahabharata. It is a story told by Krishna, an avatar (incarnation) of Viṣnu who is called *Bhagavan* ("the divine one"). Commonly referred to as simply *The Gita*, it is revered as sacred by nearly all Hindus, but especially so by Vaishnavites.

Ramayana   Although short compared to the Mahabharata (isn't everything?)*, the Ramayana is a 24,000 verse poem that tells the story of Rama of Ayodhya (another incarnation of Viṣnu). His wife, Sita (an incarnation of the goddess Laxmi), is abducted by the demon Ravana and taken to his kingdom (Lanka). Sita is rescued through the efforts of Hanuman. In the story, Hanuman is a *vanara*, and is often pictured as a monkey, (*vanara* is translated as "human with the tail of a monkey"); but, it is more likely a contraction of *vana-nara*, a term used to describe "humans who live in the forest". The tale takes on religious allegorical tones since Rama and Sita are incarnations of deities, Rama is the epitome of virtue, Sita is the ideal of love, and Hanuman is seen as loyalty, devotion, and bravery.

Holidays

There are a lot of popular Hindu holidays, although some of them may be observed primarily by one sect of Hinduism and not others. Nevertheless, there are some that are nearly universal, and even those that are not are still respected by all. Considering the most widely observed, as they occur throughout the year:

- ***Holi***   Holi is a celebration of spring, and falls in February or March. Numerous historical and mythological events in Hindu history are commemorated on this day, and this is probably the "least religious" of all of the Hindu holidays. Hindus are encouraged on Holi to disregard social norms, and to participate in unrestrained merry making. A common holi-

---

* For comparison: The Mahabharata is ~74,000 verses and 1.8 million words; the King James Version of the Bible is ~31,000 verses and 775,000 words; the Ramayana is ~24,000 verses and ~580,000 words (varies over many versions); the Qur'an is 6,346 verses and ~75,000 words; and, the Taoist *Tao Te Ching* is 81 verses and about 5,000 words.

day practice is the throwing or spraying of colored water or powders on friends, relatives, and even strangers.

- *Mahashivaratri*   A much more sedate holiday is *Mahashivaratri*, a day dedicated to meditation, fasting, and devotion to Şiva. Although obviously most important to Şaivites, most Hindus celebrate. A chant often used by devotées this day is *Om namah Shivaya* ("God, Thy name is Shiva").

- *Rama Navami*   The April birthday celebration of Lord Rama (the 7th avatar of Vişnu). The most auspicious location is the town of Ayodhya where, by tradition, Rama was born.

- *Krishna Jayanti*   The birthday celebration of Krishna (the 8th avatar of Vişnu). This falls in July or August, and is often observed with reenactments of events from the life of Krishna. Traditionally an Indian holiday only, the first political entity outside India to officially proclaim the holiday was the US State of Arizona (by then governor Janet Napolitano).

- *Raksabandhana*   A holiday on which the bonds between brothers and sisters are renewed and strengthened (essentially a celebration of the family). This also falls in July or August.

- *Kumbh Mela*   A mass pilgrimage held in the July-August time period, this occurs in two forms: every 3 years in a different city; and, the *Mahakumbh Mela* every 12th year*. It attracts both Hindus and non-Hindu participants from all over the world to participate in ritual bathing in the Ganges River. Naga paticipants (see page 248) usually participate nude (right). The 2013 Maha Kumbh Mela at Allahabad reportedly drew 120 million people. Mark Twain visited India, attended the 1895 Kumbh Mela, and later wrote the following about his experience:

---

* The pilgrimage is to the Ganges River, and takes place at the towns of Haridwar, Ujjain, and Nashik; every 12th year, it takes place in Allahabad.

It is wonderful, the power of a faith like that, that can make multitudes upon multitudes of the old and weak and the young and frail enter without hesitation or complaint upon such incredible journeys and endure the resultant miseries without repining. It is done in love, or it is done in fear; I do not know which it is. No matter what the impulse is, the act born of it is beyond imagination.   — Mark Twain (Samuel Clemens)

- **Ganesha Chaturthi**   This is a joyous festival celebrating the birth of Ganesh, and falls in August or September. Worshipped as the god of wisdom, prosperity, and good fortune, Ganesh is extremely popular and is invoked whenever a new venture is undertaken. The 10 day festival culminates when an idol* of Ganesh is brought to a local lake or river and immersed. Traditionally, this icon was made from the soil near one's home, and the immersion in a nearby lake resulted in it dissolving into the water — a process seen as symbolic of the natural cycle of creation, existence, and dissolution that occurs in nature. Unfortunately, most icons today are mass produced for the celebration, and are made of Plaster of Paris. So many icons are dissolved in local waters that lakes and streams are being seriously polluted by the dissolved plaster, and it is now a serious environmental concern; so, some suppliers have started offering "green Ganeshes" (*i.e.* environmentally friendly icons) as an alternative.

- **Dassera**   Observed in September or October, *Dassera* commemorates the victory of Rama (with assistance from Hanuman) over the demon king Ravana.

- **Navaratri**   A festival celebrating *Shakti*, the feminine aspect of Brahman, this is held in September or October. It is an extended period of celebration (*Navaratri* literally translates into English as "nine nights"), with a different manifestation of Shakti worshipped each day (*e.g.* Laxmi, Durga, *etc.*).

- **Diwali**   Perhaps the most widely and universally celebrated Hindu holiday in the year is *Diwali* (pronounced dih-

---

* Technically, idol is inappropriate, as it is a poor English translation of the Sanskrit *murti*. A murti is a representative embodiment of a Divine Spirit, and not merely a physical image. It is treated with the same respect as one would the Deity it manifests.

vah'-li). This is actually a contraction of the Sanskrit *Dipavali* (often written *Deepavali*), which translates as "row of lights". Often called the *Festival of Lights*, this is effectively the Hindu New Year. It falls in the October-November period (starting on the New Moon), and is a raucous, joyous, 5 day festival. It also welcomes the presence of Laxmi (the goddess of wealth), and is the time when banks and other institutions close their books for the year and start anew.

Small clay lamps are lit and placed in a row atop temples, houses, and even set adrift in rivers and streams. Gambling is encouraged as a way of ensuring good luck for the coming year, and – in honor of Lakshmi – female gamblers <u>always</u> win.

Chapter 21
Divergence

There are a number of groups that have been spawned by, or grown out of, the Vedic-Hindu base. These include: Buddhism (covered in depth in the next Section), Jainism, Transcendental Meditation, Divine Light Mission, Krishnamurthi Foundation, and Sathya Sai Organization. Some are quite ancient, while others are virtually contemporary. As examples of the breadth of what Hinduism has spawned, this chapter will review Jainism and the Transcendental Meditation movement.

Jainism

> *At any time, in any form and accepted name, if one is shorn of all attachment, that one is you alone. My Lord! You are one although variously appearing.*
> — Hemachandra, Anyayogavyavacchedika 29

Jainism is based on the teachings of a series of *jinas*, often rendered as "heroes" in English, but which actually translates as "those who overcome". Although each of these *jinas* is known by name, only the last three are generally accepted as historical by academics. Since the first *jina* was a giant who lived 8 to 9 million years ago, historical verification is, not surprisingly, rather sparse.

The most recent *jina* was a man named Vardhamana Jnatrputra, or Mahavira [right]. Technically, *Mahavira* is a title rather than a name (*conf* Rabbi, Doctor, Buddha, or Christ). He is best known to his followers by this title, meaning "The Great Hero". Historians generally believe that he was born in 599 BCE. Living to the age of 72, he was a contemporary of Buddha (563 – 483 BCE), and it is reported that the two men actually met and knew each other. He passed on in 527 BCE as the result of committing *salekhana* — an extreme ascetic act of fasting in which one ultimately starves to death. Mahavira was born into the Indian religious milieu of this period as an hereditary prince.

It will be seen in the next Section that Buddha proposed what is called the *middle way*; and, the question may be asked: "middle between what two points?" One point was the Brahmanic teachings of Vedism that evolved into modern Hinduism, and was already formalized by the time of Buddha. At the opposite extreme, there were ascetics who followed a life of deprivation, denial of worldly connections, and extreme monasticism — many wandering the countryside naked, denying themselves even that degree of physical comfort. Buddha himself followed this path unsuccessfully while searching for release from the bonds of worldly existence, but later moved to his *middle path*. Mahavira can be seen as being a leader and strong example of the extreme ascetic approach. He exemplified that extreme opposed to the evolving Hinduism from which Buddha generated his middle path.

The list is rarely published, but there are twenty four *jinas*, or *tirthankaras* (spiritually enlightened souls; literally, "ford makers" – *i.e.* those who help to "cross over"). They are:

1	Rishaba (Adi)	9	Suvidhi	17	Kunthu
2	Ajita	10	Shital	18	Arah
3	Sambhava	11	Shreyansa	19	Malli
4	Abhinandana	12	Vasupujya	20	Munisuvrata
5	Sumati	13	Vimala	21	Nami
6	Padmaprabhu	14	Ananta	22	Neminatha [b. 3228 BCE]
7	Suparshva	15	Dharma	23	Parshva [877-777 BCE]
8	Chandraprabhu	16	Shanti	24	Vardhamana [599-527 BCE]

Non-Jain historians only accept the historicity of Parshva and Vardhamana (Mahavira). Jainism claims such great antiquity that this is not unusual, since much of the Jain tradition had passed down orally for centuries before being committed to writing. The *Kalpa Sutra*, a Jain scripture, provides a listing of ancient orders (monastic) long assumed by historians to be fictional. Then, archæological expeditions to Mathura revealed a number of ancient inscriptions which referenced the same orders listed in the *Kalpa Sutra*. In addition, there are numerous cross references between Buddhist, Jain, and Vedic literature which tend to support each other in claims of antiquity. That all 24 *jinas* were historical will likely never be provable to non-Jains; however, many other antiquity claims of the Jains have later proven to have substantial support from non-religious sources.

The beliefs of the Jains share much of the same underlying structure as those of the Hindus and Buddhists with whom they have shared the subcontinent of India for thousands of years. They perceive the universe as existing in a series of layers, or planes of existence, which comprise both heavens and hells (in Western terminology). Everyone is bound to this set of existences as a result of *karma* (essentially the accumulated good or evil that one has done). To Jains, *karma* is seen as a sort of ethereal, primordial dust which collects on the soul and inhibits the upward transmigration of the soul through the multiple layers of existence. It is seen as a sticky substance that binds matter to the soul. *Moksha* is seen as a release from this endless succession of lives, and comes about as a result of enlightenment; but, unlike Buddhism and Hinduism, enlightenment is thought attainable only through an ascetic life.

Of all of the Vedic religions, Jainism is the staunchest proponent of *ahimsa*. As seen, *ahimsa* translates from Sanskrit into English as "non-injury", or "nonviolence". To Jains, it is resistance to the commission of any act of violence against any living entity: human, animal, or even vegetable. Superficially, an "act of violence" can be purely physical; but, to a strict Jain, it may also be mental or emotional. The result of this is that Jains are fiercely vegetarian, will not keep pets (animal enslavement is seen as an act of violence), are always willing to entertain all sides of an issue, and severely restrict acceptable professions based on how that profession might impact other lives. Ascetics wander the roads of India, often wearing cotton masks to avoid accidentally inhaling a small insect, and frequently sweep the road ahead of them with a soft broom to avoid inadvertently stepping on a crawling bug.

The Jain faith does not require the existence of a God; neither does it deny God's existence (it simply does not concern itself with it — at least not in the meaning of a Creator God). According to Jainism, all that was needed for the creation of the universe was a single perfect soul, and there are nearly an infinite number of living beings that provide that. If God does exist, then God is beyond human understanding; and since any God would be unknowable, it would be a futile endeavor to even attempt a relationship with this Deity. This effecttively makes Jainism an agnostic religion.

Theological / Spiritual Beliefs

Since "theological" refers specifically to the study of God, and since Jains do not concern themselves with God, it is actually more accurate to refer to this section as "spiritual beliefs". The following is a layman's guide to Jain spirituality and reality.

Reality falls into two separate and distinct categories: *jiva* and *ajiva* (essentially, sentient and non-sentient entities). Non-living entities (such as a rock) are composed entirely of *ajiva*; but, living entities consist of a *jiva* (the "sentient essence"; somewhat equivalent to the western concept of the *soul*) as well as a certain amount of *ajiva* (non-sentient matter) that is associated with it. Each *jiva* is spiritual, immortal, omniscient, and complete; but, the *ajiva* associated with it interferes with the *jiva*'s ability to realize its true nature. There are a seemingly infinite number of *jivas* (just look around), and each one is an eternal and discrete entity.

These *jivas* are neither interconnected nor interdependent. Each is separate and individual. Being independently eternal, they neither arise from, nor return to, some supreme jiva (which would, in essence, be God). The unencumbered jiva is venerated and worshipped as being divine; but, this is based on having reached the elevated state where they have gained release from the materiality of *ajiva* (*i.e.* spiritual release and liberation). It is not uncommon to hear Jains talk of God; but, this must not be misunderstood. To a Jain, the concept of God is not that of the western religions. God is the collective of all liberated *jivas*. Without the material trappings of *ajiva*, these liberated entitites are indistinguishable; and, there is thus a sense in which they seem to blend together into a single entity in the religious mind of a Jain.

This concept may be puzzling; so, consider the following analogy. Although people around the world talk of *America* as if it were a discrete entity, the fact is that it is really the aggregate, or collective, of individual humans who share certain qualities that make them virtually indistinguishable externally. People may talk of *America*; but, they are actually referring to this collective of more than 300 million *Americans*.

Unlike Christianity, the *jiva* is not seen to have once been perfect, only to have fallen from this divine state. Jains accept that the association of *jiva* and *ajiva* has been eternal — beginningless. This does not mean, however, that this can not be changed; and, devout Jains seek to break the association between *jiva* and *ajiva* to release the *jiva* to realize its true, eternal, omnisicient nature. What ties the *jiva* to *ajiva* is seen to be *karma*.

Although Hindus, Buddhists and Jains all accept the existence of karma, each has a somewhat different perspective on how it operates. Hindus view karma as a motive force that propels the individual through multiple lives toward the inexorable goal of release; Jains view karma as a sort of very fine dust that accumulates on the *jiva*, obscures its innate capabilities, and impedes its progress; the Buddhists usually see karma as an impeding force slowing or preventing spiritual progress[*]. The result of the Jain view (obscuring the *jiva*'s faculties) causes it to be reborn into an endless series of physical existences: *i.e.* reincarnation.

Jains see the goal of asceticism as two-fold: prevent any further accrual of karma; and, hasten the decay of that karma which is already associated with the *jiva*. When the *jiva* is finally free of all karmic association, it is also free from the cycle of rebirth. It has attained its natural, innate quality – perfection. When this happens, the *jiva* "rises" to the *siddha–loka* ("home of the perfected ones") to abide eternally in total knowledge and self-containment.

Today

There are several monastic orders within Jainism today. Lay members may follow in the path of any of these orders.

Shvetambara   The *Shvetambara* ("white clad") may be either monks or nuns. They wander India with a small alms bowl wearing only a white cloth (as either a robe, or wrap-around known as a *dhoti*). During the monsoon season, they may retreat to the Jain temples where they assist with rituals in return for food and shelter from the elements. Their split with the Digambara (*q.v.*) occurred during the 1st century CE.

---

[*] As an analogy, consider the three views of karma in automotive terms: as the accelerator (Hindu), the steering wheel (Jain), and the brakes (Buddhist).

Digambara The *Digambara* ("sky clad") are monks who have renounced all material attachment. They maintain that Mahavira was nude following his enlightenment, so they emulate this and also wander India nude (left). One of the primary areas where they disagree with the Shvetambara is in the admission of women: Shvetambara admit women to full participation, while Digambara believe for a woman to attain *moksha*, she must first be reborn male.

Sthanakavasi This began as a reform movement within the Shvetambara monastic tradition in the 17th century CE. They rejected 13 of the 45 recognized scriptures, and adopted an even stricter approach to ahimsa. It is a Sthanakavasi monk (left) who most often dons a cotton mask to keep from inhaling and killing airborne insects and microbes, and sweep the ground before him as he walks to avoid stepping on and destroying crawling insects and vermin. This order of monks (and nuns) is still often seen as a subset of the Shvetambara rather than as an independent monastic order.

Monastic progress is measured by the *gunasthana* they have achieved — a sort of scale that indicates their degree of renunciation from all ajiva attachments. At the 6th gunasthana (of 8), they take monastic vows to: observe ahimsa; avoid lying; not take that which is not freely given; renounce ownership of all possessions; and, abstain from sexual activity. Achieving the 8th (final) level is synonymous with having achieved moksha.

The lay community also works through a gradation of various levels of renunciation. There are eleven such levels (known as *pratimas*), and the end goal is to be reborn as a monk or nun. In order, these pratimas require a lay Jain to: practice correct views; take lay vows; practice equanimity (through meditation); fast on certain holy days; ensure the purity of nourishment; practice sexual abstinence by day; practice faithfulness within marriage and other material commitments; abandon household activities; abandon material possessions; renounce concerns for the householder's life; and, renounce all connections with their family.

Diet and Related Practices

Devout Jains follow dietary practices that physically reinforce their vows of ahimsa. Although followed more strictly by the monks, even laymen follow these as closely as possible.
- filtering drinking water (to remove microscopic organisms);
- eating no meat;
- eating no eggs, milk, cheese, honey or other animal products;
- eating no vegetables which are cut down or uprooted to eat;
- eating only fruit that falls from the tree (no picking); and,
- no alcohol (since it "inflames the passions").

In addition, Jains also do not:
- keep pets (enslavement);
- condone or visit zoos (captivity);
- use animals as "beasts of burden" (forced labor); or,
- travel by air (kill birds), ship (kill fish), or automobile (kill insects).

Although it may seem strange, one of the most common places to find Jains is at the local animal markets in India. There, they will spend exorbitant prices to purchase sheep, goats, cows and other animals — and then relocate them to retirement properties where they live out their natural lives being cared for and assisted. There is even a retirement home of this type in the state of Gujarat where local Jains are caring for tens of thousands of rats – most captured by hand in the sewers of Mumbai and other cities to save them from a painful governmental extermination process.

Scriptures

Although many scriptural texts have been lost to history, there remain a total of 45 Jain scriptural works – plus 1. These are all accepted by the Shvetambara sect, while the Digambara sect only accepts 32 of them as authoritative.

Kalpa Sutra The Kalpa Sutra is the "plus 1" just mentioned. It was authored later than the other texts, and consists of biographies of the 24 tirthankaras of this cycle. Although not technically scriptural (since it is non-canonical), it does belong in this general classification.

Angas   The Jain scriptures are popularly called *Angas*. This is whatever 'comes from the mouth of the Lord'. It is generally accepted that anything Mahavira taught after achieving omniscience was compiled by his followers in parts, so the Sanskrit term for "part" (*anga*) is used. Originally, there were 14 Purvas and 12 Angas that were transmitted orally; and, many (all of the Purvas, and 1 of the Angas) were lost over time. The 11 Angas still known now comprise the primary (and oldest) of the Jaina scriptures.

Upangas   Auxiliary works evolved that were based on each of the original 12 Angas, and were completed within the first century following Mahavira's passing. These are the *upangas*.

Mulasutras   Following the direction of Mahavira and his immediate successors (who were all considered omniscient), the next generation of Jain leaders were known as *Shrut Kevalis*. These prominent leaders were well versed in the Angas and Upangas, and prepared a number of subsidiary works. These are known as *sutras, cheda sutras,* or *mulasutras*. There are 4 recognized mulasutras.

Pakirnakas   There are 10 sutras that deal with subjects not otherwise addressed in the scriptures. These independent writings are also often known as the *prakirna sutras*.

Chedas   Another category of the subsidiary works by Shrut Kevalis, there are six *cheda sutras* (also known as *Chedas*).

Sutras   Finally, there are 2 sutras (also known as *chulika sutras*) that deal with issues such as the tirthankaras and the different forms of knowledge (the *Nandi sutra*), and that address the rights regarding the mode of preaching (the *Anuyogadvara Sutra*).

A Traditional Jain Blessing

Khamemi sabbajive	I forgive all beings;
sabbe jiva khamantu me	may all beings forgive me.
metti me sabbabhuyesu	I have friendship toward all,
verem majjha na kenavi	and malice toward none.

Transcendental Meditation

> *Enjoy your life and be happy. Being happy is of the utmost importance. Success in anything is through happiness. ... Under all circumstances be happy, even if you have to force it a bit .... Just think of any negativity that comes to you as a raindrop falling into the ocean of your bliss. You may not always have an ocean of bliss, but think that way anyway and it will help it come. Doubting is not blissful and does not create happiness. Be happy, healthy, and let all that love flow through your heart.* — *Maharishi Mahesh Yogi*

Founder

Mahesh Prasad Varma (right) was born on January 12, 1917 in the central region of what was then British India.* After graduating from Allahabad University in 1942 with a BS in Physics, Mahesh was a disciple of a Hindu mystic (until his mentor died in 1953). Within a couple of years, Mahesh began touring India teaching a meditation technique that had been passed down from this mentor, initially calling it *Transcendental Deep Meditation*. He later condensed that to *Transcendental Meditation* (often just referred to as *TM®*).

After about two years touring India, Mahesh expanded his range to include countries all over the globe (the US, Canada, Asia, Africa, Europe, and Australia). He appeared on television, spoke to thousands at public lectures, and authored numerous articles. This global teaching lasted over a decade (*ca.* 1958-1968); but, his world-wide fame peaked when he became the spiritual advisor to *The Beatles* in 1967. All four members of the rock group had met Mahesh, and went to India to further their meditation training. It did not go well, and all 4 eventually repudiated his influence.

---

* His birth date, place, and even name are all questionable. As an ascetic, records were of little or no importance; and, reconstructing a factual history later became problematic at best. Dates from 1911 to 1918 have been proposed, and he had relatives who used the family name of Srivastava. Allahabad University lists him on their alumni list as Mahesh C. Srivastava.

♦ Leaving India, Lennon wrote *Maharishi*, and included the line "Maharishi, what have you done? You made a fool of everyone." George Harrison convinced him to retitle the song *Sexy Sadie* to make it more generic.

Despite the loss of the Beatles, his fame grew and he generally became known as *Maharishi Mahesh Yogi* (*i.e.* "Mahesh, an ascetic practitioner of meditation through whom revelations occur from his higher consciousness"). He ended his global travels, and relocated his world headquarters from Rishikesh, India to Seelisberg, Switzerland. Among other things, he established nearly a thousand TM Training Centers, certified thousands of authorized instructors, created an organization that controls 3 to 4 billion dollars in assets, and even established a number of schools around the world. He remained active in leading a very prosperous and popular movement until the final few years of his life. Maharishi Mahesh Yogi died peacefully in his sleep at his home in The Netherlands shortly after his 91st birthday (February 5, 2008).

Practices

TM is taught through a formal instruction process that involves a total of seven steps. The cost of the training has varied from year to year and from country to country. It seems to have ranged from $35 (for a US student in the 1960s) to a high of $2,500 (the standard fee in the US in 2003). The current fee is about $1,500.

TM is a meditative technique that quiets the mind through what is known as a *mantra* (a sound "without meaning", although they often appear to be based on Vedic names for the gods). This is repeated mentally, but not audibly; and, this is used as a mechanism to enable the individual attention to transition to a quieter, less active, mental processing state. Traditional postures, breathing exercises, and movements of *hatha yoga* are used to supplement the meditation and prevent the physical body from becoming an impediment to the meditative process.

Religion?

Transcental Meditation has relied heavily on a rather secular business approach for its dissemination; it has generated a successful corporate identity with significant assets; and, it only has a peripheral connection to traditional Hindu religious views. Nevertheless, TM is definitively a religion. Why? Because the United States court system says so!

The US District Court of New Jersey* has declared that TM is inherently religious, and therefore meets the legal definition of religion. It is about as far from traditional Hinduism as one can get, and about as secular as possible and still be considered a religion; but, Transcendental Meditation is considered – both legally and academically – to be a religion.

---

* In 1977, the court heard a challenge to a New Jersey school that was teaching TM to its students. In Docket #76-341, the court ruled "TM is religious in nature", and considered it a violation of the 1st Amendment ban on the establishment of religion. Since 1994, an increasing number of schools around the country have been slowly re-adopting it — this time under the title *Quiet Time Program*.

Section VI
Buddhism

The secret of health for both mind and body is not to mourn for the past, not to worry about the future, or not to anticipate troubles, but to live in the present moment wisely and earnestly. — *Siddhartha Gautama (Buddha)*

What was India like during the 1st millennium BCE?
> — by modern standards, life would have been "primitive".

What was the predominant religion?
> — a collection of native faiths that is probably best described as *proto-Hinduism* (evolved from Vedism)

What were the politics?
> — predominantly authoritarian, autocratic, feudal states

Who was 'in charge'?
> — local kings, princes, rajas, maharajas, *et cetera*

India at this time (*ca.* 500 BCE) was a collection of small feudal states. The modern nation of India was still 2½ thousand years away, and even the unified northern empire of the great Chandragupta Maurya was about 250 years in the future. Against this political background, religion was at a stage that could be called either *early Hinduism* or *Brahminic Vedism*. Religion was thoroughly intertwined with the political state, and virtually all feudal leaders had the exclusive services of local *pandits* or *purohits* (essentially, "house priests").

Although many of the people may have not been totally comfortable with the political and religious situation at the time, those that were born into noble families had distinct advantages: they usually received a good education (which most of the population did not); they were typically isolated from the hardships of everyday life (which the common person was not); and, they had the financial resources to do essentialy whatever they chose to do (which nobody else could do). It is no surprise, then, that the founders of both Jainism and Buddhism were born into these circumstances. Both individuals were born as feudal princes:

- Vardhamana Jnatraputra, or *Mahavira*, was born as the second son of Siddhartha and Trishala (the sister of King Chetaka of Vaishali, and aunt of Queen Chellana of Magadh); he became the leader of the major ascetic sect known today as the Jains; and,

- Siddhartha Gautama, or *Buddha*, was born as the first son (and crown prince) of Śuddhodana and Mayadevi (the king and queen of the feudal Shakya kingdom in the foothills of the Himalayas); he became the founder and central figure of what is today known as Buddhism.

There are numerous similarities in the myths and stories told about Buddha and Mahavira. These similarities could indicate that followers of the two faiths frequently "borrowed" material from each other. It is also entirely possible that the stories are similar due to the similarity of their situations (both being noble births); and, these similarities alone are not sufficient to reject of even cause objections to the historical accuracy of the traditions.

Chapter 22
Buddhist Foundations

The Life of Siddhartha

As the story goes, one night in 564 BCE the Queen of the small Shakya kingdom (in the foothills of the Himalayas, along what is now the border between India and Nepal) dreamed of a white elephant with eight tusks descending down from heaven and entering through her side into her womb. After waking in the morning, she approached the local Hindu priest and asked what this had meant. It was interpreted as meaning that she had conceived a child on that night who would be "a pure and powerful being". She objected that she and King Śuddhodana had not had sexual intercourse, so conception was not possible. Nevertheless, she gave birth to a son nine months later.

When the child was born (563 BCE[*]), the king felt as if all his desires had been fulfilled in that child, and he named the young prince *Siddhartha*. His parents being Śuddhodana and Māyādevi of the Gautama clan, the child's name was thus Siddhartha Gautama. His mother, however, died just 7 days after his birth; and, her younger sister, Mahāprajāpati (also married to Śuddhodana) raised him as her own.

At the naming ceremony for the child, King Śuddhodana was told that the boy would either grow to be a great king or a great spiritual leader. This concerned the king, and he made every effort to steer him along a political, not spiritual, path. As a young prince, he grew up learning all of the traditional arts and sciences; and, it is told that he was fluent in 64 different languages, skilled in mathematics, and was an exceptionally bright student for his tutors. He was also well known for martial skills and capabilities (*e.g.* archery and fencing), and became known as *Shakyamuni*. This is a composite word comprised of *Shakya* (his father's kingdom),

---

[*] 563 BCE is the traditional birthdate for Siddhartha, although some modern scholars place it in either 483 BCE or 403 BCE.

and *muni* (literally, "the able one") — making him, literally, the "able one of Shakya".

Although his father tried to shield Siddhartha from those things that might lead him to a spiritual life (preferring him to become a great king), this was nearly impossible. On occasion, Siddhartha would visit the nearby city. All of this was overseen by a young man assigned by the king to protect Siddhartha. His role was to ensure that Siddhartha attended all of his tutoring sessions, practiced his skills, and did not encounter anything that might lead him into a religious life. This butler/man-servant/nanny was named Channa, and remained with him for nearly 30 years.

Occasionally, things would "slip through" this web of protection, and Siddhartha would encounter things he was not supposed to see. He came into contact with the ill, the elderly, and the disabled — none of which he had seen at the palace (ruins of the palace at Kapilavastu, left*). He also came into contact on one visit with a corpse — something else he had never seen. Finally, he saw a wandering Indian ascetic. Cumulatively, these encounters impressed him greatly. Having been raised in a Hindu kingdom (and therefore accepting reincarnation as an indisputable fact), he began to realize that people were born to suffer these indignities repeatedly. He became focused on finding a way to free people from the sickness, suffering, and death of an endless cycle of rebirths; and, he came to the conclusion that to accomplish this he would have to leave the palace and retire to the solitude of the forest to meditate and seek enlightenment.

Seeing that his son was depressed and likely to leave, his father arranged a party to find a suitable bride for the prince. All of the most beautiful and talented young girls in his kingdom and neighboring kingdoms were brought to the palace for Siddhartha to

---

* Kapilavastu, in the modern Indian state of Uttar Pradesh, is usually thought by Buddhists to have been the birthplace of Buddha. UNESCO believes he was born at nearby Lumbini, Nepal, and has made that a national heritage site.

meet. As a result, Siddhartha was married at the age of 16 to Yasodhara (who was about 8), a beautiful young princess (and first cousin – the daughter of his father's sister). For a while, this seemed to work, as Siddhartha and his bride settled in to the royal life. When Siddhartha was 29, Yasodhara gave birth to a son, Rahula. At this point, Siddhartha appears to have realized that life was becoming more and more involved; and, if he didn't do something soon, he would never be able to pursue the enlightenment that he knew he needed to help the world escape from its endless cycle of suffering.

So, while his wife and newborn son were sleeping, the 29 year old Shakyamuni sneaked out of the palace on his horse (Kanthaka), with the help of his personal servant (Channa). For about 6 miles, Siddhartha rode the white stallion while Channa walked alongside. Then, he dismounted, cut off his long hair with his sword, removed his silk clothing, donned the robe of a monk, and gave his jewelry, clothing, sword and horse to Channa and instructed him to take them back to the palace*.

Siddhartha tried several of the popular approaches to gaining enlightenment, and for about 6 years he followed the strict ascetic lifestyle of a wandering monk. It is not known which group of ascetics this was, for it could have been the followers of Mahavira (the Jains) or any one of a number of Hindu ascetic paths. After nearly starving himself to death, Siddhartha decided the ascetic life was not the path for him. It may have been entirely coincidental, but this was the exact same year that Mahavira starved to death following the *salekhana* ritual fast. The parallels seen between them have led many to accept that he and the five ascetics with whom he was living were, in fact, followers of Mahavira♦.

Still convinced that the opulent life of royalty and the indulgent life of the Hindu priests was not the path to enlightenment; but, now convinced that strict asceticism also wasn't the path, the 35

---

* All of these items were symbolic of his noble heritage: the sword, the fine clothing, the horse, and the hair (only the wealthy could afford the luxury of long hair).
♦ Both Jain and Buddhist sources maintain that the two men knew each other and had talked – something not likely if he had not been a close follower.

year old Siddhartha arrived at what is termed *the Middle Path*. In trying to flesh this out, he sat beneath a large Banyan tree to meditate. Remaining there all night, he confronted every temptation and diversion that Mara (a personification of Evil) could thrust on him. Tradition holds he shed "the final veils of ignorance" with the coming dawn, gaining total enlightenment and understanding.

Much like Jesus the Christ, it was later in Siddhartha's life that he was asked by his followers what (not who) he was. "Are you a god?" they asked. "No." "An angel?" "No." "A saint?" "No." "Then, what are you?" "I am awake", he answered. That response led to how he is known to this day, for the Pali word for "one who is awake" is *Buddha*.

Siddhartha (Buddha) spent the rest of his life wandering the northern Indian countryside preaching and sharing his realization with anyone and everyone who would listen. This 45 year period was not without controversy. Devadatta, a cousin of Siddhartha, had become a follower, but soon became jealous of his teacher and sought control of the growing group. It is reported that Devadatta first asked the Buddha to stand aside and let him lead the *Sangha* (community of monks). When this failed, he tried to kill his cousin on three different occasions. The first attempt was when he hired a group of archers to shoot Siddhartha. But, after meeting the Buddha, they laid down their bows and instead became followers. A second attempt involved rolling a boulder down a hill, but it hit another rock and shattered (only grazing the Buddha's foot). In his third try, Devadatta got an elephant drunk and set it loose. This also failed. Failing all this, Devadatta tried to split the group and set up an alternative sangha. There was a very brief period of success, but he ultimately failed at this as well.

At the age of 80, Buddha was given a meal as an offering by a blacksmith named Cunda. He soon became violently ill and died shortly thereafter. Traditionally, it has always been believed that he died of accidental food poisoning; however, a modern theory (Dr. Mettanando Bhikkhu and Oskar von Hinüber) maintains that he died of a mesenteric infarction (a medical condition brought on by old age with symptoms similar to food poisoning).

Chapter 23
Historical Development

I think it is helpful to have many different religions, since our human mind always likes different approaches for different dispositions. ... So from that point of view, it is better to have variety, to have many religions."
— His Holiness, Tenzin Gyatso, the XIVth Dalai Lama

Establishment

Shortly after his profound religious experience, Siddhartha began to teach any who would listen. Gradually, others began to follow him, and this formed a community of devoted followers (*Sangha*, the world's first monastic community). Following his death, the *Sangha* began to collect his teachings and to write them down to preserve them for posterity. There were disagreements, however, as to what were truly "the words of the Buddha" (the *Buddhavacana*). This was not insignificant, for the life one must live, and the path one follows to reach enlightenment, is defined in large part by which writings are seen as authoritative.

As time passed, various interpretations of Buddha's teachings produced a wide variety of philosophical schools — all of which are classified as Buddhist. In fact, Buddhism is an extremely diverse set of beliefs, and defies many of the common definitions of religion. It is thus often categorized by academics as a philosophical system, an ethical system, an historical system, *et cetera*. The primary difficulty is that Buddhism is neither monotheistic nor polytheistic; many maintain that it is atheistic. Buddhism, like Jainism, has developed a metaphysical system which has no active requirement to acknowledge the existence of God. They are not necessarily atheistic, however, for they do not generally deny the existence of God; it simply is not essential. However, they do usually deny the existence of a personal God. This often causes concern to Christians who see religion as a mechanism to worship, honor and pay homage to a person's concept of God (whatever that may be, *so long as it is a personal god*). It therefore becomes impossible for those people to categorize a system as a religion if it maintains no necessity for a personal, involved God.

But, if religion is defined on the basis of its derivation from the Latin *religio* (which meant "obligation"), Buddhism clearly complies. Although this obligation or bond is often taken to mean an obligation to God, there are several philosophical systems in the world (*e.g.* Confucianism, Jainism and Buddhism) which espouse an individual's obligation to a moral and ethical system while neither directly claiming nor explicitly denying the concept or existence of God. Based on this, these are therefore *religions*.

Divisions & Movements

Buddhism has grown and migrated throughout the entire world over the centuries. That area where it has become the most widespread is in Asia. India, the birthplace of Buddhism, has seen the virtual elimination of the religion in probably the best example in history of syncretism in action — with Hinduism reabsorbing Buddhism nearly to extinction. The rarity with which Buddhism has been predominant in an independent nation has limited the impact which it has had on world political thought. It has increased in the West, however, and is most visible in organizational structures such as the Buddhist Churches of America. As with most faiths, the geographical diversity that developed as it spread resulted in philosophical, theological, interpretive and ritualistic diversity as well. Today, along with the historical differences mentioned earlier, this accounts for the major branches of Buddhist thinking.

Theravada Buddhism

Theravada Buddhism is perhaps the oldest surviving branch, or school, of Buddhism. Following the death of Buddha, loyal monks met to plan their future. Tradition has it that there were about five hundred monks present at the meetings. When the council ended, they declared that they had captured all the words of Buddha for posterity, and that no new teaching or discourse would be added as *buddhavacana* from that point forward. Nevertheless, new teachings were added in the following centuries as accounts surfaced as much as 500 years after his death. This gradual expansion of the Buddhist canon inevitably led to internal disagreements regarding both inclusion and interpretation, and Buddhism began to evolve into various divisions. The first major division occurred over whether the potential for salvation was universal or specific. In other words, must a Buddhist seeking *nirvana* become a strict monastic devotée; or, could the laity also aspire to *nirvana*?

The predominant Buddhist position at that time placed its emphasis on each Buddhist devotée working for their own emancipation. Their ideal was an *arhat* — someone who finds the path to overcoming all ties to the material world and attains *nirvana*. Typically, it was believed that becoming an *arhat* virtually required spending one's life as a monk. As such, the sect was seen by many as being exclusive and elitist. Becoming known as *Theravadin* (or, *Theravada Buddhists*), this translates as "Way of the Elders".

The Theravadin believe that their teachings — based solely on the canon authorized by the *Sangha* at the council following the death of Buddha — is the purest form of the religion. Theravadin interpret the key truths as follows:

- the nonexistent self mistakes itself as a soul — a permanent entity;
- as a result, it clings to its belief and desire for this permanent existence — in essence, desiring what it cannot have;
- this attachment to itself leads, without exception, to attachment to other things — believing it has an enduring body, living in an enduring world, sharing that world with other enduring persons and things, acquiring enduring possessions of wealth, honor, children, reputation, *et cetera*;
- these impermanent attachments do not constitute suffering — however, accepting them as permanent when they are all impermanent inevitably leads to suffering. The cause of the suffering is desire — desirousness of all kinds (*e.g.* ambition, acquisitiveness, attachment, greed, insistence) and for all kinds (*e.g.* pleasure, well being of self and others, survival); and,
- to remove suffering, one must remove these desires — the method of which is the middle path of Buddha (neither materialistic nor ascetic), *i.e.* the *Eightfold Path*.

In Theravada Buddhist countries, the Buddhist laity tend to leave the philosophical, more difficult, and more abstruse aspects of the religion to the ordained monks. The laity goes about their daily business trying to do good, and thus build up karmic equity which they hope will lead them to become ordained monks in some future existence.

A great 3rd century BCE Mauryan (Indian) king, Ashoka, was converted to Buddhism by a Theravada monk. Just as the orthodox conversion of the Roman emperor gave significant political advantages to the orthodox sect of Christians (which is essentially what made them orthodox in the first place), the conversion of Ashoka provided opportunities for the Theravadin through which they could counter the broader appeal that more inclusive opponents had with the laity. According to tradition, King Ashoka sent teams of missionaries all over what is today India and Pakistan, as well as to neighboring kingdoms in Sri Lanka, Myanmar, and Southeast Asia — even establishing Theravada missions as far afield as Alexandria, Egypt. His renouncement of war (based on Buddhist principles) gave him tremendous influence and personal appeal in smaller, weaker kingdoms, so his missionary teams were generally well received wherever they went. His own son and daughter (Mahindra and Sanghamittra) accompanied monks to what is now Sri Lanka, and converted the Sinhalese king of that island nation. The result of Ashoka's efforts is that Theravada Buddhism today predominates in Sri Lanka, Myanmar (Burma), Thailand, Malaysia, Kampuchea (Cambodia), and Laos; it is growing elsewhere.

Mahayana Buddhism

The primary alternative to Theravada Buddhism calls itself *Mahayana Buddhism*. Sanskrit for "the greater raft", this refers to their belief that their system is broader and more inclusive. It was this group that coined the term *Hinayana* to refer to Theravada Buddhists. Meaning "the lesser raft", it was intended to "dis" the Theravadin — and, it did. It is still considered offensive by Theravadin (much as many racial and ethnic slurs are considered offensive by members of that particular group), and should be avoided.

Numerically, Mahayana is the largest branch of Buddhism, and is prevalent throughout Tibet, Nepal, China and Japan. It is composed of various syncretic schools who may even believe in God (or gods). This sect usually teaches the *boddhisattva* ideal of compassion and universal salvation. A *boddhisattva* is an individual that has the potential to become a Buddha (an enlightened individual who has been released from the eternal round of rebirths), but remains to teach and support others. Mahayana Buddhism teaches that anyone can aspire to being a *boddhisattva*, thereby making salvation potentially available to all. Mahayana Buddhists thus consider their interpretation of the teachings of Siddhartha to be more compassionate than those of the Theravadin.

In addition to the scriptural texts used by the Theravadin, Mahayana Buddhists also use a number of *sutras* (discourses) attributed to Buddha, but not recognized as such until several hundred years after his death. These sutras tend to make Mahayana Buddhism more inclusive, but Theravada Buddhists consider these sutras essentially to be forgeries.

Although King Ashoka was successful in spreading Theravada Buddhism to the south and southeast, the spread of Buddhism to the north and east was accomplished primarily by the Mahayana sect. Although there were undoubtedly earlier introductions of Buddhism into China, the first truly successful introduction occurred with a monk named *An Shih-kao*. This is important because of how he introduced Buddhism. Until this monk, Buddhism was viewed by the Chinese as a foreign religion of uncouth barbarians (*i.e.* not worthy of consideration). When An Shih-kao arrived home after studying in India, he translated Buddhist sutras into Chinese using the matching concepts translation technique.

When the American novel *Gone With the Wind* was translated into Japanese, the American civil war was a foreign, unknown event in Japan. The translators used Japanese history as the backdrop for the novel, and wrote the southern American parts using the Japanese dialect common amongst farmers on the islands of Kyûshû, Shikoku and Osumi-shôtô. This practice is known as matching concepts: since the American civil war was unknown, they substituted comparable historical concepts familiar to their target audience; since a rural, southern American dialect carries certain connotations to urban Americans that are unknown in

Japan, they substituted a Japanese dialect with comparable connotations to urban Japanese. The French translation used a similar approach: translating the southern parts into a Marseilles dialect (and the northern into a Parisian dialect).

The success of An Shih-kao's approach was tremendous. Not only was Buddhism accepted in China, but the frequent use of Taoist phraseology and examples in his translations actually led many Chinese to think that Buddhism was a new sect of Taoism. It took centuries before Buddhism developed its own identity in China. From China, Buddhism then passed to Korea and Japan.

The Japanese had a different problem than the Chinese when they were first exposed to Buddhism: the Japanese saw Buddha in the light of early Shinto beliefs, so many accepted Buddha as a "Chinese *kami*" (a Shinto spirit concept). Some members of the Soga family (one of three competing, ruling families in Japan at the time) readily accepted Buddhism because they believed they were worshipping the god that had made China so powerful. The head of the Soga family (Soga Umako) saw Buddhism as a way to break the political hold of his opponents, the Mononobe and Nakatomi clans. He built a small Buddhist chapel with an image of Buddha. Unfortunately, an epidemic broke out in Japan at that time, and Umako's foes blamed him and the image. Undaunted, Umako and the Mononobe clan waged a major battle; politics and religion became inextricably linked; and, when Umako dealt a decisive military blow to the Mononobe clan in 587 CE, the Soga claim to the emperor's throne and Buddhism's introduction to Japan, were simultaneously secured. Umako's nephew, Crown Prince Shôtoku, was made emperor; and, with Umako's approval, Shôtoku introduced Chinese Buddhist monks, scholars, artists and craftsmen into Japan. This permanently secured a place in the Japanese religious environment for Buddhism.

Mahayana Buddhism is exemplified as well in *Sunyavada* as in any other philosophy. *Sunyavada* is a philosophy of "emptiness". Note that this is emptiness, not nothingness; and, there is a difference. Ultimate Reality is called *Sunya*, which translates as void; however, it is void of distinctions, not somethingness. Anything so distinctive as Consciousness or Universality could not possibly exist in a state of emptiness. *Sunya*, itself, is considered virtually indescribable because any description distinguishes. Similarly, it cannot be grasped by intellect or rational thought, because it must be distinguished to be grasped; hence, any rational attempt to define or understand Sunya is doomed to failure before it starts.

Westerners, immersed in Aristotelian logic, balk at the inevitable use of the traditional Indian principle of *four-cornered negation* used to explain Sunya. In Western logic, the validity of Boolean operations on truth values, if explained, appears incontrovertibly logical. This causes severe problems of acceptance when Boolean algebra and Aristotelian logic do not hold. Is Sunya (voidness) existent or nonexistent? In Western logic, it must be one or the other. However, it neither is, nor is not, nor both is and is not, nor neither is nor is not, existent. (That is the core of four-cornered negation.) Is it permanent? Is it conscious? To every conceivable question, the answer remains:

- it neither is, nor is not;
- nor both is, nor is not;
- nor neither is, nor is not.

Pause here for a minute, and re-read that.

Another Mahayana concept is *suchness*. The universe can not be understood by comparing it to anything else, because we know of nothing else. We must simply know it for what it is: know it as "that". This is the concept of Suchness or Thatness. To say that a plate is not a fork does not help in knowing what a plate is; it does nothing to help define the suchness of what it is to be a plate. To be consistent with suchness, everything must be accepted for what it is. To compare it to, or distinguish it from, something else does nothing to add to our absolute knowledge of it.

To a Mahayana Buddhist, there are two types of knowledge: ordinary knowledge, which discriminates one thing from another and one kind from another; and, absolute knowledge, which apprehends such concepts as *suchness* and *Sunya*. A *buddha* or a *boddhi* (*i.e.* an enlightened person, one who is awake to reality) is one who has absolute knowledge. By contrast, a wise person is one who has a great deal of ordinary knowledge.

Is there a God? No, unless God is Sunya, the Void. However, in whatever sense there is a God, Sunya is indistinct from it. Consequently, one cannot say that Mahayana Buddhism is atheistic, for it neither is, nor is not, nor both is ... These descriptions fit the Sunyavada school of Mahayana Buddhism better than others, however all schools of Mahayana Buddhism face these same issues. The fact that there are no logical answers in Aristotelian logic to such theological questions as are constantly entertained causes no problem for the practicing Buddhist. There were ten commonly asked philosophical questions at the time of Buddha. As each was asked by his disciples, he gave the same answer: "That is a matter on which I have expressed no opinion." When asked why, he explained simply that stating an opinion on something for which he did not know the answer merely committed him to unhappiness.

Pure Land Buddhism

The *Shin* school of Mahayana Buddhism (also known as *Pure Land Buddhism*) is unlike all others in that it proscribes a faith in some Other Power as sufficient to attain *nirvana*, or salvation. As outlined above, Mahayana Buddhism maintains the *boddhisattva* ideal. *Amitabha Buddha* (or Amida) was such a boddhisattva — one who attained *arhat* status, but elected to remain on this plane of existence to help others who had not yet reached that point. In fact, he vowed to stay until all sentient beings — animals and people — reached that goal. Through countless æons, he has gathered sufficient merit to share with all who need it. All humanity needs to do is to accept the gracious offering of salvation that Amitabha offers (just as Siddhartha did). This is so different from most of the schools of Mahayana Buddhism that it is often listed as a separate sect altogether.

It is accepted that evidence of faith in this gift of grace will naturally express itself as affirmation through the repetition of the name of Buddha, or *namu Amida butsu* (usually shortened to *nembutsu*). Repetition without faith remains ineffective; however, if faith continues without the repetition, the goal will still be attained. Repetition is considered to be evidence of faith, but is not a prerequisite for it.

Is Amida God? Shin Buddhists do not consider Amida to be the Creator of the universe, but he is considered to be the saviour of man. Other *boddhisattvas* are all viewed as manifestations of Amida — even Gautama Buddha. This tends to make Shin Buddhists very tolerant of other religious traditions which claim grace is granted through acknowledgment of some Other Power. These are all (Jesus, Zoroaster, Mohammed, Krishna, *et cetera*) considered regional manifestations of Amitabha.

Another concept of Shin Buddhists is their belief in a Buddha-land (also known as the Pure Land, or Pure Realm — hence the common sect name, *Pure Land Buddhism*). This Pure Land is a wonderful place where the faithful await final enlightenment (somewhat comparable to a cross between heaven and purgatory in Roman Catholicism).

Vajrayana Buddhism

Mahayana Buddhism grew with the introduction of the Buddhist sutras. But, it didn't replace the earlier Theravadin; it grew alongside. Similarly, a new branch introduced *tantras,* which were accepted as teachings of either Siddhartha or another enlightened soul (buddha). According to the Tibetan lama Thubten Yeshe, "each one of us is a union of all universal energy. Everything that we need in order to be complete is within us right at this very moment. It is simply a matter of being able to recognize it. This is the tantric approach." This did not replace either Theravada or Mahayana, but grew alongside both. This became known as *Mantrayana* (the "vehicle of the *mantra*"). A *mantra* is a word or phrase used to focus the mind in meditation. In Tibet, this meditation was on the tantric concept that we are each a divine manifestation of universal, spiritual energy. Another name for this became *Vajrayana* (the "vehicle of the diamond", or "indestructible raft"); and, this sect may be seen as either a distinct sect or Mahayana school.

These Vajrayana Buddhists incorporated magic (in the same sense that it is usually used in the neo-pagan faiths). It involved esoteric teachings, rituals, ceremonies, initiations, incantations, sacred circles, and so on. They also maintain (as does Zen) that enlightenment is achievable in this life. The school flourished, and was the predominant influence on Buddhism as it was introduced to Tibet.

Buddhism was initially introduced to Tibet near the end of the reign of King Songtsen Gampo (Tibetan: *Srong btsan sga*) about 649 CE, and gradually grew until it flourished from 756 to 797 CE, in the reign of King Trison Detsen (*Khri srong Ide brtsan*). The Tibetan kings wanted to ensure that they were introducing the best form of Buddhism into their kingdom, so they decreed that only Indian Buddhist masters would be allowed to teach in Tibet. This effectively barred Zen and traditional Mahayana (with their Chinese practitioners) from the country, and resulted in the highly ritualistic Vajrayana Buddhism.

The indigenous religion of most of Tibet at the time Buddhism was introduced is known as Bon (pronounced *pain*). This native Tibetan religious tradition included such features as divine kingship (the earthly manifestation, incarnation or avatar of the boddhisattva *Kuan-yin*). Kuan-yin* is the boddhisattva of compassionate love. Kuan-yin is usually pictured as female in China, but often as male in Japan and Viet Nam. As a male in India, the name is Avalokiteshvara. In Tibet, a male Kuan-yin is known as *Chenrezi*, and is incarnate in the person of the Dalai Lama. Bon beliefs were supported by an oracular priestly order which had the ability to transmit divine prophecies directly from the gods to humanity. The religion was clearly polytheistic, and at that time included blood sacrifices to the various gods.

Tibetan Buddhism absorbed and adapted most of the Bon religious tradition during the first few centuries of their coexistence in Tibet. The divine kingship was perceived as not the repeated incarnations of a god, but the incarnation of Chinrezi as a lama (a monk, in Tibetan, is a *blama*); the priestly orders became monastic followers of the religion; the polytheistic pantheon was reduced to the Buddhist representation of lesser gods, buddhas, or boddhisattvas (comparable to saints in Western traditions); and, the blood sacrifices were gradually replaced with nonviolent sacrificial off-

---

* Kuan-yin is a contraction of Kuan-shi-yin. The longer name is not used out of respect and fear that it might be used inappropriately; so, the shorter, version is substituted to ensure that it is not misused.

erings. Buddhism was supported by the more powerful members of the ruling class during the eighth and ninth centuries CE, and Bon was supported by much less powerful groups. The result was the virtual eradication of Bon in most of Tibet. Bon exists to this day in northern and eastern remote areas of Tibet, and in exile in northern India (although more fully developed and organized than it once was — seemingly a necessary concession to compete with the much more 'sophisticated' Buddhism).

Early Tibetan Buddhism was re-infused with Indian Buddhism when one of the disciples of the guru Naropa returned to Tibet with his teachings of asceticism. The outgrowth of this development was several monastic orders generally considered today as orthodox orders in Tibet. One of these orders (known as the *black caps*) evolved the succession of the Great Lamas. This was adopted by other orders as well, and one (the *yellow caps*) came to refer to their leader as the *Dalai Lama* (literally, "head monk"). The *Dalai Lama* exercised both spiritual and civil authority in Tibet from the Potala Palace in Lhasa beginning in the seventeenth century. The succession of the role of Dalai Lama is different from royal succession in Europe: the successor of a deceased Dalai Lama is not the eldest son of the departed, it *is* the departed. When the Dalai Lama dies, the Great Lamas assemble a team to search the world for his reincarnation. The XIVth Dalai Lama (Tenzin Gyatso) was found as a two year old boy nearly three years after his predecessor, the XIIIth Dalai Lama (Thubten Gyatso) had passed away.

Just as *Hinayana* is offensive to Theravada Buddhists, the term *Lamaism* is offensive to Tantric Buddhists. The best known form of Tantric Buddhism is the Vajrayana Buddhism of Tibet.

The visibility of the Dalai Lama makes him one of the most widely recognized spiritual leaders in the world; and, many westerners do not know enough about the different branches of Buddhism to know exactly who is teaching what. In essence, the teachings of the Tantric Buddhists of Tibet are overwhelmingly those of orthodox Mahayana Buddhism, but with a large dose of ritual added for good measure. The Dalai Lama, as the rightful leader of Tibet (currently militarily occupied by China), is the ideal spokesman for the tradition. His serenity, wit and compassion are world renowned, and he was the recipient of the 1989 Nobel Peace Prize. As the penultimate Buddhist guru, or lama, his teachings can be viewed as representing the orthodox views of Tibetan Buddhism. What is the essence of his teaching?

> In order to generate the thought to get out of cyclic existence, it is necessary to know about the good qualities of liberation and the faults of cyclic existence that one wants to get out of. However, what is cyclic existence? As Dharmakirti says, it can be posited as the burden of mental and physical aggregates which are assumed out of contaminated action. ... When you look into it, cyclical existence can be identified as the burden of these mental and physical aggregates which we have assumed from our own contaminated actions and afflicted emotions. Once we have such contaminated aggregates, they serve as a basis of suffering in the present. Because they are under the influence of former contaminated actions and afflicted emotions, they are not under their own power. ... *So, my true religion is kindness. If you practice kindness as you live, no matter if you are learned or unlearned, whether you believe in the next life or not, whether you believe in God or Buddha or some other religion, in day to day life you have to be a kind person.*[*]

This kindness will result in less, little or no 'contaminated actions or afflicted emotions' in this life, and must produce a more spiritual and more enlightened life in some future existence. Thus, it is this kindness that is seen as ultimately breaking the hold of cyclic existence.

His Holiness, the XIVth Dalai Lama
(Jetsun Jamphel Ngawang Lobsang Yeshe Tenzin Gyatso)

---

[*] Gyatso, Tenzin [His Holiness, the XIVth Dalai Lama] (1991) *Path to Bliss* Ithaca, New York: Snow Lion Publishing

Chapter 24
Scripture, Concepts & Holidays

How ever many holy words you read, how ever many you speak, what good will they do you if you do not act upon them? — Siddhartha Gautama (Buddha)

Scripture

The very use of the term *scripture*, when applied to Buddhism, presents immediate problems for Western scholars. A similar problem arises with the idea of a *canonical* collection. Perhaps the "best" way of categorizing Buddhist texts is to divide them into two major categories: *Buddhavacana* ("the words of Buddha"), and "other texts". These other texts often consist of commentaries on either Buddhavacana or other early writings.

The more commonly referenced Buddhist texts fall into a number of different styles or forms. These include:

- *Vinaya* – a collection focused of monastic discipline;
- *Sutra* – prose discourses of varying lengths (often identified as short sutras, medium-length sutras, and long sutras);
- *Dhammapada* – a collection of sayings and aphorisms; and,
- *Perfection of Wisdom Texts* – a collection of texts (often using paradox to illustrate their point) designed to point the reader toward wisdom (the ability to see reality for what it really is).

There are literally hundreds of other texts that are also often included in the broad category of scripture; however, many of these texts are often accepted by only one of the sects or ethnic divisions that comprise Buddhism.

Concepts

Buddha was raised in Hindu society, and there are several areas where Buddhist and Hindu teachings coincide. For this reason, many Hindus consider Buddhism to be a sort of wayward branch of Hinduism (much as they do Jainism). Although there may be some merit to this view from a pragmatic viewpoint, the relationship of Buddhism to Hinduism is analogous to that of Christianity to Judaism. Even though Jesus was a Jew, there are few people in the world who would deny that Christianity is a full religious expression apart from Judaism. Similarly, it should be accepted that Buddhism is a full religious expression apart from Hinduism.

The most basic concept within Buddhist teaching is that of *nirvana*, a state of annihilation of all pain and suffering (literally, *nirvana* means a "blowing out"). This is attained by the individual Buddhist through development of mental and moral self purification. What differentiates Buddhism from Hinduism on this point is the methodology which adherents believe will lead to this self purification, and the causes of the apparent lack of purity on the mortal plane of existence.

There are three basic doctrines in Buddhist thought that encompass the underlying concepts on which the faith is built. These are known as:

- The *Three Universal Truths*;
- The *Four Noble Truths*; and,
- The *Eightfold Path to Truth*.

The *Three Universal Truths*, if they are truly universal, should be readily apparent even today. And, they appear to be.

- Nothing is ever lost in the universe
  Although form and appearance may change or even disappear, nothing ever truly "goes away"; nothing is ever lost. In 1905, Albert Einstein posited that $E=mc^2$ as the relationship that explained a mass-energy equivalence. In other words, science agrees 'nothing is ever lost in the universe'.

- Everything is subject to change
  Australian Psychologist Andrew Campbell-Watt has written that "Nothing in the world is static. Nothing remains the same. Everything is in a state of change. Those who long for stability, whereby what is present now will forever be so, are delusional. Such a situation will not and cannot exist. Change is everywhere at all times. The world and life is dynamic. Everything is in a state of flux."

- Karma (Cause and Effect) exists
  Science again agrees, as Isaac Newton's 3rd Law says that "for every action, there is an equal and opposite reaction".

What Buddha taught his followers more than 2,500 years ago has been restated in modern, physical-science terminology by Einstein, Newton, Campbell-Watt, and many, many others. These 3 Universal Truths led Buddha to postulate what are commonly known as the *Four Noble Truths*. He presented these in his very first discourse following his enlightenment (known as *Setting in Motion the Wheel of the Dharma*):

- All life is subject to misery and suffering
  Life is inherently subject to dukkha (Pali: "suffering").

- The cause of this suffering is attachment to that which is impermanent — which attachment results in a series of repeated existences
  It is craving and desire that lead to this attachment – desire for sensual pleasures, existence, and even extermination.

- Annihilation of this desire provides release from these attachments and the cycle of rebirths
  The cessation of dukkha is accompanied by a fading away and cessation of craving, the giving up and relinquishing of it, freedom from it, and nonreliance on it.

- The path to this cessation is the *eightfold path*.
  This eightfold path is seen as the means of attaining nirvana. It requires the adherent to practice:
  - right belief – *an understanding of the 4 Noble Truths*
  - right resolve – *resolve to implement this understanding*
  - right speech – *to refrain from voicing untruths*
  - right action – *to "walk the talk" (put words into action)*
  - right livelihood – *to earn one's living harmoniously*
  - right effort – *to exert oneself to implement these steps*
  - right thought – *to keep words, actions, and even one's thoughts pure and focused on truth*
  - right ecstasy – *meditate to progressively realize a true understanding of imperfection, impermanence, and non-separateness*

Holidays

There are a number of Buddhist holidays that occur throughout the year; however, they are highly culturally impacted, and calendar dates often vary from country to country and culture to culture.

Festivals are always joyful occasions; and, typically, a festival will include lay people going to the local temple to offer food to the monks and listen to a talk. In the afternoon, they will distribute food to the poor (to generate positive karma); and, in the evening, join a ceremony circling a *stupa* (a hemispherical mound holding Buddhist relics; photo is of a stupa in Sanchi, India built by Emperor Ashoka in the 3rd century BCE) three times as a sign of respect to the Buddha, the Dhamma, and the Sangha. It concludes with evening meditation and chanting of the Buddha's teachings.

New Year

Buddhists celebrate the annual New Year with a three day celebration. In Theravadin countries (*e.g.* Thailand, Myanmar, Cambodia, Sri Lanka and Laos), this begins on the 1st full moon in April. In most Mahayana areas (*e.g.* Nepal, Bhutan, or Indonesia), the New Year starts on the 1st full moon in January. This is not universal, however, as the date varies in Mahayana areas depending on the country of origin or ethnic background of the people. For example, Chinese, Koreans and Vietnamese celebrate in late January or early February (based on the lunar calendar), while Tibetans usually celebrate about a month later.

Vesak

Celebration of Buddha's birth is known as *Vesak* (or, sometimes, as *Visakah Puja*). Vesak is the biggest festival of the year, and celebrates not only his birth, but also his enlightenment and death — all on the one day. It is observed on the 1st full moon in May (except in a leap year, when the it is in June).

Magha Puja

Magha Puja occurs on the full moon in March. It is observed to commemorate an important event in the life of the Buddha, one that occurred early in his teaching life. Buddha had gone to Rajagaha, where 1,250 disciples had gathered. This gathering is known as the *Fourfold Assembly* because it consisted of four contributing factors: all 1,250 were *arhats* (enlightened souls); all of them were ordained personally by Buddha; they assembled without being called; and, it was a full moon (highly symbolic in Buddhism). This is also commonly referred to as *Sangha Day*.

Asalha Puja

Asalha Puja is the day when Buddhists pay homage to Buddha. It falls on the full moon of the 8th lunar month (usually in July). It marks the Buddha's first teaching at the Deer Park in Sarnath (near Benares). This is often referred to as *Dhamma Day*.

Uposatha

Uposatha are the ancient monthly days which are still observed in Theravadin countries. These are the days of the full moon, new moon, and two quarter-moon days. Buddhism has no "sabbath", but these days are treated similarly and occur about every 7 days.

Pavarana Day

Buddhist monks typically take a retreat during the monsoons (when they "retreat" from the flooded paths and roadways of India and Southeast Asia to take shelter in a temple). *Pavarana Day* marks the end of this "Rains Retreat" (known as the *vassa*); and, the *Kathina Ceremony* (below) is held the following month.

Kathina Ceremony

The *Kathina Ceremony* is unusual in that it is held whenever it is convenient (but within a month of Pavarana Day). New robes (or material to make them) and other necessities are offered to the monks by the lay members of the community.

Anapanasati Day

One year, at the end of the rains retreat (*vassa*), the Buddha was so pleased with the progress of the monks that he encouraged them to extend their retreat for another month. On the full moon at the end of that fourth month, he presented his instructions on mindfulness of breathing (*anapanasati*) to the assembled monks.

Abhidhamma Day

In Myanmar (Burma), *Abhidhamma Day* celebrates when the Buddha is said to have gone to heaven to teach his mother the *Abhidhamma* (the "higher teachings"). It is held on the full moon of the 7th month of the Burmese lunar year (with the new year starting in April, this puts Abhidhamma Day on the full moon in October).

In Thailand, this festival spans several days in the middle of April. People clean their houses, wash their clothes, and sprinkle perfumed water on the monks, novices and others for two or three days. They gather at the river carrying fish in glass jars to put in the water (Thailand can be so hot that ponds dry up, and fish would die if not rescued). People also go to the beach or river with buckets of water to splash each other. Once everyone is thoroughly wet, they close the day with boat races on the river.

Loy Krathong (Festival of Floating Bowls)

By the end of the *Kathina Festival* (after the monsoons), the rivers and canals are full of water. This is the time for the *Loy Krathong Festival* in Thailand. It is observed on the full moon of the 12th lunar month. To celebrate, people make bowls of leaves (filled with flowers, candles and incense), and float them in the water. As they float away, all bad luck floats away with them. The origin of *Loy Krathong* was meant to pay respect to Buddha's footprint on the beach of the Namada River in India. This is also commonly known as the *Festival of the Floating Bowls*.

The Ploughing Festival

In May, on the half-moon, two white oxen pull a gold-painted plough followed by four girls dressed in white scattering rice seeds from gold and silver baskets. This celebrates the Buddha's first moment of enlightenment, which is said to have happened when he was seven years old, while he and his father watched the fields being plowed. (This is known in Thailand as *Raek Na*).

The Elephant Festival

Historically, in India, when a wild elephant was captured, it was harnessed to a tame one in order to train it. Buddha often used this as an analogy to show that, in the same way, a person new to Buddhism should be mentored by an older Buddhist. To commemorate this teaching, the *elephant festival* is held in Thailand on the third Saturday in November. Hundreds of elephants take part in this commemoration of Buddha's teaching.

The Festival of the Tooth

Kandy is a hill city in the very center of the island country of Sri Lanka. On a small hill next to the Mahaweli River is a temple that was built specifically to house a relic of the Buddha – his tooth! The tooth is never seen, but once a year on the night of the full moon in August, there is a special procession for it. The *Dalada Maligava* is the temple.

Ulambana*

Ulambana (also known as *Ancestor Day*) is celebrated by Mahayana Buddhists for the first fifteen days of the 8th lunar month. It is believed that the gates of Hell are opened on the 1st day, and that ghosts may visit this world for 15 days. Food offerings are made to relieve the suffering of these ghosts; and, on the 15th day, people visit cemeteries to make offerings to their departed ancestors. Many of the Theravadin from Cambodia, Laos and Thailand also observe this festival.

Avalokitesvara's Birthday

This is the festival which celebrates the bodhisattva ideal represented by *Avalokitesvara* (also known as *Kuan-yin*, or *Chinrezi*), who represents the perfection of compassion in the Mahayana tradition. It is observed on the March full moon.

---

* Ulambana is similar in many of its precepts and practices to the ancient Aztec holiday of *Dia de los Muertes* (Day of the Dead), and also shares a number of common features with Halloween.

Bodhi Day (Enlightenment Day)

Bodhi Day marks Siddhartha's enlightenment as the Buddha. It is unusual in that the solar calendar is used for this holiday (celebrated the 8th of December); and, it is observed with prayer, meditation and teachings.

Chapter 25
Modern Divergence

"People can only live fully by helping others to live. When you give life to friends you truly live. Cultures can only realize their further richness by honoring other traditions. And only by respecting natural life can humanity continue to exist."
— *Daisaku Ikeda (Head of Soka Gakkai International)*

Zen

Zen has a long and torturous derivation. It has passed through numerous cultures and languages either through translation or mispronunciation. Beginning in India, and referring to a "meditative state", the word kept changing as it migrated through different languages and regions.
- *dhyāna* (Sanskrit)
- *dzyen* (Middle Chinese)
- *chán* (Modern Mandarin)
- *seon* (Korean)
- *thién* (Vietnamese)
- *zen* (Japanese)

Zen was traditionally introduced to China by an Indian monk named Bodhidharma. This was during an ancient Chinese period known as the *Southern and Northern Dynasties* (420-589 CE). He purportedly went to China to teach a 'new transmission' of Buddhist thought, one not based directly on scripture. Following Bodhidharma's death, this was picked up by a string of 6 students, making the *lineage* look like this:
- Bodhidharma [early 5th century CE],
- Dazu Huike [487-593 CE],
- Jianzhi Sengcan [?-606 CE],
- Dayi Daoxin [580-651 CE],
- Daman Hongren]601-674 CE],
- Dajian Hui-neng [638-712 CE], and
- Heze Shenhui [670-762 CE].

Bodhidharma and the first five names that follow him on this list are commonly known within Zen circles as the *Six Patriarchs*.

The fundamental goal of Zen, as it is with all of Buddhism, is *enlightenment*. Essentially, they believe that this can be: (a) attained by anyone; and, (b) may occur either suddenly or gradually.

Fundamentally, Zen sees two primary means to attain enlightenment: sudden, and gradual. *Pen-chueh* is the belief that the human mind is, from its beginning, fully enlightened (but, we are not usually aware of this). We can, however, gain sudden insight into our true nature, after which we can never return to the prior, clouded view of reality. Once this sudden awareness has occurred, *shih-chueh* is the gradual recognition and adoption of this new awareness. According to Stuart Lachs, in his 2012 *Hua t'ou: A Method of Zen Meditation*, "Our enlightenment is timeless, yet our realization of it occurs in time." The key goal, therefore, is for the Zen Buddhist to attain that sudden flash of insight into reality. Zen practices are designed to aid in attaining that insight.

Zen Beliefs

Zen is fundamentally a sub-set of Mahayana Buddhism; so, many Zen beliefs are based on Mahayana tenets.

- *Buddha nature* is the concept that all sentient beings (not just humans) possess what is known as *Buddhadhātu* (Sanskrit for "Buddha-nature"), that "spiritual" element from which awakening occurs. The Chinese had no problem accepting and adopting this concept, as it corresponded very well to their indigenous concept of the *Tao*.

- *Sunyata* refers to the illusory nature of our physical existence. When we examine the various "things" in our physical world, they dissolve into concepts, ideas, and beliefs – they physically become "no thing". The world of discrete things and objects dissolves, leaving them "empty" of inherent existence. Everything results from perception, emotion, volition, discrimination, and consciousness; nothing inherently *exists* (including us!). At first, the Chinese also accepted this, although initially equating this with their concept of *wu* (Chinese "nothingness"; but, it's not the same, as the Chinese believed in an eternal human soul).

- *Boddhisattva* is that ideal of aspiration that leads us to want to attain buddhahood, but to postpone *moksha* so that we can aid others on their path. Part of this ideal is based on the *paramitas* (the "perfection of six virtues"): *Dāna* (generosity), *Sīla* (morality), *Khanti* (patience, tolerance), *Viriya* (energy), *Dhyana* (meditation), and *Paññā* (wisdom).

Zen Practice

The principle practice of Zen is meditation. The purpose of it is to achieve that sudden flash of insight into the nothingness of the physical world, and the true nature of reality. There are several methods used to employ this, and some accompanying processes to aid in its effectiveness.

- *Zazen* ("just sitting") involves practitioners sitting comfortably in one of several proscribed positions (below) and then spending time (typically, ~an hour) in this position in meditation.

Full Lotus   *Half Lotus*   *Burmese*   *Kneeling*   *Sitting*

- *Kōans* are stories or dialogs between a lay student and their zen master. These exchanges are highly unconventional, and are designed to emphasize the non-conceptual nature of Buddhist insight. They appear to outsiders to be virtually non-sensical, and are used to instill doubt in the mind of the student regarding everything they have always accepted without questioning. There are a few koans that have become quoted so often in the West as to become trite. Do not underestimate the value or purpose of a koan; it is taken very seriously, analyzed studiously, and the student's response is evaluated carefully by the master to determine if the student is progressing on his path to realizing *satori* (that sudden insight). The purpose can be seen in a koan from a collection published by Japanese Zen masters:
    Nan-in, a Japanese master, received a professor who came to inquire about Zen.

> Nan-in served tea. He poured his visitor's cup full, and then kept on pouring.
>
> The professor watched the overflow until he no longer could restrain himself. "It is overfull. No more will go in!"
>
> "Like this cup," Nan-in said, "you are full of your own opinions and speculations. How can I show you Zen unless you first empty your cup?"

Another example (from the same collection) shows what is often expected of monks who undertake to follow Zen.

> Tanzan and Ekido were once traveling together down a muddy road. A heavy rain was still falling. Coming around a bend, they met a lovely girl in a silk kimono and sash, unable to cross the intersection.
>
> "Come on, girl" said Tanzan. Lifting her in his arms, he carried her over the mud.
>
> Ekido did not speak again until that night when they reached a lodging temple. Then he no longer could restrain himself. "We monks don't go near females," he told Tanzan, "especially not young and lovely ones. It is dangerous. Why did you do that?"
>
> "I left the girl there," said Tanzan. "Are you still carrying her?"

- *Chanting* is also often used to lull the human mind into a near state of auto-hypnosis where the physical world begins to fade from consciousness.

Zen Sects

There are several sects of Zen Buddhism, and one of the primary features which differentiates the various sects is their individual preference for how to induce this breakthrough into Reality, to make the quantum leap from *ordinary knowledge* to *absolute knowledge*. Some of the better known sects, and their names (in Japanese / Chinese) are as follows.

> ***Rinzai / Lin chi*** This sect is probably the best known in the West — not by name, but by its practice of inducing mental shock to the mind through the use of meditation on seemingly paradoxical questions such as *koans*. One of the most widely quoted Rinzai koans outside of Zen is: "What is the sound of one hand clapping?" The goal is to shock the mind

out of its preconditioned patterns and to discover that it has, in fact, been limiting itself.

Soto / Ts'ao tung This sect resorts to long periods of meditation to still the mind and allow the boundaries to melt into nothingness. This meditation technique (*zazen*), is often done sitting on the floor facing a wall for hours at a time.

Obaku / Huang po This group relies on both the Rinzai and Soto methods (meditation and *koan*), and the use of a *mantra* (repeated phrase) borrowed from the Pure Land school of Buddhism, *nembutsu*.

Soka Gakkai

A prominent branch of Mahayana Buddhism in Japan follows the teachings of a 13th century monk by the name of Nichiren Daishōnin [1222-1282 CE]. Known simply as Nichiren, it follows the *Lotus Sutra*. It is claimed that this sutra recounts an actual teaching by the Buddha toward the end of his life. It was hidden away at his death, and was not revealed to followers until several hundred years later. Nichiren accepted this Mahayana text as scripture, and taught that this is the only "direct path to enlightenment". It is believed that there are more than two million adherents to the "traditional" branches of Nichiren Buddhism.

By contrast, *Soka Gakkai* is considered "non-traditional" in Nichiren, and is often described as *shinshūkyō* (Japanese: "new religious movement"), and not included when identifying followers of Nichiren. The umbrella organization that coordinates the national Soka Gakkai groups is called *Soka Gakkai International* (SGI), and counts nearly twenty million adherents world-wide – much larger than traditional Nichiren.

Soka Gakkai is a lay religious movement founded in 1930 by a Japanese teacher, Tsunesaburo Makiguchi [1871-1944]. They were adamantly opposed to the tie between religion and politics, and opposed so-called *State Shinto*. As a result, Makiguchi and other early leaders of the group were convicted and jailed in 1943 as "thought criminals". Makiguchi died of malnutrition in prison at the age of 73. After World War II ended, the fledgling group was led by Josei Toda, who oversaw a tremendous rise in the size of the group. In 1975, Daisaku Ikeda formed SGI, and took it global. He has remained the President of SGI to the present.

Practices

Soka Gakkai adherents daily chant the phrase *nam-myoho-renge-kyo*, and recite excerpts from the Lotus Sutra. The chant literally translates into English as "devotion to the wonderful Lotus Sutra". Nichiren, quoting from the *Vimalakirti Sutra*, once said that "if the minds of living beings are impure, their land is also impure, but if their minds are pure, so is their land. There are not two lands, pure or impure in themselves. The difference lies solely in the good or evil of our minds." Nichiren was convinced that adherence to his teachings would lead to an inner peace that would inevitably be reflected in peace in the environment and society around them. SGI claims that chanting energizes the practitioner both spiritually and mentally, and makes them happier, more compassionate, wiser, more productive, and more prosperous.

SGI was excommunicated from traditional Nichiren in 1991. One of their disagreements was the SGI's heavy emphasis on the mentor-disciple relationship. SGI sees the mentor as evidence of a compassionate support of others in their pursuit of their growth.

Charter

The SGI Charter lists ten specific items, and reads as follows:

1. SGI shall contribute to peace, culture and education for the happiness and welfare of all humanity based on Buddhist respect for the sanctity of life.
2. SGI, based on the ideal of world citizenship, shall safeguard fundamental human rights and not discriminate against any individual on any grounds.
3. SGI shall respect and protect the freedom of religion and religious expression.
4. SGI shall promote an understanding of Nichiren Daishonin's Buddhism through grass-roots exchange, thereby contributing to individual happiness.
5. SGI shall, through its constituent organizations, encourage its members to contribute toward the prosperity of their respective societies as good citizens.
6. SGI shall respect the independence and autonomy of its constituent organizations in accordance with the conditions prevailing in each country.
7. SGI shall, based on the Buddhist spirit of tolerance, respect other religions, engage in dialogue and work together with them toward the resolution of fundamental issues concerning humanity.

8. SGI shall respect cultural diversity and promote cultural exchange, thereby creating an international society of mutual understanding and harmony.
9. SGI shall promote, based on the Buddhist ideal of symbiosis, the protection of nature and the environment.
10. SGI shall contribute to the promotion of education, in pursuit of truth as well as the development of scholarship, to enable all people to cultivate their individual character and enjoy fulfilling and happy lives.

Affiliations

Soka Gakkai founded a university in Japan, *Soka University*, in Hachiōji, Tokyo. Opened in 1971, the school has about 8,500 students pursuing Liberal Arts degrees in areas such as humanistic studies, peace studies, conflict resolution, *et cetera*. In 2001, they opened a related school in the United States: *Soka University of America* in Aliso Viejo, California. With nearly 400 students today, SUA offers a BA in Liberal Arts with emphasis in Environmental Studies, Humanities, Social and Behavioral Sciences, and International Studies. They also offer a Foreign Languages MA.

The founding of these universities is totally in keeping with the educational philosophy of Makiguchi. He published a 4-volume work, *Sōka Kyōikugaku Taikei* (a "value creating education system"), and had stated his belief that the purpose of a school was "to lead students to happiness".

Section VII
Other Paths

There are more things in heaven and earth, Horatio, than are dreamt of in your philosophy
— *Hamlet 1:5:166-7 (William Shakespeare)*

People need a sacred narrative. They must have a sense of larger purpose, in one form or another, however intellectualized. They will find a way to keep ancestral spirits alive.
— *Harvard Professor Dr. Edward O. Wilson*

World Religion and *Comparative Religion* texts often concentrate on these "major religions" almost to the point of exclusivity. However, identification of these faiths as the *major* faiths is not made solely on any single criterion:

- they are not the 5 largest faiths in the world – *e.g.* there are many faith practices with more adherents than Judaism, yet Judaism is always included while these others are not;

- they are not geographically biased – they nearly always include the Abrahamic faiths (from the Middle East) as well as the Vedic faiths (from south Asia);

- they are not the oldest faiths – the eras usually assigned to the formulation of these faiths varies over 5 to 6 millennia;

- they are not the faiths which have had the greatest historical impact – *e.g.* whereas Christianity and Islam have had tremendous historical impact, Buddhism has actually had very little; *et cetera*.

Their selection as the 'major world religions' is actually a result of all of these criteria; and, identification results not from any formal identification process as much as by academic consensus. That consensus, however, results in thousands of faiths being left off the list. Some of these have a significant number of adherents; some may have had a major historical impact on some part of the world; and, some may be quite small in number, but are growing rapidly in the modern world.

This final Section of 3 Chapters introduces just a few of these other faiths. Considering only the major faiths leaves a wealth of religious traditions that never get reviewed, and only scratches the surface of the variety of spiritual beliefs found around the world. No text can cover them all (there are more than 5,000 discrete religions practiced on earth), but a few others really should be introduced.

Chapter 26
East Asian Faith

Do the difficult things while they are easy and do the great things while they are small. A journey of a thousand miles must begin with a single step. — *Lao Tzu*

There are three great religions that grew out of East Asia: Shinto, Confucianism and Taoism. When later joined by Buddhism from India, the latter two became the "three ways" of the Chinese people. Although it is often difficult to separate them (with some people actually practicing all three for different occasions in their life), there are two distinct, native threads of this fabric. This is also difficult as both Confucianism and Taoism developed within what was already the prevalent, traditional Chinese thought at the time, and use terms that were already in common use at the time. Therefore, both use the same terms (while not always meaning the same thing by them).

Confucianism

In the world there are many different roads but the destination is the same. There are a hundred deliberations but the result is one. — *K'ung Fu-tzu (Confucius)*

The major question with Confucianism has always been: "Is it a religion or a philosophy?" And, this is an appropriate question — perhaps more so than for any other world tradition. There is no established God, no consistent view of an afterlife, and only a few rituals. The reason for listing it as a religion is that it is the source of ethics and morality for millions of people around the world.

History

The founder of the religion was *K'ung Fu-tzu* (literally, "Master Kong"), brought into English as *Confucius* (right). "Master" is an honorific applied to his surname (Kong); his birth name was *Kong Qiu.* Confucius was born to an older soldier and a young woman in 551 BCE. He was born in Lu (in what is now China's Shantung Province) during the Chou dynasty — an age best described as what may only generously be referred to as an era of moral laxity. His father died while he was still a child, and he was raised in a privileged environment by his mother – at the compound of the state's political leader (since his father had been a respected military officer for this leader). He became a great lover of literature, art, archery, music, and the privileged life of the nobility. His first employment was as a bookkeeper for a granary owned by one of the 3 noble families (the Chi family) in his home state.

Confucius married, had a son and a daughter, and soon earned his living by teaching the young men from the better families in the province. At the age of 50, he went to work for the Duke of Lu (*i.e.* the Chinese feudal equivalent of a Duke) in the administration of the duchy. He did this for five years; but, by the age of 55, he became disillusioned with the Duke's neglect of his subjects to pursue young women. He resigned (or was fired) at 55 and left to look for similar work in other provinces.

Despite his abilities, no other province would engage him; and, he once again supported himself through teaching. In 484 BCE, at the age of 67, he was invited back to Lu by a new Duke to be his advisor. Although he returned home, he declined the post to spend his remaining years editing the classics of literature. He died at his home in 479 BCE at the age of 72. A contemporary of Buddha, Mahavira and Li Erh (Taoism), Confucius developed an approach to morals and ethics which he preached and taught throughout the region. In his final years, as an old man, he taught this ethical system to his disciples in Shantung.

Where it "fits"

In its modern form, it is not easy to separate Confucian thought from Buddhist and Taoist thought — since two or even all three of these traditions are often practiced by adherents in a unified, integrated mode. Taoism provides a connection with nature; Buddhist thought provides the religious tone of an Ultimate Reality and an afterlife; and, Confucianism provides the ethical foundation on which to base a moral life. But, it was a unique tradition.

Philosophical (or Ethical) Confucianism

Essentially, Confucius taught that there were five basic principles to which humanity must adhere:

- ***Jen*** – the relationship between two people. Essentially, it is kindness and benevolence between strangers, and is the Confucian version of the Golden Rule. Confucius taught that this must be practiced and exhibited until it took root in the very consciousness of the people. Note that he taught this during the most violent and fratricidal period in Chinese history.

- ***Chun tzu*** – a state of moral maturity, a trait exhibited by a person who is fully capable of leading society back from the brink of disaster and ruin. It is exemplified by a loyalty to the state and a dedication to the basic rights of the people at the local level.

- ***Li*** – respect and, to a lesser degree, ritual. It is simply *the way things ought to be done*. Dr. Huston Smith provides the illustrative example of the French expression *savoir faire* (literally meaning "to know to do"), which indicates a state in which the appropriate action is most certainly going to occur. It is essentially a principle of righteousness and harmony.

- ***Te***, as it is also used in Taoism, is *power*. It is the power that allows one person to rule over another. It includes a responsibility for the ruler to be just and fair, and the citizen to be loyal and dutiful. It represents, as do many Chinese terms, the entire reciprocal relationship.

- ***Wen*** – what might be called *the humanities*. Dr. Smith refers to *wen* as *the arts of peace*. It is the essence and the totality of society in both their æsthetic and spiritual application.

Other concepts, closely related to these, include: *yi* (the reciprocity of activity between friends, and basic honesty in business relationships – often described as the "internalization" of *li*); and, *hsiao* (which embraces the various stages of familial love – love of parents, love of children, love of siblings, *et cetera*).

There was a strong current of ancestral respect and admiration which ran throughout the teachings of Confucius. He believed that respect for one's elders was the practice of *hsiao* in its most ele-

mental form; and, respect for one's forebears became a hallmark of Chinese philosophical and religious beliefs. In total, however, he identifed 5 specific relationahips. Each of these relationships, although often unequal, displayed a level of power and responsibility on <u>both</u> sides. He identified these relationships as:
- Ruler — Subject;
- Husband — Wife;
- Parent — Child;
- Elder sibling — Younger sibling; and,
- Elder friend — Younger friend.

Religious Confucianism

Much of what has been described so far is more philosophy than religion. As Confucianism grew as a religion, it did so through syncretistic melding of the Confucian moral philosophy with the surrounding religions of Buddhism and Taoism. The result, as we can see, is a broad union of these three sources under the heading of 'Religious Confucianism'. The elements of the philosophy are there, but are brought into religious fruition through a bonding with <u>both</u> Taoism and Buddhism.

Drawing heavily from a description by Dr. Douglas K. Chung, religious Confucianism promulgates several principles:

- *In the beginning — nothing.* There is no personal God that predates existence as we know it.
- *Ultimate Reality* (the *Tao*) is the cause of change (*I*) and, as a consequence, generates the two primal forms: *yang* (energy) and *yin* (passiveness). In their ethereal forms, *yin* and *yang* represent the essence of tension present in all material systems: light and dark, weak and strong, male and female, forceful and passive, *et cetera*. The result of the interaction of these two primal essences creates all that exists; and, it all exists within a framework of interdependence of all creation.
- The dynamic tension that exists produces continual change. This is thus the 'natural order of things'. The natural world, the universe, and human nature are inherently good. Acceptance of the dynamism of change caused by the tension of *yin* and *yang* allows humans to discover the real person, and to cherish the principle of change that underlies all existence.

- There are four basic principles of change:
  - *Change is easy.* As the basic "way" (*Tao*) of existence, there is no natural resistance to it;
  - *Change is transformational.* A change in the *yin* of something automatically produces a change in the *yang*. The result is a cycle of expansion and contraction;
  - The only thing in existence that does not change is the fact that there will always be change; and,
  - That transformation which is "best" is that which improves both the individual and the environment — through growth and development.
- Any search for change (the ever present principle of change) first reflects upon:
  - the state of the individual in the environment;
  - timing (the appropriateness of change at this time);
  - the mean (the Golden Path) in the environment (the mean is considered to be a strategic position — the best from which to work with change. The *Tao* always resides at the mean);
  - the receptivity of the *yin* and *yang* forces to be altered or compromised; and,
  - the integration of the particular within the general environment (*i.e.* the specific system within the economic, political and social realms).
- *All existence is interconnected.* This pattern extends from the relationships between individuals up through the relationships of friends, families, elders, and the state, to the world. What defines the merit of the individual is part of a chain of existence which runs from ancient ancestors to an undetermined future. As such, one can only acquire and manifest humanity with and through others. In western terminology, humans are a *social animal*.
- *Society functions best when the entire chain is understood.* Individuals who find the truth and maintain it optimize the relationships between the individual and the whole. This inevitably transforms society.

Taoism

To understand others is to be knowledgeable;
To understand yourself is to be wise.
To conquer others is to have strength;
To conquer yourself is to be strong.
To know when you have enough is to be rich.
To go forward with strength is to have ambition.
To not lose your place is to last long.
To die but not be forgotten — that is true long life.
— Lao-tzu *(Te Tao Ching;* chapter 33)

Taoism is the epitome of what Dr. Huston Smith was saying when he referred to the relative characters of western, eastern and southern religions. He wrote that "the religions of the West (Judaism, Christianity, and Islam) have accented the problem of humanity's relation to nature; those of East Asia (Confucianism, Taoism, and Shinto) have stressed the social problem; and those of India (Hinduism, Buddhism, and Jainism) have attended primarily to the psychological issue." He proposed that nature, being far more difficult to bend to the will of humanity in East Asia than in Europe, became something to admire and revere, but not to be subjugated. As such, intellectual activities tended to emphasize social structure, which was more amenable to being disciplined than nature.

The primary textual source for Taoism is the *Tao Te Ching*. Dr. Douglas K. Chung has written that this book can be used "as a guide to the cultivation of the self as well as a political manual for social transformation at both the micro and macro levels." The text is attributed by the faithful to an old man named *Li Erh* in the sixth century BCE. Also known as *Lao-tzu* ("Old Master"), specifics about his physical historicity are difficult to ascertain. Although we can be virtually certain that he was an historical figure, very little detail is known. Fortunately, this is not really all that important, since Taoism is not a religion of personality. Lao-tzu is seen as neither an incarnation of God nor a great prophet. He was the author / collector of 'bits of wisdom' distilled for the average person to assimilate — a systemization of much of what Chinese philosophy had accepted for centuries. The *Tao Te Ching* is the collection and systematic presentation of that wisdom.

Near the end of 1973, archæologists in Hunan Province in China made a valuable discovery in the small village of Ma-wang-tui: the tomb of the son of Li Ts'ang (the Marquis of Tai, and Prime Minister of Changsa). His burial had been accompanied by a virtual library of texts — for many of which modern historians had only the name (assuming the actual text had been lost forever). Among these scrolls were two copies of the Lao-tzu work: one copied about 200 BCE; the other predating it, and originating sometime prior to 206 BCE. These texts were at least 200 to 300 years older than any previously known texts, and those that had been known were so-called received texts (copied and handed down many times). There are no major differences in either content or philosophy between the Ma-wang-tui texts and those which have been known for nearly 2,000 years. The only significant difference was that the order of the two sections of the work was reversed. Therefore, when Dr. Robert G. Henricks translated the Ma-wang-tui text, he published it as the *Te Tao Ching*. It is from this translation that the epigraph at the start of this section is taken.

Taoism evolved in a land and time where social transformation was, as it was with Confucianism, a primary goal. That does not mean, however, that there was no interest in a religious tradition more attuned to either nature or the human psyche — only that social transformation was primary. Consequently, Taoism has come to take three distinct and different forms over the years. These can be recognized as Philosophical, Religious and Natural Taoism.

Philosophical Taoism

The term *Tao* means "path, road, or way". In the strictest sense, *Tao* is too immense to be properly understood by humans. In this sense, it is comparable to the concept of an infinite God. Whereas many traditions consider God to be personal, the Tao is impersonal. It is the way of transcendent, Ultimate Reality. It is the great creative essence of the universe; it is the spiritual center from which all reality flows. It is eternal; it exists without beginning, and without end. For humanity, however, it is also unknowable — it is simply too profound and all encompassing to be understood by human intelligence.

This eternal essence, this way, to which all creation adheres, can be experienced and witnessed in small part through its reflection or manifestation. For the Tao is not only ineffable and indescribable, it is also the underlying source of creative energy behind the universe itself. As such, it is the *way of the universe*. It is expressed in nature, and all that nature exhibits. Finally, Tao can be seen to be the unity of the way we choose to live and the way of Reality. It is the path we must follow to succeed in this life. What success means in this sense helps to define whether one is following Religious Taoism, Natural Taoism, or Philosophical Taoism. The philosophical approach to the Tao does not need to define success. It is sufficient just that we recognize that there is an essence to the universe, that this essence is structured and organized, and that the way of this essence can be observed through the ways it is manifested in the universe we see. The adherent of Philosophical Taoism is therefore supporting what can be described as an *attitude toward life*. One seeks true wisdom and knowledge, and the highest achievement in Philosophical Taoism would be to live a life that is calm, serene, and sagacious. This form of Taoism is most often seen outside of Chinese communities.

Religious Taoism

Religious Taoism defines success in life as falling in line with the Tao, yielding to it, and relinquishing all resistance to the inevitable flow of life. The goal becomes to draw more of life's essence from adherence to the Tao, so as to be able to influence the Tao. In this type of Taoism, often known as *Tao Chiao* ("church Taoism"), there are significant similarities with neighbouring Buddhism as well as the local Chinese animist religious traditions of 2,500 years ago. The result is a ritualistic melding of traditions which are difficult to isolate or define.

The early indigenous faith of China was clearly polytheistic, and Religious Taoism appears to follow in this path. Although the *Tao* is Ultimate Reality, and is an undivided essence (which would seem to make Taoism monotheistic), Religious Taoism recognizes numerous gods and goddesses (which appear to make it polytheistic); a clean categorization of *Tao Chiao* is simply not possible.

Gods and goddesses which are generally acknowledged in *Tao Chiao* include:

- *T'ai-shang Lao-chun* is the deified version of Lao-tzu, and is seen in Tao Chiao as a sort of divine prophet.

- *Yuan-shih t'ien-tsun* is the 1st of the *Three Pure Ones*, and instructs humans from his heavenly perspective. He is the embodiment of virtue, and the source of all Truth.

- *Ling-pao t'ien-tsun* is the 2nd of the *Three Pure Ones*, and regulates yin and yang, and to "mete out time". He is also known as *Tao-chun* (Lord of the Way).

- *Tao-te t'ien-tsun* is the 3rd member of this Taoist "trinity", and his role is to visit the material world in a variety of identities, and to bring humanity to the way of the Tao.

- *Yu-huang* is the closest Taoist deity to the western concept of God. Known as the *Jade Emperor*, humans ultimately must answer to Him for their actions, good or bad. He is supreme, and all other Taoist gods defer to Him.

- *Hsi-wang Mu* is the *Mother Empress of the West*, Hsi-wang Mu lives in the Kunlun Mountains in the west of China, and guards the doorway to the heavens. She has the power to grant longevity and immortality, and there is a tree in the middle of her garden whose fruit bestows immortality, making the eater "like the gods". Whereas the Tree of Life in the Garden of Eden is usually pictured as bearing apples, the Tree of Immortality in Hsi-wang Mu's garden bears peaches.

- *Tou-mu* was originally a Hindu goddess venerated as the patron goddess of healers.

- *T'ai-i t'ien-tsun* is the *Celestial Lord of the Great Beginning*, and presides over the realm of the dead. He is the personification of compassion.

In addition to these, there are many others. Three that have become fairly easily found in the west are the three *star gods* – so called because they are believed to reside on the three stars on Orion's Belt in that constellation. They were apparently historical, physical individuals who were deified following their deaths as a result of the merit they had gathered while on earth. Known collectively as the *San Hsing* (or *San Xing*), that name literally means "three stars". Individually, they are:

- *Fu hsing* is the god of good luck and happiness. Emperor Wu Ti ordered all of the midgets in Dazhou brought to the Imperial Court for his entertainment. Yang Cheng, governor of Dazhou, appealed to the Emperor, and they were allowed to remain with their families. This merit brought deification as *Fu Hsing* around 580 CE.

- *Lu hsing* is the god of wealth and career. In life, he was a scholar by the name of Shi Fen, who was a favorite of Emperor Jing (2nd century BCE). He was known to teach avoidance of corruption or greed in one's professional life, and was deified as a god (actually, like the others, more accurately as an *ascended master*) following his passing.

- *Shou hsing* is the god of long life. Born Zhao-Yen, he was prophesied to die of chronic illness by the age of 19. Selflessly, he offered his lunch to two old men playing checkers in a field, and the two (who were, in fact, the gods of birth and death) rewarded his kindness with immortality.

Natural Taoism

This is the material application of the spiritual essence of Taoism. This may be easier to understand if the three forms of Taoism are put into financial terms (paraphrasing Dr. Huston Smith):

- *Philosophical Taoists* try to improve the bottom line through austerity;

- *Religious Taoists* attempt to use corporate structure and tax shelters to improve the bottom line; but,

- *Natural Taoists* improve the balance sheet by expanding top line growth. This results in a number of beliefs and practices which are designed to enhance life and longevity through increasing the *qi* (or *ch'i*, "life force").

The list of material experiments they conducted, and the practices that followed from these experiments, is impressive. Diet, sexual practices, herbalism, exercises, yoga, meditation, breathing regimens, *et cetera* were developed to aid in the process of increasing one's *qi*. The well known Chinese regimen of *Tai Chi Chuan*, the medical practice of acupuncture, Chinese traditional herbal medicine, and the macro-biotic diet all developed in this manner.

One of the most familiar aspects of Taoism is the division of the universe into *yin* and *yang*. These are seen as complementary forces of the Tao which together form completeness and unity. They are frequently displayed symbolically as a circle divided into two forms — one white and one black — which each resemble a curved drop of water (right). This symbol is frequently seen in the field of martial arts, and is central to the flag of South Korea. It represents the 2 complementary forces of nature: masculine and feminine, dark and light, cold and hot, passive and active, *et cetera*. Although very similar to Religious Confucianism, there are distinct differences between Taoist and Confucianist ideas of yin and yang. Taoists accept a natural balance of yin and yang in the universe, and that yielding to the universal harmony of these forces keeps us from wasting *qi*. The result is a religion that is often more attuned to nature and the universe than any other. It should not be surprising that Taoists are often part of the green political movement wherever they happen to live.

Dr. Huston Smith identified Taoism as one of the "socially focused" religions, rather than one of those that are "nature focused". This may seem to contradict what was just said; but, it doesn't. The western religions tend to focus on the concept of *dominion* over nature, whereas Taoism tends to focus on the concept of being *in tune* with nature — and society.

In his excellent introductory book, *The Tao of Pooh*, author Benjamin Hoff identifies seven Taoist *principles* that he considers essential ingredients of Religious Taoism. Using a combination of terms (both traditional and Hoff's) for these, they are:

- *P'u* — the "uncarved block". Hoff says "things in their original simplicity contain their own natural power, power that is easily spoiled and lost when that simplicity is changed."

- *Absolute knowledge* — although this may seem somewhat anti-intellectual at first, it really is not. It is a dependence on what Buddhist's call *absolute knowledge* rather than *ordinary knowledge*. This is based on the premise that "while the scholarly intellect may be useful for analyzing certain things, deeper and broader matters are beyond its limited reach."

- *Suchness* — it is critical in Taoism to recognize that things are simply as they are, and can't be forced into being something else. They also can not be described by making comparisons to other things. "Every thing has its own Inner Nature [which,] when relied on, can not be fooled. ... The Way of Self-Reliance starts with recognizing who we are, what we've got to work with, and what works best for us."

- *Wu wei* — *i.e.* "without doing, causing or making". In modern terms it is to "go with the flow". It refers to not forcing something to go against the fundamental nature of things.

- *El Dorado* — it seems as if most people are seeking some Great Reward; they are searching for their personal El Dorado. The problem is that they are so caught up in the search for it, that they neglect the true value of suchness, the way things simply are. Spanish conquistadors wandered the American south looking for the "city of gold" (*el d'or ado*). They were so focused on this goal that they completely missed many things of real value (both cultural and material) that they encountered on their travels.

- *Valuation* — "To take control of our lives and accomplish something of lasting value, sooner or later we need to learn to Believe. ... We simply need to believe in the power that's within us, and use it." Taoists resist the temptation to transfer our responsibilities and our burdens onto the shoulders of some God or other Deity.

- *T'ai Hsü* — this is the "Great Nothing", or "Great Void". It is free from all characteristics, but present in everything. It is the undefinable, the indescribable. It is not nothing; it is the Great Something – devoid of distinctions and characteristics. It is the Taoist version of the Buddhist *sunyavada*.

Taoism Summary

Taoism is summarized by Paul Wildish as follows:

- The *Tao-te-Ching* tells us that the Tao is the limitless void, unnameable and unknowable.

- The Tao transforms itself from the non-material to the material through the processes of *yin* and *yang*.

- All processes are subject to cyclic change governed in our material world by the Five Elements.

- Life is governed by the Three Treasures of *ching* (essence), *ch'i* (energy) and *shen* (spirit). The exchange and intermingling of the elements is the context in which Man lives, and creates perfection.

- Man is too often unable to see this natural perfection and is led by his ego to concern himself only with the accumulation of material wealth and the pursuit of desire. Some come to recognize this emptiness and folly and are able to follow the 'teaching without words.'

- In order to follow the Way successfully, one must take the course of *wu wei*, or non-action, and act only instinctively in accord with Nature.

- The adept must perfect stillness and blend with the energies of the body to become more a spirit than a material form.

- At the end of his life, the adept is serenely perfected. When the moment of death arrives, the ego is dissipated and consciousness expands to become the limitless void of the Tao.

Shinto

Shinto is the native religion of Japan. As such, it significantly pre-dates the arrival of Buddhism (which the Japanese readily accepted and adapted in the various schools of Zen). When something is the only religious practice that there is, there is no need to have a name for it. In the case of Shinto, there was therefore no name for this set of spiritual beliefs until Buddhism was introduced from China. At that time, it became necessary to distinguish between the two belief systems; so, they became *kami no michi*

(Japanese: "The Way of the Kami") and *seon* (the Korean term for the new Buddhist import from China, *ch'an*). The Japanese pronounced the Korean *Seon* as *Zen*; and, since Kami is a difficult word to translate into Chinese, the Buddhist missionaries substituted the word "gods" for "kami" in The Way of the Kami, and thus translated *kami no michi* as *Shen Tao* (Chinese: "way of the gods").

The key to this religious faith, *Shen Tao* (in Chinese) or *Shinto* (as pronounced in Japan), is that unusual Japanese word that the Chinese could not adequately translate: *kami*. Technically, *kami* refers to a feeling of awe, wonder, and veneration for the essence, spirit, soul, jiva, or numinous quality of something. Typically, *kami* is treated as being synonymous with the western term *soul*; but, it included awe and veneration of inanimate objects as well. So, either you acknowledge that trees, rocks, lakes and mountains have souls, or you have to acknowledge that *kami* is not exactly the same as *soul*. Traditionally, there are eight million kami[*]; however, since there are now well over one hundred million Japanese, this number has become woefully inadequate.

Shinto evolved from a merger of this reverence for nature with an agricultural fertility cult that was present in ancient Japan (likely dating to the *Ainu* — the indigenous people of Japan before the Japanese arrived). As a result, there are a number of Shinto rituals that seem to evoke images of the ancient fertility rituals:

- worship of Amaterasu at the Ise shrine;
- planting ceremonies;
- harvest celebrations; and,
- even the veneration of "sacred trees".

History

The earliest Shinto practices were oral, and often involved the use of *miko* (female shamans). It wasn't until the successful introduction of Buddhism that Shinto leaders began to commit their re-

---

[*] In ancient Japanese, eight was considered "holy". The reason is not well understood, but it is believed to be related to the fact they used eight to express large, vague numbers (*e.g.* many, or millions and millions, *et cetera*). "Eight million kami" thus could be translated as "millions and millions of kami".

ligious practices to writing. The earliest compilations were the *Kojiki* (712 CE) and *Nihongi* (720 CE), recounting two kami who descended from heaven on a rainbow. The union of *Izanagi* (male) and *Izanami* (female) resulted in the Japanese islands and many "new" kami. These included *Amaterasu* (Sun Goddess), *Susanoo* (Storm God), and *Tsukiyomi* (Moon God). *Amaterasu* had a grandson *Ninigi*, who had a great grandson, *Jimmu* — the first human in the line (and, the first Emperor of Japan). As a result, traditional Shinto faith held the Emperor to be divine, and all Japanese to be children of the *kami*. Jimmu's reign as Emperor is dated to 660 BCE. Because Shinto considers everything to have come from the kami, it considers life itself to be divine. Worship, therefore, is not a human attempt to gain the favor of blessings from the kami, but is an attempt to share, through ritual, a fellowship with the kami.

In 1853, the American Naval Commodore Matthew C. Perry arrived in Tokyo and found a Japan that was led by an Emperor who was dependent on the military to remain in office. Perry insisted that Japan open its ports to the United States; and, this introduced western technology and concepts to Japan. Japanese life and ideas quickly began to change; and, in 1867, the military leader of Japan (the *shogun*) resigned. The following year, 1868, Emperor Meiji (right) became the ruler of all aspects of Japanese life (political, spiritual and military). One of his first acts was to demarcate a distinct line between the Shinto and Buddhist priesthood — a line that had blurred under the military rule.

State Shinto

Buddhist leaders had taught that the kami were really Buddhist boddhisattvas; in 1872, this teaching was made illegal. As a matter of patriotic loyalty, all Japanese citizens were required to participate in what became known as **State Shintoism**. They were free to practice Buddhist, Confucianist, Taoist, or sectarian Shintoism in private; but, they were obliged to publicly participate in the ceremonies, rituals and obligations of State Shinto (which supported the Imperial claim of divinity). In fact, the Japanese Constitution adopted in 1889 (known as the *Meiji Constitution*) stated that Japanese citizens would be allowed to enjoy freedom of religion only "within certain bounds of order and loyalty".

The Emperor, as the direct descendant of Amaterasu, was a deified figure. This assured the Japanese people of victory in war, and success in peace. When soldiers during World War II failed in an assigned mission, it was not unusual for them to commit *hara-kiri* (ritual suicide). It was this same religious devotion that made Japanese pilots volunteer for *kamikaze* flights*. When Japan surrendered in 1945, one of the terms of the surrender (which they were forced to accept) was a public denial by Emperor Hirohito of his divinity. Despite this, many faithful Shinto adherents refused to accept his forced denial right up to his death in 1989. Today, with Akihito as Emperor, State Shinto is gone — settling into a sort of national religious unity emphasizing ethnic devotion and worship at religious sites operated by Shrine Shinto (below).

Shrine Shinto

From the earliest days of Shinto until 1945, State Shinto and Shrine Shinto could not be separated. Although without any collected Scripture *per se*, the *Kojiki* and the *Nihongi* (both mentioned above) served as sources for Shinto mythology, and the *Engishiki* (927 CE) as a collection of prayers and blessings. With State Shinto abolished by the constitutional changes of 1945, Shrine Shinto is best perceived as "church Shinto", where adherents participate in religious and spiritual rituals and ceremonies that are still officially sanctioned by the Japanese government. Even after the Emperor disavowed divinity, the Japanese government and Shinto religious leaders maintained an extraordinarily close relationship that continues today, and Shinto shrines are maintained by government funding in much the same way that National Parks are maintained in the United States.

Sectarian Shinto

The Japanese government's Agency for Cultural Affairs divides Sectarian Shinto into three distinct groups: traditional sects, mountain worship sects, and revelatory sects. The first group is

---

* *kami kaze* ("divine wind") refers to 2 naval battles (1274 and 1281 CE) in which a surprise wind crushed a superior Mongolian navy, enabling victory.

mostly sects that have existed within Shinto since the late 19th century; although, if a new sect emerges, the government would almost certainly classify it under this heading.

Typically, the revelatory sects are those that base their teachings on the individual religious experience (revelation) of an adherent. There are five such groups officially recognized. There are three sects which worship, or show reverence to, the kami of holy mountains (specifically, Mount Fuji and Mount Ontake). After the new Meiji Constitution, there were thirteen officially recognized sects* in the 1890s.

Beliefs

With so many different sects of Shinto, it is difficult to make blanket statements. Nevertheless, there are some consistent beliefs which can be identified:

- Amaterasu, the Sun Goddess, is the most common specific object of worship;
- Amaterasu is not seen as the Ultimate Reality as much as a sort of "guardian spirit" for the Japanese people;
- there is an over-riding respect for the power and order seen in the universe;
- adherents accept the Japanese island chain as a special creation of the gods, and consider certain physical features (such as Mount Fuji) as a sacred blessing;
- the focus of the human-kami relationship is seen blessing the Japanese people, not all humanity — they see their religious duty as a duty to their "ethnic extended family", the Japanese people;
- society is best served by an inequality of roles, with women subservient to fathers, husbands, brothers, and even sons;
- similar to the Confucian *chain of existence*, Shinto adherents see themselves as part of an extended family that in-

---

* Tenrikyo, Konkokyo, Kurozumikyo, Fuso-kyo, Izumo-oyashiro-kyo, Jikko-kyo, Misogi-kyo, Shinshu-kyo, Shinto-shuseiha, Shinri-kyo, Shinto Taisei-kyo, Ontake-kyo and Shinto Taikyo.

cludes blood relatives, all other Japanese, and ancestors long deceased — and, there is a reverence for each;
- ethical behavior is governed by devotion to family, Japanese society and country; and,
- upon death, the body is cremated, and the individual soul joins its ancestors.

In Summary

The Shinto prayer that follows has been used to open every session of the Japanese parliament since the mid-1950s.

> Let us be grateful for *kami*'s grace and ancestors' benevolence, and with bright and pure *makoto* [sincerity or true heart] perform religious services.
>
> Let us work for people and the world, and serve as representatives of the *kami* to make society firm and sound. In accordance with the Emperor's will, let us be harmonious and peaceful, and pray for the nation's development as well as the world's coexistence and co-prosperity.*

Shinto is most likely about the same "age" as Confucianism and Taoism, but does not share the same Chinese folk religion background they have. Confucianism and Taoism are both overwhelmingly followed by Chinese people; however, neither of them comes close to Shinto in being classified an "ethnic religion". Shinto is not a religion that desires to become a global, international presence; it is a religion firmly rooted in Japanese history and culture, and is unabashedly a faith of the Japanese, by the Japanese, and for the Japanese.

---

* Quoted from *The General Principles of Shinto Life* proclaimed in 1956 by the Association of Shinto Shrines.

Chapter 27
African Faith

O Mother, advocate for the whole world!
What a remarkable Mother I have!
O Mother, a pillar, a refuge!
O Mother, to whom all prostrate in greeting
Before one enters her habitation!
I am justly proud of my Mother.
O Mother who arrives,
Who arrives majestic and offers water to all!

— traditional Yoruban prayer

Yoruba

The Atlantic coast of Africa has a huge curve that surrounds the Gulf of Guinea (circled area on map to the right). Along the northern side of the gulf are several modern African nations that can be grouped together under the heading of *West Africa*. These comprise the homelands of most of the people taken to the Americas in the slave trade. Those nations involved include Côte d'Ivoire (*i.e.* the Ivory Coast), Ghana, Togo, Benin, and Nigeria. Other countries that might also be included in this grouping would be Liberia (west of Ivory Coast) and Cameroon (southeast of Nigeria). The heart of the British slave trade was the cities of the Yoruba people (primarily Benin, Togo, and Nigeria), a culture that was unusually urban in native Africa. The name *Yoruba* describes a number of semi-independent peoples only loosely tied together by geography, language, history, and religion, and constitute the remnants of the once powerful Oyo kingdom. Archæologists and historians date the Oyo kingdom to sometime before 850 CE, and it is probably much older.

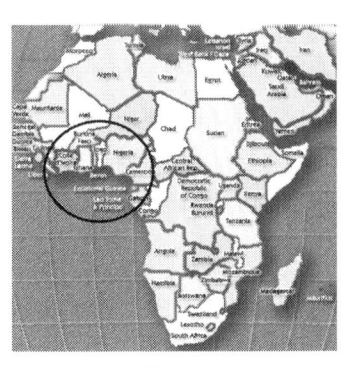

Traditionally, the Yoruba center religious beliefs on a pantheon of deities known as *orisha*. This would classify their faith as polytheistic; but, just as it was with Hinduism, life is not that easy. At the top of this pantheon of *orisha* is the "High God", *Olódùmarè*. This god is thought to be so far beyond the human condition that:

- He is not the "creator god" (He delegated that task to an orisha); and,
- there are no temples, shrines or sacred sites for the worship of Olódùmarè directly, since He is only worshipped indirectly through the orisha.

The orisha are a combination of primordial spirits who existed with Olódùmarè before the universe was created, the spirits of revered leaders who have passed to the spirit world, and the spiritual essence of rivers, hills and mountains of cultural significance to the Yoruba people.

Perhaps the most popular of the orisha is *Shango*. Shango is seen as the embodiment of creativity and originality, and is represented as the god of thunder and lightning. There are believed to be more shrines for the worship of Shango than any other orisha. Shango worshippers become such for a variety of reasons: taught by their parents, visions in dreams, desire for creativity and success, *et cetera*. A large majority of the Shango faithful are female, and even male Shango priests dress as females for rituals (it is said that Shango *prefers* women). Most wooden carvings and figures of Shango also show females (often at his feet). Shango's symbol is the *oshe Shango*, a double-edged stone axe. During ceremonies, the Shango priest/ess (usually female) dances to a chorus of staccato drum rhythms, and waves the axe fiercely, emulating lightning arising from storm clouds.

Female worshippers often hold their breasts aloft in respect to Shango, and wood carvings used as support posts for houses and temples often depict female Yoruba kneeling in respect, holding breasts aloft (effectively the "prayer position"). Figures in this position are known as *olumeye*, which means "one who knows honor"; and, they are often found on altars. In perhaps the most famous carving of this type, the olumeye (left) is depicted as a young bride — with her hair arranged in the wedding style, and wearing strands of waist beads signifying virginity.

Yoruba rituals for orisha are referred to as *egungun*. These rituals are both mischievous and spontaneous. Unlike religious rituals in most of the world's religions, they tend to be creative and improvisational. During one egungun video recorded by Margaret Thompson Drewal, a priestess in the ritual left her assigned area and ran through the spectators (*i.e.* congregation) fondling both men and women of her choosing, often sneaking up behind them and "goosing" them. This was considered mischievous, and was improvised, not planned. It is considered typical of a Yoruba ritual. These rituals are more than just celebrations; they are transformational journeys from the worldly realm of knowledge to the realm of the orisha.

Above Shango and the other orisha is *Olódùmarè*, which translates into English as "the Almighty". He has been described by Yoruba writers as "the creator of all things, the almighty and all-knowing, the giver of life and breath, and the final judge of mankind." This concept of an almighty God is so overwhelming and remote to the Yoruba that they cannot relate to Olódùmarè in their everyday reality; hence, the worhip of the lesser, more functionally specific orisha.

Although Shango may be one of (if not the) most popularly worshipped orisha, the most powerful is generally considered to be Ogun. Ogun is the god of war, god of the hunt (for food), and god of metal work. As such, he serves as the patron deity of blacksmiths, warriors, and anyone else who uses metal in their occupations. He also presides over all deals and contracts. In American courts, witnesses were traditionally asked to place their hand on a Bible while swearing to "tell the truth". In Yoruban areas, witnesses are asked to kiss a machete (the sacred symbol of Ogun), since they consider Ogun to be wrathful in his vengeance. If one were to break a pact made in his name, swift and terrible retribution is expected to quickly follow.

Why should an American, thousands of miles away from the Yoruban homeland, care about their religious beliefs? Because many of their descendents live in the United States and other North and South American countries, and many still practice religions related to the ancestral *Yoruba* or its closest relative, *Fon*.

The Yoruba Diaspora

The majority of Jews in the world today do not live in the traditional homeland of Israel. They live in other parts of the world as a result of what is known as the *diaspora*. This means "a dispersion of an originally homogeneous people" Although often used as a virtual synonym for the dispersal of the Jews, it technically refers to any people who have been 'scattered to the four corners of the globe'. The Jews were typically driven from their homes by those who hated, resented, or misunderstood them; the Yoruba were taken from their homelands to serve as slaves to the highest bidder. The results, however, were the same: a diaspora. When slaves practicing Yoruba arrived at their destination, it was common for their new "owners" to be fearful of their strange, unfamiliar, African religion; so, the slaves were forced to conceal their beliefs (to avoid harsh, often brutal, punishment) by masquerading them as a form of Christianity. Over time, these "beliefs in costume" evolved into new, syncretic religions.

Religions that resulted from practicing Yoruba (and the closely related Fon) with a Christian veneer include such religions as:
- Voudun (also known as Voudoun or Voodoo)
- Santeria (also known as Regla de Ocha)
- Macumba
- Candomble
- Umbanda
- *and many others*

Voudun

Voudun, also known as Voudoun and Voodoo, developed in Haiti from the merging of Fon (a close relative of Yoruba) and Roman Catholicism (the French-flavored Christian religion of their owners). It is similar in many respects to Candomblé and Umbanda (derived from Portuguese-flavored Catholicism) that developed along similar paths in Brazil.

Followers of Voudun accept the reality of the physical world as well as three distinct levels of divinity. These are:
- *Gran Met* (Grand Master), also known as *Bondye* (from French "bon Dieu", meaning "good God"). Ruling over the

entire spirit world, but so far removed that He is not worshipped directly, He is essentially a version of Olódùmarè;
- *Loas*, or *Lwas*, are lesser divinities, and are central to their religious system (these are, effectively, the *orisha* with a Fon pseudonym); and,
- the *dead*, which are both ancestral spirits and the spirits of saints, and are always present and available to the practitioner of Voudun.

Just as many religions distinguish between bishops, priests, and the laity, Voudun distinguishes between the:
- *Asogwe* (who can ordain others to their calling);
- *Sur Pointe* (equivalent to a seminary student);
- *Vodouisant* (a priest, *Hougan*, or priestess, *Mambo*); and,
- *Kanzo* (lay member).

Worship of a *Lwa* usually takes place under the direction of a *Vodouisant* at a ceremonial dance known as a *Rada*; and, the *Lwa* are typically called with drumming and chanting. Behaving much like channelling or possession in western esoteric beliefs, an individual is thus *mounted* (*i.e.* "possessed") by the *Lwa*. Some of the better known *Lwa* are:
- *Damballah*, a primordial serpent deity who, with his consort, created the universe;
- *Ayida*, the consort of Damballah, manifested as a rainbow;
- *Baron Samedi*, the *Lwa* of the dead;
- *Ogoun*, a warrior with great martial abilities, and related to both *Shango* and *Ogun*;
- *Erzuli*, the wife of *Ogoun*, and manifestation of femininity and love (similar to Venus);
- *Agwe*, the untamed sea; and,
- *Legba*, or *Papa Legba*, the guardian of crossroads (as is the Yoruban orisha *Eleggua*), who must be consulted before all other *Lwas*.

Voudun began when African slaves in Haiti were forced either to practice Roman Catholicism under their French masters or be beaten. The name is most likely from *vœu dieu*, which in French is literally a "prayer to God". *Candomblé*, a Brazilian equivalent, was named for the coffee plantation celebration attended by the black slaves. Similarly, *Umbanda*, another Brazilian slave religion, is from the Hindi *aum-gandha* (meaning "divine principle"), and is a syncretic mix of Yoruba and the religions of British slaves brought in from India (primarily Hindu). In close contact with Candomblé adherents, Umbanda adherents "borrowed" a great deal from them, and also communicate with Catholic saints through the auspices of intercessories (typically, ancestors).

Beliefs

Typically, adherents of *Voudun*, *Candomblé*, and *Umbanda*:

- accept that humans have both a physical body and a spiritual body;
- accept that spirits (discarnate souls) are frequently in contact with those in the physical world;
- believe humans can learn to contact and get assistance from these spirits in order to provide physical healing and spiritual growth;
- use animals for sacrifice in rituals;
- make priests or priestesses (*Voudouisants* in Voudun; *Babalao* in Candomblé and Umbanda) responsible for sacrificial animals, and conduct these rituals and sacrifices; and,
- accept that there are no "evil spirits", but only mischievous or misbehaving spiritual entities.

Santeria

Santeria (also known as *Regla de Ocha*, *La Regla Lucumi* and *Lukumi*) was a parallel development in Cuba. The many names for the faith are all related:

- *Santeria* – the "Way of the Saints";
- *Regla de Ocha* – the "Rule of the Orisha";
- *La Regla Lucumi* – the "Rule of Friends" (*i.e.* the orisha);
- *Lukumi* – "Friends"; and,
- *Macumba* – an offensive term sometimes used as a synonym for Santeria.

In fact, just as Quaker and Protestant were intended by religious leaders of the day to be demeaning and pejorative, but were later adopted by the targets of the insults, Santeria was intended by the Spanish in Cuba to demean the slaves' religion, but has now generally been accepted by adherents of the faith. The Spanish Catholics who controlled Cuba thought that their "new Catholic slaves" spent far too much attention and devotion to the saints, and far too little on God. Since their Yoruban religion worshipped Olódùmarè (God) indirectly, through the orisha, it only made sense that they would transfer this practice to the Catholicism they were forced to adopt.

When new slaves arrived in Cuba from the African coast, they were baptized on the dock by the presiding Catholic priest, making them superficially Roman Catholic. Slave owners did not want 'pagan slaves', so slaves that refused the baptism were either sent elsewhere or killed on the spot. Those who were baptized managed to keep their Yoruban religion alive by simply substituting names. Although there were obviously different alignments in different groups, a typical arrangement would have been:

- *Babalú Ayé* (orisha of health) = *Saint Lazarus* (patron saint of the sick);
- *Shango* (orisha of thunder & lightning) = *Saint Barbara* (who controls thunder & lightning);
- *Elleggua* or *Elebga* (controlling crossroads) = *Saint Anthony* (who controls gates and crossed roads);
- *Obatala* (orisha of creation and spirituality) = *Christ*;
- *Ogun* or *Oggán* (orisha of war) = *Saint Peter* (patron saint of war); and,
- *Osun* or *Oshun* (orisha of wealth and sensuality) = *Our Lady of Charity* (who also controls money and sensuality);
- *et cetera*

Adherents of Santeria are commonly found in Cuba, the Dominican Republic, Argentina, Brazil, Colombia, Venezuela, México, the United States (primarily Florida, New Jersey, New York City, Los Angeles, and Puerto Rico), France and the Netherlands. Santeria had been actively suppressed in Cuba since the 1959 revolution; but, they finally recognized this as a losing battle, and the oppression stopped under the new constitution of 1992 As a result, the popularity of Santeria in Cuba exploded during the 1990s. Estimates usually put adherents around 800,000 in the United States, with 300,000 of those in New York City and about 60,000 in Florida. Much more conservative estimates put the US adherents at about 40,000; however, with the large Cuban-American population, this appears to be far too low.

Beliefs

Santeria has been oppressed for so long that most adherents do not want to talk about their religion. Nevertheless, there are some basic themes that are pretty well established:
- God is known as *Olódùmarè* or *Olorun*, owner of heaven;
- God is the creator and preserver of *orisha*, or lesser deities;
- each orisha has an associated Christian saint;
- the orisha need food (in the form of animal sacrifice and human praise);
- at animal sacrificial rituals (most often using chickens, but also sometimes goats or other small animals), the blood of the animal is collected and offered to the orisha;
- it is believed this offering brings good luck, purification and the forgiveness of sins;
- dancing, chanting and drumming at rituals are believed to lead to the "religious experience" of actual possession by an orisha (known as *being mounted*);
- human ancestors, known as *Ara Orun* (the "people of heaven"), are called upon for moral guidance; and,
- the names of the ancestral spirits are recited at family gatherings and ceremonies.

Practices

Santeria is an "initiation religion" (much like the Druids 1500 years ago, or the Rosicrucians today). As a result, very little information is released to the general public regarding their beliefs, rituals, symbolism or practices. This is compounded by the fact that Santerians are not, as Islam puts it, "people of the book" – any book. The traditions of the faith, like most aboriginal religions, are preserved through initiation and oral tradition. Nevertheless, there are some things that are known about it.
- Rituals usually open with an invocation to *Olódùmarè*;
- drums are used to provide traditional African rhythms;

- dancing is done to honor and invoke specific orisha;
- animals may be sacrificed during some of the rituals;
- the priest (*Santeros* or *Babalochas*) or priestess (*Santeras* or *Iyalochas*) undergoes years of study, training, and apprenticeship in the rituals and oral traditions of the faith, and undergoes a period of solitude prior to being initiated as a priest or priestess; and,
- *Botanicas* are specialty shops that cater to Santerian supplies (selling charms, herbs, potions, drums, musical instruments, *et cetera*).

Legal Rights

Many Americans have their cultural sensibilities offended by Santeria – particularly by the animal sacrifices. Santerians respond that (a) the animals are killed in a humane manner, which is better than can be said for the chicken you buy at the store; (b) animal sacrifices were common in ancient Israel, and only ended after the Romans destroyed the temple; (c) the animals are not "wasted", but are usually eaten after the ritual; (d) the orisha require the sustenance, so the sacrifices need to continue; (e) the sacrifices have been a part of Santeria (and Yoruba before it) for over a thousand years; and, (f) the US Constitution guarantees them "freedom of religion".

Although often practiced out of public view, there are several Santerian churches that have incorporated under US law. For example, *The Church of the Lukumi Babalu Ayé* was formed in the early 1970s in southern Florida; *The African Theological Archministry* was formed in South Carolina in the late 1970s; and, *The Church of the Seven African Powers* was founded in Florida during the 1980s. Each of these churches maintains an international membership that is believed to be significant.

These churches commune with the orisha through prayer, ritual divination, and offerings (known as *ebo*). Although ebo may refer specifically to animal sacrifice, it is much broader than that; and, animals are generally only used in important situations (*e.g.* death, sickness or serious misfortune). In less severe situations, offerings may consist of candy, fruit, candles, *et cetera*.

Animal sacrifices are done quickly, and with as little pain to the animal as possible; the meat is usually eaten by the participants after the ritual; but, on rare occasions, the carcass of the animal is disposed of following the ritual. Nonetheless, the city of Hialeah, Florida felt that the Church of the Lukumi Babalu Ayé posed a health problem for the city, and passed a series of ordinances making it illegal to "kill, toment, torture, or mutilate an animal in a public or private ritual or ceremony not for the primary purpose of food consumption." Since eating the animal was never the primary reason for the sacrifice, this made all animal sacrifices illegal. Oba (Santeros) Ernesto Pichardo, the founder of the church, claimed it was an abridgment of their freedom of religion, and fought the new ordinances in the courts – all the way to the US Supreme Court. He won. In the court's decision, Justice Anthony Kennedy wrote that "although the practice of animal sacrifice may seem abhorrent to some, religious belief need not be acceptable, logical, consistent, or comprehensible to others in order to merit First Amendment protection."

Final Note on Santeria

On the *I Love Lucy* television sitcom, Desi Arnaz sang "Babalú Ayé", a Cuban rendition with rhythmic drums; at the start of the final season, he left the "Tropicana" and started his own club: *The Ricky Ricardo Babaloo Club*. The words to his song clearly invoke the Santerian orisha of health, and the new "club" he supposedly owned again invoked this orisha. So, Santeria has even entered mainstream America.

In another example, the sidekick of cartoon sheriff Quick Draw McGraw was named *Baba-Looey*. Quick Draw and Baba-Looey were first introduced in 1959, shortly after the *I Love Lucy* series. Born in New Mexico, growing up in Santa Fe (later, the barrios of Los Angeles), and coming from Cuban–American ancestry, cartoonist Bill Hanna (of Hanna-Barbera) was well aware of the fact that he was naming Quick Draw's burro sidekick after a Santerian orisha.

Chapter 28
Neo-Pagan Faith

"Eight words the Wiccan Rede fulfill, An it harm none do what ye will" — *Doreen Valiente*

Perhaps nothing in the field of religion is so hotly debated as the modern history of Paganism. To understand what is so contentious, one needs to start with a basic description of what it is.

An *Earth Religion* is considered to be any religion whose main tenet is that the worshipper is in harmony with the Earth and with all life. Such religions oppose the idea that the world is a resource to be subdued and exploited. Most (but not all) of these *Earth Religions* are generally classified as *Neo-Pagan*. The ancient Latin word for a rural farmer (*i.e.* "country dweller") living outside the city was *paganus*; and, it is from this word that the modern English *pagan* is derived. As the Roman Empire was converting to Christianity, the rural communities were continuing to practice the ancient, oral, agricultural religion; thus, this pre-Christian religion, followed by the *pagani*, became known as the *pagan religion*. A *Neo-Pagan* is thus someone who follows a modern re-creation, re-vitalization or continuation of an ancient pagan faith. *Wicca* (the proper term for what is commonly known as witchcraft) is the largest of these neo-pagan religious systems. Other well known examples include Druidry (a Celtic faith) and Ásatrú (the faith of the Vikings of Scandinavia).

Where the controversy arises is over whether they are:
(a) the original, true pagan faiths 'brought to light';
(b) re-creations of the original pagan faiths, as faithful to the originals as possible; or,
(c) new, unrelated developments that claim the old religions as their base to give them a certain credibility.

Although some adherents believe they are following the uninterrupted, continuous practice of the original religions, the facts just do not support this; therefore, the only real question facing anthropologists and other academics interested in the neo-pagan religions is the degree of accuracy with which these new versions have been constructed.

The general consensus seems to be that they are quite accurate; at least they do not conflict in any meaningful way from what is known historically and scientifically. But, even accepting them at face value, there is another problem: not only is the neo-pagan movement a highly diverse group, but even sub-sets such as Wicca are highly diverse and often poorly defined.

Wicca

History

Wicca is the proper name for what is often referred to as witchcraft. This is a form of paganism practiced for thousands of years prior to what amounted to a three-pronged attack over 500 years that effectively destroyed it: the Inquisition (conducted by the Roman Catholic church); the abuse, jailings, and hangings of accused witches in colonial America; and, the *burning times* (the Wiccan term for the tens of thousands of suspected witches burned at the stake across Europe) in the Middle Ages.

Beliefs

Modern Wicca is essentially a reconnection with the life-force of nature, both on this planet and in the stars and space beyond. Through rituals employed at the new and full moons and at festival times, adherents strive to put themselves in tune with these natural forces. They honor the gods and goddesses as visualizations of immanent nature. They are, on the surface, a polytheistic belief system in tune with the natural world. Wiccans generally believe that we each have within ourselves the capacity to reach out and experience a oneness with all Life; and, their rituals attempt to establish that contact. What they are not is a group that flies around on broomsticks with pointy hats. This was a caricature promoted by Christian opponents who saw, but misunderstood, a traditional agricultural ritual commonly conducted at either the Spring equinox or May Day.

Different sects take their inspiration from different ethnic traditions, such as Celtic, Greek, Norse, Italian, *et cetera*. Others base their systems on the writings or teachings of a modern founder such as Gerald Gardner, Z Budapest, or Starhawk. Despite this apparent diversity, it is nearly universal for the branches of Wicca to openly embrace a feminist attitude. In reality, Wicca – all sects – is based on an agricultural religion that is at heart monotheistic*.

The most commonly held beliefs include:

- the immanence and transcendance of Deity (be it god, goddess, or both);
- the interconnectedness of all life — with every living entity connected spiritually to every other living entity;
- divinity manifesting itself through all living beings (nature itself being divine);
- images of the gods and goddesses being recognized not as idols, but more as visual reminders of the various aspects and powers of a much greater divinity; and,
- the *Wiccan Rede* — "An' it harm none, do what you will." ("an'" being an archaic way of saying "and if"). This is the basic statement of Wiccan ethics.

Wiccans do not accept the concept of the devil, a personification of a supreme spirit of evil and unrighteousness. They see Satan as an invention of Middle Eastern thought — fundamental to some of the religions of that region (*e.g.* Zoroastrianism, Christianity, Judaism and Islam), but foreign to their belief system. The gods of Wicca are in no way connected with Satanic practice. Since most Wiccans do not even believe Satan exists, they certainly do not worship him. Historically, the gods of an older religion are often branded as the devils of a newer one in order to promote conversion. This clearly occurred with Wicca, as the *horned god* of Wicca (Cernunnos, *aka* Pan, above right) is the image typically associated with *Satan*, despite the fact that there is absolutely no historical, theological, or legitimate connection.

---

* Most Wiccans accept a single Deity while interacting with it through both female and male anthropomorphic forms (*i.e.* god and goddess) for convenience. They find it easier to relate to Deity if the form is aligned with the traits it represents (*e.g.* a loving goddess, a protective god). Recognizing that this is for human convenience, all of the gods and goddesses are One (*i.e.* monotheism).

Practices

Wicca is one of the most varied religions in the world with regard to the basic format of its practice. Although the "traditional" format is in a small group (typically no more than 13) known as a *coven*, Wicca is also often practiced in large congregations, or — even more often — by what are known as *solitaries* (who practice their faith individually, without the support of a group of any size). It is estimated that more than half of all practicing Wiccans are solitaries. Despite these differences in format, some of the more common practices include:
- rituals at 8 specific points in the solar year (the *Sabbats*);
- monthly rituals that coincide with the full moon (*Esbats*);
- rituals and celebrations generally being preferred outdoors, under the stars, in touch with nature; and,
- constructing ritual space by drawing out a circle and consecrating it for use in the service — with a new circle created each time there is a ritual or celebration.

The Circle Within a sacred circle, two primary activities occur: celebration and magic. Celebration is the more important at the major seasonal holy days, or *Sabbats*. It is at these times that the myth of the holiday is played out in ritual drama, dancing, singing, feasting and general revelry. It is more common for magic to be performed at the *Esbats*, based on the phases of the moon. Magic to most Wiccans involves psychic healing, the focus of energy to achieve positive results, and aids to the spiritual development of members of the coven. It is seen as an art form — a conscious direction of the will to a desired end through strict discipline to specific principles. Wiccans believe that "whatever is sent out will return three-fold", so they are extremely careful and conscientious to keep their use of magic positive.

There is probably no religion on earth that is more dependent on its symbolism than Wicca. As such, the "tools" that Wicca uses as part of this symbolism are critical. There are several such tools that are basic to nearly all Wiccans; and, these include:
- an *athame* — a ritual knife (often with an intricate white or metallic handle), used both as a tool to define space (such as in casting a sacred circle – similar to the use of a laser

pointer) and as a conductor of energy — it is never used profanely (*i.e.* to cut anything);

- a *pentagram* (a five pointed star often, but not always, surrounded by a circle) — used to represent the "Aristotelian elements" (earth, air, fire, and water – plus spirit) — or, alternatively,
  - a *container of salt* (usually a small dish) — to represent the earth element;
  - a *censer or bell* — to symbolize the air element;
  - a *candle* — used to symbolize the fire element;
  - a *chalice of water* — for the water element; and,
  - either an *ankh* or *quartz crystal* — to symbolize the spirit element;
- other "minor" tools are often added to supplement or substitute for these "major" tools. These may include a *broom*, a *sword*, a *cauldron* and others.

Wiccans, as do most neo-pagan faiths, often refer to the *Wheel of the Year* (a concept that all life on earth is cyclic). As such, the eight *Sabbats* are evenly spaced markers throughout the year that indicate what the gods are "doing" at that time of year; generally, an entire mythology is employed that anthropomorphizes these seasonal agricultural events. The eight Sabbats (all of which run from sundown to sundown) are:

- **Samhain** (pronounced sow'-en) — the New Year. Mythologically, it is believed that the veil between the worlds of life and death are weakest at this time, and ancestors often walk among the living. They are welcomed with feasts by their relatives, and often grant blessings from the "other world". On the modern calendar, this is October 31st — Halloween. In México, it has been known as the *Dia de los muertes* (Day of the Dead) since Aztec days.
- **Yule** — the winter solstice (December 21st — when daylight is at its shortest, and the sun is "reborn"). Some celebrate a *Festival of Light* to commemorate the Mother Goddess giving birth to the Sun God. The name *Yule* is from the Norse word *Juul*, meaning "wheel, or log" —

when the Wheel of the Year again turns to make the days longer. Many traditional Norse pagan traditions (*e.g.* the Yule log, the fir tree being brought into the house, placing candles or lights on it, the use of bells, wassailing, *et cetera*) were brought into Christianity by Norse converts.

- ***Imbolc*** — "February Eve" (also called *Oimelc* and *Brigid*), this falls about January 31st. It is a celebration of the revival of life. It is usually celebrated with candles or bonfires to commemorate the now evident warming of the earth, and the various names all derive from this. *Imbolc* is Old Irish and means "sustenance"; *Oimelc* is also Irish, and means "ewe's milk" (this is lambing time for sheep); and, *Brigid* is the Celtic Fire Goddess, the "patroness" of smiths and others who use fire in their work. The modern form of this ancient holiday is *Groundhog Day*.

- ***Ostara*** — the vernal equinox (March 21st) — when day and night are exactly 12 hours each. The Germanic and Anglo-Saxon goddess of the dawn, *Eostre* (after whom Easter is named), is the tutelary goddess of this day. She heralds the return of the sun and the rebirth of nature.

- ***Beltane*** is planting time (April 30th, or May Eve). It is a joyous holiday with singing and dancing around a *May pole* (a phallic symbol of fertility), and *May* is derived from an Old Norse word meaning "to shoot out new growth". The ancient Romans had a 5 day celebration at this time known as the *Festival of Flora* (the goddess of flowers). Literally, *Beltane* means "Bel's fires" and refers to the practice of blessing the cattle between bonfires to ensure their fertility and growth of the herd in the coming year. A common Celtic tradition to celebrate May Day was to dance around the May Pole. This began as the *Morris Dance*, a pagan dance ritual at Beltane that is continued to this day in Great Britain (often without realizing its pagan roots). The Cotswold version of the dance, related to the Spanish *fandango*, is performed annually by the all-male Gloucestershire Morris Dancers.

- ***Litha*** — "Midsummer Eve". Immortalized by Shakespeare, this is the longest day of the year (June 21st); and, life and light are celebrated as abundant. It is a time when the first fruits of the season are ready (*conf.* modern *Strawberry Festivals*). It was on this day that ancient Chinese agricultural religions (pre-Taoist, Confucianist, or Buddhist) celebrated the *Festival of Li* (the Goddess of Light), and the ancient civilization of Crete celebrated the *Festival of Rhea* (the Mountain Mother whose breath created all).

- *Lammas* (aka **Lughnasadh**) — July 31st, serves the Celtic and Germanic peoples as a festival to honor the "birth of their culture" and the Sun God *Lugh* (known as *Lleu* to the Welsh and *Lugus* in Gaul). The Irish celebrated with races and games held in his name — the original source of the annual summer picnic held by businesses, churches, and social groups. This was often mixed with *Lammas*, the Saxon Feast of Bread, at which the first grain harvest was eaten in ritual loaves. The old English folksong *John Barleycorn* tells the story of the death and transformation of the Barley God on this day.

- *Mabon* — the final Sabbat of the pagan year. Day and night are again in balance at this time (September 21st, the autumnal equinox), and a harvest festival is held to thank the Goddess for providing sufficient sustenance to feed them through the pending winter. This is the source of the *Harvest Festival* that is still celebrated in many agricultural communities. Since farmers often labored far from home (only returning after the harvest), this is also known as *Harvest Home* — the source of the *Homecoming* tradition followed by many schools.

This brings us back to Samhain, the Wiccan New Year. Virtually all of these festivals coincide with modern secular or Christian holidays[*]; and, this is no coincidence. These days were community celebrations, and were kept largely intact as pagans converted to Christianity (although rededicated to the Christian God, saints, prophets or events). In many, the pagan traditions are still apparent.

---

[*] Samhain = All Saints Day; Yule = Christmas; Imbolc = Groundhog Day; Ostara = Easter; Beltane = May Day; Litha = Strawberry Festivals; Lughnasadh = Feast of St Peter in Chains (Loaf Mass); and, Mabon = Homecoming

Summary

During a tax reform drive in 1986, a proposed amendment would have barred Wicca and other neo-pagan churches from the same tax exemption granted to other religions. Amendments are known by their primary sponsor, and this one was called the *Helms Amendment* (Jesse Helms, R–NC). The amendment was soundly defeated after extensive lobbying by the *ACLU* (American Civil Liberties Union), *COG* (Covenant of the Goddess), *Circle Sanctuary* (a Wisconsin Wiccan group), *Church and School of Wicca* (one of the largest Wiccan organizations; located in Helms' home state of North Carolina), and others. Wicca is not the only religion that would have been impacted had the amendment passed; Druidism, Ásatrú, Santeria, Voudun and others would also have lost out.

Some of the better known Wiccan sects, or denominations (usually called *traditions*), are:

- ***Tuatha de Danaan*** is, in Irish, the "people of the Goddess Danu"; these are *færies*. They honor the pre-historic gods of the Irish, Scottish and Welsh — the færies, elven (elves), leprechauns, and pwca (*conf* kami and orisha).

- ***Gardnerian*** follows the work of Gerald Gardner [1884-1964], the modern founder of Wicca. Gardner, an Englishman, was introduced to Wicca by an *hereditary witch*. Although it no longer dominates the Craft as it once did, it remains the largest tradition within Wicca.

- ***Alexandrian*** was founded by Alexander Sanders. Based largely on the Gardnerian tradition, it has a greater emphasis on ceremonial magic.

- ***Dianic*** is a broad tradition that is generally more feminist in outlook than most others, and is matriarchal in organization. It emphasizes rediscovering female divinity.

- ***Hereditary*** are highly secretive forms of Wicca that have been handed down in families for generations, and which often pre-date Gardner and other modern founders.

- ***Celtic*** is a grouping of covens and solitaries that base their faith on Celtic mythology and history. Typically, deities are known by Celtic names (such as *Cerridwen* and *Cernunnos*, the goddess and horned god, respectively).

- *Færie* see Tuatha de Danaan (above)

- *Seax Wica* was founded by Raymond Buckland (right) in 1973, and is essentially Gardnerian Wicca organized along Saxon lines and emphasizing an egalitarian structure rather than the hierarchical structure common in the Gardnerian tradition. Buckland is often thought of as the "dean" of modern Wicca, and has authored several authoritative texts.

- *W.A.S. (Witchcraft as a Science)* was founded in Salem, Massachusetts in 1955 by Laurie Cabot (right). A self-proclaimed witch (declared Salem's "official witch" in 1977 by the City Council, State legislature, and Governor Mike Dukakis), Cabot teaches that Wicca is a science as well as religion and art. She teaches past life regression as well as a variety of Wiccan related sciences. Over 20,000 people have graduated from her courses, and been initiated into Wicca; and, Laurie is well-known and well-liked by residents of the Salem area (including the author).

Prior to a Wiccan ritual, the High Priest(ess) walks a circle with the athame in their hand, defining the sacred space. When the ritual begins, the High Priest(ess) walks around inside the perimeter of the sacred circle (clockwise), and invites the "guardian spirits" of the 4 compass points to join the ritual. The altar is set up (frequently on a table inside the sacred circle) facing east. (S)he then invites the god and goddess (the primary deities in nearly all forms of Wicca) to attend (they are never "summoned"). Following the ritual, they are all blessed as they depart, and the sacred circle is released back to nature by again walking the perimeter (again clockwise, in nearly all traditions).

Magic

It is impossible to discuss Wicca without discussing magic. It forms a major part of the practice of the faith (Hollywood has made it the only part; but, that is just the movie industry doing what it does best: misunderstanding religion). Many religious rituals would be considered magic by non-adherents; but, Wicca is unusual in that it has no problem with the use of the word. Their only concern is that it not be confused with "stage magic" (*i.e.* illusion and mis-direction). As a result, Wiccans often differentiate between them by spelling them *magic* (stage magic) and *magick* (religious magic).

Magic can be divided into 2 discrete categories: *inductive magic*, and *sympathetic magic*. Wiccans nearly always practice sympathetic magic.

Inductive Magic is the use of a word, phrase, action, or other human intervention in an attempt to control or impact the outcome of something – an action unrelated to the desired outcome. An example of inductive magic would be crossing your fingers. There is no connection between crossing your fingers and your team scoring a touchdown 2,000 miles away – yet people often cross their fingers at tense times during a game.

Sympathetic Magic is another human intervention used to try to control or impact the outcome of something; but, it is clearly related to the intended outcome. It relies on the *Hermetic principle* often stated as "as above, so below". Essentially, the concept is the same as it is for traditional astrology:
- Deity made the stars;
- Deity made you;
- everything (including you) therefore reflects and displays Deific intent and design;
- since all reflects Deity, everything is reflecting a common source, and there is a connection between all events.
- If we can discern Deific design in the stars, we should be able to recognize that same design in our lives.

An example of sympathetic magic is when someone thinks that the afternoon shower was caused by their earlier watering of the lawn, or washing their car.

Appendix: Photo Credits

Page Credit / Authorization to Use

4-13 Feuerbach, Tylor, Frazer, Freud, Durkheim, Marx, Eliade, Geertz, Dean, and James are all used under license by *Creative Commons Attribution 2.0* (licensing details at http://creativecommons.org/licenses/by/2.0/).

19-20 Sweatlodge, Sufi, and ascetic are in the public domain.

21 Maharishi Mahesh Yogi and Rajneesh are used under license by *Creative Commons Attribution 2.0* (http://creativecommons.org/licenses/by/2.0/).

22-23 Leary, Alpert and Metzger are all used under license by *Creative Commons Attribution 2.0* (http://creativecommons.org/licenses/by/2.0/).

24-26 Cayce, Krishnamurti and Singer are used under *Creative Commons Attribution 2.0* (licensing at http://creativecommons.org/licenses/by/2.0/).

27 Huston Smith is used under license by *Creative Commons Attribution 2.0* (licensing details at http://creativecommons.org/licenses/by/2.0/).

28 Goldfish cartoon used under MicroSoft® software license.

34 The clip art of Bob Dobbs (which dates to the 1940s) and the Mark of Dobbs are both in the public domain.

36-37 Pastafarian images are used with the permission of Bobby Henderson.

42 Portrait of Rev. William Paley [1743 – 1805] is in the public domain.

46 Portrait of Blaise Pascal [1623 – 1662] is in the public domain.

48 Portrait of Saint Anselm [1033 – 1109] is in the public domain.

49 Photo portrait of Dr William Lane Craig [b.1949] is from an advertising campaign for his participation in televised religious debates, and is thus in the public domain.

51 The photo of Dr Edwin Powell Hubble [1889 - 1953] has been released into the public domain by the copyright holder.

52 The photo of Drs Stephen William Hawking [b.1942] is in the public domain by virtue of the fact that it is owned by NASA, a US governmental agency.

54 Portrait of CS Lewis [1898 – 1963] is by Arthur Strong, from 1947. Its use here is claimed to be used under fair use as: (1) it is a historically significant photo of a famous individual; (2) it is being used solely for informational purposes; and, (3) its inclusion adds significantly to this work because it shows the subject of the article on him.

58 Viracocha photo is public domain as it is from the Peruvian government.

Page	Credit / Authorization to Use
59	Quetzlcoatl statue from temple at Teotihuacan; photo taken by author.
61	Photo of ziggurat is used in compliance with the copyright assignment terms of the University of Texas, the copyright owner.
62	Hera statue at Palazza Nuovo in Rome.
63	Poseidon statue in Athens Zeus statue at Palazza Nuovo in Rome..
65	Ancient distribution map of Italy developed by the author.
67	Marble bust of Emperor Domitian in the Musée du Louvre, Paris, France.
68	Graphic representation of Paut Neteru developed by the author.
69	Pictures of Anubis and Ammut are of antiquities, and are public domain.
78	Map of the Middle East is modified from a US government produced map (CIA), and is thus public domain.
80	Photo credit for the picture of Yuya's mummy is due G. Elliot Smith, who originally published this photo in The Royal Mummies (Le Caire: Imprimerie de L'institut Francais d'archeologie Orientale). Published in 1912, this is now in the public domain.
81	Source of Zoroaster picture unknown. Its use is claimed to be used under fair use as: (1) it is a historically significant photo of a famous individual; (2) it is being used solely for informational purposes; and, (3) inclusion adds significantly to this work because it shows the founder of a major world faith.
82	The map of primary Zoroastrian flight routes was developed by the author
83	Photo of Fire Temple in India taken by author.
87	Illustration of Farovahar is of an ancient religious symbol, and is thus in the public domain.
92	*David and Abishag* by Pedro Américo is from 1879, and public domain.
147	All of the icon photos are of Russian Orthodox icons in the personal collection of the author.
148	Credit for the picture of *St Peter's Basilica* is due the Italian Tourist Board (public domain).
152	Photo of Castle Church taken by the author.
153	Portrait of Martin Luther by Lucas Cranach der Ältere in 1529 is now in the public domain. Portrait of John Calvin originally puslished in The Hundred Greatest Men (New York: D Appleton & co.) was published in 1885, and is now in the public domain

Appendix: Photo Credits   349

Page	Credit / Authorization to Use
158	Painting of Saint Jerome is by Peter Paul Reubens (*ca.* 1628), and is in the public domain. Drawing of John Wyclif is from the *Project Gutenberg eBooks*, and is used in compliance with Fair Use Standards.
159	William Tyndale is used under license by *Creative Commons Attribution 2.0* (licensing details at http://creativecommons.org/licenses/by/2.0/).
160	King James I of England is used under license by *Creative Commons Attribution 2.0* (licensing at http://creativecommons.org/licenses/by/2.0/).
172	Mary Baker Eddy is used under license by *Creative Commons Attribution 2.0* (licensing details at http://creativecommons.org/licenses/by/2.0/).
174	Photo of the Christian Science Ctr (*The Mother Church*) is by the author.
175	Painting of Joseph Smith, Jr is in the archives of the Church of Jesus Christ of Latter Day Saints, and is in the public domain.
176	Painting of Brigham Young is in the archives of the Church of Jesus Christ of Latter Day Saints, and is in the public domain.
178	Photo of Charles Taze Russell is from 1885, and is in the public domain.
183	Drawing of Fox dates from *circa* 1800, and is in the public domain.
193	Photo of *Kaaba* in Mecca is from the Saudi Travel Bureau, and is in the public domain.
198	Map of Islamic Umayyad Dynasty is original to these notes.
205	Photo of Mriza Ghulam Ahmad was taken in 1901, and all copyrights have expired.
207	Representation of the Qur'an is of published material from the public domain.
217	Photo of Bahá'u'lláh was his Turkish passport photo. As a government document, this was never copyright protected, although it would have expired even if it were.
221	Guru Nanak is used under license by *Creative Commons Attribution 2.0* (details available at http://creativecommons.org/licenses/by/2.0/).
225	The 5 photos of the "five K's" are taken from Indian government publications, and are thus all in the public domain.
226	Image of the *Harimandar Sahib* is from a UNESCO publication, and therefore not copyright protected.
229	Photo of Ossama bin Laden is from a US Government "Wanted" flyer, and was not copyright protected.

Page	Credit / Authorization to Use
241	Bronze statue of Shiva is a replica in the author's collection.
	The Krishna painting is several hundred years old, and is public domain.
242	Painting of Brahma is from the 15th century, and is at the Government Museum in Chennai, Tamil Nadu, India.
243	Nandi statue at Chamundi Hills, Mysuru, India; photo by the author.
257	Copyright for the photo of Nagas at 2005 Khumb Mela celebration in Ujjain, Madhya Pradesh, India is held by Christopher Martin (UK), and photo is used by permission.
261	Photo by author of statue of Mahavira at shrine in Girnar, Gujarat, India
266	Both photos of Jain adherents (Digambara and Sthanakavasi) are owned by the Government of India, and are therefore in the public domain.
269	Photo of Maharishi Mahesh Yogi is Copyright 2010 Global Good News, and is used in compliance with Fair Use standards.
276	Kapilavastu photo is used under license by *Creative Commons Attribution ShareAlike 2.5*.
290	Photo of His Holiness, the XIVth Dalai Lama is copyrighted by The Tibetan Foundation, a government entity, and is under the Fair Use doctrine.
294	Photo of the Great Stupa at Sanchi, India was taken by Joel Suganth, and was published under (and is used here) the *Creative Commons Attribution Share Alike 3.0 Unported*.
301	All of the zazen yoga position drawings are from Dummies.com, owned by John Wiley & Sons inc. Copyright is held be the publisher, and use here is under the academic standards of Fair Use.
309	Drawing of Confucius is believed to be from the 11th or 12th century.
314	Drawing of Lau-tzu os from the 14th century.
319	The yin-yang symbol is in the public domain.
323	Photo of Emperor Meiji is owned by the country of Nippon (Japan).
327	Map of the Gulf of Guinea area of west Africa developed by the author based on a map of Africa that is in the public domain.
328	The carved column of a bride is in the London Natural History Museum.
339	Clip art of Cernunnos is used under MicroSoft® software license.
341	Photo is of pentacle in the private collection of the author.

Made in the USA
Middletown, DE
28 August 2015